Finding a Common Thread

Other works of interest from St. Augustine's Press

Plato, *The Symposium of Plato* (the Shelley Translation)

Aristotle, *On Poetics* (trans. by Seth Benardete and Michael Davis

Aristotle, *Physics, Or Natural Hearing*

St. Augustine, *On Order [De Ordine]*

St. Augustine, *The St. Augustine LifeGuide*

Thomas Aquinas, *Commentary on the Epistle to the Hebrews*

Thomas Aquinas, *Commentaries on St. Paul's Epistles to Timothy, Titus, and Philemon*

Thomas Aquinas, *Treatise on Law: The Complete Text*

Thomas Aquinas, *Treatise on Human Nature: The Complete Text*

Thomas Aquinas, *Disputed Questions on Virtue*

Thomas Aquinas, *Commentary on Aristotle's Nicomachean Ethics*

Thomas Aquinas, *Commentary on Aristotle's Metaphysics*

Thomas Aquinas, *Commentary on Aristotle's De Anima*

Thomas Aquinas, *Commentary on Aristotle's Physics*

Henry of Ghent, *Summa of Ordinary Questions: On the Possibility of Human Knowledge*

John of St. Thomas, *Intro. to the Summa Theologiae of Thomas Aquinas*

Robert Hugh Benson, *Lord of the World*

LaRochefoucauld, *Maxims*

William of Ockham, *Ockham's Theory of Terms*

William of Ockham, *Ockham's Theory of Propositions*

Friedrich Nietzsche, *On the Future of Our Educational Institutions*

Friedrich Nietzsche, *Prefaces to Unwritten Works*

St.Anselm, *Proslogion*

Averroes, *Averroes' Middle Commentaries on Aristotle's Categories*

Averroes, *Averroes' Commentary on Aristotle's Poetics*

John C. Calhoun, *A Disquisition on Government*

John Poinsot, *Tractatus de Signis*

Finding a Common Thread

Reading Great Texts from Homer to O'Connor

Edited by

Robert C. Roberts, Scott H. Moore,
and Donald D. Schmeltekopf

Introduction by Robert C. Roberts

St. Augustine's Press
South Bend, Indiana

Manufactured in the United States of America

1 2 3 4 5 6 19 18 17 16 15 14 13

Library of Congress Cataloging in Publication Data
Finding a common thread:
reading great texts from Homer to O'Connor /
edited by Robert C. Roberts, Scott H. Moore, and Donald D.
Schmeltekopf; introduction by Robert C. Roberts.
p. cm.
ISBN 978-1-58731-254-0 (paperbound: alk. paper)
1. Literature – History and criticism. 2. Christianity and literature.
3. Books and reading. 4. Best books. I. Roberts, Robert Campbell,
1942– II. Moore, Scott H., 1964– III. Schmeltekopf, Donald D.
PN49.F559 2012
809'.93382 – dc23 2011039529

∞ The paper used in this publication meets the minimum requirements of the American National Standard for Information Sciences – Permanence of Paper for Printed Materials, ANSI Z39.48-1984.

St. Augustine's Press
www.staugustine.net

Table of Contents

Preface

The reading and teaching of great texts is a long tradition in the Anglophone world, beginning in Oxford and Cambridge in the 12th century and being carried to America by the Puritans in the 17th century. Because the Puritans who founded Harvard in 1636 were educated at Oxford and Cambridge, it was only natural that they too would embrace the great texts tradition. As additional colleges were established in America over the next two centuries, they all had one thing in common: the reading of great texts after the pattern of Harvard! Since virtually all of these schools were founded and animated by Christian concerns, the purpose of reading great texts was not merely to enhance culture, but also to inculcate wisdom, i.e., for the sake of faith in the triune God, for the life of piety, and for moral truth.

The growth of the research university beginning in the second half of the 19th century, and with it the specialization of knowledge by disciplines, resulted in unprecedented advances in science and technology. Indeed, the quantitative methodologies of these fields appeared so convincing that most of the social sciences also embraced them. But a price was to be paid: the tradition of the great texts, and with it the moral formation of students, came to be increasingly marginalized in the modern research university and eventually in most undergraduate colleges as well. Several schools made some efforts to sustain the tradition, as in Columbia's western civilization course (1919), "Plan II" at the University of Texas (1935), Harvard's core curriculum (1946), Chicago's great books program (1946), and Yale's directed studies program (1947). But the overwhelming majority of colleges and universities in America today—including some just named—have abandoned the tradition of reading great texts, even in the humanities, in exchange for mere introductory courses in the disciplines.

On the contemporary higher education scene, however, interest in recovering the great texts tradition is reviving, as at Baylor University. Indeed, this book is a product of the growing presence and importance of Baylor's Great Texts Program. The effort began with the adoption in 1992 of the Baylor Interdisciplinary Core. This general education curriculum includes a series of interdisciplinary courses, including one in the humanities, that follows a great text sequence of reading. Even more significant, perhaps, is the development of a Great Texts major in Baylor's Honors College. This major has become the centerpiece of the Honors College, and is currently supported by ten full-time faculty members.

A noteworthy feature of Baylor's work in great texts is our commitment to put the great texts in conversation with the Christian tradition, reading and interpreting them not from an allegedly neutral and "value-free" perspective, but solidly within the 2000-year old Christian tradition. This feature informs the chapters in this book and, we believe, contributes to its distinctive quality. To press this intention, the editors organized two consultations lasting two and a half days each to discuss the papers submitted for this volume. Each author received the benefit of critical discussion by his or her colleagues. Not only did these exchanges strengthen each chapter, they also enabled us to bring coherence to the entire project and contributed to the liberal education of several of us! As the introductory chapter indicates, the grounding theme of the book is "wisdom as the end of education."

The editors wish to thank all the authors for their contributions. We also thank Darin Davis, director of Baylor's Institute for Faith and Learning, and the Center for Ministry Effectiveness and Educational Leadership, for their financial support of our consultations. Without that support it is doubtful this project would have been possible. In addition, we wish to recognize the work of Julie Covington and Douglas Henry for their helpful arrangements throughout both consultations.

Donald D. Schmeltekopf
Scott H. Moore
Robert C. Roberts

June 2010

Reading Texts and Nurturing Wisdom
Introduction

The specialization of the academic disciplines in the contemporary research university has brought colossal advances in scientific knowledge and technology. The sheer number of facts "we" know, and the countless ways research has allowed "us" to manipulate our environment and our bodies, justify the awe with which we contemplate our accomplishments and the academic institutions on which they largely depend. Less publicly visible, but still impressive, are the accomplishments of specialization in the humanities. We know ever more historical facts about ever more focused topics in ever smaller time periods. We have increasingly detailed knowledge of languages and their history, and better and better established texts of historical documents. We owe much of this knowledge to meticulous, highly specialized scholarly work.

But this specialization has come at a cost, a cost largely hidden and not negligible. The evolution of the modern research university and the very specialization that drives it so efficiently have entailed a costly forgetfulness of the original intent of a university education. This forgetfulness is so profound that it is in fact a change of heart, a change of aim, a change in what we care about. And as such, it is a change in the kind of persons the university aims to nurture and shape, and in the kind of faculty it prizes and employs.

The great universities of the world were formed to train the keepers of wisdom. They were formed to educate an elite in an understanding of the nature, value, and purpose of human life so that that elite might convey such understanding, as far as possible, to the people, and so maintain, and possibly improve, the wellbeing of the larger society and its members. Wellbeing, in this connection, was only secondarily the sort of thing that could be fostered by technological advance; wellbeing was primarily a state of character, a disposition of the will and the affections, a "moral" understanding of oneself, one's fellow human beings, and the universe we dwell in. The change of purpose that I speak of is forgetfulness, in many parts or possibly even in the whole of the research university, of the goal of educating whole persons with some semblance of wisdom. In its place we aim to train in techniques, whether in legal debate and medical practice, or quantum physical research, the refinement of fiber-optic transmission, the establishing of an ancient text, the mastery of medieval French, or the writing of professional papers in epistemology and metaphysics.

Wisdom is the aim the contemporary university has "forgotten." The present collection of essays on "great texts" from Homer to O'Connor hopes to contribute to a possible recovery of something like this ancient aim of higher education.

Wisdom as the End of Education

One salient, if ironic, example of the disciplinary hypertrophy and narrowing of focus mentioned above is the philosophical discipline of epistemology. Until late in the 20th century, Anglo-American epistemology focused its considerable analytic resourcefulness on one epistemic good, which it called "knowledge." Knowledge, in the preferred sense, was roughly *justified true belief.* Thus you (usually) have knowledge when you sincerely assent to a proposition, *and* that proposition is true, *and* you have an adequate justification for sincerely assenting to it. Perhaps this particular focus reflects the emphasis on knowledge in the contemporary university.[1]

Lately some epistemologists have come to think that knowledge, so conceived, has been overrated (see, for example, Kvanvig 2003). *Understanding* is a much more substantial and valuable fruit of intellectual development and of our endeavors to increase it. Given the talent in the field, it seems to some of us lookers-on that it took the professional epistemologists a surprisingly long time to figure this out. To those involved with reading and teaching great texts it has always been pretty obvious that "knowledge" as the epistemologists understood it is not the aim of a university education, or of reading great texts.

The epistemologists who have begun to turn their attention to understanding would all agree, I think, that understanding involves grasping connections and seeing relationships among things, whether the things be parts of a sentence, parts of an engine, parts of a theory, causes and effects, historical events, texts incorporated in or incorporating other texts, or certain truths (on the one hand) and oneself (on the other). Understanding is making some kind of sense of things, appreciating some significance or rational order in them. It comes in degrees. It can be shallow or deep, minimal or extensive, barely or richly articulated, crude or subtle, trivial or important. Wisdom, I take it, is a kind of understanding, namely understanding that is deep, extensive, subtle, and important. And it is important because its objects are human life and all that bears most importantly on the quality of a human life.

Wisdom, then, is not just any understanding. We can imagine a professor with an encyclopedic knowledge of some complex text – say, Dostoevsky's *The Brothers Karamazov* – who also has an extensive grasp of the interconnection of the details of the story to one another and to the whole. Further, this professor understands the text very well in relation to Dostoevsky's other works, his letters and notebooks, the events of Dostoevsky's life and literary influences on his work, the political and social conditions in relation to which the novel was written, and so forth. *But* – her knowledge of the text does not amount to wisdom. How could this be, given that *The Brothers Karamazov* is about human life and all that bears most importantly on the quality of a human life? How could this extensive understanding not amount to wisdom?

Ancient Greek and Greek-inspired philosophy aimed at wisdom, and at least from Socrates to the Hellenistic philosophers thought of wisdom as a trait to be cultivated through intellectual-moral disciplines designed to shape not only one's intellect, in some narrow sense, but also one's affections, desires, loves – one's goals – in life (see Hadot 1995). Thus the various strategies for gaining wisdom in the ancient world could be called, in the words of a title by Martha Nussbaum (1992), "therapies of desire."[2] Without the disciplined education of our desires, none of us is happy or healthy; we all need therapy. So the ancients' answer to the question at the end of the last paragraph would be, "To have all that knowledge and understanding of *The Brothers Karamazov*, and yet not have gained wisdom, our imagined professor would have to lack the appropriate love or desire, and the organization of her knowledge and understanding around this desire."

Now it's hard to imagine anyone accomplishing the kind of understanding that I have imagined our professor to have of Dostoevsky's great book without her being passionate about anything at all. Perhaps she always aspired, since her youth, to be an important professor at an important university, and that ambition drove her to her current understanding of the book. Or maybe ever since she was a child she has loved to solve puzzles, and *The Brothers Karamazov* and its authorial, political, and social background provided a fund of just the kinds of puzzles she likes to solve, and her understanding has grown out of solving one after another.

The ancient philosophers would not have thought either of these passions to be the kind that grounds wisdom. Neither professional ambition nor the pleasure of puzzle solving betokens an aim worthy to be the ultimate aim of a human spirit. For Plato, the desire that could ground wisdom was the love of the transcendent Good; for Aristotle, it was the desire for human wellbeing (*eudaimonia*); for the Stoics, love of the rational order in the universe. For Dostoevsky himself, it was the love of Christ. One sees a pattern here, a pattern that shows by contrast why the loves I have imagined our professor having are not the kind to inform wisdom.

So if wisdom is to be acquired through a reading of the great texts, that reading must not only advance the student's facility at making connections among parts of a text, or between a text and its historical background, or among the texts in the syllabus, but must also foster an understanding of the reader's life in the context of this universe in which we find ourselves, so that the reader can be growing in his or her desire for the good. No one can acquire wisdom without a conception of the good that is consistent enough to enable him or her to learn to love it. Each of the ancient schools taught and presupposed in its therapy of desire a particular conception of the good, and it is hard to see how it could have done otherwise. It did so, too, in a pluralistic context, in vivid awareness that its own conception was not the only option in the market.

One of the difficulties of making wisdom an aim of education in the typical modern research university is that such a university can presuppose no shared conception of the human good. It can presuppose, at any given point in its evolving history, a particular conception of good chemistry, good engineering, good mathematics, good textual research, good United States history, and (more controversially) good sociology, good psychology, good literary theory. But it cannot presuppose any particular conception of what it is for a human being to live a fulfilled and excellent life, or of the metaphysical background (the conception of reality) that might correspond to and justify such a life. Nor can it sanction any particular scheme of moral formation for its students. The best it can do in this regard is to foster a more or less promiscuous tolerance of just about any character formation and behavior imaginable (except intolerance, with which it may identify any effort to proselytize or nurture its students in certain proscribed ancient religious outlooks).

An advantage, then, of a frankly Christian university is that it can presuppose such a framework, a metaphysics, a conception of the good for human beings, as is needed for the holistic formation of its students. It can, with a good conscience, intentionally go about teaching the great texts, which all embody and express one wisdom or another, in a wisdom-oriented way. It can approach the texts, whether pagan, Christian, other-religious, or post-Christian, from a passionate and metaphysical standpoint that is commodious for nurturing actual, and not merely hypothetical or experimental, wisdom in its students.

The Essays in this Volume

This book contains eighteen chapters by people who teach great texts in the university, offering guidance on how to read a diversity of particular texts from the western tradition crossing an expanse of about 2700 years. The period begins in paganism and is dominated for 1500 years by Christian writers, after which some of the great writers are "post-Christian." Most, but not all the authors of the essays in this volume teach in Christian institutions of higher education, and most of the authors teach at Baylor University, where an apparently successful experiment is being conducted on reviving the teaching of great texts in the undergraduate curriculum. The essays here offered are the product of conversations among friends committed to a fairly uniform vision of what the teaching of great texts is all about. Not all of our texts are official members of the "Great Books" canon. Some are simply favorites of the essay's author. In the case of at least one author (Robert Kruschwitz) the chapter offers an argument that the text in question warrants a place in a great texts curriculum.

I will now introduce the essays, not in the order of our table of contents, but according to their contribution to the project of instilling Christian wisdom in ourselves (the professors) and our students. Accordingly, a particular analysis of the concept of Christian wisdom will guide the introduction of the essays. That analysis includes six points, of which the first is,

1) Wisdom is a heartfelt understanding of the good for human beings where that good is "ethical" but not narrowly so (not just a knowledge of duty, for example); for the wise person the good is also beautiful, attractive, interesting, desirable. Wisdom, thus, has an "aesthetic" dimension.

Early in the history of the church, the fathers who developed a distinctly biblical and Christian wisdom appropriated Plato's *Symposium.* It therefore stands as a prime example of a pagan work read with the faith-whetted intellectual appetite of the Christian community. Under Douglas Henry's guidance (chapter 3) the class will read the *Symposium* with special attention to two powerful loci that can occasion the learning of Christian wisdom. Plato's beautiful account of *Erôs'* ascent from the sensory savoring desire of beautiful particulars to the intellectual savoring desire of perfect eternal universal Beauty is plausibly read as a somewhat short-falling anticipation of a similar progress of the soul towards God. The other locus is the comedy of Alcibiades' drunken lovesick speech in praise of Socrates, whom he compares to a grotesque but seductive satyr-doll that secretly encloses sublime images of the gods. Thus Alcibiades, despite his own spiritual grotesqueness, seems to have a vision for the good that can penetrate through appearance to the deeper reality. Such vision for the hidden good is an aspect of wisdom, but Christians have also supposed that all people, as spiritual creatures, are subject to this power, and thus harbor an inclination and ability to see God.

Anthony Esolen's beautiful chapter (9), itself a song, guides our reading of Dante to let the *Comedy* impress on us that paganism yearns for a beauty it cannot grasp and points to a fellowship beyond its power to craft. At its best, human reason unaided by God's self-manifestation is driven by a love that finds fulfillment only in God's free gift of life and the community that gift makes possible. Wisdom is more than the power to explain, or even to choose reliably the best course of action. It is also the capacity to appreciate, to *taste* the goodness of the good and to *see* and *feel* the limits and deficits of what stands in need of completion. "Rationalism," as the typical pathology of modern academic life, is literally errant, a kind of wandering blindness, and Christian wisdom involves a heartfelt appreciation of rationalism's foolishness. Dante's *Comedy*, then, in its very songlike or poetic beauty, can contribute to our wisdom, if only we manage to read it well.

Paul Contino (chapter 16) appeals to Dostoevsky's own interpretive guidance in taking *The Brothers Karamazov* as a work intended to transform the reader's taste and consciousness. The beauty to which the book sensitizes us is the "severe" beauty of Christ, thus a good that requires a special cultivation of our seeing to recognize and care about. As in the *Symposium*, this is a beauty of which more easily recognizable beauties (like that of Grushenka, or the novel itself) partake, so that the latter can conduct us to the profoundest beauty. They can serve as conduits toward what is more deeply and transcendently lovable because, as Christians and Platonists believe, the ultimately good is singular and has no contrariety within Himself. Yet as soon as we begin to appreciate the beauty that we must love if we are to be wise, we find that it accuses and challenges us. Because we ourselves are distorted, we do not see clearly. We do not love or think aright, and so our glimpses of undistorted truth alarm us, and we shrink back into our more comfortable and trivial loves. But Dostoevsky's hope is that, as we read *The Brothers Karamazov*, the beauty of the book and of its main characters – Alyosha Karamazov and Father Zosima – will draw us toward a more mature love of the One they both serve.

2) Wisdom tends to create, and to presuppose, a narrative unity of the life of the wise individual, a sense of his or her own identity, an understanding of his life as having a "point," as making sense.

In her essay on Virgil's *Aeneid* (chapter 5), Julia Hejduk explores interpretations of the "darkness" of Virgil's depiction of human life, the senselessness of Dido's and Turnus's misfortunes, and the personal unfulfillment of Aeneas's heroism and hard work. In contrast with the egoism of the Greek heroes, Aeneas aims to found a community; he lives a "sacrificial" life. But he does so in a world governed by egoistic gods with "unassuageable thirst for the power and honor represented by blood sacrifices," so that theology is no resource for making personal sense of individual people's lives. From the personal point of view, the pessimism of the book of Ecclesiastes seems to have the final word:

> "Meaningless! Meaningless!"
> says the Teacher.
> "Utterly meaningless!
> Everything is meaningless" (1.2).

Ovid seems to revel in Virgil's darkness, drawing the shades even further closed, but also, like a frivolous existentialist, losing Virgil's moral seriousness. A recent novelist seeks to deny the darkness by patching up Virgil's narrative, "correcting" such details as Aeneas' practice of human sacrifice and the disaster in which many erotic attachments end. Hejduk ends her essay commending Dante's Christian treatment of Virgil as the one that simultaneously preserves Virgil's honesty and makes satisfying individual sense of lives of sacrifice. Since honesty and sense-making are aspects of the virtue of wisdom, Hejduk's guidance in our reading of the *Aeneid* can function as a tutorial in wisdom.

3) The self-understanding of the wise individual places her in a "world" – physical, social, and cultural. The sense of her identity involves a sense of belonging to a community of thought and value.

Barry Harvey's essay (chapter 10) on Catherine of Siena's *The Dialogue* presents her work as "a form of spiritual exercise" in which she holds together "what may seem to us to be contrary tendencies: contemplation and the active life, prayer and corporeal works of mercy, reason and revelation, the acquisition of virtue and absolute dependence on God's grace, the life of the mind and the life of the affections, [and] the importance of ascetic discipline and the inclusion of the laity who walk the ordinary way of love." On Harvey's reading of *The Dialogue*, Catherine does not think that wisdom is acquired through private ecstatic ("mystical") experiences of God (though she had such experiences). Christian love of neighbor and God is the necessary foundation of wisdom, which is spiritual union with God, and this cannot be achieved apart from a discipline of prayer, worship, study, and works of mercy. Harvey also deepens our understanding of *The Dialogue* by placing it with respect to changes that were taking place in the church's understanding of theology, liturgy, and ethics in the years leading up to Catherine's authorship. In some ways Catherine resists, and in others she reflects, these changes.

In Beth Newman's guide (chapter 12) to reading Teresa of Avila's *Las Moradas*, (known by the somewhat misleading English title of *The Interior Castle*), Newman advises us to take the work as an exposition of Scripture by a loyal and active, albeit critical and reforming, member of the body of Christ, the church. Since some read *Las Moradas* as an exercise in spiritual solipsism or as offering a doctrine-less and generic "spirituality," it is perhaps the more striking to try reading this book, which is so obviously preoccupied with self-knowledge and the nature and development of the soul, in full appreciation that we are "bodily" in two senses: we *have* members, which we are to put into intelligent motion on behalf of our Lord Christ; and we *are* members, organic functional parts of the Lord's body, the church. Nevertheless, the book is clearly about the various possible spiritual states of a soul and how to acquire the better ones by prayer. It is a book about Christian practice, and thus a handbook of the practical side of Christian wisdom.

Few ideas are more central to Christian wisdom than the distinctively Christian understanding of evil and the related concept of violence. Ralph Wood reads Flannery O'Connor's *The Violent Bear It Away* as an instructive fictional exploration of these ideas. A series of discussions of this shocking novel in a college or university context that allows for free and serious use of Christian theology as an interpretive key might serve to jar our students and ourselves out of the secular habits of thought about our identity and our life that our culture daily encourages in us.

Our culture is "therapeutic," utilitarian, and spiritually reductive. It encourages us to demythologize and naturalize evil; it encourages us to think of the human good not as the venturesome, possibly unpleasant, and arduous following of God's will, but what Wood calls "anthropoid contentment." It tends to idealize human autonomy rather than honoring obedience to the call of God. It tends to think of mentally defective people as "useless" and to suppose that both they and we would be better off if they did not exist.

By contrast, O'Connor's novel encourages us to consider that evil might be a palpable and transcendent – indeed, a personal force – in the world, and that our good might consist in a suffering obedience to God found in the one community of love that refuses to regard anyone as "useless." It is hard to imagine how O'Connor's vision could be given the serious, wisdom-engendering reading it deserves in a classroom dominated by the very cultural ideas she is seeking to undermine.

4) Since the wise person has a sense of belonging to a particular community of thought and value, catechesis ("theological" education, getting clear on what we believe) is an essential part of becoming wise.

Phillip Donnelly (chapter 14) sets John Milton's *Paradise Lost* in two primary contexts, that of Milton's political convictions concerning the relation of the English monarchy to religious belief and practice, and that of a debate over the limits of philosophy as a source of wisdom. Milton writes the story of the fall in epic form, using literary devices inherited from both pagan antiquity and the practices of biblical interpretation developed by Christian poets and theologians, to give nothing less than a general biblical account of the ways of God with man. In so doing, Milton defends a conception of human wisdom that requires particular divine revelation and shows how creation and providence are compatible with real human freedom and responsibility.

On Donnelly's proposed reading, Milton is in silent dialogue with Plato, particularly with Plato's idea of the proper moral-intellectual formation of the soul in the *Republic*. Milton differs from Plato on the place of literary art in the best development of virtue, both "intellectual" and "moral." In symmetry with the created contingency of the world, our knowledge both of that world and of who we are and what our good is has an unavoidably informational or empirical character, according to Milton. We cannot know by thought and imagination alone what we need to know to live the best possible human life. Philosophical dialectic, even combined, as Plato combines it, with literary artfulness, does not provide a sufficient education of mind and heart. We need revelation if we are to be rightly formed as human beings. No matter how smart we are, true ethics is not something we can just "think up." Nevertheless, our moral and intellectual *appropriation* of that revelation requires thought. So something like Plato's dialectic, or the method of "triall by what is contrary," is a crucial device in our spiritual development. A reading of *Paradise Lost* that takes seriously the cues to which Donnelly's essay calls our attention will be a context for students to think carefully about their own moral education and that of anyone for whose formation they may in the future be responsible. In this way, such a distinctively Christian reading will be an occasion for their deepening in wisdom.

Two loci of wisdom on which students will focus as they read James Joyce's *Portrait of the Artist as a Young Man* under the guidance of Dominic Manganiello (chapter 18) are the nature and development of the soul, and the nature and purpose of art. In the case of both loci Joyce's book is a brilliant inversion of health and truth as these have been understood by the most profound thinkers and artists of the Christian tradition, and cannot be properly understood except as against the background of the tradition it inverts. Both the brilliance and the inversion can be instructive for those who wish to nurture and be nurtured in that tradition. The novel teaches that the finest soul finds its own creative way, not in submission to God through acceptance of church teaching, but in the experimental dismantling of received tradition and in refusing direction by external authority. And it teaches that art, as a reification of the artist's own creative brilliance and erotic energy, rather than God, is the proper object of uncompromising devotion. The starkness and fineness of the contrast between these conceptions of life and art can deepen the reader's appreciation of the Christian way.

In the modern context, the doctrine of human sin marks off the Christian consciousness from much that is taught in the surrounding culture. In his essay on Thomas Aquinas's *On Evil*, Robert Kruschwitz (chapter 8) proposes the use of a text that is not included in traditional great texts curricula (indeed, it was only recently published in English). He argues that Aquinas's discussion of the seven capital vices, which has historical roots in monastic "therapeutic" (or prophylactic) exercises for combating destructive sin, is especially well adapted to the ethical and spiritual aspirations of our current generation of college students. An appreciation of human frailty, dysfunction, and sin – in short, an understanding of what prevents us from being happy and healthy human beings – is surely an essential aspect of Christian wisdom, and Aquinas's *On Evil* is vastly superior, for this purpose, to the texts that are conventionally read in undergraduate ethics courses.

By the time Aquinas rethinks the ancient schema of human pathology, the social context of discussion has moved from the monastery, with its immediate spiritual-practical goal of soul formation, to the university, with its more intellectualist aims. Still, the medieval university was a Christian university, with a strongly shared conception of the human good and a general commitment to the Christian formation of persons. And our contemporary Christian universities and colleges, while far from being monasteries, are more congenial institutional settings for nurture in self-understanding than their secular counterparts. Texts like *On Evil* offer occasion for basic instruction in Christian doctrine, without which full-fledged Christian wisdom is not possible.

5. The sense of belonging is a historical consciousness, a kind of cultural "memory"; the wise person knows and understands his antecedents, and sees himself and his present world in terms of them.

The theme of John O'Callaghan's chapter (17) is that of active forgetting and remembering of who we are and who has formed us. In *On the Genealogy of Morals* Friedrich Nietzsche proposes that if we are to come to know ourselves, to become truly healthy and mature as human beings, to become wise, we must engage in a certain active "forgetting." On O'Callaghan's reading, Nietzsche accepts a project that has been under way since the earliest modern philosophy, namely the project of making ourselves *autonomous*. The foil against which the project is a rebellion is any understanding of ourselves in which we acknowledge our indebtedness to others, but the paradigm case is Christianity, which teaches that God made us in his own image and requires obedience from us. Thus Augustine comes to know himself by accepting Catholic teaching, and so coming by introspection to see that he is made in the image of the triune God. Modern philosophers (Descartes and Kant get special attention) throw off the authority of the church but do not complete the movement towards autonomy. Descartes continues to believe that he is made in the image of God and allows himself to be bound by the limits of truth, while Kant finds in pure practical reason a moral law to which he must submit. According to Nietzsche, these philosophers' failure to achieve autonomy, and thus wisdom and happiness, is that they did not discover and use active forgetting, along with its defiance of truth. They continue to remember the tradition they have inherited from previous philosophers and the church. They continue to remember where they came from. Nietzsche's contribution, which according to him marks a major turning point in the history of philosophy, is that you can actively forget your debts to your tradition and thus become a truly self-made man!

While acknowledging that a number of Christian approaches to *King Lear* are possible, Roger Lundin (chapter 13) leads us in a reading that places the work at the same time in the historical setting of broad cultural change and the intimate context of wrenching personal loss. The historical context is the onset of "modernity," that period in which "nature" comes to be conceived as an impersonal mechanical force with which human beings vie for mastery according to the disjunction: master nature for your own advantage or, to your detriment, be mastered by it (or by others who have learned to master it). Accordingly, modernity evacuates from nature any suggestion of providence.

When King Lear foolishly abdicates his throne he thereby forsakes the protections of social convention associated with his position, and lays himself open to human ambition and malice and thus to the senseless forces of nature. For Lear, the nature in which he is subjected to the storm by his ambitious, unloving daughters is not a theoretical matter for historical-cultural analysis, but a question of the meaning of his own life. So to understand Lear's agony and his personal need to make sense of his life in the face of nature, the reader needs to have some personal reference for Lear's desolation, some point of connection in his or her own life by which to begin to appreciate what Lear is going through. Lundin reports his own growth in understanding *King Lear* (and thus life as a human being) as turning crucially on a personal loss. Any of us can supply an analogous story of our own. However, understanding does not come from "personal experience" alone, but from our ways of *framing* our experience. And Lundin testifies to the importance of Christian theology, especially modern theology, in the formation of his understanding of himself through great literature.

In his reading of Augustine's *Confessions*, Michael Foley (chapter 6) charts Augustine's use and abuse of classic books as they figured in his development. He shows how Augustine's understanding of these books reflected moral stages in his life, such that as he moved from waywardness to more perfect attunement to the moral Author of the universe, he also moved from being a worse, to being a better, reader of excellent texts. Thus the model of excellent reading suggested by the *Confessions* is that it cannot be separated from a positive process of moral progress on the part of the reader. "The lesson for us as educators," writes Foley, "is to be as solicitous about our students' formation as we are about their accumulation of facts or truths." This is wisdom for teachers, and will counsel a special kind of care in the selection and interpretation of texts in the classroom. But it is also wisdom for the students, because a reading of the *Confessions* that highlights the roles of texts in Augustine's conversion along the lines that Foley commends will occasion reflective awareness, on the part of our students, of this intrinsic connection between the intellectual and moral virtues of the excellent reader.

Scott Moore's guide to Homer's *Odyssey* (chapter 2) calls the reader's attention to three features of this epic comedy: the much-revisited theme of descent into hell, and the contestable Homeric virtues of wisdom and justice. Moore is especially keen that our students should appreciate how each of these themes is taken up, criticized, transformed, and deepened in the great texts of the subsequent millennia. All of these features provide opportunities for wisdom-cultivating discussion of the text. It can be instructive to read the account of Odysseus' descent into the underworld in juxtaposition with the other descent stories that Moore mentions, and then to think of all the pagan ones in the light of the fact that our Lord himself, as part of his ministry, descended into hell. Another focus for discussions of the *Odyssey* is the virtues of the heroes. In particular, their conceptions of wisdom and justice seem (or ought to seem) very alien to the mind of Christ, and so to our minds if we are growing in Christian virtues. But as Moore points out, relatively modern people like Machiavelli (and we might think too of Nietzsche) may be, in their thinking about virtues, more like Homer than like Christians. In these ways and in many others a reading of the *Odyssey* provides an enormously rich environment of ideas for the cultivation of Christian wisdom.

6. The wise person is "discerning," knowing how to divide, separate, and distinguish, appreciating differences, but is also alive to similarity, analogy, and continuity among ideas.

In my chapter on Aristotle's *Nicomachean Ethics* (chapter 4) I propose a number of ways we can read Aristotle's *Ethics* in juxtaposition to the New Testament so as to increase our powers of ethical discernment – our understanding of our own ethical outlook, as well as Aristotle's. I then discuss at greater length two major convergences, namely, the concept of virtues and that of friendship. I suggest that Aristotle's actual method of analyzing virtue concepts is more similar to the New Testament's approach than he claims, though the particular virtues he promotes are more different from New Testament virtues than most people realize. I then argue that Aristotle has conflicting models of friendship – one that conceives it as a kind of justice, and one that models it on generosity. The generosity model bears greater resemblance to New Testament agape, but one feature of Aristotle's view goes on partially to undermine the resemblance.

If we are actively trying to live the Christian life, as many students and faculty members in Christian universities do, this distinction-making will bear significantly on our own self-understanding, desiring, feeling, and acting, and this understanding will verge toward wisdom. Wisdom involves knowing who we are and where we stand. As Christians we are heirs of both Aristotle and the New Testament, but the New Testament is normative for us in a way that Aristotle is not. Thus as we grapple with the details of Aristotle's great book in the light of the New Testament, we not only become better at making clear distinctions about character, motivation, and our ultimate good, but we also piece together the genealogy of our morals.

Christians often regard Kant's moral philosophy as a fount of much that is wrong with "enlightenment" rationalism as it has influenced modern intellectual life, and indeed many of the essays in the present volume can be read as protests against such rationalism. Kyla Ebels-Duggan's essay (chapter 15) contributes valuably to this volume by warning people like us against a too hasty dismissal of Kant's moral thought, and as an example of charitable and wise Christian reading. Ebels-Duggan does not, in the end, save Kant from all Christian criticism, but in her admirably clear exposition of the *Groundwork* she extracts the teeth from a number of objections that are popular among Christian intellectuals.

David Lyle Jeffrey's reading of *Canterbury Tales* (chapter 11) illustrates a general truth about reading great Christian texts: the kind of "secularizing" reading that is sometimes promoted in colleges and research universities obscures the Christian purpose, and thus the way the text actually works. Such reading guarantees that the reader will misunderstand the text. If the text is designed, as Jeffrey argues *Canterbury Tales* is designed, to transform the reader by "placing" him or her, affectively-cum-intellectually, in the one true story, then to read the work while intentionally or unintentionally ignoring the author's purpose is to misunderstand the text, and even more importantly, to fail to gain from the text the understanding of oneself that it aims to engender. Wisdom is a readiness to read with an ear prepared, to hear in the words of the text their import for life. It is thus a kind of "hearing-as," the hearing of one thing in terms of another, which in the *Canterbury Tales* is often another text. To read *Canterbury Tales* well, to read them with understanding, is to hear the texts alluded to in the present text, but more than this, it is to appreciate the personal significance of the allusion.

To appreciate this significance is in many cases of the *Canterbury Tales* to hear a kind of incongruity that reflects on the character of the tale's teller, on his or her wisdom or lack thereof. To hear such incongruity with appreciation is to be amused in the sense of to *find funny* or *humorous*. But to find something funny is, at least for the moment, to take a personal *position* with regard to some norm of the way things ought to be. So when we hear Palamon and Arcite alluding to Boethius' *Consolation of Philosophy*, but doing so in a way that reveals a grotesque moral misunderstanding of the words they allude to, and we find their misunderstanding amusing, we take, for the moment, a personal or spiritual position on what the real meaning of the Boethius text is. That text is morally serious, so our amusement at Palamon's and Arcite's misunderstanding involves *us* in taking a morally serious position (again, I say, possibly only for the moment, and maybe even in spite of ourselves). By contrast, no such morally serious position is entailed by our amusement at the incongruity of the "moustache kiss."

The *Canterbury Tales* encloses levels or graded kinds of humor, and the capacity to appreciate the bawdy stories is decidedly on the low end of the grading scale. A course in which the aim of reading is to cultivate wisdom will aim to move the students *up* the grading scale to levels that make demands for some modicum of wisdom on the part of the readers. As Jeffrey suggests, this progress will involve training the students in other texts, in terms of which the students will learn to "hear" the Canterbury tales and so, understanding, experience the amusement that expresses their incipient or growing wisdom. The tales, Jeffrey alerts us, are arranged in three series, the tellers in each successive series representing an intellectual and affective advance in the ascent to wisdom or virtue as the pilgrims advance toward the Canterbury Cathedral where they will dismount and enter to make their confession and communicate with Him who is the Word made flesh. Thus the early, more carnal, narrators must be heard in conjunction with the later, more integrated, ones if the reading is to convey the effect that Chaucer intended on heart and understanding.

Sarah-Jane Murray (chapter 7) discerns a formative purpose in the narrative poems (*Lais*) of Marie de France. The *Lais* are entertaining, often funny, stories about knights and ladies falling (often unlawfully) in love, and of rivals doing one another in out of envy, and the comeuppances they suffer in consequence of their folly. Marie illustrates how one sin, if not repented of, leads to another and so on to yet others, miring the sinner in a sticky mass of troubles, not only for himself but for those around him. Murray comments that Marie is "famous for her ambiguity" and regards the poems she composes as complex and "obscure." However, Murray helps us to see that we can lighten much of the obscurity by reading the *Lais* as informed by biblical understanding and undertaken with Christian purpose.

The poems' success in mediating the reader's growth in wisdom depends on the reader's allusive sensitivity, in particular her sensitivity to biblical allusions, because they carry with them, for biblically literate people, a standpoint from which to understand the otherwise indeterminate value of the characters' actions. This biblical and theological understanding, which the teacher of great texts will need to make explicit for 21st century students, contrasts rather starkly with the sensuous (Ovidian) outlook of many of the stories' characters.

In *Guigemar*, for example, Marie does not overtly moralize; indeed, she ends the story with Guigemar's jubilation at recovering his adulterous beloved, heedless that he has thereby "brought down and destroyed a whole country." Marie leaves it to the reader to sense that, despite the entertainment the story has provided him, and the "happiness" of its "hero," the Ovidian picture of love that it presents is deeply distressing. That this distress is particularly characteristic of a biblically oriented reader becomes, perhaps, clearer with Murray's guidance in reading *Laüstic*. Again, the theme is knightly adultery (sexually unconsummated, in the present instance). Seen in the light of Marie's biblical conception of love, the lovers' nightly trysts at the windows of their adjacent houses, which the lady in question excuses to her husband by blaming a nightingale (*laüstic*) for her sleeplessness, acquire a comic cast. When the angry husband kills the bird, the wife, in a fit of self-pity, sends her lover the carcass, for which he orders a portable shrine to be built so that he may be forever reminded of his beloved. Murray disagrees with scholars who interpret this *lai* as a celebration of courtly love. On a reading that credits Marie with a more intelligent Christian irony, the knight's undying devotion to the dead bird indicates, rather, the idolatrous character of such "love." For readers who might be tempted to feel otherwise, a careful reading of *Guigemar* and *Laüstic* can be a tutorial in Christian discernment. But Marie's characters are not all Ovidian reprobates. For example, the leading female characters in *Fresne* and *Eliduc* are likely to shock the modern reader with their redemptive and healing sacrificial love.

Conclusion

The eighteen papers in this volume, each about a text that might figure in a syllabus of "great texts," aim to help the teacher who would approach such texts with a single and unified pedagogical goal. The goal we propose is one of holistic character formation. That is, we read each text for its contribution to the integrated intellectual, moral, and aesthetic development of the reader (whether that reader be the "teacher" or the "student"). Since the activity of reading has its effect on character by way of intellect and imagination, it has seemed fitting to call our character ideal "wisdom." In this Introduction, I have argued that such a goal is best achieved in a community with a shared conception of the human good (since each of our texts is, in its own way, *about* the human good).

The notion of the good that dominated the best human thought in the West during the middle centuries of the period covered by our texts is the Christian one – a notion articulated, no doubt, in a diversity of Christian ways. Moreover, intellectual communities inspired by and seeking the human good as the Christian tradition conceives it actually exist at this moment (they are represented by the authors of this volume). For these reasons, the Christian community seems a natural context for such an endeavor, and Christian wisdom an appropriate goal. The reader who is not committed to this life and goal may still take interest in this volume of essays, as displaying a possible model (or anti-model) for an intellectual life that is similarly unified but differently conceived.

References

Aeschylus 1953. *Oresteia*. Trans. Richard Lattimore. Chicago: University of Chicago Press.

Aristotle 2004. *Nicomachean Ethics*. Trans. J. A. K. Thompson. New York: Penguin Classics.

Balthasar, Hans Urs von 2000. *Mysterium Paschale: The Mystery of Easter.* Trans. Aidan Nichols, O.P. San Francisco: Ignatius Press.

Campbell, Joseph 2008. *The Hero with a Thousand Faces,* 3rd ed. Novato, California: New World Library.

Euripides 1998. *Euripides I*. Eds. David R. Slavitt and Palmer Bovie. Philadelphia: University of Pennsylvania Press.

Fagles, Robert 1996. "Notes on the Translation" in *The Odyssey*. New York: Penguin Books.

Heaney, Seamus 1961. *The Cure at Troy: A Version of Sophocles' "Philoctetes."* New York: Farrar, Straus and Giroux.

Herzog, Don 2006. *Cunning*. Princeton: Princeton University Press.

Homer 1996. *The Odyssey*. Trans. Robert Fagles. New York: Penguin Books.

Hume, David 2006. *Essays: Moral, Political, and Literary*. New York: Cosimo Classics.

Lewis, C. S. 2000. "Myth Became Fact" in *Essay Collection and Other Short Pieces*. Ed. Lesley Walmsley. London: HarperCollins.

Liddell, H. G., and Robert Scott, Eds. 1982. *Greek-English Lexicon*. Abridged Ed. Oxford: Oxford University Press.

Machiavelli, Niccolò 1998. *The Prince*. 2nd ed. Trans. Harvey C. Mansfield. Chicago: University of Chicago Press.

MacIntyre, Alasdair 1984. *After Virtue*. 2nd ed. Notre Dame, Indiana: University of Notre Dame Press.

Milton, John 1992. "Paradise Lost" in *The Complete English Poems*. Ed. Gordon Campbell. New York: Knopf Publishers.

Modern Library 1998. "100 Best Novels." http://www.randomhouse.com/modernlibrary/100bestnovels.html

Ratzinger, Joseph 2009. *Credo for Today: What Christians Believe*. Trans.
Michael J. Miller, et al. San Francisco: Ignatius Press.

Reeves, James, Ed. 1965. *The Cassell Book of English Poetry*. New York: Harper and Row Publishers.

Homer
The Odyssey

Many of the "common threads" that bind the great texts and their authors to one another have their origins in Homer. Tradition places this blind poet from the island of Chios in the eighth century BC and something like a Trojan War itself some four hundred years prior to that. From the point of view of one seeking to understand the common threads that run through the Greats or to join their conversation so as to grow in human wisdom, it matters little whether "Homer" names one or more distinct, historical individuals who composed the *Iliad* and the *Odyssey* or an early school of poets who collected and redacted the oral traditions that narrated a Trojan War shrouded in mystery and tragedy half a millennium earlier. In either case, "Homer" still names the human source of these two extraordinary epics, which are often the portal through which readers of great texts first travel as they seek to understand the human predicament and the quest for happiness, virtue, and understanding that marks the life well lived.

Homer's *Odyssey* is, of course, the epic "sequel" to the *Iliad*. While the *Iliad* offers a window onto the struggle between the Achaeans and the Trojans and culminates with the death of valiant Hector, the *Odyssey* is the famed account of the Greek hero Odysseus and his journey from Troy to his home on the western island of Ithaca, his son Telemachus's search both for his father and himself, and his wife Penelope's attempt to be faithful to the gods and to her husband while protecting their homeland. The epic concludes with their common struggles to reclaim and restore their rightful kingdom.

Many students will have read selections from the *Odyssey* in their high school literature classes, and even more will have read summaries from Edith Hamilton or another modern author. Moreover, they will have encountered the *Odyssey* in countless ways through popular culture, and this familiarity gives readers a sense that they know the story and the difficulties that Odysseus must face.

Such an assumption is partly justified. The *Odyssey* does provide western culture (from the ancient to the contemporary) with some of its most enduring themes and episodes. The subject matter of the *Odyssey* (together with the *Iliad*) is the basis for much Greek tragedy; Virgil's *Aeneid* is an attempt to provide Imperial Rome with an epic worthy of the one Homer provided for the

Greeks by continuing the Trojan thread after the defeat at home. Not only do Augustine, Dante, Rabelais, Shakespeare, Cervantes, and countless others draw explicitly on the *Odyssey*; re-telling and re-interpreting Odysseus's wanderings becomes a device by which many more recent authors re-present the human journey. James Joyce's *Ulysses* is frequently recognized as one of the most important literary works of the twentieth century.[1]

Yet the *Odyssey* remains an unknown text for many contemporary readers. The *Odyssey* they know is almost exclusively the portion that Odysseus recounts to King Alcinous and the Phaeacians. Here we find most of Odysseus's "adventures": the hallucinations brought on by the Lotus-eaters, the struggle with Polyphemus the Cyclops, the near arrival to Ithaca thwarted by the crew's curiosity about Aeolus's bag, the escape from the Laestrygonian cannibals, the bewitchment by Circe, the journey into Hell, the temptations of the Sirens, Scylla and Charybdis, the slaughter of Helios's cattle. These adventures just *are* the *Odyssey* for most of our students and the larger culture as well. It is all they know, and all they think they need to know. Most are surprised to discover that this long "tale" by Odysseus comprises only a small portion of the *Odyssey* itself. In fact, it is limited to Books 9–12 of the text.

Most contemporary readers thus have very little sense of the plight and the difficulties faced by Telemachus, despite the fact that the narrative begins (after the first one hundred lines) with the son rather than with the father. Athena ends Odysseus's long exile by beseeching Zeus to send Hermes to Calypso and convince her to free the long-suffering hero and send herself to Telemachus to enact a four-fold plan: rouse him to bravery, inspire him to confront the suitors ruining their household, send him off to find his father, and most importantly "make [known] his name throughout the mortal world."[2] In much the same way, the role of Penelope (from beginning to end) is often overlooked or forgotten. Convincing self-possessed Penelope and winning back her acceptance proves to be the final challenge that wily Odysseus must overcome. The text concludes with an epilogue (Book 24) that raises as many questions as it answers and initiates a quest for the discovery of justice that moves through the western canon from retribution to litigation and beyond.

Perhaps no question engenders more disagreement than whether Odysseus is a sympathetic character. The master of exploits, the man of pain, he was more often reviled than praised in the ancient world. Should the modern reader rejoice at his triumphs or lament them? Are his strengths virtues? Attempts to answer these questions bring to light the contested character of the concepts of virtue, wisdom, and justice. Is Odysseus virtuous, wise, or just? What are we to make of the inheritance that the *Odyssey* bequeaths to the western canon? What, especially, are Christian readers to make of this text and its ambiguous hero?

One can approach answers to these questions by reading and rereading the *Odyssey* within the context of the canon as a whole. As one returns to the *Odyssey*, one sees that its themes and questions prefigure many of the very same issues that get played out throughout the canon of later great texts. What must one do to fulfill one's obligations to God or the gods? What virtues or strengths of character are necessary for success in life? What is justice and how is it achieved and sustained? What is the connection between one's right relationship to God and the development of those necessary virtues or personal characteristics that enable one to be happy and successful? What if justice and happiness conflict? What if my greatest strengths of character contain the seeds of my own undoing? The questions that Odysseus must confront as he moves across the wine-dark sea become some of the most important issues for the authors of the great texts across the centuries.

To reflect on these questions, consider three representative features of the epic that play formative roles in the development of the canon. These features are the descent into Hell, the *Odyssey*'s representation of virtue and wisdom, and the quest for justice. In each case, the epic presents a complex body of thought informed by heroic assumptions with which the canon grapples again and again over the next two and a half millennia.

Descent into Hell

Odysseus's descent (*katabasis*) into the underworld inaugurates an important theme that will be repeated through much of the western canon. Most of Book 11 is comprised of Odysseus's retelling of his journey to the Kingdom of the Dead. On Odysseus's version of the story, after an entire year on Circe's island Circe tells him that he must journey to the House of Death to consult with Tiresias. The blind seer of Thebes will give Odysseus the wisdom he needs to journey safely to Ithaca, including instructions for performing a ritual sacrifice without which he cannot return.

Tiresias tells Odysseus that he and his crew may reach home, if he has the power to rein in their wild desires "and curb your own, what's more" (11, 119). He is warned not to touch the sacred cattle of Helios, the god of the sun, and what will happen to him and his men if they cannot control their desires. According to Tiresias, if the cattle are harmed, his ship and crew will be lost, and even if Odysseus survives, "you'll come home late and come a broken man – all shipmates lost, alone in a stranger's ship – and you will find a world of pain at home" (11, 129–32). Tiresias knows that Odysseus will triumph over his adversaries, but his long journey and his sufferings will have changed both him and his home in ways that can never be restored. Finally, Tiresias prophesies how and when Odysseus himself will die and what obligations to Poseidon (Odysseus's sworn enemy) and the other gods he must make to die an honored death. Following his exchange with Tiresias, Odysseus converses with other shades from their previous lives, including his mother Anticleia, Agamemnon, Ajax, Achilles, and more.

Note three things about Odysseus's descent into the underworld. First, Homer bequeaths to the reader a geography of the underworld which will be repeated, elaborated, and transformed throughout the canon. Most important in this regard are the rivers found in Hades. Homer names four: Acheron, Periphlegethon, Cocytus, and Styx. These are, respectively, the Rivers of Grief, Fire, Tears, and Hate. In Homer, these rivers principally demarcate the boundaries of and within Erebus, the underworld. (Initially, it appears that Odysseus is merely at the entrance of the underworld and the shades come to him.) Much later (though recounted earlier in the narrative), Calypso will swear by the River Styx to convince Odysseus that she is not devising some new plot against him (5, 205). Robert Fagles notes that Styx was "the guarantor of oaths sworn by the gods." In Hesiod's *Theogony,* any god who swears falsely by Styx is paralyzed and excluded from the assemblies of the gods (Fagles 1996, 507).

Building on the Homeric geography of the underworld, Ovid and Virgil will add the River Lethe, which Dante places in the Garden of Eden atop Mount Purgatory. In *The Purgatorio*, Lethe is the river the pilgrim must cross to forget his sins and the grief that those sins have produced. It is connected with Eunoë through which one's memories of good actions are rekindled (Canto 28). John Milton will offer the most famous re-description of the Odyssey's underworld rivers in Book 2 of *Paradise Lost*:

> Of four infernal rivers, that disgorge
> Into the burning lake their baleful streams –
> Abhorrèd Styx, the flood of deadly hate;
> Sad Acheron of sorrow, black and deep;
> Cocytus, named of lamentation loud
> Heard on the rueful stream; fierce Phlegeton
> Whose wave of torrent fire inflame with rage.
> Far off from these, a slow and silent stream,
> Lethe, the river of oblivion, rolls
> Her watery labyrinth, whereof who drinks
> Forthwith his former state and being forgets –
> Forgets both joy and grief, pleasure and pain.
> (Milton, "Paradise Lost" 2.1654–56)

It is clear that Christian poets like Dante and Milton take up the pagan geography of the underworld and transform it into essential elements of the Christian myth, expanding and appropriating relevant aspects into metaphors that illumine Christian understandings of both the origins of sin and the final destiny of humankind.

Second, Odysseus's descent into the underworld establishes a pattern and a precedent that is repeated time and again in western literature, becoming an essential dimension in the development of the epic hero. Aeneas, like Odysseus before him, journeys into the underworld in search of that wisdom which can be garnered only by those who pass from this world. Apollodorus, and later Ovid, also recount journeys into the underworld, especially that of Orpheus. Dante the pilgrim's journey is not principally in pursuit of knowledge; his is the journey of the soul to God, but such a soul must pass through Hell before he can even arrive on Mount Purgatory, let alone ascend into Heaven. Once again, one must pass through Hell to reach the final destination.

Milton's Satan famously prefers reigning in Hell to serving in Heaven, subverting Achilles' claim to Odysseus that "I'd rather slave on earth for another man – some dirt-poor tenant farmer who scrapes to keep alive – than rule down here over all the breathless dead" (9, 556–58). And the convention is employed in countless instances in modern and contemporary literature: Shakespeare, Bunyan, Goethe, Dostoevsky, Melville, Conrad, Joyce, Eliot, Williams, Proust, Bulgakov, Tolkien, Orwell, Sartre, Murdoch – far too many to name. The descent into Hell, whether literal or metaphorical, has become one of the most common conventions in western literature.

Third, Christian belief affirms that Christ himself descended into Hell. The "Harrowing of Hell" is the belief that following Christ's crucifixion, he descended into Hell (Eph. 4:9), both proving that Death could not hold him (Acts 2:31) and proclaiming the gospel to those who had died before (1 Pet. 3:19, 4:6). This doctrine is of such significance as to be included in most major creeds and confessions of faith, including the Apostles' Creed. The Christian must face some difficult questions here. The creeds teach this belief as an essential element of orthodox belief and thus no mere convention. Is it mere coincidence that what pagan religions taught as myth, the Christian faith now teaches as true?

C. S. Lewis famously argued, "The heart of Christianity is a myth which is also a fact. The old myth of the Dying God, *without ceasing to be myth*, comes down from the heaven of legend and imagination to the earth of history." For Lewis, the crucial element for identifying the "myth which is also a fact" is the claim to historicity. "We pass from a Balder or an Osiris, dying nobody knows when or where, to a historical Person crucified (it is all in order) *under Pontius Pilate*. By becoming fact it does not cease to be myth: that is the miracle." Lewis concludes, "To be truly Christian we must both assent to the historical fact and also receive the myth (fact though it has become) with the same imaginative embrace which we accord to all myths. The one is hardly more necessary than the other" (2000, 141; italics in the original).

Perhaps Lewis's explanation is persuasive for understanding Christ's crucifixion or incarnation. Will it suffice also for this troublesome notion of Christ's descent into Hell, an event explicitly recorded by none of the canonical evangelists? St. Matthew (12:40) records Jesus prophesying that "Just as Jonah was three days and three nights in the belly of the great fish, so will the Son of Man be three days and three nights in the heart of the earth," but none of the gospel writers offers an account of Jesus's descent into Hell. The appeal to Jonah does not help the modern reader distinguish mere literary convention from historical narrative. In the words of Pope Benedict XVI, this doctrine "seems to call most of all for 'demythologization'" (Ratzinger 2009, 82).

Is this really a question for history? That is, between Good Friday and Easter Sunday, did the person of Jesus of Nazareth, after being crucified under the orders of the Roman governor Pontius Pilate, actually proceed into the depths of Hell? While in Hell, did Christ preach and liberate captive souls? Christian expositors through the ages have wrestled with how to understand this belief.

There are numerous avenues for understanding this difficult affirmation. One might simply declare that the descent into Hell is nothing more than a literary convention. Joseph Campbell (2008), for instance, argues that Christ's life, death, and return are best understood through the rubric of the Hero's Journey. Christ's alleged descent is simply one more trial for him to overcome. Myth does not become historical Fact. Or one might want to reject any alleged similarity at all between Christ's descent and that of the epic heroes. One could accomplish this either by re-examining the scriptural sources on which the doctrine is based or reinterpreting the theological significance of the claim in a new light. The creedal reference to Christ's descent is usually assumed to be taken from 1 Peter 3:19–20 and 4:6. 1 Peter speaks of Christ making a proclamation "even to the dead" and to the "spirits in prison." The passage, however, mentions those who lived in the days of Noah and is keen to connect the dying and rising again with baptism. Should such an oblique reference be understood as a "descent into Hell"? The doctrine can also be reinterpreted in the light of larger, more comprehensive Christian doctrines. Some theologians, such as Hans Urs von Balthasar, have emphasized the descent's role in soteriology and have argued that the descent demonstrates Christ's suffering rather than his triumph (2000, 160–87).

Here we see a major difference between the epic literary convention and Christian doctrine. Odysseus descends into the Kingdom of the Dead to gather information, not only how he might find his way home but also what religious obligations he must perform for the gods to ensure his arrival. Christ's descent into Hell is not a quest for information. On the surface, the traditional interpretation of Christ's descent seems to parallel more closely the myth of Orpheus, who descends into the Underworld to retrieve his beloved Eurydice and bring her back to the land of the living. One might be tempted to interpret Christ's liberation of the souls in the prison of the dead along these lines. Of course, Orpheus's vanity and anxiety cause him to fail, and the similarity between the myths falls apart.

The more important question for the interpretation of the *Odyssey* turns on Odysseus's quest for wisdom and information. The closest parallel within the *Odyssey* is Menelaus's search for and capture of Proteus. Menelaus asks the Old Man of the sea essentially the same question Odysseus will ask of Tiresias, "How can I cross the swarming sea and reach home at last?" (4, 528). And yet, Menelaus's labor pales in comparison to that of Odysseus.

Does Odysseus find the wisdom that he is seeking in the Kingdom of the Dead? Yes, he does, and in this way Odysseus is certainly more of an exemplar for Aeneas or for the character Dante than he is for Christ. And yet there may remain important similarities. The descent into Hell may illumine something necessary for goodness and flourishing. In the *Odyssey*, Odysseus learns from Tiresias what his religious obligations are (the ritual sacrifice necessary to return), and he is reminded by Agamemnon of the benefit of a cunning, secret arrival to Ithaca. But how is this knowledge related to wisdom, and is Odysseus's cunning virtuous?

Wisdom and Virtue

The epic's depiction of human virtues and especially of wisdom is one of the most striking challenges to the sensibilities of the contemporary reader. The heroic virtues, as embodied in the heroes Achilles, Hector, Odysseus, Agamemnon, Ajax, and others celebrate those human characteristics or traits which were necessary to flourish in the heroic age. Chief among the heroic virtues was courage and related characteristics such as strength, speed, renown, fidelity, and cunning. (Whether they are also the traits most valued by Homer can be questioned since both the *Iliad* and the *Odyssey* contain hints of a critical attitude toward the heroic virtues.)

The heroic story is a story of contests of strength, of battles for dominance, advantage, and revenge. For the heroes, the good itself, the good after which it is unquestionably natural to seek, is *honor*. Honor is *recognized superiority* – having important people look at one and recognize one's greatness. The world of the heroes is a deeply competitive world, and the terms of competition – the criteria of greatness – are nobility of birth, physical prowess, wealth, daring, and skill. These are the heroic virtues. They are the standards of rank and achievement, and these produce *kudos* (fame) in life and *kleos* (glory) after death which rank among the most important achievements in Heroic life.

The *Greek-English Lexicon* of Liddell and Scott gives, as the first definition of *arête* (virtue), "*goodness*, *excellence* of any kind; but in Homer, like

Latin *virtus* (from *vir*), *manhood, prowess, valor*; also, *manly beauty, dignity,* etc." (Liddell 1982, 100). Alasdair MacIntyre comments, "a fast runner displays the *aretê* of his feet (*Iliad* 20, 411) and a son excels his father in every kind of *aretê* – as athlete, as soldier and in mind (*Iliad* 15, 642)" (MacIntyre 1984, 122). A virtue, then, is essentially an excellence, a quality that makes an individual an excellent human being. By the end of the fifth century BC, the nature and character of these excellences have become a contested matter. In Plato's dialogue the *Meno*, Socrates questions Meno on the nature of virtue, seeking to identify what is common to all virtue. In the *Republic*, Plato emphasizes the four virtues of wisdom, courage, temperance, and justice. In other dialogues, like the *Euthyphro*, piety takes center stage. By the mid-fourth century, Aristotle will, in his *Nicomachean Ethics*, expand both the number and kinds of virtue, distinguishing between "moral" and "intellectual" virtues (Book 6). Throughout the Greek tradition, a human virtue is a human excellence.

What is the "excellence" for which Odysseus is best known? Odysseus is repeatedly described as "cunning," and his most common epithets refer to this central aspect of his character: wily Odysseus, crafty Odysseus, the man of twists and turns.

Homer himself probably does not wholeheartedly endorse Odysseus's cunning, and later Greek literature and the subsequent western literary tradition is decidedly mixed on the question. David Hume links Odysseus's cunning with "fraud" and notes that "the sage Ulysses in the Greek poet seems to delight in lies and fictions, and often employs them without any necessity or even advantage" (2006, 233). Sometimes the advantage is patent: Odysseus's cunning is credited for the wooden horse episode at Troy, and thus the Achaean victory; it is what enables him to deceive Polyphemus to save himself and his men, and it is magnificently on display when he deceives the suitors into believing that he is an old man and not the king returned from his journeys. Is this sort of cunning – cunning as deceptive guile – a virtue?

Within the heroic framework, Odysseus is credited with being wise. His cunning directly contributes to his success in battle, it is part and parcel of his courage, it serves his fidelity to his men and family, and it is intimately connected with what the reader assumes is his wisdom. But Odysseus's cunning is not best understood as wisdom or a species of wisdom. It is neither *sophia* nor *phronêsis* (prudence or practical wisdom). It is perhaps best understood as cleverness (*deinotês*).

In Book 6 of the *Nicomachean Ethics* Aristotle, writing four hundred years after Homer, distinguishes *phronêsis* from cleverness. According to Aristotle, cleverness is a capacity for finding what is needed to fulfill an end. If the aim or end of a person's cleverness is noble, then his cleverness is praiseworthy. If its goal is unscrupulousness or some other bad end, then cleverness is not to be praised. According to Aristotle, "this is why we call both prudent and unscrupulous people clever." But one cannot be prudent without being good, and "wickedness distorts the vision and causes serious error about the principles of conduct" (*Nicomachean Ethics*, 1144a). Thus it would seem that Odysseus's cleverness is praiseworthy only if it is directed toward a noble end. Is Odysseus's clever cunning directed toward a noble goal and thus good and virtuous?

If one accepts the heroic notion of the good as honor achieved through high birth, strength, skill, and domination of others, then we will have to admit that Odysseus is honorable. Even where his deceitfulness seems to have no practical purpose, it does serve a heroic purpose. MacIntyre notes that cunning is an important heroic virtue "because cunning may have its achievements where courage is lacking or courage fails" (1984, 123). Moreover, deceit and trickery are ways of dominating. The tricked one looks diminished, looks the fool, is passive and out of control of the situation, while the trickster is the agent and in control. Odysseus has no practical need to taunt the defeated Polyphemus as he makes his escape, but it serves the heroic purpose of deliciously accenting Odysseus's triumph and revenge. (True, he pays dearly for it, and by the end of the poem he has presumably learned to direct his desire for dominance and revenge in such a way as to cause himself less trouble. But then again, maybe not; see the discussion of Book 24 below.)

Yet throughout the western canon, Odysseus is rarely viewed as a man of virtue, and his cunning is often his most despised trait. In Sophocles' play *Philoctetes*, he is presented as deceitful and malicious, attempting to manipulate both Philoctetes (whom he had abandoned many years earlier) and Neoptolemos (Achilles' young son). He is depicted as a liar and a coward, and in the end, he is successful neither in persuading Neoptolemos to betray Philoctetes nor in convincing Philoctetes to join the Greek forces in Troy. Heracles must appear to persuade his old friend of what Odysseus cannot. And in Euripides' tragedies Odysseus is even worse. In *Hecuba* he is the "sweet-talking, forked-tongued, glad-handing son of Laertes" (Euripides 1997, 83) who breaks his promise to Polyxena before callously taking her to be sacrificed in memory of Achilles. *Trojan Women* shows more of the same. By the fifth century in Athens, Odysseus has ceased to be a hero or exemplar; indeed, he has lost even his courage and any effective cunning.

The Odysseus that we meet in the Eighth Circle of Dante's Hell is not being punished for wrath or lust or avarice – all of which he was surely guilty. He is being punished for deception and is found in the pouch where fraudulent counselors are clothed in the fires of their own deceit. That trait for which he is best known and most highly praised in the *Odyssey* becomes the sin that defines his damnation.

If Dante damns Odyssean guile, Niccoló Machiavelli praises it all the more. Machiavelli's prince is indeed a "man of twists and turns." He suggests that the prince who desires to consolidate and maintain his position as lord paramount "needs to have a spirit disposed to change as the winds of fortune and variations of things command him, and . . . not to depart from good, when possible, but know how to enter into evil when forced by necessity" (Machiavelli 1998, 70). And though Machiavelli does not cite Odysseus in *The Prince* (though he does appeal to Achilles on two occasions), Odysseus is an apt illustration of the transformation of Aristotelian virtue into Machiavellian *virtù*, that capacity which anticipates and tames the river of fortune.

It was the pursuit of fortune, Odysseus tells Dante in the *Commedia*, that led to his abandonment of wife, son, and father in pursuit of greater glory and adventure, a folly that takes him to within sight of Mount Purgatory, only to have the seas rise up and seal his fate. And yet it is this picture of the pursuit of life as vigor and excitement which carried the image of Odysseus into the nineteenth century. Alfred Lord Tennyson praises Dante's Odysseus, not Homer's, in his famed poem "Ulysses" (Reeves 1965, 793). In this dramatic monologue, Tennyson imagines the man of twists and turns as he grows weary of tending to Ithaca and longs to set out across the seas once more, in search of new adventures: "I cannot rest from travel: I will drink / Life to the lees." Honor and glory, not cunning, have become the defining characteristics of the speaker. "I am become a name; / For always roaming with a hungry heart . . . Myself not least, but honoured of them all." Tennyson's Odysseus will not rest in contentment or contemplation. "How dull it is to pause, to make an end, / To rust unburnished, not to shine in use!" His desire is "To follow knowledge like a sinking star, / Beyond the utmost bound of human thought." The poem concludes with a call to arms and adventure:

> ". . . Come my friends,
> 'Tis not too late to seek a newer world.
> . . . .
> Tho' much is taken, much abides; and though
> We are not now that strength which in old days
> Moved earth and heaven; that which we are, we are;
> One equal temper of heroic hearts,
> Made weak by time and fate, but strong in will
> To strive, to seek, to find, and not to yield.
> (Tennyson, "Ulysses")

However rousing Tennyson's portrayal may have seemed to nineteenth-century readers, it is deeply at odds with the picture of Odysseus which emerged from antiquity and into the medieval period. In truth, it tells us more about the Victorian quest for a British Empire upon which the sun never set than it does about "the man of twists and turns driven time and again off course." Perhaps this is as it should be, for Odysseus's wanderings have often served to illustrate and reflect the character and commitments of Homer's readers, whether this is seen in Sophocles' scoundrel, Tennyson's mariner, or Joyce's tragic anti-hero, Leopold Bloom.

Justice

As the *Odyssey* offers a window on competing conceptions of virtue and wisdom, so too does it lead its readers to the difficult subject of justice. Justice in the *Odyssey* is primarily *rectificatory* or *corrective*. That is, it is a matter of rectifying or setting right what is not right. In the *Odyssey* such justice is primarily accomplished by vengeance. Just as the *Iliad* begins and continues well into the story with Achilles' sullen effort to get back at Agamemnon for unfairly depriving him of his prize Briseis, so the *Odyssey* begins with Athena pleading with Zeus to end the unjust exile that long-suffering Odysseus has endured on account of Poseidon's curse. Poseidon himself is exacting rectificatory justice for the blinding of his son Polyphemus. The Trojan War had been fought because of perceived injustice, and many of Odysseus's "adventures" find their source in the experience of some injustice, whether such was done to his own men by Circe or Polyphemus, or to Helios's cattle by his own men, or most importantly, by the reckless suitors who have taken control of Odysseus's household over the course of two decades. In almost every case, vengeance is the order of the day. As MacIntyre notes, "In heroic societies life is the standard of value. If someone kills you, my friend or brother, I owe you their death and when I have paid my debt to you, their friend or brother owes them my death. The more extended my system of kinsmen and friends, the more liabilities I shall incur of a kind that may end in my death" (1984, 124).

Rightly understood, justice, of course, is much more than merely a corrective for wrongs committed against another. Aristotle, in fact, describes justice as "not a part of virtue but the whole of it, and the injustice contrary to it is not a part of but the whole of vice" (Aristotle, 1130a). Though just as quickly as he makes this claim he acknowledges that the *universal* understanding of justice must be set to one side so that one can investigate the *particular* forms of justice which are required by a community. Space in the current essay does not permit a full discussion of the differences between the types of particular justice that Aristotle discusses in Book 5 of the *Nicomachean Ethics*. What is important to note is that justice in the *Odyssey* is but a slice out of the much thicker concept of justice that evolved out of Greek and biblical materials over the next twenty-five or thirty centuries. By itself heroic justice was an inherently unstable slice, one on which the realities of human nature make an insistent demand, over time, for the development of the other aspects of the concept. A brief look at two episodes in which we see the pursuit of justice on this understanding of it will suggest how problematic the notion is for the epic as a whole.

First, the account of Agamemnon's murder and death is told no less than five times (and mentioned in passing even more often). It is not surprising that the death of Agamemnon and the curse on the house of Atreus would become one of the great narratives in ancient Greek literature, given its prominent role in the *Odyssey*. By its very nature, culpability in this narrative is deeply complicated. There is Aegisthus's vengeance arising from Atreus's slaughter of Thyestes's other children; Agamemnon's three-fold offense against Clytemnestra (the murder of Iphigenia, the abandonment of Argos, and the return with Cassandra); and Clytemnestra's own unfaithfulness with Aegisthus. In time, Orestes will avenge the death of his father by murdering both Aegisthus and his mother Clytemnestra.

In the opening sequence of the *Odyssey* in the Olympian court, Zeus reflects on Orestes' vengeance as an example of how justice as retribution is achieved. Athena will also appeal to Orestes' example to inspire Telemachus to assume the mantle of his own manhood and its responsibilities. "You must not cling to your boyhood any longer – it's time you were a man. Haven't you heard what glory Prince Orestes won throughout the world when he killed that cunning, murderous Aegisthus, who'd killed his famous father?" (I, 341–345). But Orestes does not only win glory throughout the world. He also brings on himself the wrath of the Furies who pursue their own vengeance for his matricide.

Aeschylus's presentation of this narrative in the *Oresteia* trilogy (some three hundred years later) emphasizes the inadequacy of heroic justice understood as retribution. Ultimately Athena demands that Orestes be tried by a jury of Athenians. The significance of the move from vengeance to litigation cannot be overestimated.

Already, however, by the conclusion of the *Odyssey*, it is clear that justice as vengeance cannot be sustained, as is suggested by our second example, Odysseus's slaughter of the suitors and the necessary debt of vengeance against Odysseus that the suitors' families thus owe to their slain fathers and brothers. While it is clear that vengeance cannot be sustained, it is far from clear how the heroic actors can do otherwise. In what is surely a model for Aeschylus, Athena here simply effects a ceasefire and a cessation of hostilities, without any litigation or consideration of evidence. Part of what makes the conclusion to the *Odyssey* so unsatisfying to the social sensibilities of later Greek readers, not to speak of Christians or their modern liberal heirs, is its facile notion of ultimate justice. Having slain the suitors and been reunited with Penelope, Odysseus rises early the following morning to go in pursuit of sheep and cattle to replenish what the suitors had squandered and to meet in battle their many kinsmen who will rise against him in defense of their slain sons and brothers.

The conclusion, however, is abrupt. As Odysseus, Telemachus, Laertes, and four servants rush into battle against Eupithes, the father of Antinous, and the other kinsmen of the suitors, Athena inspires the aged Laertes to pray to Zeus and fling his long spear into Eupithes – which he does with great success. At this very moment, however, Athena calls for a truce: "shed no more blood – make peace at once!" (24, 585). Remarkably, they obey her; even Odysseus obeys, though he is first inclined to pursue even those who have dropped their weapons. The epic ends with the note that Athena "handed down her pacts of peace between both sides for all the years to come – the daughter of Zeus whose shield is storm and thunder, yes, but the goddess still kept Mentor's build and voice" (24, 599–602).

The sudden image of the peaceful kingdom could not be more odd or improbable if Homer had employed the functionally equivalent locution from northern European fairy tales: "and they lived happily ever after." The reference to Mentor is intriguing, but it seems primarily to denote Athena's dual role as protector and advisor. The reader is certain that the drama cannot end in this way. The debt owed to the dead must be paid; the security of Ithaca requires that the challengers be vanquished; and the need for honor and glory (*kleos*) of and by the heroic warriors ensures that these demands will be met. If a divine order for peace and the end of hostilities could be sufficient to produce a truce, then it could have been accomplished many years before on the ringing plains of windy Troy.

What the unsatisfying conclusion does produce, however, is the long line of dramatic works that struggle with the conflicting demands of honor, fidelity, and the transformation of the heroic conception of justice. This can be seen in the roll call of fifth century tragedies: the *Oedipus* cycle, *Iphigenia in Aulis, Electra, Trojan Women, Oresteia,* and many more. The philosophical work produced in the early and mid-fourth century will turn explicitly to the question of the nature of justice in the wake of the political failures of the Athenian state at the end of the fifth century. When Socrates is persuaded to return to the fire to "have a talk" with Polemarchus, Cephalus, and the rest, he is returning to discuss the unanswered questions which have their origin in the Homeric epics, questions which neither poet nor politician have satisfactorily addressed.

Conclusion

Here we see the beginning of a common thread. The pursuit of wisdom, virtue, and justice leads one on paths through great difficulties, even perhaps on a tour of Purgatory and Hell. It is not surprising that the word "odyssey" has taken on the connotations of any journey through which the traveler is transformed by unexpected trials and tribulations. Reading Greats is itself a kind of odyssey, one in which new challenges ever lie before the reader. Even as we are challenged to reconsider and reevaluate our heroes and their virtues, the quest for the security and serenity of the penultimate scenes never grows old. Most of us find that we, like Joyce and countless others, discover new names for Polyphemus, Circe, Antinous, and all the rest, but the struggle to overcome their enchantments and challenges rarely diminishes. The *Odyssey* confronts us even when we are reading texts whose subjects and sources seem to be worlds away from Homer's wine-dark sea. And yet each new journey, both with the text and with its heirs, prepares us for the next one. It equips us to pursue wisdom and justice even through the gates of Hell – with or against Odysseus, the man of twists and turns driven time and again off course.

The Odysseus we meet in Sophocles' *Philoctetes* is a far cry from the man of pain given to us by Homer or the audacious sailor described by Tennyson. Seamus Heaney's version of Hercules' last words to Philoctetes is perhaps an apt conclusion for those who would venture out again and again with Odysseus, again and again with those Greats which challenge and transform us in the hope of wisdom and justice.

> So hope for a great sea-change
> On the far side of revenge.
> Believe that a further shore
> Is reachable from here.
> Believe in miracles
> And cures and healing wells.[3]
> (Heaney 1961, 77)

Scott H. Moore

References

Aeschylus 1953. *Oresteia*. Trans. Richard Lattimore. Chicago: University of Chicago Press.

Aristotle 2004. *Nicomachean Ethics*. Trans. J. A. K. Thompson. New York: Penguin Classics.

Balthasar, Hans Urs von 2000. *Mysterium Paschale: The Mystery of Easter.* Trans. Aidan Nichols, O.P. San Francisco: Ignatius Press.

Campbell, Joseph 2008. *The Hero with a Thousand Faces,* 3rd ed. Novato, California: New World Library.

Euripides 1998. *Euripides I*. Eds. David R. Slavitt and Palmer Bovie. Philadelphia: University of Pennsylvania Press.

Fagles, Robert 1996. "Notes on the Translation" in *The Odyssey*. New York: Penguin Books.

Heaney, Seamus 1961. *The Cure at Troy: A Version of Sophocles' "Philoctetes."* New York: Farrar, Straus and Giroux.

Herzog, Don 2006. *Cunning*. Princeton: Princeton University Press.

Homer 1996. *The Odyssey*. Trans. Robert Fagles. New York: Penguin Books.

Hume, David 2006. *Essays: Moral, Political, and Literary*. New York: Cosimo Classics.

Lewis, C. S. 2000. "Myth Became Fact" in *Essay Collection and Other Short Pieces*. Ed. Lesley Walmsley. London: HarperCollins.

Liddell, H. G., and Robert Scott, Eds. 1982. *Greek-English Lexicon*. Abridged Ed. Oxford: Oxford University Press.

Machiavelli, Niccolò 1998. *The Prince*. 2nd ed. Trans. Harvey C. Mansfield. Chicago: University of Chicago Press.

MacIntyre, Alasdair 1984. *After Virtue*. 2nd ed. Notre Dame, Indiana: University of Notre Dame Press.

Milton, John 1992. "Paradise Lost" in *The Complete English Poems*. Ed. Gordon Campbell. New York: Knopf Publishers.

Modern Library 1998. "100 Best Novels." http://www.randomhouse.com/modernlibrary/100bestnovels.html

Ratzinger, Joseph 2009. *Credo for Today: What Christians Believe*. Trans. Michael J. Miller, et al. San Francisco: Ignatius Press.

Reeves, James, Ed. 1965. *The Cassell Book of English Poetry*. New York: Harper and Row Publishers.

Plato
The Symposium

Thoughtful readers of Plato quickly come to wonder about the human aspiration to seek and see what is good, as well as the longing for God sometimes prompted by desire for the good. In Plato, after all, we find an unprecedented apprehension of the ways that love and knowledge, together with one or another kind of seeing, are intertwined; a stirring vision of the unity of truth, beauty, and goodness; and a persistent intuition of the need for God. Because Plato's conception of the good depends finally on seeing God, Christians, among others, have compelling reasons to study him carefully, and especially his most artfully composed dialogue, the *Symposium*.[1]

In what follows, I make a case for such. I begin by accounting for Plato's favorable reception during Christianity's first half-millennium, for the *Symposium* is accredited within a wider tradition of admiration of Plato. I then explore two of its principal themes. The first is the way human longing finds its crowning fulfillment in a vision of the divine. The second is the way morally well formed desire helps us see what really matters, for often appearances deceive and truth is hidden. Jointly taken, the fit object of our deepest longing – the divine – is for Plato something to which we are naturally oriented, but which is not necessarily obvious to us. Two memorable metaphors in the *Symposium* carry the themes: Diotima's ladder of love and the Sileni of Alcibiades. Of course, though Plato gestures in Christian directions, his ideas fall short of the faith, so along the way I also note the *Symposium*'s key shortcomings vis-à-vis Christianity.

Early Christian Reception of Plato

From almost the beginning, Christians discerned in Plato an example of one by whom God's "invisible attributes, namely, his eternal power and divine nature, have been clearly perceived, ever since the creation of the world, in the things that have been made" (Rom 1:20 ESV).[2] It takes only modest transpositions to identify God as the "Being that is beyond being, surpassing it in dignity and power," to which he appeals at *Republic* 509b or to name as God what *Timaeus* 28c characterizes as the "Maker and Father of everything."[3]

Like Christians, Plato understands the limitation of human reason in matters of divinity. One cannot read Socrates' and Glaucon's exchange at *Republic*

509, for instance, without encountering repeated expressions of the boundaries reason bumps into in its quest to identify the Good. Furthermore, Plato's dialogues show a consistent predilection to approach the subject of God with humility and reverence – indeed with a sense of human frailty characteristic of genuine piety. Plato's work lacks any notion of the moral or noetic effects of sin, yet because he has chastened confidence in the power of *logos*, Christian interpreters widely agree that "Plato's acknowledgement of God . . . , fitfully intelligible but not yet visible in the Word made flesh, gives to his writing a value unique in the pre-Christian world" (Beckett 2006, 38).

Favorable Christian consideration of Plato's philosophy appears early among the Church Fathers. The late Pope John Paul II observes that "Christian proclamation was engaged from the very first with the philosophical currents of the time" (John Paul II 1998, 49). He cites Justin, Clement of Alexandria, Origin, the Cappadocian Fathers, Dionysius the Areopagite, and Augustine as seminal theologians who grapple thoughtfully with Greek philosophy and especially Platonic thought (John Paul II 1998, 52–54). To be sure, they neither merely endorsed Platonism nor naively tacked on Christian trappings. Justin insisted that "the only sure and profitable philosophy" was Christianity, and Clement regarded the gospel as "the true philosophy" for which Greek thought was only a propaedeutic (John Paul II 1998, 52). In their own ways, though, they admired the beauty and goodness of the truth in Plato's work, and maintained that truth, wherever it is found, is the common possession of human beings and a treasure to be honored by Christians. With Plato in mind, Justin writes in his *Second Apology*:

> Whatever things were rightly said among all men, are the property of us Christians. For next to God, we worship and love the Word who is from the unbegotten and ineffable God, [and] all the writers were able to see realities darkly through the sowing of the implanted word that was in them. (Justin Martyr 1994, chap. 13)

Similarly, in *The Stromata* Clement writes:

> For God is the cause of all good things; but of some primarily, as of the Old and the New Testament; and of others by consequence, as philosophy. Perchance, too, philosophy was given to the Greeks directly and primarily, till the Lord should call the Greeks. For this was a schoolmaster to bring "the Hellenic mind," as the law, the Hebrews, "to Christ." Philosophy, therefore, was a preparation, paving the way for him who is perfected in Christ. (Clement of Alexandria 1994, 1.5)

While acknowledging the need for revelation, the Church Fathers emphasize Plato's penetrating sense of a divinely created, ordered, and rationally apprehensible cosmos.[4]

Sustaining three centuries of esteem for Plato, Augustine writes in his *Confessions* that "some books of the Platonists translated from Greek into Latin" (7.9) providentially taught him the *preambula fidei*. Augustine thereby grants Plato a place among his spiritual teachers, for Plato facilitated his intellectual conversion and prepared the way for his will's conversion to the love of God in Christ. Platonism subsequently served Augustine as a rich point of departure for the elaboration of complex theological ideas. In *The City of God* he writes, "We prefer the Platonists to all others" because "these, by knowing God, have discovered where to find the cause by which the universe was established, and the light by which truth is to be perceived, and the fount at which we may drink of happiness" (8.10). With Augustine's partiality to Plato in view, Josef Pieper, commenting on *Republic* 507d–509b, notes "how it was possible for Augustine to see in the Platonic theory of ideas a presentiment of the wisdom of the divine *logos*, conceived as the ultimate embodiment of all the archetypes" (Pieper 2006, 164). So, in both of these ways – as intellectually useful preparation for conversion and as an intellectual system well suited for the theological elaboration of the faith – Augustine secures Plato's significance among Christians for all time.

From the beginning, then, Christians have valued Plato's dialogues for four reasons. First, they confirm the evidence of God's "eternal power and divine nature" to the light of human reason. Second, they offer an extended narrative argument on behalf of the humble wisdom-lover's contemplation of God – an argument that suggests the furthest extent to which reason can orient us to our divine source and end.[5] Third, they were more congenial to Christian teaching than the prevailing alternatives of stoicism, skepticism, and various forms of gnosticism. Indeed, as in Augustine's case, they could even provide intellectually sound direction to prepare one for the gospel. Fourth, Plato's dialogues and the philosophical tradition that they underwrote opened up fresh, theologically rigorous, and culturally relevant ways of articulating the faith. In short, from the earliest days of Christian reflection, many have held that Plato's dialogues confirm scriptural teaching about reason's power to discern God; instantiate a rationally sophisticated aspiration to see God; open the mind to the gospel; and provide a philosophically rich vocabulary for the theological articulation of Christian faith.

Longing, Ascent, and the Vision of God in the Symposium

Among all the dialogues, the *Symposium,* a friendly dinner party featuring a speech-making contest on the subject of love, emphatically merits Christian readers' abiding attention. C. S. Lewis regarded the *Symposium* as executed with such artfulness and vision that he cites it as the *locus classicus par excellence* of Platonism. He bemoans the plight of the "average student [who] wants to find out something about Platonism," yet "the very last thing he thinks of doing is to take a translation of Plato off the library shelf and read the *Symposium*," for "first-hand knowledge is not only more worth acquiring than second-hand knowledge, but is usually much easier and more delightful to acquire" (Lewis 2002, 3). I wholeheartedly endorse Lewis's judgment, so I hope my readers will study the original more intently, give it pride of place among Plato's dialogues, and find delight and help in its lessons.

Of the many reasons for Christians to grapple with the *Symposium*, two come to the fore. Lucy Beckett notes the first of these:

> The *Symposium* is the book in which Plato comes closest to writing of the love of God, in particular of how we may find our way from our experience of human love to a love of God's goodness, beauty and truth in which human love is not cancelled but taken up into a greater reality. (Beckett 2006, 49)

Beckett has in view the great middle part of the dialogue where Socrates recounts "the speech about love I once heard from a woman of Mantinea, Diotima – a woman who was wise about many things besides this" (201d). In her myth of the birth of Eros, the offspring of Poros and Penia (203b–e), and even more in the rites of love by which one ascends to a transcendent end that even the wisest may scarcely attain (210a–212a), Diotima gives us an inspiring vision of human life raised to its highest level. Emphasis on the speech that Socrates borrows from Diotima (and makes his own) has ancient precedent, for Origen notes in *Against Celsus* that "the words of Socrates regarding Eros in the Symposium of Plato . . . are put in the mouth of Socrates as being more appropriate than what was said regarding [Eros] by all the others at the Symposium" (4.34). Though the *Symposium* must be read as a whole to grasp a variety of crucial insights, the metaphorical ladder of ascent at the heart of the dialogue concentrates the text's most memorable philosophical insights.

By the time Socrates relates Diotima's speech on love, the dialogue has introduced a splendidly variegated series of encomia of Eros. Through the first part of the dialogue, Phaedrus, Pausanias, Eryximachus, Aristophanes, and Agathon take turns speaking of Love's merits. Because of the competitive context of the speechmaking, the stakes are higher with each successive speech, for winning the laurel crown of victory at evening's end depends upon besting one's fellows. When Agathon makes his speech, he therefore calls attention to how he intends to surpass everyone, saying that while the others spoke merely about the blessings that Eros bestows on humanity, he will speak about the excellences of the god himself (195a). With his speech so framed, Agathon's conquest appears assured. Since the symposium is in honor of Agathon's first victory over Athens's tragedians, a plausible direction for the dialogue would be to cap off a grand day by giving the man of the hour all-around victory at his own party. That is precisely what Plato does not offer us.

Agathon – whose name literally identifies him as a "good" man – gives us, in eloquent language, a nominally good man's understanding of Love's nature and benefits. But Socrates complicates matters by responding,

> I thought you should tell the truth about whatever you praise . . . . But now it appears that this is not what it is to praise anything whatsoever; rather, it is to apply to the object the grandest and the most beautiful qualities, whether he actually has them or not. (198d–e)

Socrates argues that Agathon's speech contains almost nothing true about Love at all. Love desires beauty and goodness in all of their manifestations, but insofar as Love desires beauty and goodness, it lacks them, for "a thing that desires desires something of which it is in need; otherwise, if it were not in need, it would not desire it" (200b). Agathon allows the point, admits that he didn't know what he was talking about, and concedes that he cannot challenge Socrates – which is to say, the truth.

That brings us back to the conversation with Diotima that Socrates reports once having. Diotima's questions revealed Socrates to be ignorant about Eros in much the way that Agathon's speech showed ignorance of his nature. However, Socrates learned something about Eros by asking a question that Agathon did not: If Eros is neither beautiful nor good, is Eros ugly and bad (201e)? After rebuking Socrates' near-blasphemy, Diotima explains that some things occupy a position between beauty and ugliness, wisdom and ignorance, goodness and badness, and immortality and mortality. Eros is just such a being. Insofar as Eros does not possess beauty, wisdom, goodness, and immortality, he is neither blessed nor divine. Yet because Eros is not ugly, ignorant, bad, or mortal, he calls for our special attention. To help Socrates understand, Diotima tells a story that takes us to the apogee of the *Symposium*.

Eros longingly, lovingly seeks what he does not of his own resources possess – beauty, wisdom, goodness, and immortality.

> As the son of Poros [resourcefulness] and Penia [poverty], his lot in life is set to be like theirs. In the first place, he is always poor, and he's far from being delicate and beautiful (as ordinary people think he is); instead, he is tough and shriveled and shoeless and homeless, always lying on the dirt without a bed, sleeping at people's doorsteps and in roadsides under the sky, having his mother's nature, always living with Need. But on his father's side he is a schemer after the beautiful and the good; he is brave, impetuous, and intense, an awesome hunter, always weaving snares, resourceful in his pursuit of intelligence, a lover of wisdom through all his life, a genius with enchantments, potions, and clever pleadings. . . . He is in between wisdom and ignorance as well. In fact, you see, none of the gods loves wisdom or wants to become wise – for

> they are wise – and no one else who is wise already loves wisdom; on the other hand, no one who is ignorant will love wisdom either or want to become wise. For what's especially difficult about being ignorant is that you are content with yourself, even though you're neither beautiful and good nor intelligent. (203c–204a)

In Diotima's story we catch a glimpse of the nature not only of Eros, but of philosophy as well. Notwithstanding deprivation and poverty, Eros resourcefully strives to obtain the beauty, goodness, and truth for which he longs. Living between wisdom and ignorance, Eros cannot be content with subrational pretence, yet neither does he have full understanding. These are the qualities of the true philosopher, who desires and pursues the good while not fully possessing it. Indeed, Eros archetypically embodies a universal human desire for happiness, because "what makes happy people happy [is] . . . possessing good things," and "this desire for happiness, this kind of love . . . is common to all" (205a).

In a theologically significant turn, Diotima takes her account one auspicious step forward. What Eros, philosophers, and every human being really desire is to possess the good, true, and beautiful forever. But if it is true that "love is wanting to possess the good forever" (206a), as Socrates admits, then what we truly want is immortality (207a, d). In our love for transcendent goods that we do not create, sustain, or possess of our own selves, we desire to ascend to the divine.

The *Symposium* inspires its readers to look toward the gates of heaven through the myth told by Diotima, the wise woman whose name identifies her as "one honored by god." If we have followed her story, we cannot but share in a love of good things enjoyed forever, understand that divine immortality is the only guarantor of such a transcendent hope, and consequently long to see and to be united with God forever. To have discerned the profundity of the love that orients human beings toward God is one of Plato's considerable accomplishments.

Yet left in these abstract terms, the *Symposium* would offer us a finely wrought philosophical dialogue, but a less than fully human account of the love and knowledge that seeks the divine source and end of life. For Plato the highest fulfillment of human longing – the sight of "the Beautiful itself, absolute, pure, unmixed, not polluted by human flesh or colors or any other great nonsense of mortality" (211e) – is reached by way of the natural loves common to all humankind. Two claims are crucial. First, ardent love of the divine is open to and possible for everyone. "Even you, Socrates," Diotima allows, "could probably come to be initiated into these rites of love" (210a). In the universal experience of desire and longing is found a point of departure for the highest reaches to which the human soul can attain. Second, the divinely blessed pinnacle of human existence begins with the love of another person. The *Symposium* intimates that we make our way from "our experience of human love to a love of God's goodness, beauty and truth in which human love is not cancelled but taken up into a greater reality" (Beckett 2006, 49). The love of God is not an alternative to but rather a fulfillment of our love of one another. On both counts the *Symposium* offers us a prescient philosophical grasp of elementary points of Christian doctrine that are more clearly revealed in the teachings of scripture.

But before turning to the famous Ladder of Love or Stairway of Ascent, Diotima also admits difficulty to Socrates: this "is the final and highest mystery, and I don't know if you are capable of it" (210a). Plato anticipates that not every reader, and surely not every person, will follow Love all the way to its fitting conclusion in the contemplation of the divine. Even with sound instruction from divine seers or wise elders, not all will give themselves up to the love of God. But Diotima hopes Socrates will try. She describes the disciplining of human longing such that it strives finally for the sight of God. The Ladder of Love moves in stepwise ascent from the love of a particular beautiful body, to a universalized love of all beautiful bodies, to the love of beautiful souls which are "more valuable" than mere bodies, to the love of beautifully ordered laws that help cultivate admirable souls, to the love of beautiful knowledge of a vast and glorious quality. At the penultimate stage of the ascent:

> The lover is turned to the great sea of beauty, and, gazing upon this, he gives birth to many gloriously beautiful ideas and theories, in unstinting love of wisdom, until, having grown and been strengthened there, he catches sight of such knowledge, and it is the knowledge of such beauty . . . . (210d–e)

She breaks off her account here to insist that Socrates pay greater heed than ever before, for the very "goal of Loving" is at hand. From the topmost rung of the ladder one may espy Beauty itself, the thing that "always is and neither comes to be nor passes away, neither waxes nor wanes" (211a), that which is "itself by itself with itself, . . . always one in form; and all the other beautiful things share in that, in such a way that when those others come to be or pass away, this does not become the least bit smaller or greater nor suffer any change" (211b).

> This is what it is to go aright, or be led by another, into the mystery of Love: one goes always upwards for the sake of this Beauty, starting out from beautiful things and using them like rising stairs: from one body to two and from two to all beautiful bodies, then from beautiful bodies to beautiful customs, and from customs to learning beautiful things, and

> from these lessons he arrives in the end at this lesson, which is learning of this very Beauty, so that in the end he comes to know just what it is to be beautiful. (211c)

Herein the true lover beholds Beauty in the right way and abides with it, and the result is true virtue (212a). Better still, the "love of the gods belongs to anyone who has given birth to true virtue and nourished it, and if any human being could become immortal, it would be he" (212b).

Plato's vision of the mutually interdependent relation of love, knowledge, and the divine strongly influenced Christian thought. Augustine did more to show the proto-Christian tendencies of Platonism than any other up to his day. Thus, we find him in the *Confessions* movingly reflecting on a day near the end of his mother's life, when "she and I stood alone leaning in a window, which looked inwards to the garden within the house where we were staying, at Ostia on the Tiber" (9.10). As Augustine and Monica rested, preparing for the voyage across the Mediterranean and home to Africa, they shared in a remarkable and grace-filled experience of ascent.

> [O]ur conversation had brought us to this point, that any pleasure whatsoever of the bodily senses, in any brightness whatsoever of corporeal light, seemed to us not worthy . . . even of mention. Rising as our love flamed upward towards that Selfsame, we passed in review the various levels of bodily things, up to the heavens themselves, whence sun and moon and stars shine upon this earth. And higher still we soared, thinking in our minds and speaking and marveling at Your works: and so we came to our own souls, and went beyond them to come at last to that region of richness unending, where You feed Israel forever with the food of truth: and there life is that Wisdom by which all things are made, both the things that have been and the things that are yet to be. . . . [W]hile we were thus talking of His Wisdom and panting for it, with all the effort of our heart we did for one instant attain to touch it; then sighing, and leaving the first fruits of our spirit bound to it, we returned to the sound of our own tongue, in which a word has both beginning and ending. (9.10)

It is almost worth learning Plato's *Symposium* just to understand and honor the Christian experience of longing, love, ascent, and vision that Augustine here so tenderly recalls. Although he may be the first great mind to adapt Platonism so thoroughly for Christian purposes, he is far from the last.

The Surprising Treasures of the Sileni of Alcibiades

Christian admiration of the *Symposium* also grows out of another rich metaphor. It grounds a second principal reason for serious study of the dialogue. Near the end, after a raucous entry and flamboyant flirtation with Socrates, Alcibiades is invited to give a final speech in praise of Eros. Given the spectacular heights to which Socrates' account of Diotima's speech tends, Plato could not plausibly allow another encomium of love to follow. Alcibiades declines the invitation. Instead, at Eryximachus' suggestion, Alcibiades speaks in praise of Socrates. Yet Alcibiades's late arrival at the party and his speech, laden as it is with erotically charged misconduct and double entendres, would appear to serve the dialogue poorly and to leave its *philosophical* readers with an anticlimactic conclusion, even supposing that they delight in the theatrical excesses of Socrates' young protégé. Even if we imagine that Alcibiades's part in the dialogue offers a dramatically interesting finale, it does not initially seem to provide an intellectually fulfilling conclusion.

To the contrary, Alcibiades's encomium of Socrates, far from abandoning the central concerns of the *Symposium*, offers us an illuminating instantiation of the way of life commended by the text. Socrates is the consummate and archetypal lover, he has been initiated into the rites of love through Diotima's aid, and his capacity for the kind of love that elevates human life to its highest potential is what Plato has in view. Pierre Hadot writes:

> Throughout the dialogue, but especially in the speeches of Diotima and Alcibiades, we notice that the features of the figure of Eros tend to become confused with those of the figure of Socrates. In the last analysis, the reason they become so closely enmeshed is that Eros and Socrates personify – one mythically, the other historically – the figure of the philosopher. This is the profound meaning of the dialogue. (Hadot 2002, 41)

Lest we leave the *Symposium* with only an ethereal and ineffectual love of wisdom, Plato brings us down from the heady metaphysics of Diotima's speech and into the real life of a peculiar human lover, his own teacher, Socrates.[6]

Alcibiades begins his encomium of Socrates by giving the symposiasts an image of Socrates. Socrates is like a satyr or silenus in the pattern of the mythic Marsyas whose wild, insatiable lechery was a commonplace. The stories have it that Marsyas, no mere rapacious debaucher, fashioned with his aulos the most affecting enchantments the human ear has ever heard, so that "his melodies have in themselves the power to possess and so reveal those people who are ready for the god and his mysteries" (215c). As Alcibiades develops the theme of his speech, he claims that Socrates is "much more marvelous than Marsyas, who needed instruments to cast his spells on people" (215c), for Socrates needs "no instruments; you do exactly what [Marsyas] does, but with words alone" (215d). He says to Socrates: "Let anyone – man, woman, or child – listen to you or even to a poor account of what you say – and we are all transported, completely possessed" (215d). Alcibiades has suffered the effects of which he speaks. In the dramatic setting of the dialogue Plato makes it clear that Alcibiades's otherwise seemingly exaggerated claims about Socrates are meant earnestly. In the most compelling way, then, Alcibiades casts Socrates in the role of an accomplished lover who almost effortlessly incites desire in others. Interpretive caution is needed, however, for likening Socrates to a satyr or a silenus is not in itself the most important feature of Alcibiades's portraiture. A couple of details call for attention.

First, Alcibiades likens Socrates not to a predatorial satyr, but instead a special kind of *statue* of a satyr:

> I'll try to praise Socrates, my friends, but I'll have to use an image. And though he may think I'm trying to make fun of him, I assure you my image is no joke: it aims at the truth. Look at him! Isn't he just like a statue of Silenus? You know the kind of statue I mean; you'll find them in any shop in town. It's a Silenus sitting, his flute or his pipes in his hands, and it's hollow. It's split right down the middle, and inside it's full of tiny statues of the gods. Now look at him again! Isn't he also just like the satyr Marsyas? (215a–b)

Alcibiades immediately leaves to the side the essential feature of the image he offers. Instead of telling us how Socrates resembles "a statue of Silenus," Alcibiades begins to relate the variety of ways in which Socrates is, like a satyr, "impudent, contemptuous, and vile" (215b). Except for one passing mention along the way (216e–217a), it is only in his closing lines, as an afterthought, that Alcibiades returns to the crucial detail of his image of Socrates (cf. 221e–222a).

In the ingenious image of a Silenus statue Plato helps us resist "assuming homology between visible appearance and the reality within" (Steiner 2001, 89).[7] Making such a misplaced assumption is "a mistake against which much of Platonic philosophy is directed" (Hunter 2004, 100). The implications of Alcibiades's image of Socrates are numerous. For one, we are meant to understand that the shabbily clad, pug-faced, unshod Socrates – never mind his gussied-up presentation at Agathon's party – must not be mistaken as a dodgy degenerate. Alcibiades himself confesses, "I once caught him when he was open like Silenus' statues, and I had a glimpse of the figures he keeps hidden within: they were so godlike – so bright and beautiful, so utterly amazing – that I no longer had a choice – I just had to do whatever he told me" (217a). More importantly, we should understand that the image of a Silenus statue conveys something about the essential nature of wisdom. Alcibiades intimates as much when he likens Socrates' "ideas and arguments" to "those hollow statues of Silenus" (221e):

> If you were to listen to his arguments, at first they'd strike you as totally ridiculous; they're clothed in words as coarse as the hides worn by the

> most vulgar satyrs. He's always going on about pack asses, or blacksmiths, or cobblers, or tanners; he's always making the same tired old points in the same tired old words. If you are foolish, or simply unfamiliar with him, you'd find it impossible not to laugh at his arguments. But if you see them when they open up like the statues, if you go behind their surface, you'll realize that no other arguments make any sense. They're truly worthy of a god, bursting with figures of virtue inside. They're of great – no, of the greatest – importance for anyone who wants to become a truly good man. (221e–222a)

Virtuous people, virtuous arguments, and even virtue itself seldom attract admiration from those who look merely at appearances, concern themselves with superficialities, or obsess about what others see at first glance. Yet what *hoi polloi* find repulsive, troublesome, contentious, impractical, absurd, and laughable may for genuine wisdom lovers represent the greatest treasures.

Christians easily resonate with Plato's recognition of the gap between what seems and what is. Scripture puts the point clearly:

> Has not God made foolish the wisdom of the world? . . . [But] the foolishness of God is wiser than men, and the weakness of God is stronger than men. . . . God chose what is foolish in the world to shame the wise; God chose what is weak in the world to shame the strong; God chose what is low and despised in the world, even things that are not, to bring to nothing things that are, so that no human being might boast in the presence of God. (1 Cor 1:20, 25; 27–29 ESV)

The worldly wisdom that Paul devalues is not real wisdom; he sees no rift between reason and faith. Instead, Paul has in view the gap between conventional wisdom about well-ordered human life and the counter-cultural ways of Jesus' followers, the ones "who have turned the world upside down" (Acts 17:6 ESV). Plato obviously does not see the tension between conventional wisdom and true wisdom exactly as Paul does. For Paul it is most radically expressed in the brutal execution of the innocent Son of God, Jesus of Nazareth. Nevertheless, Plato's sense of the incongruence between appearance and reality, and his lament at the breach between the commonplaces by which we order our lives and the truth by which we should order them, is a pagan prototype of the inside-out, upside-down world of the gospel of the crucified Christ. As Beckett says, "It is not the case that Plato's philosophy makes sense of the revelation of God in Christ, but that the revelation of God in Christ . . . makes sense of Plato's philosophy, the sense that Plato himself could not make" (Beckett 2006, 53).

I have been attending to the first of two surprising truths about Socrates that are occluded by Alcibiades's emphasis on Socrates' satyr-like qualities. It is that the most important features of Socrates, the most significant lessons to which reason brings us, and the most crucial principles by which we should order our lives, require us to look past superficial appearances, beyond the coarse exterior which Plato likens to the statue of Silenus. Let me now address the second one.

In the *Symposium* Plato voices a range of judgments about the appropriate relation between the lover (*erastes*) and his beloved (*eromenos*). In each instance the desire of the lover for his beloved is assumed, barring intemperance, manipulation, or other defects of character. How a lover may be rightly disposed to his beloved is addressed, and the appropriate response of a beloved to a lover receives attention, but no one questions the consummation of erotic desire.

In these regards, Alcibiades's likening of Socrates to Marsyas initially appears to follow the precedent of the dialogue's prior speeches. According to classical mythology, the sileni, oldest of the satyrs, were inveterate debauchers whose perpetually erect phalluses occasioned their shameless seduction of others. In the terms employed above, Silenus occupies the role of an *erastes*, or lover, skillfully practicing sexual inducements upon his *eromenos*, or beloved. Marsyas, the famed satyr whose moving music facilitated his many conquests, fits the model perfectly, and it is Marsyas among all of the sileni to whom Alcibiades compares Socrates.

The difficulty is that Socrates does not fit the model of Marsyas. The more Alcibiades describes his longstanding friendship with Socrates, the more complicated the relationship becomes. Given the conventional features of Athenian pederasty, Socrates, the elder of the two, might be imagined as the *erastes*, with the attractive, socially ascendant Alcibiades as his *eromenos*. This matches Alcibiades's own expectations, as he tells his colleagues. To his credit, he anticipated from Socrates an opportunity to be taught "everything he knew" (217a), for "my heart, or my soul, or whatever you want to call it, [had] been struck and bitten by philosophy" (218a). Socrates exemplifies the wisdom, temperance, courage, and justice that Alcibiades lacks, to the extent that Alcibiades worries that his life is "no better than the most miserable slave's" and that his "life isn't worth living" (215e–216a). To Alcibiades's dismay, however, Socrates will have none of it, for he turns out to have no sexual interest in Alcibiades at all, notwithstanding his unparalleled beauty. Instead, he treats him kindly as a father or older brother would (219c–d). Alcibiades reproaches Socrates as a poor *erastes*; he is "indeed a paradoxical satyr, who does *seem* not to need anything such as food, drink, money, warm clothing, or sex" (Hunter 2004, 101). Moreover, Alcibiades gives us an account of himself that reveals what a poor *eromenos* he is. Instead of chastely forestalling interest on the part of others, Socrates in particular, Alcibiades casts himself in the role of the lover. He confesses that after a number of ineffectual encounters with

Socrates, "what I did was to invite him to dinner, as if *I* were his lover and he my young prey" (217c). As a result, Alcibiades finds himself pursuing Socrates endlessly and hopelessly. Alcibiades ends his encomium of Socrates with a stern warning to Agathon: "He has deceived us all: he presents himself as your lover, and, before you know it, you're in love with him yourself!" (222b).

What should we make of such a mixed-up role reversal? The explanation for Socrates' chaste conduct toward Alcibiades rests in the understanding of Love he learned from Diotima. Plato gives plenty of indication that Socrates loves Alcibiades dearly, and that Socrates devotedly loves many other friends as well. But as a corollary of his determined and disciplined love of divine Beauty, Socrates cares about more than immediate gratification of the erotic desire physical beauty incites. What he seeks to know and to love is the inner man. He wants to see others "open up like the statues," as it were, and to find the souls of his friends "bursting with figures of virtue inside" (222a). Socrates is thus set apart from those whose reciprocated affection stays at the level of mutual gratification. He spurns mere *quid pro quo* sexual intercourse, for it lacks fecundity, has no self-transcendent orientation, and falls short of the ascent to God that he aspires to. Socrates loves his friends, then, and seeks their good. However, he neither loves them for their own sake nor really for his own sake. Rather, Socrates loves his friends insofar as they provide an opportunity to cherish a particular manifestation of the Truth, Beauty, and Goodness that claim his attention and his life. By resisting the advances of those uninitiated into the rites of Love, and by exemplifying for them a "love of the gods [that] belongs to anyone who has given birth to true virtue and nourished it" (212a), Socrates shows them a higher way. He makes this very point at the end of his encomium: "Once persuaded, I try to persuade others too that human nature can find no better workmate for acquiring [immortality] than Love. That's why I say that every man must honor Love, why I honor the rites of Love myself and practice them with special diligence, and why I commend them to others" (212b).

For Christian readers, Plato's account of Socrates' love for his friends strikes both a harmonious and a dissonant note. To a "human love [that] is not cancelled but taken up into a greater reality" grounded in the love of God, we can only assent (Beckett 2006, 29). Augustine teaches essentially the same lesson when he reflects in the *Confessions* on his own bitter experiences of failed human love, and when he confesses, "Blessed is the man that loves Thee, O God, and his friend in Thee, and his enemy for Thee" (4.9). He explains:

> Wherever the soul of man turns, unless towards God, it cleaves to sorrow, even though the things outside God and outside itself to which it cleaves may be things of beauty. For these lovely things would be noth-

> ing at all unless they were from Him. . . . In all such things let my soul praise You, O God, Creator of all things, but let it not cleave too close in love to them through the senses of the body. For they go their way and are no more; and they rend the soul with desires that can destroy it, for it longs to be one with the things it loves and to repose in them. But in them is no place of repose, because they do not abide. (4.10)

Augustine invites his readers to learn from him: "if material things please you . . . [and] if souls please you, then love them in God . . . . Love them, I say, in Him, and draw as many souls with you to Him as you can . . ." (4.12). Though Socrates' love of the divine lacks the benefit of God's self-revelation to Israel or incarnation in Jesus Christ, the *Symposium's* Socratic model of taking the love of a friend up into the love of God seems basically sound.

The dissonance we detect in the character of Socrates' love of his friends is connected to Plato's sharp body-soul dualism, combined with an apparently scant appreciation for materiality. In Socrates we find a sublimated eroticism that does not value embodied life and love to the degree it should. As Beckett once again puts so well:

> Plato's thought . . . is flawed, for a Christian, only by his unsurprising separation of the soul from the body, a dualism that with his conviction that the soul is immortal he had no way of avoiding. His belief in God awaits its completion in the light of the Incarnation and Resurrection of Christ and of the revelation of the Holy Trinity. (Beckett 2006, 51)

Making allowances for a deep-rooted dualism, Socrates' positioning of human love in an ordered series of loves oriented towards God gets much right.

I ended the previous section by commending study of the *Symposium* in order to appreciate Augustine's contemplative vision of God in the *Confessions*. It is almost as profitable to study the *Symposium* to understand another, later Christian text by Erasmus, *The Sileni of Alcibiades*. With Alcibiades's statue of Silenus in mind, Erasmus describes Socrates as not worth a nickel. "He had the face of a country bumpkin, a bit like that of an ox, and a snub nose always running with snot. You would have thought he was dull and stupid, good only at pulling faces" (Erasmus 1999, 169). After other abusive but true claims about Socrates, Erasmus presents a view of the inner treasures within the crude exterior: "But if you open up this Silenus, who is outwardly so ridiculous, you find within someone who is closer to being a god than a man, a great and lofty spirit, the epitome of a true philosopher" (170). Then, in an unexpectedly capacious fashion, Erasmus identifies other children of wisdom as sileni, including Antisthenes, Diogenes the Cynic, and Epictetus the slave-born Stoic. Of them he explains:

> This is the nature of things truly worth having: what is most valuable

> about them is hidden away and concealed, while what is visible on the surface appears beneath contempt. They hide their treasure beneath a coarse and worthless shell, and do not let the uninitiated catch even a glimpse of it. Vulgar and trivial things have a quite different character. They please at first sight, and their best qualities are immediately visible to any passerby. But if you look more closely, you will find that they are the opposite of what you would think from their appearance and reputation. (171)

Erasmus recognizes wisdom in storing up heavenly treasures out of sight, in lives hidden from the world by their plainness. However, he has a more stunning point to offer.

> And was not Christ, too, a marvelous Silenus – if I may be permitted to speak of him in such terms? I cannot see why all those who take pride in calling themselves Christian do not feel an obligation to make their best efforts to copy this aspect of his nature. If you look at the outside of this Silenus, what, judging by normal standards, could be more contemptible or despicable? His parents were insignificant and penniless. His home was a shack. He was poor himself, and his disciples were few in number and equally insignificant, drawn from the tax collector's office and the fisherman's nets. Then think of his life – a life without pleasure, during which he endured hunger and exhaustion, insults and mockery, that finally ended on the cross. . . . But if you have the opportunity to look at the inside of this Silenus, if Christ deigns to show himself, our immortal God, to the purified eyes of your soul, what an indescribable treasure you will find; in this muck, what a pearl; in this humility, what grandeur; in this poverty, what wealth; in this weakness, what immeasurable strength; in this disgrace, what glory; in these labors, what perfect peace; and finally in that bitter death, the never-failing source of everlasting life! (171–172)

Though Christ could have ruled the temporal world, exercised matchless power, amassed material treasure, and silenced the sophists of his day, "he chose to be a Silenus, and it is this example that he wanted his disciples and friends, that is, all Christians, to imitate" (172). More could be said of Erasmus' asseverations about other Sileni – the prophets, John the Baptist, the apostles, Martin of Tours, the sacraments of the church, and the holy scriptures – to say nothing of the strict examination of conscience called for by Erasmus' charge that the "majority of men are Sileni turned inside out" (173). Here, though, let me simply reiterate the importance of reading Plato's *Symposium* in order to understand the Christian thought and texts that follow for thousands of years thereafter.

Conclusion

Plato's *Symposium* is a philosophical dialogue without equal, judged by its overall artfulness, development of character, insight, influence, subtlety, and wit. It sets the philosophical life, indeed all of human life, within a divinely ordered hierarchy that begins in the love of another person; ascends to the love of truth, beauty, and goodness; and reaches its culmination in the love of the divine source and end of everything. The eloquence and persuasiveness of the *Symposium* made its legacy immediate and enduring. Its import within Christianity was established in the earliest centuries by the Church Fathers and has continued unabated to the present.

The legacy of Plato's *Symposium* lives on. Consider Evelyn Waugh's great book, *Brideshead Revisited*, where we read that "to know and love one other human being is the root of all wisdom" (Waugh 1993, 39), and in which Waugh explores how divine grace can draw one up through human love to the love of God. Or think of Iris Murdoch, who never strays far from Plato in either her fiction or philosophy. In her novel *The Nice and the Good*, John Ducane reflects, "No love is entirely without worth . . . . But it is in the nature of love to discern good, and the best love is in some part of at any rate a love of what is good" (Murdoch 1978, 344). Elsewhere Murdoch calls for a "moral philosophy in which the concept of love . . . can once again be made central" (Murdoch 2001, 45), and she ends it by citing Plato's use of "ordinary human love [as] . . . striking evidence of a transcendent principle of good" (73). Or think of Simone Weil, in whom T. S. Eliot recognized a "genius akin to that of the saints" (Eliot 2002, viii). Weil wrote essays entitled "God in Plato" and books such as *Intimations of Christianity among the Ancient Greeks*, and she argues that "it is only in so far as the soul orients itself towards what ought to be loved, that is to say in so far as it loves God, that it is qualified to know and understand" (Weil 1968, 104). And I already have repeatedly invoked Beckett, for whom Diotima's ladder of ascent prompts the remark: "A Christian reader will be most of all impressed by the consequences of this vision, which are consequences for the soul in the life of God" (Beckett 2006, 50). It always has been so for Christian students of the *Symposium*. Plato's vision leaves a lasting impression, for it uncovers a deeply rooted longing, teaches us how to discern better the appearance of its satisfaction from true fulfillment, and orients us ultimately to God.

Douglas V. Henry

References

Augustine. 1998. *The City of God Against the Pagans*. Trans. and ed. R. W. Dyson. Cambridge Texts in the History of Political Thought. New York: Cambridge University Press.

Augustine. 2006. *Confessions*. Trans. F. J. Sheed. Ed. Michael P. Foley. 2nd ed. Indianapolis: Hackett Publishing Company.

Beckett, Lucy. 2006. *In the Light of Christ: Writings in the Western Tradition*. San Francisco: Ignatius Press.

Bury, R. G. 1932. *The Symposium of Plato*, 2nd edition. Cambridge: W. Heffer and Sons.

Clement of Alexandria. 1994. *The Stromata, or Miscellanies*. In Vol. 2 of *Ante-Nicene Fathers: The Writings of the Fathers Down to A.D. 325*. Ed. Alexander Roberts and James Donaldson. Peabody, MA: Hendrickson Publishers. Repr., Buffalo: NY: Christian Literature Publishing Company, 1885.

Eliot, T. S. 2002. Preface to *The Need for Roots: Prelude to a Declaration of Duties Towards Mankind*, by Simone Weil. Trans. Arthur Wills. New York: Routledge Classics.

Erasmus, Desiderius. 1999. *The Sileni of Alcibiades*. In *Utopia*, by Thomas More. Ed. and trans. David Wooten. Indianapolis: Hackett Publishing Company.

Hadot, Pierre. 2002. *What is Ancient Philosophy?* Trans. Michael Chase. Cambridge, MA: Belknap Press of Harvard University Press.

Hunter, Richard. 2004. *Plato's* Symposium. Oxford Approaches to Classical Literature. New York: Oxford University Press.

John Paul II. 1998. *Fides et Ratio*. Boston: Pauline Books.

Lewis, C. S. 2002. Introduction to *On the Incarnation*, by St. Athanasius. Trans. and ed. A Religious of C.S.M.V. Crestwood, NY: St. Vladimir's Seminary Press.

Justin Martyr. 1994. *The Second Apology*. In Vol. 1 of *Ante-Nicene Fathers: The Writings of the Fathers Down to A.D. 325*. Ed. Alexander Roberts and James Donaldson. Peabody, MA: Hendrickson Publishers. Repr., Buffalo: NY: Christian Literature Publishing Company, 1885.

Murdoch, Iris. 1978. *The Nice and the Good*. New York: Penguin Books.

——— 2001. On 'God' and 'Good.' In *The Sovereignty of Good*. New York: Routledge Classics.

Origen. 1994. *Against Celsus*. In Vol. 4 of *Ante-Nicene Fathers: The Writings of the Fathers Down to A.D. 325*. Ed. Alexander Roberts and James

Donaldson. Peabody, MA: Hendrickson Publishers. Repr., Buffalo: NY: Christian Literature Publishing Company, 1885.

Pieper, Josef. 2006. On the Platonic Idea of Philosophy. In *For the Love of Wisdom: Essays on the Nature of Philosophy*. Ed. Berthold Wald. Trans. Roger Wasserman. San Francisco: Ignatius Press.

Plato. 1989. *Symposium*. Trans. Alexander Nehamas and Paul Woodruff. Indianapolis: Hackett Publishing Company.

C. Riedweg, C. 1987. *Mysterienterminologie bei Platon, Philon und Klemens von Alexandrien* New York: Gruyter, 1987.

Sheffield, F. 2001. "Alcibiades' Speech: A Satiric Drama," *Greece and Rome*, vol. 48: 193-209.

Steiner, Deborah. 1996. For Love of a Statue: A Reading of Plato's *Symposium* 215A–B. *Ramus* 25: 89–111.

——— 2001. *Images in Mind: Statues in Archaic and Classical Greek Literature and Thought*. Princeton: Princeton University Press.

Weil, Simone. 1968. *Science, Necessity, and the Love of God*, trans. Richard Rees. London: Oxford University Press.

Aristotle
Nicomachean Ethics[1]

Introduction

On nearly every page of *Nicomachean Ethics* we meet themes at which Aristotle's thought intersects the New Testament, and at every point of intersection Christian and Aristotelian thought illuminate one another, sometimes by supplementation, sometimes by the starkest contrast.

Aristotle thinks the highest human happiness is impossible without the contemplation of god, but he does not think that god created the world or cares about it. In Christian thought the knowledge of God is intimately connected with moral practice, indeed one cannot know God without loving one's neighbor; while for Aristotle theological knowledge differs so much from moral knowledge that one of the most vexing questions addressed in Aristotle scholarship is how his ethics can conceive the excellent human life as unified. Aristotle's god categorically does not issue commands, but the Father of Jesus Christ does.

The notion of a human virtue is central to Aristotle's ethical thought, and in the letters of the New Testament we encounter lists of Christian virtues, sometimes called the fruit of the Holy Spirit; but the Christian and Aristotelian lists of virtues overlap only partially, and sometimes a Christian virtue is an Aristotelian vice, and vice-versa. Aristotle says we acquire moral virtues through habituation – repeated performance of the actions characteristic of a virtue – and takes this mechanism almost to rule out moral conversions in adulthood. The New Testament writers would not deny (indeed, would stress) the effects of habituation, but in addition they think that God can transform people quite abruptly. Aristotle seems confident that some people become perfected in virtue in this life; Christian belief in the tenacity of sin tends to the contrary opinion, but our Lord urges us to seek perfection.

The narrative of God's interactions with his chosen people Israel provides the framework for New Testament ethics; while Aristotle inherits, and to some extent uses in his ethics, the theological narratives of the ancient Greek poets, his ethics deeply revises the ethics of the heroic age of Greece without, seemingly, any alternative *story* to provide its backbone. For Aristotle, ethics is a branch of politics, in the quite literal sense that ethical perfection depends on living in a well-structured city; Christians may also believe such a thing, but that city is not to be found among currently possible earthly cities. In the current order of things, we are resident aliens, who must work out our virtues in significant friction with societal structures – sometimes even the church.

Aristotle and the apostle Paul both devote attention to human weakness of will – the intentional doing of what one knows to be undermining one's wellbeing – but Aristotle explains it as a kind of ignorance, and Paul explains it as perversity. For Aristotle, practical wisdom is central to the good life and a crucial basis for each of the other moral virtues, but Paul says that the wisdom of the Greeks is foolishness and that Christ is our wisdom. Is Aristotelian practical wisdom really contrary to the mind of Christ?

Aristotle gives another central place in his ethics to a kind of love that he calls *philia* (friendship), while the New Testament gives an even more central place to a kind of love that it calls *agape*. How do friendship and *agape* compare? A related issue is that of human equality. Though Aristotle makes the virtue of justice turn on the concept of equality, his ethics is strongly elitist; he believes that some human beings are slaves by nature (see *Politics*, Book 1), while New Testament ethics is radically egalitarian: Onesimus is Philemon's brother, "both in the flesh and in the Lord" (Philem. 16). Without denying that we are very *un*equal, along the lines that Aristotle emphasizes (intelligence, gender, beauty, strength, temperament, family connections, education, wealth), the apostolic witness supposes that all human beings are equal as created in the image of God.

Aristotle lavishes a perhaps surprising attention on the concept of pleasure, presumably because he thinks it a special index of virtue, pretty closely related to happiness, and a necessary aspect of fully engaged intelligent human activity;[2] the many biblical references to joy and pleasure make for a natural locus of comparison. Finally (and I'm not suggesting that this list of Bible/Aristotle themes is complete), Aristotle and the Bible each have a concept of blessedness or happiness or complete wellbeing. The two concepts are neither completely different nor the same, and a comparison of them will throw light on both.

In this short paper I want to convey an idea about how to read Aristotle's *Ethics* in the context of Christian higher education. Such reading has at least the following goals: to familiarize students with an astonishingly great text about human nature and wellbeing; to cultivate the student's ability to think philosophically about the issues in the text; to deepen the student's understanding of the conceptual framework of Christian ethics and especially its bearing on topics like the ones listed above; and to teach the student the more general skill of reading a great text simultaneously for what it says and for its relevance to his own understanding of himself and the world. To make my reflections concrete, I'll devote the rest of this paper to two topics that loom rather large in Aristotle's text: the virtues and friendship.

Aristotelian and Christian virtues

Aristotle's account of the virtues is at the center of his ethical thought. In the famous Function Argument (1.7) he concludes that the distinctively human good (*eudaimonia*, or happiness) is rational activity of the soul in accordance with virtue. In Book 2 he establishes that the moral virtues are dispositions to perform actions and to feel emotions in ways that conform to the correct principles. We are born with a nature that makes it *possible* for us to acquire the virtues, but *actually* to acquire them we have to perform virtuous actions, feel virtuous emotions, and think virtuous thoughts. The moral life is an active life, and we learn the virtues through proper actualizations of our potentialities. In Book 3 Aristotle shows that we can be properly praised for our virtues and blamed for our vices because our good and bad traits of character come from actions (and passions) that we voluntarily perform or undergo. Virtues enable us to choose excellent actions by deliberating well and then acting in accordance with our deliberations.

After discussing general features of the virtues from 1.13 to 3.5, from the middle of Book 3 to the end of Book 6 Aristotle gives accounts of particular virtues, such as courage, temperance, and justice, as well as several other excellences. His discussions vary in length from one chapter ("ready wit" [Ross] in 4.8) to a whole book (justice in Book 5). To each of the virtues corresponds a generically human activity-type (or a family of such types), and the virtue is an ability and inclination to perform the activity in the proper way, thus achieving one of the "ends" or fulfillments of human life. For example, eating, drinking, and sexual activity are generically human types of activity governed by the virtue of temperance, and temperance is the ability and inclination to perform these activities properly (rationally – according to the right "rule" or *logos*); but the right performance of such activities is one of the ends proper to human life, thus a part of the "final" end of *eudaimonia* or wellbeing or happiness. Similarly, the activities of distributing goods, trade, making legal judgments, and meting out honors and punishments, are the generically human activity-types governed by the virtue of justice, and justice is the ability and inclination to perform such activities well; and right performance of such activities is one of the ends proper to human life. And so forth for the other virtues. The totality of these activities is the ultimate goal of human life, complete human fulfillment or *eudaimonia*. Here is a chart roughly coordinating human activities, virtues, and ends. (*See chart on following page*).

Aristotle tries to characterize in a general way the "right rule" that governs the virtues. The doctrine of the mean is the claim that every moral virtue occupies a point on a continuum of something quantifiable, and that point specifies the virtuous disposition, as contrasted with vicious or less virtuous ones. The vices lie at the extremes of these continua: one of defect and one of

ACTIVITIES (*energeiai*) aspects of human living	**VIRTUES (*aretai*), aspects of human excellence**	**ENDS (*telê*), aspects of success in human living**
Facing fearsome things	Courage (*andreia*) (3.6–9)	The noble (protecting one's state, gaining honor)
Eating, drinking, sexual intercourse	Temperance (*sophrôsunê*) (3.10–12)	Health, reproduction, enjoyment
Giving (freely), acquiring, and retaining wealth	Liberality (*eleutheriotês*) (4.1)	Self-expansion, helping others, its own sake
Giving freely of large public gifts	Magnificence (*megaloprepeia*) (4.2)	Self-expansion, public benefit
All the activities cumulatively of political life	Magnanimity (*megalopsuchia*) (4.3)	Being honorable
Seeking and receiving lesser honors	Proper ambition (nameless) (4.4)	Having honor
Dealing with offenses against oneself and one's own	Good temper (*praotês*) (4.5)	Maintaining friendly intercourse
General social intercourse about "touchy" issues	Politic integrity (nameless) (4.6)	Social order
Self-characterization	Modesty (nameless) (4.7)	Being known by fellows
Exchanging pleasantries	Ready wit (*eutrapelia*) (4.8)	Amusing social intercourse
Dealing with one's own moral faults	Shame (*aidôs*) (4.9)	Moral maturity
Distributing goods, meting out honors and punishments, transacting business	Justice (*dikaiosunê*) (5)	Bringing about justice in the activities to which it applies
Syllogistic reasoning	Scientific knowledge (*epistêmê*) (6.3)	Getting true conclusions from premises
Production	Art (*technê*) (6.4)	Products
Deliberation about and perception of what to do	Practical wisdom (*phronêsis*) (6.5)	Virtuous actions
Induction, understanding, contemplation	Intuitive reason (*nous*) (6.6)	Getting truth, understanding, contemplation
Induction and understanding, plus syllogism	Philosophic wisdom (*sophia*) (6.7)	Getting true conclusions from premises
Deliberation about what to do	Excellence in deliberation (*euboulia*) (6.9)	Acting well
Making evaluative judgments	Understanding (*sunesis*) (6.10)	Truth about practical matters
Judging cases of justice / injustice	Understanding about equity (*gnômê*) (6.11)	Avoiding unnecessary condemnation
General or inclusive: Living a human life	**General or inclusive:** According to virtue	**General or inclusive:** Living a human life well (in accordance with the human virtues); i.e., ***EUDAIMONIA***

excess. Thus courage is a disposition to experience a medial amount of fear and of confidence (that is, neither too much nor too little) in threatening situations (especially warfare), and good temper is a disposition to experience a medial amount of anger in response to others' transgressions against oneself and one's own relatives, friends, possessions, and so forth.

But in explaining the mean, Aristotle regularly forsakes the language of quantity for the language of what is "right" or "due." For example, good temper is not just a matter of having the right *amount* of anger, but of getting angry on the right occasions, toward the right persons, for the right reasons, and so forth. Thus Aristotle's explanation seems to show the inadequacy of the original quantitative explanation (that is, the identification of what is "right" or "rational" by location in the middle of a continuum). Then in the opening chapter of Book 6 he admits that the doctrine of the mean (quantitatively *or* qualitatively formulated) is woefully uninformative: "if a man had only this knowledge he would be none the wiser" (1138b29, Ross, 137), and says that in what follows he will state the rule more precisely. He never does.

Aristotle's usual way of sorting out conceptual matters (exemplified, for example, by his discussion of what *eudaimonia* is in 1.4–12) is to survey the diverse opinions of the many and the wise, subject them to critical evaluation, and then formulate his own view of the matter, attempting to find valuable insights among the diverse opinions and to preserve as much as possible from them. If we read Aristotle as applying this approach, if less overtly, to his accounts of the virtues, then we can see that the real "rule" for what constitutes the traits of the ideally functioning human being is not the doctrine of the mean, even in its preferable non-quantitative formulation, but is derived by a critical acceptance of the best of current culture. The doctrine of the mean indicates Aristotle's (failed) aspiration to virtue-norms that completely transcend culture.

The Virtue of Aristotelian Courage

Consider Aristotle's discussion of courage. It is of middling length – four chapters (3.6–9). He begins by reiterating that courage is "a mean concerning feelings of fear and confidence" (3.6, 1115a7, Crisp, 48). But it is more concerned with fear than with confidence (3.9, 1117a32–35), and is concerned with only some kinds of fears, namely, those experienced in the perils of battle (3.6, 1115a21, 25–35). It is not appropriate to fear poverty or disease, but people who are fearless[3] of these things are not thereby courageous (the person who is fearless about losing his property displays a different virtue: liberality). Aristotle allows that the courageous person will be fearless also in other contexts than war, for example, in disasters at sea (1115a35–b5); but such fearlessness is not the kind that warrants attribution of courage. The limitation of courage to the context of battle may be a vestige of the Homeric ethic, though Aristotle's ethics is not generally Homeric.[4]

In chapter 7, he drops the insistence on the battle context and says merely that "the courageous person is the one who endures and fears – and likewise is confident about – the right things, for the right reason, in the right way, and at the right time; for the courageous person feels and acts in accordance with the merits of the case, and as reason requires" (3.7, 1115b17–20, Crisp, 50). We have already seen that what "reason requires" cannot be determined by a merely quantitative measure, since the rule *only in battle* is not a matter of the quantity of anything, yet *only in battle* seems to be part of the rule for what constitutes the virtue. The same is true of "for the right reason." He now tells us that committing suicide is never courageous (even, presumably, if the suicide's fear is somewhere midway between zero and all-out panic) because he does it to escape the pain of poverty or love (1116a13–15), and neither of these motives is the right kind of reason.

In 3.8 Aristotle gives us a catalog of states that may appear to be courage but are not. Here the military theme returns, and he quotes or alludes to Homer several times. *Citizen courage* is the disposition to do, in the face of threat from an enemy, actions like those of the courageous person, out of a desire to avoid "legal penalties and opprobrium" (1116a19–20, Crisp, 51). Fear of shame is fear of dishonor (*atimia*), and honor (*timê*) is what is due to what is noble (*to kalon*), and genuinely courageous men act for the sake of the noble. So to the extent that citizen courage is motivated by fear of opprobrium, it is pretty similar to real courage, but differs in being more motivated by others' disdainful response to one's deeds, while genuine courage is motivated by the noble itself. *Courage under threat of punishment* is less like real courage. Here soldiers act "courageously" out of fear of punishment rather than fear of shame. *Courage as knowledge* is the disposition to perform actions that look outwardly courageous, but are due to the soldier's awareness that he is in no real danger, because he knows the circumstances of war or is proficient with weapons. *Courage as spirit* (*thumos*) is the disposition to do "courageous" actions, not for the sake of the noble, but out of a kind of (blind) raging enthusiasm, like a wounded animal that attacks the hunter. *Courage as ignorance* is displayed when a man acts "courageously" because he does not recognize the danger he is in.

Let us summarize the conditions that Aristotle has detailed for the kind of courage he discusses. Courage is a disposition

- to *perform actions*
- in situations of *threat to one's life*
- with *knowledge* of the threat
- on the *battlefield*
- *not solely out of "spirit"* but possibly with the *help of spirit*
- for *the sake of the noble*
- while feeling *fear, neither too much nor too little*, for one's life, and

• feeling *confidence, neither too much nor too* little,[5] in one's ability to act well.

The above, then, is a kind of rule for Aristotelian courage. My point about Aristotle's analysis of this virtue is that the concept cannot be derived from either of the two principles *find the mean with respect to fear and confidence*, or *fear and feel confident rightly*. The second formula is clearly preferable, but as Aristotle himself points out at the beginning of Book 6, to have an adequately informative rule we still need somehow to find out what fearing and feeling confident rightly *amounts to*. And we have also seen that courage is more specific than fearing rightly, because one can fear rightly the loss of one's property (while feeling confident that one can act well) without exhibiting Aristotelian courage. I suggest that Aristotle's semi-covert approach to specifying the rules governing the virtues is pretty much the same as his overt approach to specifying the nature of *eudaimonia*. He consults what the many and the wise say or think it is, and sorts out these suggestions critically by setting them against one another and by applying logical criteria and his own observations of life and human nature. In other words, he starts with the ethical outlook of his community, and refines and formulates it by applying philosophy and psychology to it. Aristotle never formulates the rule for Aristotelian courage, unless we take the whole discussion in 3.6–9 to be the "formula."

Aristotle takes the virtues he discusses to be dispositions that make it possible to live the good life as he understands it. Reading broadly in the *Nicomachean Ethics*, we can see that the best human life, as Aristotle distills it from the opinions of the many and the wise of his culture, has the following features: self-sufficiency as opposed to dependency (see 10.6–8), agency as opposed to passivity (1.8, 1098b30–33), power over others (1.2, 1194b8–11) or just power (10.7, 1178a1), superiority to others (4.3), being honored by others for one's agency, power, and superiority (4.3), non-conflictual relations with all others (5.1, *Politics* 5) and friendship with some of the best (8–9). From this list of broad aspects of human excellence, it is not difficult to understand why courage would be a major virtue for Aristotle.

New Testament Virtues

In a parallel way, the writers of the New Testament[6] discuss the traits that they take to be the dispositions to live the good life as *they* understand it. Having a different understanding of the good life, they also have a different list of virtues. Here is a list of major New Testament virtues: faith (*pistis*), hope (*elpis*), love (*agapê*), forgiveness (*aphesis*), humility (*tapeinophrosunê*), gratitude (*charis, eucharistia*), peace (*eirênê*), patience (*makrothumia, hupomonê*), self-control (*enkrateia*), compassion (*splanchna*), and meekness or gentleness (*praütês*).

Comparing the two lists, we are struck with how little they overlap. Faith fits us to be related personally to a personal God and to accept for ourselves the work his Son has done on our behalf. Hope gives us a happy relationship with an eschatological state of ourselves and the world. Aristotle has no counterpart of these virtues because both of the corresponding parts of the good life are missing from his understanding of it. He does have the quasi-virtue of friendship (more on this below), but would not regard the indiscriminate love of neighbor (*agapê*) as a good thing. Aristotle's virtue vocabulary overlaps that of the New Testament in the word *praütês* (in Aristotle *praotês* – gentleness, mildness, meekness; for Aristotle the word designates the mean with respect to anger, and he says that the gentle person will tend to be "indulgent" [*suvgnômonikos*] with those who injure him [4.5, 1126a3]). This indulgence is akin to forgiveness, and some scholars translate the word so,[7] but the concept is not that of forgiveness.[8] In his discussion of magnanimity (4.3), Aristotle almost directly rejects gratitude as a desirable trait, saying that the magnanimous (that is, great-souled) man prefers not to think about benefits he has received, because the beneficiary is inferior to the benefactor, and the great-souled man wants to be superior. Similarly, Aristotle will reject humility as a "slavish" trait, and thus closer to vice than to virtue. On self-control (*enkrateia*) the New Testament virtue vocabulary again overlaps Aristotle, but self-control is only a quasi-virtue for Aristotle, since it implies that its possessor has impulses that are inappropriate enough to need controlling. In listing self-control among the fruit of the Holy Spirit (Gal. 5.23), the apostle Paul shows himself less "perfectionist" and in a way less optimistic than Aristotle about human potential. The Aristotelian virtue that is closest to self-control is temperance (*sôphrosunê*), which is the perfection of one's physical appetite-dispositions. Christians have tended to think that, while our impulses are certainly subject to improvement, we will probably always, in this life, need to be prepared to control errant ones when they beset us. Compassion is an important Christian virtue, no doubt an aspect of *agapê*. Aristotle discusses compassion (*eleos*, however, not *splangchna*) in *Rhetoric* 2.8, but treats it only as a passion, not as a virtue.

How does the New Testament present virtues? We have seen that Aristotle tries, unsuccessfully, to give what we might call a "theory" of virtue, a general and fairly simple formula that is supposed to be a template from which a more specific formula can be formed, that specifies what any particular virtue is. Thus the general form of a virtue is that it is a mean state, and any particular virtue-type is a mean state with respect to some kind of thing that is quantifiable (fear and confidence, anger, bodily appetites, etc.). However, I have suggested that the actual normative content of his accounts of the particular virtues is presented in less formal "discussions" that involve the presentation of examples with appended observations, the comparison of real examples of the virtue with simulacra, the critical consideration of what the many and the wise of Aristotle's culture think that the virtue in question is, and so forth.

The New Testament is not a work of philosophy, and generally does not go in for definitions and theoretical formulae. Occasionally we will see a formula such as "Faith is the assurance of things hoped for, the conviction of things not seen" (Heb. 11.1), but such sayings are better taken, not as strict definitions, but as remarks or wise sayings that highlight some aspect of the concept (in this case, of faith) for some particular pastoral purpose. Such remarks might correspond to one of the remarks about the nature of courage that I derived above from Aristotle's more extensive discussion of the virtue. But, not being philosophy, the New Testament also does not attempt to summarize the main features of virtues, as I did at the end of my discussion of Aristotle on courage. Even that is more abstract and formulaic than what the New Testament writers typically do. The New Testament consists mostly of stories (the Gospels and Acts of the Apostles) and pastoral teaching and exhortation (the letters of the apostles and the teachings of Jesus in the Gospels). Were we to write something more systematic, and thus more like Aristotelian analysis, about the virtue concepts in the New Testament, we would have to assemble the parts of the concepts from these stories and pastoral teachings, and then fill in some gaps to answer questions about the concept that are not addressed in the New Testament. This is just the kind of thing that Thomas Aquinas, consulting Aristotle, the Bible, and the church fathers, gives us in his discussions of the virtues in the Second Part of the *Summa Theologiae*.

Aquinas is perhaps the greatest of the many "Aristotelians" who read Aristotle in the light of earlier great texts of the Christian tradition. Aquinas's treatment of courage is fairly typical. While courage is not found in the *lists* of virtues scattered through the New Testament, clearly Jesus and, after Pentecost, the apostles and many subsequent believers, *exemplify* courage when they act on behalf of God in ways they well understand as jeopardizing their lives and wellbeing. Accordingly Aquinas, while following Aristotle quite closely, alters the Aristotelian account to reflect the features of courage that belong specifically to the Christian outlook. He retains the idea that courage is essentially a disposition with respect to fear and is paradigmatically exemplified by one who faces death in battle. But that person is now not the soldier but the Christian martyr, and the battle is not in defense of the city-state but of the kingdom of God, and the action is not that of slaying the enemy but that of enduring the enemy's onslaughts, and the "noble" is explicitly the love of God and his righteousness (see Aquinas 1966, Questions 123–4, especially 124 article 2).

New Testament Humility

Let us briefly consider the important New Testament virtue of humility. It comes in for less exposition than virtues like faith and love, but more than such virtues as self-control and perseverance. So with respect to the amount of exposition, it is perhaps analogous to Aristotle's courage. Paul addresses humility in Phil. 2.1–11, and it is plausible to read the story of Jesus washing the disciples' feet in John 13.1–20 as illustrating some of Paul's points. Furthermore, the attitude expressed by John the Baptist when he speaks of his joy at hearing the bridegroom's voice and comments "He must become greater; I must become less" (John 3.22–30) seems to exemplify the trait whose paradigm is the incarnate Lord. The concept of humility that is in play in these passages is that of a high-minded indifference to prestige. The humble person does not "insist" on the privileges and honors of his high status (if he has such), nor does he seek or long for the privileges and honors of high status (if he lacks such), except insofar as these are needed in the pursuit of some good end that he seeks. Thus according to Phil. 2, Jesus did not insist on his divine status as making him more important or giving him prestige or honor, but was willing to take on the nature of a servant out of love for humanity and to bring about our rescue.

Similarly, John the Baptist does not mind being eclipsed by the greater Jesus, but simply rejoices in the work of his Master. This willingness to have the status of a servant for the sake of some great good is illustrated in the footwashing scene of John 13, but we see there that Jesus' humility is not a forgetfulness of his lordship, for he comments about what he has just done, "You call me 'teacher' and 'Lord,' and rightly so, for that is what I am. …I have set you an example, that you should do as I have done for you" (13.13, 15). Thus humility is quite different from self-hatred, feeling humiliated, low self-estimate, shyness, or contrition (awareness of one's own moral pollution). It is instead a kind of self-forgetfulness that is quite compatible with bold action, enthusiastic pursuit of something good, and frank acknowledgment of one's own talents and abilities, and even one's moral purity. However, it does seem incompatible with Aristotelian magnanimity, which on Aristotle's account is the virtue exhibited by a person who possesses all the virtues in the highest degree. The writer of *Nicomachean Ethics* 4.3 would most likely have contempt for the central character of John 13.

I have just sketched, ever so briefly, a concept of humility by drawing on the New Testament in somewhat the way Aristotle draws on the many and the wise of his culture to generate his sketches of the virtues in *Nicomachean Ethics*. The New Testament is a kind of sourcebook for Christian thinking about the virtues, and can be juxtaposed, in this regard, with the reading of Aristotle's great book in the Christian college or university, to the better understanding of both texts and, for the Christian student, the better understanding of his own spiritual tradition's ethical outlook. Aristotle's pedagogical purpose for *Nicomachean Ethics* is to cultivate those who are morally and intellectually up to it in the most articulate, critical, and profound practical wisdom available to people of his culture (2.2, 1103b26–32). Christian teachers of great texts can use Aristotle's text to a similar purpose of our own.

Aristotelian Friendship and New Testament Love

Friendship is a topic that naturally interests college students, and a discussion of Aristotle's profound account of it, with the New Testament in mind, can deepen students' wisdom about this important aspect of life.

Aristotle opens the discussion of friendship that occupies Books 8 and 9 by saying that friendship "is a virtue or involves virtue" (8.1, 1155a3, Crisp, 143). It differs from paradigm virtues in being a relationship between two people. Most virtues *make for* good relationships with others; but they are traits of individuals, not relationships. A good marriage requires the parties to have some virtues; but however good it may be, a good marriage is not a virtue.

Aristotle's account of friendship appears to be based on a schema of what attracts and thus motivates human beings: Everything that seems "lovable" to us humans does so under the appearance of a) the pleasant, b) the useful, or c) the good in itself. But Mike's friendship with Joe is more than Mike's being attracted to Joe because Joe seems pleasant, useful, or good to him; it is also his wishing Joe well. But it is more than this, since friendship is a *reciprocal* well-wishing; if Joe does not wish Mike well, then no amount of Mike's wishing Joe well will constitute a friendship. But a friendship is also more than a reciprocal well-wishing of mutually attracted parties; the well-wishing must be mutually *recognized*. If it remains unknown to each that the other wishes him well, there is still no friendship, despite all the mutual well-wishing. Adding some further conditions of friendship that emerge as Aristotle's account unfolds, we can say that friendship is (at least)

- a *reciprocal* and
- *equal* and
- *mutually recognized* and
- *fairly stable*
- *well-wishing* and *well-doing*
- *between two persons*
- based on *an attraction to one another* because of
- *pleasure, usefulness,* or *goodness,* and
- leading them *to enjoy one another's company* and
- *to want to spend time together* and
- *pursue activities together.*

The three kinds of attraction make for three kinds of friendship: friendships of pleasure, friendships of utility, and friendships of virtue. But these are not all equally friendship, for the friendship of virtue is true friendship, while the other two are "incidental" friendships (*kata sumbebêkos*, 1156a17). They are friendships only by analogy (1157a33) with the friendship of virtue.

Aristotle's argument for the centrality of the friendship of virtue appears to be this. The attraction of friendship is essentially *to the other person*, for we are not friends with utilities and pleasures, or with non-personal things that provide utility and pleasure. We are not friends with our cars. Thus true friendship is only for someone who is good *as a human being*, not for someone who is good merely *as a source of pleasure* or *as useful in some respect*. But only the virtues, not pleasantness or utility, make a person good *as a human being*. Thus the other two kinds of friendships are "incidental." This argument is borne out by the consideration that friendship is thought to be relatively stable and permanent, but friendships based on utility and pleasure dissolve as soon as the utility or pleasure ceases, while true friendships, as based on virtues, depend on more permanent properties of the friends.

Aristotle's account of friendship harbors a tension by which it moves both away from and toward the New Testament concept of love. On the one hand, it strongly emphasizes the equality and reciprocity conditions, and thus tends to model friendship on the virtue of justice. Because friendship between two people accomplishes the same thing that justice would, "when people are friends, they have no need of justice" (8.1, 1155a27, Crisp, 144). This, I think, is the main stream of his account. The less prominent stream models friendship on a virtue that resembles New Testament generosity (not exactly what Aristotle calls liberality [*eleutheriotês*, see 4.1]). Here the well-wishing / well-doing condition and the attraction condition are prominent, though the attraction does not fit comfortably into any of the usual categories of the pleasant, the useful, and the good. Let us look first at the justice-strand in Aristotle's discussion, then at the generosity-strand.

The equality and reciprocity conditions signal the justice model of friendship. Jesus both nods to and violates the equality condition when in John's Gospel (15.12–17) he calls the disciples his friends (*philoi*). He violates it when he lays it down as a condition of their being his friends that they obey him. We will not take it as an overture of friendship if someone offers to be our friend only if we agree to obey his commands. But then Jesus says something that suggests that the notion of equality does have some bearing on his concept of friendship: the master does not share with his servant the rationale for his commandments; he expects "blind" obedience. But Jesus has brought the disciples to understand (to some extent) the motives behind the kingdom of God. "No longer do I call you servants (*doulous*), for the servant does not know what his master is doing; but I have called you friends, for all that I have heard from my Father I have made known to you" (15.15). Friendship of the disciple with Jesus is a very unequal and only partially reciprocal relationship. What about friendship among ordinary sinners? Neither Jesus nor the apostolic writers teach much about friendship as a special kind of love, but if we take their teachings about *agapê* as bearing on the nature of friendship as well, we will surely suppose that genuine friendships will not require perfect reciprocity or equality of benefit.

Aristotle sometimes writes as though they do. We learn in Book 5 that distributive justice is essentially a kind of equality – not arithmetical, but proportional (see 1131a15–30). Consider a law firm in which a senior partner earns twice as much as the junior partner for an hour of her work. On Aristotle's analysis, this arrangement can be just despite the numerical inequality of the earning, if the pay that each gets is proportional to her "merit." Merit might be measured in terms of years of seniority or level of competence or of education, etc. Thus the formula for distributive justice, where A and B are persons, G is some distributable good (like money or honor), and M is some kind of merit, is

$$\frac{\text{A's share of } \mathbf{M}}{\text{B's share of } \mathbf{M}} = \frac{\text{A's share of } \mathbf{G}}{\text{B's share of } \mathbf{G}}$$

In ideal friendships, the partners are equal in merit (chiefly virtue) and also give and take equally of love and the other benefits of friendship. But some relationships that deserve the name of friendships are unequal in these ways – parent / child, husband / wife, ruler / subject. Here Aristotle applies the above principle of distributive justice, and makes the G in question affection or love (*philêsis*):

> In all friendships involving superiority, the affection must be proportional as well. The better, that is to say, must be loved more than he loves, and so must the more useful, and each of the others likewise; when the affection is in accordance with merit, then a kind of equality results, which is of course thought to be a mark of friendship. (8.7, 1158b23–28, Crisp, 152)

The implication of Aristotle's view seems to be that a true friendship can obtain between father and son, or husband and wife, only if the inferior loves the superior more than the superior loves the inferior, so that the inequality of the *persons* is compensated by the inequality of the *love*. Thus a case in which a virtuous father loves his less virtuous son more than the son loves his father, or in which they love each other equally, falls short of being perfect friendship, because it fails to satisfy the equality condition.

To Christian ears this is a pretty strange doctrine; the strict give and take and the computation of merit seem foreign to friendship, as to other kinds of love. In fact, it seems that the more meritorious is a person's love for another, the *less* will his love need requital. The virtue on which friendships should be chiefly modeled is generosity, not justice.

Aristotle seems to share our intuition. He says that young people's friendships, in which they give each other pleasure, are more like true friendship than the friendship of utility because there is more generosity (*to eleutherion*, 1158a22) in them. In the chapter following the one from which I most recently quoted, Aristotle gives further voice to this intuition.

> But friendship seems to consist more in loving than in being loved, as is indicated by the enjoyment a mother finds in love. Sometimes she will give her own child to others to bring up, and though she loves him because she knows him, she does not seek to be loved in return, if it is impossible to have both. It seems enough for her to see the child doing well, and she loves him even if, because he does not know her, he gives her none of the things appropriate to a mother. (8.8, 1159a28–36, Crisp, 153; see also 9.4, 1168a6–7)

Here the equality and reciprocity conditions of friendship seem to have dropped out of the picture altogether. The well-wishing and well-doing may even be a one-way affair, with the satisfaction the friend experiences being entirely in the wellbeing of the beloved. The affection or attraction to her child that moves the mother to wish him well and promote his wellbeing does not seem to fit any of the standard Aristotelian bases of attraction. Obviously it is not the child's utility that motivates the mother, nor the pleasure the child gives by being beautiful or funny or ingratiating (Aristotle imagines that the mother foregoes such pleasure), nor does the mother admire the child for his virtue. How then do we explain the mother's (and by implication possibly other friends') well-wishing and well-doing?

In 9.7 Aristotle explains why benefactors love their beneficiaries more than beneficiaries their benefactors. He rejects the proposal that the beneficiary is a debtor and the benefactor nurtures him to protect his investment: benefactors, says Aristotle, love their *beneficiaries*, but creditors do not *love* their debtors; they just want payment. A better analogy is artists' relation to their works.

> The position of the benefactor then resembles that of the artist; the recipient of his bounty is his handiwork, and he therefore loves him more than his handiwork loves its maker. The reason for this is that being is to all people something worthy of choice and love, and we exist by virtue of actuality (that is, by living and acting); and the product is, as it were, the producer in actuality, so he is fond of his product, because he is fond of his own existence. And this is natural, since what he is in capacity, his product reveals in actuality. (1168a4–10. The first sentence is Rackham's translation, 547; after that, Crisp's, 173.)

In this way, benefactors see their beneficiaries in much the same way as poets, who "have an excessive liking for their own poems, and are fond of them as if they were their own children" (1168a1–2, Crisp, 173), see their works. In accordance with the idea that the benefactor loves the beneficiary as the product of his own activity, Aristotle also notes that "everyone is more fond of what has cost them effort" (1168a22, Crisp, 174), and says that this is why mothers are fonder of their children than fathers are.

So the generosity we see in the case of the benefactor and the parent, while it does not demand reciprocity, seems to avoid doing so by stressing the "superiority" of the one who "loves." The lover revels in his agency and creativity, relegating the beloved, in his eyes, to a status of receiver, of dependency and creaturehood. We see the same pattern of thought in Aristotle's discussion of the great-souled man, who is "the sort of person to do good, but is ashamed to be a beneficiary himself, since doing good is characteristic of a superior, receiving it of an inferior" (1124b10–11, Crisp, 70). The lover's activity is parasitic on the beloved's passivity, and activity is where excellence and full being are.

Aristotle's account may correctly describe some parents' love for their children. It may correctly describe the behavior of many benefactors. But by Christian lights it is not ideal. Indeed, it might well be called a sinful love. The New Testament summarily assigns all of us to creaturely, responsive, status: "We love because he first loved us" (I John 4.19). Jesus warns against lording it over others. "…those who are supposed to rule over the Gentiles lord it over them. But it shall not be so among you…" (Mark 10.35–45), but Aristotelian generosity has a subtle lording character.

Nor does the New Testament make it a condition of the virtuous person's love that the one he loves be virtuous. Instead, it stresses forgiveness, forbearance, gratitude, humility, and highlights human imperfection.

> Put on, then, as God's chosen ones, holy and beloved, compassion, kindness, lowliness, meekness, and patience, forbearing one another and, if one has a complaint against another, forgiving each other; as the Lord has forgiven you, so you also must forgive. And above all these put on love, which binds everything together in perfect harmony. And let the peace of Christ rule in your hearts, to which indeed you were called in the one body. And be thankful. (Col. 3.12–15)

Jesus bids us be perfect as our heavenly Father is perfect, by loving in a world filled with imperfect individuals. "You have heard that it was said, 'You shall love your neighbor and hate your enemy.' But I say to you, Love your enemies and pray for those who persecute you, so that you may be children of your Father who is in heaven; for he makes his sun rise on the evil and the good, and sends rain on the just and the unjust" (see Matt. 5.43–48).

Christians may agree with Aristotle that friendship, as a special kind of love, is selective, and in particular that the best kind of friendship selects the friend, in part, for his virtues, and to this extent the relation between the two is equal and reciprocal: *each* is virtuous, and each appreciates the other's virtue. But once in the friendship, there is no strict give and take; the dominant attitude of each to the other is a non-Aristotelian generosity in which the status of each as giver is rather dim to himself, and his status as receiver of good things, first from God but also from his friend, dominates his consciousness. To the extent that each gives, either expecting something in return or feeling the superior power of his own position as giver, the friendship is not of a distinctively Christian kind.

Conclusion

Reading the *Nicomachean Ethics* in the context of a Christian university education is a wonderful occasion for enhancing the student's skill at critically reading a very deep text that is full of insights and wisdom, but hails from an alien ethical world. It can be an occasion for thinking carefully and comparatively about human nature and its mature realization in the form of ethical and spiritual virtues and the relationships with others that such virtues make possible. For the Christian student, placing Aristotle under the light of deep expressions of our own moral tradition may make the reading more exciting and more likely to be engaged and critical. Casting an Aristotelian light on the moral thought of our own community can bring the contours of that thought into edifying salience, thus contributing to the holistic Christian educational goal of developing character while sharpening intellect.

References

Aquinas 1966. *Summa Theologiae*, vol. 42. Trans. Anthony Ross, O. P. and P. G. Walsh. New York and London: McGraw-Hill Book Company.

Aristotle 1934. *Nicomachean Ethics*. Trans. H. Rackham. Cambridge, Mass.: Harvard University Press.

Aristotle 1980. *Nicomachean Ethics*. Trans. W. D. Ross, rev. J. L. Ackrill and J. O. Urmson. Oxford: Oxford University Press.

Aristotle 2000. *Nicomachean Ethics*. Trans. Roger Crisp. Cambridge: Cambridge University Press.

Bible 1973. *The Oxford Annotated Bible with the Apocrypha*, Revised Standard Version. New York: Oxford University Press.

Brewer, Talbot 2009. *The Retrieval of Ethics*. Oxford: Oxford University Press.

Griswold, Charles 2007. *Forgiveness: A Philosophical Exploration*. Cambridge: Cambridge University Press.

Nussbaum, Martha 1996. "Aristotle on Emotions and Rational Persuasion" in *Essays on Aristotle's Rhetoric*. Ed. Amélie Rorty. Berkeley: University of California Press.

Plato 1997. *Laches*. Trans. Rosamond Kent Sprague. In *Plato: Complete Works*. Ed. John M. Cooper. Indianapolis: Hackett Publishing Company.

Virgil
The Aeneid

A paper on reading the *Aeneid* as a "great text" should begin by acknowledging that, for most of the two millennia since its publication, it was *the* great text: "to describe the epic as a bestseller would make sense only if the customary noun were 'betterseller.'"[1] Virgil was considered for many centuries the primary representative and repository of all the wisdom of pagan antiquity. Macrobius' *Saturnalia* upholds Virgil's supreme authority on all matters against encroachments by pesky Christians; conversely, because of the perceived prophecy of Christ's birth in the Fourth Eclogue, Christians were able to claim the poet as in some sense their own.[2] Augustine may have expressed regret over his tears for Dido and his fascination with the "wanderings of some Aeneas or other" (*Conf.* 1.13), but Virgil's words and themes still resonate throughout his works to the end, and the *Aeneid* is the starting point for his arguments against the religion and *mores* of Rome in the *City of God*.[3] In the Middle Ages, Virgil's works were subjected to Christian allegorization and even quarried for prophecies: the common practice of the *Sortes Virgilianae*, in which lines selected at random were thought to provide supernaturally guided instruction, shows that Virgil's stature was scarcely lower than that of the Bible.

Even without the supernatural bridge of the Fourth Eclogue, medieval Christians could fit the *Aeneid* into their own moral and theological framework. There is a certain appeal to the Neoplatonist reading of Bernard Silvestris (a twelfth-century Chartrian writer of a commentary on most of *Aeneid* 1–6), in which Aeneas's journey recapitulates allegorically the soul's journey toward perfection. This model of trial and spiritual growth in Aeneas's travels from Troy to Italy harmonizes readily with the Judeo-Christian grand narrative: Virgil's suffering hero shares much with the Jews in the desert, Jesus in the wilderness, each human soul on its pilgrimage from the Egypt or Babylon of sin to the Jerusalem of salvation. The idea of human life as a battle also appears to accord with the *Aeneid*'s second half: like Hercules defeating the monster Cacus (whose name in Greek means "bad guy"), goodness will triumph in the end.

And yet, the more deeply we enter into the story of the *Aeneid*, the more we must reconsider or discard such generalizations. Allegorization is a convenient means of sanitization: if Dido equals "lust," then of course Aeneas had to leave her, and good riddance.[4] The problem is that this is not the story Virgil tells. Dido was a wise and competent ruler, in command of herself and her people, until Aeneas arrived and she began to be poisoned by cruel and self-serving gods. As she laments in a moment of clarity before her suicide,

> "Happy, oh, too happy, if only the Trojan
> keels had never touched our shores."[5]
> (4.657–58)

Neither Troy nor Carthage nor the cities of Italy are depicted as worse than the civilization Aeneas will found: all are thriving, just, cultured, and religious. What makes Virgil so endlessly fascinating is his refusal to simplify moral issues, his vivid and sympathetic portrayal of the humans who, though flawed, suffer primarily from being on the losing side. Dido and Turnus fall, not because they have too little faith, but because they have too much – because they put their trust in the justice of a god who happens to be supporting the other team.[6] Moreover, whatever the long-term beneficial effects of Aeneas's conquest of Italy, he himself, within the poem, achieves neither transcendence nor happiness.

In the present paper, I would like to focus on the idea of "sacrifice" as an interpretive key to many aspects of the *Aeneid* and a touchstone for both its affinities with and its departures from Christianity. The literal and the figurative aspects of sacrifice are of crucial importance to the poem, and their interaction – in ways that, for the modern reader, may be counterintuitive – reveals much about Virgil's conception of the human condition. Literally, "sacrifice" means the ritual slaughter of living creatures, animal or human, an act that for the Romans was the means of securing the *pax deorum* or "state of peace with the gods." Figuratively, "sacrifice" has come to mean "to forfeit something of value in order to obtain something of higher value." As the Christian must make many (figurative) sacrifices in order to participate internally and externally in the Kingdom of God, so Aeneas has to make many (figurative) sacrifices in order to found proto-Rome – in Virgil's inimitable summary, *tantae molis erat Romanam condere gentem*, "Of such tremendous weight it was to found the Roman nation" (1.33). But Christianity is also founded on a literal sacrifice, the slaughter of a perfect victim as the only means (for reasons that exceed human understanding) of reconciling us to God. It is here, I suggest, that Virgil parts company with Christianity. For in the *Aeneid*'s universe the gods' unassuageable thirst for the power and honor represented by blood sacrifices means that human efforts can never satisfy them, and indeed, Virgil implies that the effect of the slaughter will always be to engender more.

In his essay contrasting the community-minded "secondary epic" of Virgil with the self-centered "primary epic" of Homer, C. S. Lewis writes, "It is not thanks to the Fourth Eclogue alone that [Virgil] has become almost a great Christian poet."[7] The *Aeneid*'s unique role in the western canon derives from this "almost," from its being so nearly Christian and yet, ultimately, so antithetical to the divine love and joy at the heart of the Christian message. After sketching some of the historical, literary, and religious background that would have informed Virgil's ancient audience, I shall briefly discuss three fictional responses to the poem: one from the generation after Virgil (Ovid's *Metamorphoses*) that amplifies the *Aeneid*'s darkness, one from 2008 (Ursula Le Guin's *Lavinia*) that "corrects" it, and one from seven hundred years ago (Dante's *Divine Comedy*) that transfigures it.

Historical Background

Unlike the Homeric epics, which were composed before written history and have the timeless quality of myth, the *Aeneid* is permeated by the historical consciousness that distinguishes Rome from Greece. And Roman history is primarily a history of war. In addition to the foreign conquests that turned a tiny asylum for fugitives into the world's greatest empire, civil war was woven into the very fabric of Rome. The foundational act was one of fratricide, Romulus killing his brother Remus in a quarrel over who would found the new city; Virgil's formative years had been dominated by a series of civil wars (49–31 BC), those between Julius Caesar and Pompey, Augustus and Pompey's sons, and most recently Augustus and Mark Antony. Despite the attempts of Augustan propaganda to emasculate Antony and demonize his lover Cleopatra, Antony was a Roman with a substantial following of Romans. Many readers locate the *Aeneid*'s darkness in Virgil's ambivalence about Augustus's acquisition of power – which in his early years included such atrocities as the sacrifice of 300 Roman aristocrats at the altar of Julius Caesar – and about the possibility of a just and lasting peace.[8]

This historical consciousness appears most prominently in the *Aeneid* in the three great set-pieces of Roman history (Jupiter's prophecy, 1.254–96; the parade of Roman statesmen in the Underworld, 6.756–886; and the shield of Aeneas, 8.626–731), but it is also important to an understanding of the poem's narrative trajectory as a whole. The Battle of Actium on Aeneas's shield is a paradigmatic representation of the official view, the gorgeous East with its dog-headed gods warring against Augustus and the traditional Roman pantheon; yet the many allusive connections between Cleopatra and Dido belie this facile caricature. If Aeneas is most prominently an Augustus figure, in his tragic affair with a powerful, passionate, and suicidal African queen he also has much in common with Antony. In the Italian war that dominates the poem's second half, Virgil stresses the essential equality of the "two peoples" with an anguished question near the end of the poem:

> Did it please you, Jupiter, for peoples
> destined for eternal peace to clash with such strife?
> (12.503–504)

Jupiter's ultimate promise to Juno has the Italians keep their *mores*, their language, their religious rites, and their name, with the Trojans contributing only to the gene pool (12.834–37) – hardly a triumphant conquest by a superior culture.

Literary Background

Roman literature is uncompromisingly "intertextual," with much of its richness and meaning deriving from allusions to other texts. Many of these authors (such as Apollonius, Lucretius, Callimachus, and Propertius) normally fall outside the Great Texts curriculum; fortunately, however, the Homeric epics and at least some Greek tragedies are likely to be included. It is well known that the two halves of the *Aeneid* (1–6 = wandering, 7–12 = war) largely recapitulate the *Odyssey* and *Iliad*, respectively, and that the story of Pallas-Turnus-Aeneas echoes that of Patroclus-Hector-Achilles; the Trojans in the *Aeneid* come to play the role of the Greeks in the *Iliad*. The story of Dido and the war in Italy show both formal and thematic affinities with Greek tragedy.[9]

One specific example of "comparing and contrasting" may illustrate the rewards to be gleaned from reading texts in community rather than in isolation. In *Iliad* 16, Zeus famously grieves for his son Sarpedon, wishing he could rescue him from death:

> Seeing them, the son of crooked-scheming Kronos pitied them,
> and addressed Hera, his wife and sister: "O woe is me,
> that in my eyes Sarpedon, dearest of men, is fated
> to be vanquished at the hand of Patroclus son of Menoitios.
> The heart in me strains two ways in my breast as I ponder it,
> whether to snatch him up while he's alive from the tearful
> battle and place him in the fertile land of Lycia,
> or to vanquish him now at the hands of the son of Menoitios."
> (*Il.* 16.431–38)

Hera convinces him that to go against Fate (*Moira*) would result in cosmic chaos, and Zeus reluctantly concedes, sending down "bloody drops" generally interpreted as tears of blood (*Il.* 16.459). In the corresponding scene in the *Aeneid*, the neophyte god Hercules weeps over the impending death of young Pallas, and Jupiter responds with a speech about the inevitability of Fate:

> Hercules heard the youth and suppressed a mighty groan
> within the depth of his heart and poured forth empty tears.
> Then the father addressed his son with friendly words:

"The day for each man is fixed, short and irrecoverable
is everyone's time for life; but to stretch out fame through deeds,
this is the task of virtue. Beneath the high walls of Troy
so many sons of gods have fallen – nay, along with them
fell Sarpedon, my progeny; for Turnus, too,
his Fate is calling and he's come to the limit of his given time."
So he speaks, and turns his eyes away from the Rutulian fields.
(10.464–73)

The mention of Sarpedon in Jupiter's speech alerts the reader (if it were not obvious already) to compare the scene with that of Sarpedon's death in *Iliad* 16. But notice the stark contrast: not a word from Jupiter indicates pity for mortals; he shows no sorrow over or desire to alter the dictates of Fate; and instead of weeping tears of blood, he "turns his eyes away," a gesture that elsewhere in literature indicates either indifference or contempt. Though some readers may feel that the "awkwardness" and "inferiority" of Virgil's scene compared to Homer's "cannot have been Virgil's intention,"[10] another interpretation is that the deliberate contrast indicates Jupiter's obsession with power and fame at the expense of all else.

Religious Background

While the broad differences between Virgilian and Homeric gods are largely accessible to readers of the texts in translation, some less familiar aspects of Roman religion are also important to understanding the poem.[11] I give here just the briefest outline of three cultic "texts" that would have belonged to the ancient reader's competence: the nature of Roman sacrifice, legends surrounding the death of Aeneas, and the cult of the Rex Nemorensis.

In Roman sacrifice, the figurative and literal aspects overlapped only partially. The Romans did not win over the gods with good intentions: what mattered was sacrificing the right animal, in the right way, with the right words. To trip up in any of these areas constituted a *piaculum*, a ritual error that needed to be atoned for by a further sacrifice (also called a *piaculum*). Aeneas, despite his trademark *pietas*, frequently performs sacrifices that do not conform to the standard.[12] For instance, Helenus exhorts Aeneas in the strongest possible terms to worship Juno *first* upon reaching Italy (3.435–40); when Aeneas arrives, he prays *first*, not to Juno, but to Minerva – though he says that he has followed Helenus' instructions (3.543–47). Similarly, in a dream vision, the god of the Tiber orders him to get up and perform a sacrifice to Juno at first dawn, then offer a sacrifice to himself (8.59–62); when Aeneas awakens at sunrise, he offers a prayer *to the river nymphs and Tiber*, equips his fleet, and *then* offers the sacrifice of the white sow to Juno (8.68–85). In both of these episodes Aeneas believes that he has followed instructions correctly, and yet in both of them it is made clear that he has not. Juno has shown herself obsessed with sacrifices to herself: her opening speech concludes, "Does anyone adore the divinity of Juno hereafter, or will they as suppliant place an offering (*honor*) upon her altars?" (1.43–44). The final word of Jupiter in the poem responds to this question, for he assures his wife that "no race will be equal [to the Romans] in giving you sacrifices (*honores*)" (12.840). Yet in the very act of attempting to please the goddess, Aeneas twice commits ritual errors that make his offerings worse than useless, for a botched sacrifice requires another in expiation.

Another feature that would have been familiar to Virgil's audience is the legend of Aeneas's own death and apotheosis. Though the accounts vary, most agree on certain fundamental points: Aeneas disappeared into or near the Numicus river, his body was never found, and he was consequently worshiped as a god. The ambiguity many have seen in the *Aeneid* as a whole is nicely encapsulated in the mystery surrounding Aeneas's death: the disappearance of his body could be explained by either the best possible fate, apotheosis, or the worst possible fate, drowning and being washed out to sea without burial.[13] Jupiter tells both Venus and Juno that Aeneas is destined for divinity. Yet the *Aeneid* also shows an almost obsessive repetition of deaths by drowning and men being lost at sea: Orontes the helmsman thrown overboard during the first storm (1.113–17), Misenus losing a conch-blowing contest with the sea-god and lying unburied on the shore of Italy (6.162–74), and most prominently Palinurus, the helmsman whom Neptune claims for himself in order to grant Aeneas safe passage to Italy (5.835–71, 6.337–83). Palinurus is often seen as the paradigmatic sacrificial victim, the "one head given for many"; yet ancient readers were rightly puzzled that, apparently, *two* of Aeneas's comrades died by drowning and lay unburied on the shore. Moreover, what is most prominent in Palinurus' death is his unwillingness, which is so extreme that he tears the rudder off in his fall. Of all ritual errors requiring expiation by another sacrifice, the manifest unwillingness of the victim was the worst.

The final feature that may surprise the modern reader is the cult of the Rex Nemorensis, or "King of the Wood," which the fourth-century commentator Servius tells us about in his comment on the Golden Bough (and which is the starting point for Frazer's monumental socio-anthropological work of that name).[14] I have argued at length that a sustained allusion to this cult is a crucial aspect of the *Aeneid*, so I shall simply summarize a few features here. In the grove of Diana at Nemi lived a priest-"king," always a fugitive slave, who guarded her sacred tree. A Challenger was required to break off a bough from the tree, beat the reigning Rex in a swordfight preceded by a ritual chase, and sacrifice him at Diana's altar to become the new King of the Wood. The breaking off of the bough as a prelude to the combat suggests a symbolic equation between human and tree that finds many resonances in the *Aeneid*.[15] The cult, moreover, had a dual affinity with Greek tragedy, for Orestes and Hippolytus were both associated with its founding.

Even a casual reading should reveal the importance of these themes. "Tree violation" brings to mind Polydorus, whose voice finally emanates from the tree Aeneas assaults three times, even after it bleeds human blood (3.22–68); the Golden Bough, which the Sibyl said would be either easy or impossible to break off (6.146–48), but which famously "hesitates" (6.210–11); and the sacred tree of Faunus, which the Trojans had cut down to level the battlefield, but whose stump holds fast Aeneas's spear (12.766–87). Equally important is the equation of human and tree represented by the "trophy" (*tropaeum*), a tree-trunk monument commemorating victory over a fallen warrior:[16] Aeneas hanging the armor of Mezentius piece by piece upon an oak tree, turning it into an effigy of the dead king (11.5–16), is a perverse Homeric "arming scene" mirrored in the arming of Turnus (12.87–95). When Aeneas in his final words declares that Turnus is "clothed in the spoils of my own people" (12.947), he echoes the words of Mezentius, who had vowed to make his son Lausus into a *tropaeum* "clothed in the spoils of Aeneas" (10.775–76). Aeneas's chasing of Turnus (12.733–90), the simile comparing their swordfight to bulls fighting to decide "who will rule the grove" (12.719), the assimilation of Turnus to a *tropaeum*, Aeneas's "sacrifice" of his enemy at the poem's shocking close (*immolat*, 12.949) – all of these recall the cult of the Rex Nemorensis, with its unending cycle of human sacrifice.[17] And the implications of that cult are that the victor, ultimately, will become a sacrificial victim himself.

An Ancient Response: Ovid's Metamorphoses

The role of Virgil in western literature is rather like that of Plato in western philosophy: you can agree or disagree, but you cannot escape it.[18] Ovid's *Metamorphoses*, a sprawling epic (not to mention comedy, tragedy, didactic, elegy, and every other genre imaginable) from the origin of time to the Roman present, is so saturated with Virgilian echoes that an attempt even to characterize the relationship between the two authors is daunting. One example of Ovidian "amplification," again centering on the figure of Jupiter, will have to suffice. For Virgil, the association between Augustus (ruler of the Roman empire) and Jupiter (ruler of the universe) is merely implicit and incomplete. After the gods' assembly in *Aeneid* 10, for instance, he shakes all Olympus with his nod, rises from his golden throne, and is accompanied to the threshold by the inhabitants of heaven (10.115–17) – a fairly subtle reference to the gestures of the leader of the Roman senate. Ovid, on the other hand, leaves no room for doubt in his description of the divine assembly hall:

> This is the place that, if my words should be given audacity,

> I wouldn't fear to call the Palatine of the great sky.
> (*Met.* 1.175–76)

Where Virgil's Jupiter shakes Olympus with his nod, Ovid's tosses his mane about "three and four times" (*Met.* 1.179–80) – and the word he uses for hair happens to be *caesaries*, with "Caesar" right inside.[19] For Virgil, Juno is the primary exponent of wrath (*ira*), with Jupiter's ire evinced more by his actions (such as punishment by thunderbolt) and his statement at the end that the two are alike in their "floods of wrath" (12.831); Ovid's Jupiter, on the other hand, conceives "wrath huge and worthy of Jupiter" (*Met.* 1.166) and stirs up the passions of the sycophantic assembly.[20] In the *Aeneid*, Jupiter's rapes are felt only in their consequences, most prominently in the lament of Juturna near the poem's end;[21] Ovid displays them repeatedly and graphically. Such comparisons could go on indefinitely, and students reading both the *Aeneid* and the *Metamorphoses* will find much to discuss in the two poets' reflections on the nature of power, divinity, and love.

A Modern Response: Ursula Le Guin's Lavinia

Ursula Le Guin, one of the foremost fantasy writers of our era,[22] has recently produced a fascinating fictional interpretation of Virgil's epic. The shadowy figure of Aeneas's eventual bride becomes a fully realized character, delivering in a first-person narrative her version of the events told by "her" poet Virgil, whose specter summarizes for her early in the novel the story of the *Aeneid*. This gives both Virgil and Lavinia the opportunity to "correct" his version. For instance, when Lavinia queries, "You know everything, don't you?", the poet's ghost responds, "No, I know very little. And what I thought I knew of you – what little I thought of at all – was stupid, conventional, unimagined. I thought you were a blonde!" (Le Guin 2008, 58). The most glaring error of which Lavinia later accuses the poet has to do with Aeneas's actions following the deaths of Pallas and Mezentius:

> The fury went out of Aeneas then. He went back to where Pallas lay and gave orders, in tears, that the boy's body be wrapped to carry back to his father, Evander, with a guard of honor, though not with slaves to be sacrificed, as the poet said; I do not know how my poet could think his own Italian people would commit such barbarity. Perhaps the Greeks might. Though all my poet sang was true and is true, yet there are small mistakes in the truth of it, and I have tried to mend those tiny rents in the great fabric as I tell my part in it. (Le Guin 2008, 143–44)

I have suggested that this "small mistake in the truth," the performance of a human sacrifice, is in fact an interpretive key to the poem. Lavinia herself makes a "small mistake" in saying that Virgil described the sacrificial victims as "slaves": they were aristocratic young warriors, four sons of Ufens (also the name of a river) and four sons of Sulmo (also the name of Ovid's birthplace). Virgil is here assimilating Aeneas to Homer's Achilles, who sacrifices twelve youths to the shade of Patroclus; Aeneas sacrifices only eight, but unlike Homer's, Virgil's youths are given an identity that associates them with the Italian countryside. More importantly, as I have argued at length, what the *Aeneid* both depicts and prophesies is an endless cycle of human sacrifice. Unlike the final sacrifice of Turnus, which occurs in a moment of fury and wrath (and for which Le Guin's Lavinia tells us Aeneas felt obsessive remorse), that of the eight youths occurs in cold blood amid pomp and ceremony (11.81–84), and it is no coincidence that the youths march in parade with captive leaders bearing tree trunks "clothed in the enemy's arms" (11.83). Both groups foreshadow the sacrifice of Turnus, "clothed in the spoils of my people" (12.947), simultaneously the tree and the priest-king in the cult of the Rex Nemorensis.

Though Le Guin's Italians and Trojans are both religious peoples, she has understandably edited out the Olympian gods entirely: "The Homeric use of quarrelsome deities to motivate, illuminate, and interfere with human choices and emotions doesn't work well in a novel, so the Greco-Roman gods, an intrinsic element of the poem, are no part of my story" (Le Guin 2008, 275). This is a common and perhaps necessary feature in post-modern adaptations of Greco-Roman myths; and yet ancient texts are not comprehensible in themselves without this "intrinsic element." Attempts to reduce the gods to abstractions are unsatisfying, for Virgil's gods can exhibit the same sort of complexity as his humans: for instance, if Juno merely represents the forces of disorder or chaos or irrationality, why is it that she shows "pity for [Dido's] long suffering" (4.693)? The role of the gods in the *Aeneid* is central. Virgil formulates the problem of evil at the beginning of the poem:

> Muse, relate the causes to me, by what wounded divinity,
> or through what grief the queen of the gods impelled a man
> marked by righteousness (*pietas*) to unroll so many misfortunes, undergo
> so many labors. Is such wrath in the hearts of the gods above?
> (1.8–11)

Virgil's answer is an unequivocal "Yes," as is made evident by the trajectory of the narrative and by the statement of Jupiter, in his final speech, that he and Juno are alike in the "floods of wrath beneath [their] hearts" (12.831).

Another "mistake" Le Guin's Lavinia implicitly corrects throughout concerns the nature of erotic love and the possibility of its resulting in human happiness. Le Guin follows Virgil's cue in depicting Lavinia's mother Amata (whose name means "beloved") as emotionally unbalanced and in love with Turnus. (In Roman society, where girls in their teens routinely married men in their thirties or older, such attractions between mothers- and sons-in-law would not have been uncommon.) But where Le Guin departs from most modern interpretations is in her insistence that Lavinia despises the arrogant Turnus and loves the virtuous Aeneas, with whom she has a blissfully happy marriage until the latter's death in battle; the mysterious disappearance of Aeneas's body into a river is yet another important Virgilian theme Le Guin "corrects." For Virgil, Lavinia is a pale character who bursts into violent color, literally, only with her spectacular blush at her mother's last speech to Turnus:

> Lavinia received her mother's speech with tears,
> bathing her burning cheeks, on which a very great blush
> suffused its fire and spread throughout her heated face.
> As when someone violates Indian ivory with bloody
> purple, or when lilies mingled with many roses
> grow red, such colors did the virgin give on her face.
> (12.64–69)

It is essential to Le Guin's story that Lavinia love Aeneas and Aeneas only; her blush under Turnus' gaze in an early scene is merely from embarrassment at the brute's presumptuous stare (Le Guin 2008, 19). But a more likely interpretation of Virgil's text is that the imagery of flame, blood, violation, and erotic flowers signals Lavinia's amorous attachment to Turnus,[23] thus further problematizing the morality and consequences of the Trojans' conquest of Italy.

A Christian Response: Dante's Divine Comedy

Near the end of *Middlemarch*, George Eliot describes the epic journey that is marriage as "the conquest or irremediable loss of that complete union which makes the advancing years a climax, and age the harvest of sweet memories in common." Much the same could be said of the progress of the soul in the *Divine Comedy*, where the "partners" are duty and desire: if the Fall represents the divorce of these two, the Atonement represents their remarriage, and the pilgrim's journey culminates in the "complete union" that sanctifies all memories. Perfect freedom is the inability to will anything but the Good. In the world of the *Aeneid*, by contrast, desire and duty align only when Aeneas surrenders to his lust for vengeance.

Though Dante does not express disapproval of Aeneas himself, he recognizes that erotic love in Virgil's unredeemed world brings only destruction of both the individual and the community. Virgil describes love the same way as the plague.[24] Dido's burning passion for Aeneas turns into the flames that engulf both her and the civilization she has so competently built – happy, confident, fulfilled, until Aeneas came and her love for him destroyed everything. Dante's last words to Virgil in the *Comedy*, after he has finally laid eyes on Beatrice and wants to share the thrilling news with his master, are a translation of Dido's words to her sister, "I recognize the signs of the ancient flame" (*Purg.* 30.48; *Aen.* 4.23). As the pilgrim completes his journey of purification, he is about to experience the transfiguration of earthly sexual desire into that perfect Love which is God Himself, the bliss and the *telos* of all His creatures.[25] And when Dante turns around, he finds, like Orpheus with Eurydice, that Virgil has disappeared forever. The difference between the two poets, between paganism and Christianity, is summarized in this moment: Virgil can never know the love that brings redemption.

What Virgil does know is the "harsh pain of a great love polluted" (*Aen.* 5.5–6). In the terrible parting of Aeneas from Dido appears starkly the conflict of *pietas* that is one of the *Aeneid*'s central themes. Dido has fainted, in a foreshadowing of her death; her limbs collapse and her attendants carry her into her *thalamos*, a Greek word meaning both "bridal chamber" and "tomb" (4.391–92). Aeneas longs to comfort her, but instead he knows he must follow the commands of the gods:

> But righteous (*pius*) Aeneas, although he longs to soothe her grief
> with consolation and to avert cares with his words,
> groaning greatly, his heart staggered with great love,
> nevertheless obeys the gods' orders and returns to his fleet.
> (4.393–96)

The word *pius* here, representing Aeneas's outstanding quality, is both ironically inappropriate and ironically appropriate: the problem is that his *pietas* pulls him apart, with loyalty to the woman he loves striving impossibly against loyalty to a Fate he does not want and a land he has never seen. He is *pius* both because of and in spite of his desire to stay and comfort her. The English offspring of Latin *pietas*, "pity" and "piety," could be said to summarize Aeneas's dilemma:[26] his pity for Dido urges him to stay, while his piety toward the gods urges him to leave.

Dante exhibits a similar emotional turmoil in his own response to Paulo and Francesca, whose disordered love places them in the "crowd where Dido is" (*Inf.* 5.85). The pilgrim's response to their grief is a brilliant conflation of both of Virgil's lovers:

> While the one spirit was speaking this,
>   the other was weeping; so that from pity (*pietà*)
>   I fainted, just as if I were dying,
> and fell the way a dead body falls.
> (*Inf.* 5.139–42)

Dante collapses like Dido, and it is *pietà* that causes him to do so. Aeneas in his chilling parting speech to Dido tells her that if Fate were allowing him to arrange his life as he wanted, he would be...*back in Troy* (4.340–44), a slap in the face for which generations of readers have not forgiven him. Yet the omniscient narrator, a more reliable source than Aeneas's words, tells us that his heart is staggered by great love. He obeys out of stern necessity the commands of gods who are indifferent to his happiness or that of any other mortal. The pilgrim Dante, by contrast, must leave behind disordered erotic love for the creature in order to enter fully into the real and lasting Love of the creator.

In addition to his profound sympathy for the tragic love of Dido and Aeneas, Dante also shows his awareness of Virgil's sorrow for the carnage entailed by the Trojans' conquest of Italy. His one-tercet summary of the *Aeneid*'s second half is astonishingly "modern" in its depiction of the parity of the two sides:

> He will be the salvation of that humble Italy
> for which died the virgin Camilla,
> and Euryalus and Turnus and Nisus, of wounds.
> (*Inf.* 1.106–108)

Far from demonizing Camilla as a bloodthirsty Amazon, Dante practically canonizes her: she died for her country, and "the virgin" (*la vergine*) connotes innocence, youthfulness, and femininity, with perhaps even a hint of the Christian resonances of holy virginity. The intertwining of Italian with Trojan names (Italian-Trojan-Italian-Trojan) suggests the equality of the peoples; all are represented as dying for their country, with the compact phrase "of wounds" underscoring their suffering. Here we hear clearly that voice of regret which has assumed such prominence in recent interpretations of the *Aeneid*.[27]

For Dante, the darkness of the *Aeneid* does not lie in flawed political structures, past or present, or in human passions or the human will to power. Augustus is simply "the good Augustus" (*Inf.* 1.71); Aeneas is the "just son of Anchises" (*Inf.* 1.73–74). Virgil the character is denied happiness for one reason only: he lived "in the time of the false and lying gods" (*Inf.* 1.72), and consequently he "did not worship God rightly" (*Inf.* 4.38). Here Dante is in complete agreement with Augustine, who quite frankly calls the pagan gods demons whose primary desire is to thwart human happiness:

> Do not seek out the false and lying gods; rather, cast them away and scorn them, blazing forth into true freedom. They are not gods, they are evil spirits, for whom your eternal happiness is a punishment. It seems that Juno does not begrudge the Trojans (from whom you derive your origin in the flesh) the Roman citadel so much as those demons, whom you still consider gods, begrudge the entire human race its eternal home. (*City of God* 2.29)

My one modification to this verdict would be to implicate Jupiter as well as Juno in the disregard for human happiness.[28]

And yet, despite the absence of divine and the destructiveness of human love, Virgil remains for Dante the "almost" Christian poet. Nowhere is this more explicit than in the encomium of Virgil by Statius, who bestows on him the highest praise a Christian poet can give:

> "You acted like a man who goes by night,
> who carries the lamp behind and doesn't help himself,
> but makes the people in back of him learned,
> when you said, 'The age is being renewed;
> justice returns, and the first human time,
> and a new offspring descends from the sky.'
> Through you I became a poet, through you, a Christian."
> (*Purg*. 22.67–73)

Statius explains that the extraordinary phenomenon of his conversion to Christianity came about through Virgil's prophetic words in the Fourth Eclogue. However we may feel about this Christian "reader response," a crucial point for Dante's Statius is that Virgil did not understand the purport of his own words or derive any happiness from them. *Il lume dietro*, "the lamp behind": this poignant image encapsulates the sacrificial paradigm that pulses through the Aeneid, a pre-Christian paradigm in which the one sacrificed receives no reward. Like the Jews, whom Augustine describes as those who "carried in your hands the lamp of the law in order to show the way to others while you remained in darkness,"[29] Virgil was, for Dante, incapable of knowing himself the joy that his light would bring to others.

That Virgil should be forever denied the vision of God toward which he has been leading his pupil is a source of enduring pain and bewilderment to readers of the *Comedy*.[30] How is it that the teacher who repeatedly brings hope to the despairing pilgrim could be without hope himself? Could Virgil not have turned around, just once, to see the vision illuminated by the lamp he himself was carrying behind him? As Virgil's best Christian reader, Dante knew that Virgil could know happiness only in losing it, could experience the supreme consummation only as a moment of supreme loss. In the "almost" Christian *Aeneid*, sacrifice means suffering without compensation for the victim, death without resurrection. Dante's Virgil may play the role of a Sibyl or an Anchises in guiding his pupil through the afterlife, but Virgil also, at the pivotal moment, plays the role of Aeneas himself. His loss of the beatific vision is not a judgment on Virgil's soul; it is a comment on Virgil's poem.

References

Allan, Mowbray 1989. "Does Dante Hope for Virgil's Salvation?" *Modern Language Notes* 104: 193–205.

Ball, Robert 1991. "Theological Semantics: Virgil's *Pietas* and Dante's *Pietà*," in Jacoff and Schnapp (1991), 19–36.

Benko, Stephen 1980. "Virgil's Fourth Eclogue in Christian Interpretation," *Aufstieg und Niedergang der Römischen Welt* 2.31.1: 646–705.

Comparetti, Domenico 1997. *Vergil in the Middle Ages*. Orig. pub. 1885. Princeton: Princeton Univ. Press.

Dyson, Julia T. 1996. "Dido the Epicurean," *Classical Antiquity* 15: 203–21.

——— 1999. "Lilies and Violence: Lavinia's Blush in the Song of Orpheus," *Classical Philology* 94: 281–88.

——— 2001. *King of the Wood: The Sacrificial Victor in Virgil's* Aeneid. Norman, OK: Univ. of Oklahoma Press.

Fagles, Robert, trans. 2006. *Virgil: The Aeneid*. New York: Viking Penguin.

Fitzgerald, Robert, trans. 1990. *Virgil: The Aeneid*. New York: Viking Classics.

Galinsky, G. Karl, ed. 1974. *Perspectives of Roman Poetry: A Classics Symposium*. Austin, TX: Univ. of Texas Press.

Goold, G. P. 1970. "Servius and the Helen Episode," in Harrison (1990), 60–126.

Hardie, Philip R. 1993. *The Epic Successors of Virgil: A Study in the Dynamics of a Tradition*. Cambridge: Cambridge Univ. Press.

Harrison, Edward L. 1989. "The Tragedy of Dido," *Échos du Monde Classique* 33: 1–21.

Harrison, S. J., ed. 1990. *Oxford Readings in Vergil's "Aeneid."* Oxford: Oxford Univ. Press.

Hawkins, Peter S. 1991. "Dido, Beatrice, and the Signs of Ancient Love," in Jacoff and Schnapp (1991), 113–30.

Hejduk, Julia D. 2009a. "Ovid and Religion," in Knox (2009), 45–58.

——— 2009b. "Jupiter's *Aeneid*: *Fama* and *Imperium*," *Classical Antiquity* 28: 279–327.

Jacoff, Rachel, and Jeffrey T. Schnapp 1991. *The Poetry of Allusion: Virgil and Ovid in Dante's Commedia*. Stanford: Stanford Univ. Press.

Jenkyns, Richard 1985. "Pathos, Tragedy and Hope in the *Aeneid*," *Journal of Roman Studies* 75: 60–77.

Kallendorf, Craig 2007. *The Other Virgil: 'Pessimistic' Readings of the* Aeneid *in Early Modern Culture*. Oxford: Oxford Univ. Press.

Knox, Peter E., ed. 2009. *A Companion to Ovid*. Malden, MA and Oxford: Oxford Univ. Press.

Le Guin, Ursula K. 2008. *Lavinia*. Boston and New York: Mariner Books.

Lewis, C. S. 1942. *A Preface to Paradise Lost*. Oxford: Oxford Univ. Press.

Lyne, R. O. A. M. 1987. *Further Voices in Vergil's Aeneid*. Oxford: Oxford Univ. Press.

MacCormack, Sabine 1998. *The Shadows of Poetry: Vergil in the Mind of Augustus*. Berkeley, Los Angeles, and London: Univ. of California Press.

Mackie, C. J. 1990. "*Quisquis in arma vocas*: Turnus and Jupiter in the *Aeneid*," *Antichthon* 24: 79–85.

Mazzotta, Giuseppe 1979. *Dante, Poet of the Desert: History and Allegory in the Divine Comedy*. Princeton: Princeton Univ. Press.

Panoussi, Vassiliki 2009. *Greek Tragedy in Vergil's Aeneid: Ritual, Empire, and Intertext*. Cambridge: Cambridge Univ. Press.

Parry, Adam 1963. "The Two Voices of Virgil's *Aeneid*," *Arion* 2: 66–80.

Perkell, Christine G. 1997. "The Lament of Juturna: Pathos and Interpretation in the *Aeneid*," *Transactions of the American Philological Association* 127: 257–86.

———, ed. 1999. *Reading Vergil's Aeneid: An Interpretive Guide*. Norman, OK: Univ. of Oklahoma Press.

Putnam, Michael C. J., and Jan M. Ziolkowski, eds. 2008. *The Virgilian Tradition: The First Fifteen Hundred Years*. New Haven and London: Yale Univ. Press.

Reckford, Kenneth J. 1961. "Latent Tragedy in *Aeneid* VII, 1–285," *American Journal of Philology* 82: 252–69.

——— 1974. "Some Trees in Virgil and Tolkien," in Galinsky (1974), 57–91.

Schmidt, Ernst A. 2001. "The Meaning of Vergil's *Aeneid*: American and German Approaches," *Classical World* 94: 145–71.

Segal, Charles P. 2001. "Jupiter in Ovid's *Metamorphoses*," *Arion* 9: 78–99.

Shippey, Tom 2000. *J. R. R. Tolkien: Author of the Century*. Boston and New York: Houghton Mifflin Harcourt.

Thomas, Richard F. 1988. *Virgil. Georgics. Volume 2: Books III–IV*. Cambridge: Cambridge Univ. Press.

——— 2001. *Virgil and the Augustan Reception*. Cambridge: Cambridge Univ. Press.

Watkins, John 1995. *The Specter of Dido: Spenser and Virgilian Epic*. New Haven and London: Yale Univ. Press.

Ziolkowski, Jan M. 1997. Introduction to Comparetti (1997), vii–xxxvii.

St. Augustine
The Confessions

It is a testimony to St. Augustine's skills as a writer and thinker that, despite the daunting and still-growing mountain of secondary scholarship on the *Confessions* (to which this prosaic pebble is now added), there is still more to say about his extraordinary autobiography. The difference between a good book and a great book, we are told, is that a good book can be enjoyed and profited from in a single reading, but a great book enriches and surprises us with something new no matter how many times we read it. By this criterion, the *Confessions* readily qualifies as a great book.

Part of the *Confessions*' greatness lies in its deceptive simplicity. Despite its fairly straightforward plotline and the fact that Augustine is able to sustain his reader's interest by relying on mankind's unceasing interest in the love lives of others,[1] the *Confessions* has numerous and perplexing depths – it is, as our students often remind us, a "hard book." This, interestingly, appears to have been Augustine's intention all along. As he notes elsewhere, things that are acquired easily and without effort tend to be held cheap and in low regard (*On Christian Doctrine* 2.6.7) while things that "are sought with some difficulty are discovered with much more pleasure" (2.6.8). In the *Confessions* Augustine likens Scripture to a "thick-leaved orchard" in which its more attentive readers find "fruit hidden" behind its opaque foliage and "flutter about with joy" before eating it (12.28.38) – this before saying how he himself would like to imitate biblical poetics (12.31.42).

In keeping with the spirit of a great texts conversation and in an effort to uncover some of the *Confessions*' hidden fruits, I would like to consider the *Confessions*' references to other classical writings. For one thing is certain: the *Confessions* is a book about other books. There is not a single one of the thirteen Books of the *Confessions* in which a literary work is not mentioned, and there is not a single stage in Augustine's literate life that is not profoundly shaped by what he reads: the destructive effect of reading Virgil and Aristotle, the enlightening effect of reading Cicero and the Platonists, the salvific effect of reading St. Paul in the garden, and so on. More than once, Augustine's happiness hinges on his profiting or not profiting from a book; his life is a vivid illustration of Emerson's remark that "books are the best of things if well used; if abused, among the worst."

Puzzling Treatment

But the *Confessions* is a hard book, and while the ubiquity of literary discussions in the *Confessions* is easy to recognize, most readers continue to be puzzled by the oddities of some of Augustine's treatments. His diatribe in Book 1 against the poets (especially Virgil) strikes the classicist as shrill, while his dismissal of Aristotle in Book 4 seems only to confirm a rank Platonic bias. Such stark judgments by Augustine are all the more perplexing given the fact that he draws heavily from the supposedly pernicious sources he is condemning. In Book 1 he castigates himself for taking Dido's plight too seriously, but in Book 5 he adorns the story of his own departure to Rome in imagery strongly reminiscent of the scene in the *Aeneid* where Dido is left weeping on the shores of Carthage (*Conf.* 1.13.20–22, 5.8.15 vs. *Aen.* 4.576ff).[2] In Book 1 he condemns Terence for favorably portraying an *exemplum stupri*, a model of fornication, but in Book 10 he quotes Terence approvingly for his own reflections on why truth begets hatred (1.16.26, 10.23.34). In Book 3 he praises Cicero's *Hortensius* yet makes the unfair criticism (unfair for a work composed in 45 B.C.) that it lacks the name of Christ; he then goes on to use the book as an excuse to join the Manicheans (3.4.7–6.10). In Book 4 he implicates Aristotle in his materialist understanding of God, yet in Book 11 he draws from Aristotle to articulate a notion of time free from materialist misconceptions (4.16.28, 11.26.33–27.35). Is Augustine a hypocrite or perhaps a schizophrenic? The inconsistencies between his pious censures and his allusive dependence have led at least one renowned Augustinian scholar to sniff at the "anachronistic bias" of this "acrimonious account" (Hagendahl 1967, 445).

The Ordo of the Confessions

The key, I contend, to understanding Augustine's use of literary compositions lies in the structure of the narration of his past in Books 1 through 9, a narration that is at first blush equally puzzling. First, Augustine's autobiography does not always proceed in chronological order: Augustine tells us that he was nineteen when he read Aristotle's *Categories*, but he mentions this incident in Book 4, which concerns his life at the age of twenty-six. Second, Augustine names only some of the people in his life. The friend whose death utterly devastated him is not named in Book 4, nor is his mistress, the mother of his son Adeodatus; even his mother Monica is mentioned by name only once: at the very end of Book 9 (9.13.37). On the other hand, relatively casual acquaintances such as Ponticianus are named without hesitation (8.6.14). Adding to this puzzle is the fact that, with only one exception, no proper names of Augustine's friends or family are given in the first half of the narration (1.1.1–5.7.13), while the second half abounds in proper names: Alypius, Nebribius, Simplicianus, Victorinus, etc.

Details such as these tended to confound the specialists, leading them to draw various erroneous conclusions. Silence on the mistress's name, for instance, was construed by some feminists as proof of misogyny, while the ostensibly rambling inclusion of events was evidence enough for one of the mid-twentieth-century's titans of Augustinian studies, H. -I. Marrou, to proclaim, "Augustin compose mal" (Marrou 1938, 61).[3] Twenty years ago, however, two scholars discovered independently of each other that the first nine Books of the *Confessions* are arranged chiastically, with the middle of the middle Book – that is Book 5, in between chapters seven and eight – serving as the pivot of its two wings (Crosson 1990 and Stephany 1989; I will be drawing primarily from the analysis of one of those authors, Frederick Crosson). Significantly, the midpoint occurs at the place where Augustine departs Carthage for Rome. The entire first half of the narration, then, takes place in Africa (Thagaste, Madaura, and Carthage) while the entire second half takes place in Italy (Rome, Milan, Cassiciacum, and Ostia). The "African" half (1.1.1–5.7.13) is saturated with the language of descent, for Augustine is spiraling downward away from God; on the other hand, the "Italian" half (5.8.14–9.13.37) contains numerous images of ascent, for he is gradually returning to God. The narrative midpoint is again significant: it is at 5.7.13 that Augustine describes his encounter with the Manichean bishop Faustus as paradoxically liberating, for it was in meeting Faustus that he finally saw the bankruptcy of Manichaeism, and it was in seeing the bankruptcy of Manichaeism that he began his journey to the Catholic faith. As Augustine puts it, Faustus unwittingly started the unbinding "of the snare that held me" (5.7.13); though he still had a long way to go, Augustine had hit his rock bottom and was now turning a corner.

Finally, faithful to the chiastic structure, the Books in each narrative half bear a relation to each other (see diagram below). Particularly significant is the cluster of Books 2 and 8, 3 and 7, and 4 and 6, which reflect the Platonic tripartite division of the soul into the concupiscible, rational, and irascible, respectively. (see diagram on the next page)

Crosson's theory about the chiastic structure of the first nine Books helps explain the *Confessions*' various anomalies. The dearth of names in the African half, for example, is the result of two principles. The first is that Augustine only names those who have been "instrumental (whether knowingly or not) in the path of ascent towards God" (Crosson 1990, 88). Faustus is named because he unwittingly helps Augustine to reject Manichaeism, while Augustine's friend in Book 4, who was the object of an excessive and unhealthy love, is not (this despite the fact that the friend dies a baptized Christian). The "friends unfriendly" in Book 2 who goad him to steal pears are obviously not instruments of the good and thus go unnamed, but the true friends in Book 8 who tell him pious stories and encourage him to convert are (hence each is mentioned by name).

CHIASTIC STRUCTURE OF BOOKS ONE THROUGH NINE

1-Birth (his) -Born into "living death" (original sin) -Reading "bad" poetry–Terence, Vergil -Hates Greek		9-Deaths (Monica, Adeodatus, etc.) -Reborn to new life (baptism) -Reading good poetry (Psalm 4) -Uses Greek word (only time)
2-Garden & pear tree -Bad friends, "friends unfriendly" -Sexual lust	*[concupiscible part of soul]*	8-Garden & fig tree -Good friends -Sexual continence
3-Intellectual birth: Cicero -Intellectual corruption: Manichees	*[rational part]*	7-Intellectual flowering: Platonists correct Manichean errors
4-Worldly pursuits -Pride, ambition -Loss of friend, mortality	*[trascible]*	6-Rejection of worldly ambition -True friends (Alypius & Nebridius) -Discussion of soul's immortality
5.1–5.7-Uprooting of false *scientia* -(astronomy discredits Manich'n astrology) -False bishop Faustus		5.8–5.14-Planting of true *scientia* (Ambrose explains figurative sense) -True bishop Ambrose

5.7–5.8
Augustine leaves Carthage for Rome
(middle of Book Five)

No Names. Descent Away from God	Many Names. Ascent Back to God
AFRICA	ITALY
(Three parts of the soul as disordered)	(Three parts of the soul as well-ordered)

The second principle concerns the nature of friendship. Augustine's descent into sin is also a move away from community: the more he is estranged from God, the more he becomes alienated from himself and others; and the more he returns to God, the more he participates in true fellowship. As Augustine states in one of his addresses to God, "Blessed is the man who loves you and his friend in you" (4.9.14). Paradoxically, it is when Augustine learns to subordinate the love of his friends to his love of God that he is for the first time capable of loving them for who they truly are; but his friends are in a sense nameless to him when they are the object or catalyst of an inordinate love that skews their proper identity.

The narrative chiasm also explains the story's chronological discrepancies. If, as Crosson argues, Book 4 is about the irascible part of the soul in its disordered state, then we can see why Augustine relates his reading of Aristotle's *Categories* here rather than elsewhere, for the point of the vignette is to illustrate his enormous pride and vainglory prior to conversion.

Misuse and Reuse

Moreover, the chiastic structure reveals a dynamic pattern of godless "misuse" and godly "reuse," where the good use of things is largely contingent on the degree to which Augustine the user has been morally, intellectually, and religiously converted. When Augustine, unconverted and unrepentant, is spiraling away from God in the first half of the narrative, he abuses all of the things around him and concerning him because, with his own desires in a state of turmoil, he is incapable of using anything properly. Conversely, when Augustine begins his ascent back to God in the second half through a multiform and ongoing conversion, the very things that were once "deadly" to him now serve as occasions of grace rather than sin since Augustine's soul has now gained the wherewithal to make good use of them. Augustine's narrative, in other words, is driven at least in part by a poetics of use and abuse that in many cases has more to do with the agent than with the object, with the condition of the user than with the qualities of what is being used.[4]

The pattern of godless misuse and godly reuse extends to persons, exemplified, as we have just seen, by Augustine's selective naming. And it is also true for different kinds of goods, for things that are dismissed in the earlier part of the *Confessions* as occasions or instruments of sin have a strange tendency to reemerge later in the work but in a more positive light. The things in question can be places, such as bathhouses (in Book 2 they are the scene of Patricius's vulgar boasts about his son's pubescence, but in Book 9 they enable a bereaved Augustine to weep for his deceased mother [2.3.6, 9.12.32]). The things can be objects, such as a fig tree (Augustine foolishly believes that Manichean elders have power over theophorous weeping figs in Book 3, while in Book 8 Augustine, before reading the theocentric passages of St. Paul, wisely sheds real tears under a fig tree [3.10.16, 8.12.28.]). They can also be activities: in Book 4 Augustine rejects the bibliomancy of randomly reading a verse for personal guidance, yet this is precisely what he does in response to the voice admonishing him to "take and read" in Book 8 (4.3.5; 8.12.29).[5] And they can even be languages: in Book 1 Augustine says he had little use for Greek as a boy, while in Book 9 is found the only Greek word besides *philosophia* in the *Confessions*.[6] The latter is a delightfully subtle confirmation of the chiastic thesis as well as an answer to Augustine's prayer – made, significantly, when he discusses his boyhood aversion to Greek – that he may one day use well whatever he has learned (1.15.24).

And the things can be books. Just as the very items or activities that led Augustine down a path of misery are the same ones that, when re-ordered, help him in his return to God, so too are the same authors who were initially so harmful to him "redeemed" in Augustine's eyes once his eyes have been healed and strengthened to see things properly. To illustrate this point, I will scrutinize Augustine's use of two classical authors, Aristotle and Cicero (Virgil, alas, would require a much larger treatment[7]).

Aristotle

In 4.16.28, Augustine mentions the *Categories* of Aristotle for the first – and nominally, the only – time:[8]

> And what did it profit me that, when I was just twenty years old and there came into my hands a certain Aristotelian work called the *Ten Categories*, I read it and understood it, alone?[9]

For the young Augustine, comprehending a difficult subject matter without any assistance was a cause of glee, especially since several of his instructors and their learned colleagues were eager but unable to boast of similar mastery. Yet by the time he writes the *Confessions*, Augustine realizes that his easy grasp of the *Categories* was an occasion for downfall, puffing up his pride and serving as a stumbling-block to God.

> What did this profit me, seeing that it harmed me when, imagining that whatever had being was included within these ten categories, I tried in this way to understand even you, my God, wonderfully simple and immutable?[10]

The *Categories*, it appears, led Augustine down the erroneous path of trying to fit God into one of the *praedicamenta* of substance, quality, quantity, etc. There thus seems to be ample reason to concur with James O'Donnell's conclusion that for Augustine, the "theoretical instruments" of Aristotle were "defective" by virtue of Aristotle's "ignorance of the truth about God" (O'Donnell 1992, 2: 266).[11]

Nevertheless, on the basis of the testimony of the *Confessions*, it is perhaps safer to conclude that the defects in question belong more to the young Augustine than to Aristotle. Augustine does not offer a direct critique of the *Categories*, stressing instead his own culpability in whatever errors they may have occasioned. He was the one, not Aristotle, who persisted in imagining that whatever had being was to be placed in one of the categories. And he was the one who did so out of the impression that God was someone "subject to His own greatness or beauty, so that they were in Him as in a subject, like in bodies" (4.16.29). Such a carnal conception of God can hardly be associated with the *Categories*, which does not treat of being *qua* being or intelligible realities *per se*, let alone deity.[12] But it is much associated with the young Augustine, who continually struggled with metaphysical materialism until he read the books of the Platonists later in his life. Augustine's conclusion to Book 4 sums up nicely the thrust of his point here: none of the ostensibly good things to which he had been exposed, be it Aristotle or the liberal arts, could be of any use to him as long as he held that God was a sort of luminous body (4.16.31).

If this is the case, Augustine's discussion of the *Categories* is not a condemnation of Peripatetic thought but an illustration of his own depravity at that time in his life. For though Augustine understood (or should have understood) that the *Categories* was not about God, he nevertheless, out of pride and vanity, used the work to misconceive God. Book 4, which according to the chiastic structure concerns the part of the soul from which springs pride, begins with Augustine's pride in the liberal arts and ends on the same point. And it is in this same Book that Augustine mentions that he was being rebuffed by God because God "resists the proud" (4.16.26). Augustine's treatment of the *Categories* is, in fact, primarily in terms of pride, first as an occasion of pride in others, and then in himself (4.16.28, 29).[13]

The theme of 4.16.28 and 29, then, is not the demerits of Aristotle's *Categories*, but of Augustine's misuse of those *Categories*, a misuse precipitated on the one hand by his lack of intellectual conversion, which would have enabled him to differentiate material and spiritual substances, and on the other by his lack of moral conversion, which would have granted him the humility to approach God in a more fertile manner.

But if the *Categories* was misused by an intellectually and morally callow Augustine, it invites the question whether an older and wiser Augustine ever makes good use of it. I contend that he does in several places, the clearest and most significant of which occurs in *Confessions* 12.29.40, where Augustine lifts Aristotle's discussion of the four kinds of priority from *Categories* 14a25–14b20. In that section of the *Categories*, Aristotle examines what it means to say that one thing is prior to another. Initially, he posits that there are four possibilities: 1) priority of time (*chronos*), where A is said to be prior to B if it is older than or came before B (*Categ.* 14a27); 2) priority of existence or being (*einai*), where A is prior to B if A's existence follows from B's, but B's does not follow from A's (14a30–31); 3) priority of arrangement (*taxis*), where one thing is said to be prior to another according to some order, such as letters being prior to syllables (14b1); and 4) priority of nature (*phusis*), where one thing is said to be prior to another if it is honored more (14b5). Aristotle, however, does not seem entirely happy with the fourth priority, remarking that this is how "the many" (*hoi polloi*) tend to speak. Perhaps this is why he goes on to describe it as the most different from, or "alien to" (*allotri?tatos*), the others (14b7). Aristotle's ambivalence is compounded by his unexpectedly adding a fifth priority, one in which "of two things whose existence follows from each other… one which is in any way the cause of the other is prior by nature to it" (14b10). The example Aristotle gives is the *fact* that a man exists and the *statement*, "A man exists." Each follows from the other but they do not reciprocally cause each other, for the fact causes the statement to be true, not vice versa. Significantly, Aristotle also refers to the fifth kind as a priority by nature (*phusis*).

The odd way in which Aristotle lists the priorities serves two purposes. First, Aristotle's ambivalence about the fourth priority underscores its dubious status as a natural priority. To honor one thing more than another is indeed a kind of priority, but it is a priority of human convention or whim, not nature. By stating that priority of honor is what is *thought* to be prior by nature by ordinary men and women, Aristotle is implicitly drawing our attention to the difficulty that the vast majority of human beings have in properly differentiating personal or conventional opinions about reality from reality itself. What the many consider natural is, upon deeper reflection, revealed to be nothing more than personal or cultural bias. On the other hand, the fifth kind of priority, the kind that is grasped by someone capable of differentiating different modes of being (i.e., a philosopher), is truly "natural" (*physei*). Further, by listing the fifth priority separately as he does, Aristotle underscores its differences from the first four. Unlike the other kinds of priority, which compare simple things to each other, the fifth is a comparison of things from different modes, of a thing existing in reality and a truth existing in the mind.[14]

In Book 12 of the *Confessions* Augustine also lists four kinds of priority: eternity (*aeternitas*), time (*tempus*), choice (*electio*), and origin (*origo*) (12.29.40). Augustine describes them in the following way: Something is said to be prior by "eternity, as God [is prior to] all things; by time, as the flower [is prior to] the fruit; by choice, as the fruit [is prior to] the flower; by origin, as the sound [is prior to] the song."[15]

These priorities are introduced in an attempt to clarify a possible interpretation (not Augustine's own) of the Genesis verse, "In the beginning God made," as meaning, "First God made" (12.28.38). To avoid a possible contradiction with the rest of the Genesis passage, the subscriber to this view would need to understand "first" in a non-temporal sense – hence the need to explore different notions of priority.

Despite differences in nomenclature, a comparison of Aristotle's and Augustine's lists reveals striking similarities. Augustine, for example, keeps Aristotle's initial topography of four priorities[16] but readily accepts Aristotle's unstated demotion of the fourth, the so-called priority by nature, to a priority of human whim. Thus in his own list Augustine will refer to the "priority of choice" (*electio*) and give as its example the fact that most people, hard-nosed utilitarians that they are, will choose the delicious and nutritious fruit over the pretty but useless flower. There is also an affinity, if not identity, between Augustine's "priority of origin" and Aristotle's "priority of order." Not only is Augustine's example of sound and song comparable to Aristotle's example of letter and syllable, but his renaming of it in terms of origin conforms to

Aristotle's treatment of this priority as a logical ordering of first principles and propositions, the former of which constitutes the starting point for the latter.[17] Even the priorities most distinct from each other, Aristotle's "priority of existence" and Augustine's "priority of eternity," betray an intriguing compatibility. For Aristotle, the priority of existence means that A's existence follows from B's, but B's does not follow from A's. Were one to substitute "God" and "all things" (the two referents Augustine uses to exemplify the priority of eternity) for A and B, one would arrive at the following statement: *God is prior to all things as God's existence follows from the existence of all things, but the existence of all things does not follow from God's existence*. Such a compatibility by no means suggests that the two priorities are the same; on the contrary, as A. Solignac notes in his explication of 12.29.40, the priority of eternity is the only one of Augustine's that requires a uniquely Christian view of God "immutably creating mutable beings" (Augustine 1962, 612, fn 26).[18] But if so, then Augustine's priority of eternity would mark a development of Aristotle's priority of existence in light of divine revelation. Thanks to the proficiency wrought by his ongoing conversions, Augustine has indeed learned to make good use of the *Categories*.[19]

Cicero

Cicero is one of Augustine's chief sources of information about classical philosophy as well as one of the most important intellectual influences in his life. It is not surprising, then, to find the noted Roman statesman occupying such a prominent position in the *Confessions*.[20] One of the few writers cited with approval in Book 1 and the author of the work that begins Augustine's profound turn to a life of truth-seeking, Cicero is mentioned by name four times in the *Confessions*.[21] Yet even Augustine's reading of Cicero's *Hortensius* at the age of eighteen and his subsequent transformation by no means guarantees a proper use of the book. Despite its initial impact, which, all told, is enormously beneficial, Augustine's response to the *Hortensius* also perpetuates and even deepens his moral and intellectual decline.

In Book 3, Augustine tells us that he read Cicero's *Hortensius* as a part of his regular course of studies in rhetoric. His teachers had assigned the book, he tells us, merely to "sharpen his tongue" (3.4.7). But by attending to its content rather than its style, Augustine gained from it a much different lesson:

> This book of [Cicero's], called the *Hortensius*, contains an exhortation to philosophy. Truly it changed my affections, it changed my prayers to you yourself, O Lord, and it made me have utterly different purposes and desires. Suddenly all vain hope seemed worthless to me, and with an incredible burning in my heart I longed after the immortality of wisdom and began to rise up, that I might return to you.[22]

Augustine goes on to say that the book inspired him to "fly away from earthly things" and to seek wisdom itself as opposed to this or that philosophical school, and that it so accurately refutes philosophical errors that it can be considered a virtual embodiment of Colossians 2:8: "Beware lest any man cheat you by philosophy and vain deceits." If the book has any flaws, it is the disappointing omission of Christ's name, which Augustine had learned to love from his infancy (3.4.8). Thanks to a sensitive and attentive reading of the *Hortensius*, Augustine's intellectual conversion has begun in earnest.

Nevertheless, the young Augustine seems to have neglected at least three aspects of the *Hortensius*. The first is the dialogue's call for chastity as a precondition for the intellectually erotic life. Augustine himself alludes to this call later on in Book 8. Reminiscing on the dozen or so years that had transpired since his first reading of the *Hortensius*, Augustine reflects: "And I, a miserable young man, miserable especially at the beginning of my manhood, had even then begged for chastity from you, and I had said, 'Give me chastity and continence, but not yet.'"[23] This remark, as well as the broader passage in which it occurs, suggests that Augustine knew about the importance of sexual continence from the beginning of his turn to wisdom, and that his famously impish prayer was not a recent petition on the eve of his moral conversion but one he had been making ever since he read the *Hortensius*.

Second, Augustine does not explicitly acknowledge in Book 3 the *Hortensius*' teaching about a God or *summum bonum* that is intelligible rather than sensible. In 7.1.1, however, Augustine mentions that he knew God was not in the form of a human body ever since he learned about philosophy;[24] and his citation of Col. 2:8 in Book 3 amounts to stating that the *Hortensius* offers a vigorous rejection of philosophical materialism.[25] As we shall see below, Augustine elsewhere maintains that the Platonists' crucial distinction between the sensible and the intelligible, the distinction that Augustine at last comes to understand in Book 7, is present in Cicero as well;[26] indeed, according to Augustine, it is even to be found in the *Hortensius*.[27] Yet despite the value Cicero's writings in general and the *Hortensius* in particular have in leading one to the comprehension of a reality not intrinsically conditioned by space, matter, or time, it appears to have been underutilized or overlooked by the young Augustine. In *On the Happy Life*, Augustine tells Theodorus that while the *Hortensius* inflamed him with the love of philosophy, he still remained in a fog that confused his course (1.4), a fog that was at least partly due to his intellectual materialism.

Third, the young Augustine does not fully appropriate the lesson he learned about preferring substance to style. It was because Augustine, in contradistinction to his obsequious and shallow peers, admired Cicero's heart rather than his tongue, that his life was so profoundly altered. Yet in the very next scene when Augustine turns to the sacred scriptures he is repulsed by their humble "mode" and thus incapable of appreciating their hidden depths (3.5.9). Augustine's inconsistency is all the more ironic given that the eponymous Hortensius, who as a rhetorician was more interested in word-mongering than truth-seeking, receives the butt of the dialogue's criticisms for precisely such superficiality.

All of this negligence on Augustine's part not only leads him away from the wisdom he is now so keen to attain, but each failing conspires in such a way as to bring him into the deadly error of Manichaeism. Immediately following his uplifting reading of the *Hortensius* and his disastrous reading of the Bible, Augustine falls in with the Manichean sect (3.6.10). Augustine is attracted to the Manicheans because they promise the wisdom to which the *Hortensius* points and they nominally overcome the dialogue's only apparent weakness, its failure to mention Christ (in contrast to Cicero, the names of God, Jesus, and the Holy Spirit were forever on the lips of the Manicheans [3.6.10]). Moreover, the Manicheans are able to take advantage of Augustine's selective or defective appropriation of the *Hortensius*. Augustine is able to postpone the demands of continence by becoming a member of the sect (which, despite the claims of its elders, requires no moral transformation), just as he can ignore the need to understand intelligible reality by instead immersing himself in their materialist metaphysics. All of this is possible because Augustine is moved by the Manicheans' grandiloquent bombast, the very kind of bombast he should have learned to see through thanks to Cicero's pointed critique of Hortensius, to say nothing of Augustine's own successful method in reading the dialogue.

Significantly, it is only as Augustine is sequentially delivered from each of these errors that he more or less acknowledges that he knew better all along (he alludes to the *Hortensius'* teaching on immaterial things and on chastity in Books 7 and 8, not in Book 3). This delay in informing the reader about the full contents of the *Hortensius* dramatizes, I would suggest, a culpable "under-use" of the text, viz., a reading that is essentially accurate but, because of the contrary wishes of the reader, conveniently de-emphasizes part of its teaching. While it is true that Augustine never fully forgot the lessons of the *Hortensius* and had been thinking of them all along, his postponed revelation of these things until the ascending chiastic leg of the narrative suggests that despite his ample good use of the book as a young man, he still did not use it as much as he could have, nor did he fully appropriate its wisdom until after his conversion.

This under-use of the *Hortensius* raises two further questions. First, if the young Augustine did not fully plumb the resources of Cicero's dialogue, in what ways does he ever progress in his reading of the *Hortensius* or of Cicero's works as a whole? Augustine gives at least a partial answer to this query by discussing the school to which Cicero belonged: the Academics. In 5.10.19,

Augustine mentions that the Academics, the disciples of the Third or New Academy headed by Carneades in the second century BC who were renowned for their universal skepticism, seemed to him the wisest of philosophers because they doubted everything and taught that no one can affirm anything as true. But Augustine quickly qualifies his characterization: "It *seemed* clear to me that they thought this way, as is commonly held, *for I did not yet understand their meaning*."[28] Augustine's hesitance about Academic doctrine is surpassed only by the surprising content of his explanatory clause. Surely, no historian of philosophy would dispute Augustine's summary in Book 5 of the Academics' teachings, and yet Augustine is essentially stating here that the summary is misleading, that the common perception about Academic doctrine belies its "real meaning."

To learn of Augustine's thoughts about that real meaning, one must look beyond the *Confessions* to three principal sources: Epistles 1 and 118, and *Against the Academics*. In these writings Augustine conjectures that Cicero and the philosophers of the New Academy held "views far different from what is commonly believed about them" (Ep. 1.1).[29] In fact, rather than reject the Platonic quest for wisdom as unattainable, the Academics both subscribed to and maintained all of Plato's philosophy, especially his seminal distinction between the sensible and the intelligible (Ep. 118.3.16). But because the insight into intelligible, non-material reality is one which the vast majority of human beings have enormous difficulty in attaining, the first Platonists were unsuccessful in changing public opinion on the matter. Instead, the materialist philosophies of the Stoics and Epicureans came to dominate popular and intellectual circles during the centuries following Socrates' death (Ep. 118.3.17). Given this situation, the few remaining Platonists were faced with a dilemma: either they publicly uphold the distinction between the sensible and the intelligible and suffer not only persecution and ridicule but the fate of watching carnal-minded men reject and distort Plato's teaching; or, they conceal what they know, contenting themselves instead with attacking and refuting the emaciated philosophies of Zeno and Epicurus (Ep. 118.3.16,17, 20; *Against the Academics* 3.17.37).

According to Augustine, the Academics chose the latter course. Hiding their own opinions, they set out instead to expose the folly of materialist metaphysics;[30] yet they also left clues in their writings about their own convictions for the most careful of readers to find. In so doing they refreshed a tiny elite of men (*paucissimi homines*) with the true "Platonic fountain" (Ep. 1.1)[31] at the same time that they protected this limpid stream from the flesh-enthralled[32] "herd" whose heavy hoofs and clumsy categories would have only muddied the waters in their attempt to drink (Ep. 1.1). (Augustine's unflattering animal moniker is deliberate, "for what," he muses, "is more bovine than thinking that the soul is a body?"[33]) Indeed, true philosophy would have remained in hiding indefinitely were it not for the remarkable rise of Christianity which, by helping a critical mass of believers to move from the visible to the invisible, single-handedly defeated philosophical materialism and thus enabled Platonists to teach in the open again (Ep. 118.3.20; *Against the Academics* 3.19.42). Ironically, a philosopher like Plotinus, living as he did in the wake of the Incarnation, was able to promote an explicit Platonism after centuries of concealment because the very faith he so contemned made a discussion on non-material substances possible again (Ep. 118.3.21, 118.5.33).

What Augustine comes to recognize in the writings of Cicero and the Academics,[34] therefore, is what the political philosopher Leo Strauss referred to as "esotericism," i.e., a method of writing that is capable of conveying difficult and dangerous truths to a very small (and perceptive) group of readers without exposing the greater majority of readers to things they would be incapable of fruitfully appropriating and which would thus only cause them harm.[35] Defined thus, esotericism is not an occultish or pseudo-mystical phenomenon but a pedagogically and politically sensitive mode of writing that enables the philosopher to communicate his teachings to an audience capable of understanding them properly, all without ruining others or endangering his own life in the process.[36] As Augustine puts it, the esoteric writer hides his opinion from the sluggish and reveals it to the alert.[37]

Of course, Augustine knew none of this at the time. When he was twenty-eight years old (the age recounted in Book 5) he still thought that the Academics believed what they wrote and wrote what they believed. This, as it turns out, was a providential mistake, for in inspiring Augustine to imitate their doubts (which he thought they seriously entertained), the Academics led him away from the Manicheans altogether (5.14.24). (This may in fact be the only case of a salubrious misreading in the *Confessions*.) When or how Augustine does come to learn of this esoteric art is never made clear, though one possibility, interestingly enough, is that he learns of it through a right reading of the Bible. When in 6.11.18 Augustine again refers to the Academics and their public teachings, he this time poses a question: "O great men! O Academics! Can nothing be comprehended with certainty for directing one's life?" Now, however, Augustine is able to answer their cognitive doubts with a confidence grounded in something he has recently discovered: "Indeed it can, and so let us seek *more* diligently and let us not despair. For behold, the things which seemed absurd in the Church's books *are not absurd now*, and can be respectably understood in another sense."[38]

That "other sense" is Scripture's hidden allegorical level of meaning, revealed to Augustine by Ambrose and relayed early in Books 5 and 6 (cf.

6.5.8). Could Augustine have learned to look for multiple levels of meaning in a philosophical text from Ambrose's biblical exegesis? Once he had begun to see from a proper understanding of the Old Testament's carnal descriptions of God how the apparent meaning of a passage can be strikingly different from its real meaning, did Augustine then go on to suspect that the Academics' exoteric positions were strikingly different from their esoteric convictions? Possibly, though it is difficult to say either way, since Augustine also recognizes significant differences between Scripture's divine poetics and philosophical esotericism. One thing, however, is certain: by the time he is baptized, Augustine reads the Academics in a fundamentally different manner than when he first picked up a book by their most celebrated author.

The second question raised by Augustine's initial under-use of the *Hortensius* is whether he ever returns later to Cicero and the *Hortensius* and re-uses them. The *Hortensius* is, of course, mentioned again in Book 8, but this occurrence is more of a retrospective evaluation than a post-conversion re-use. The question of a possible re-use is also complicated by the badly mutilated condition of the extant *Hortensius* manuscript, a condition that renders our recognition of any number of subtle allusions to the dialogue difficult.

Happily, however, we are capable of discerning at least one important clue Augustine has left for us in Book 9. It is there that Augustine describes his first four writings as a convert, the so-called Cassiciacum dialogues. Though Augustine now has reservations about their haughty tone, he is quick to mention that they are nevertheless authentically Christian works, "written in the service of the Lord."[39] Curiously, Augustine also relays in the same chapter a disagreement he had with Alypius over their publication. Alypius, Augustine tells us, wanted to omit the name of Christ from the works so that they would be "redolent of the cedars of the gymnasia," while Augustine successfully insisted that the name remain. The account of this incident is significant for two reasons. First, it connects the Cassiciacum dialogues to Cicero's philosophical dialogues, a number of which take place in one of his two gymnasia; second, it recalls the only deficiency that Augustine could find with the *Hortensius*, namely, that it lacked the name of Christ. These details suggest that Augustine is able at last to make good use of the *Hortensius* at Verecundus's villa in Cassiciacum because he now knows not only the name of Christ but the person, and that the fruits of this good use may be found in the writings written during that time (significantly, the only Ciceronian work mentioned by name in the Cassiciacum dialogues is the *Hortensius*[40]). Augustine's successful re-use of Cicero, in other words, is his own Cassiciacum collection, the only works by Augustine that carefully imitate the content and conventions of a Ciceronian dialogue but with one notable exception: they include the saving name of Jesus Christ.[41] Augustine does not simply re-use the *Hortensius*: he perfects it by redressing its one gaping lacuna.

Conclusion

The use and abuse of books in Augustine's life is relevant to a discussion on a Christian university's engagement of secular learning for two reasons. First, the pattern reveals a theology of progress via conversion broadly understood. Contrary to Enlightenment notions of education that focus on the dissemination of information while abstracting from personal formation as a precondition for the proper analysis and reception of data,[42] Augustine emphasizes a moral and intellectual reorientation towards the good. This reorientation, or conversion, enables the mind to "read" things well, while its absence virtually assures the abuse or "misreading" of those same things. This is especially the case with books, which will be well-used or ill-used, not insofar as one possesses a high IQ or the proper set of techniques, but to the degree that one has been morally, intellectually, and religiously converted. The lesson for us as educators is to be as solicitous about our students' general formation as we are about their accumulation of facts or truths.

Second, Augustine's theology of conversion may explain why the librarious pattern of abuse and re-use is for the most part inconspicuous. Virgil, Terence, Aristotle, etc., are first mentioned critically by name, but their positive reuse surfaces in the text silently, without their names. The *Confessions* has an oddly "revisal" quality, wherein the first word on a subject is not the last and the last word on the subject is not pronounced. But why is the last not pronounced, that is, not explicitly articulated? Why is Terence named in Book 1 but not in Book 10? Why is Aristotle openly discussed in Book 4 but not in Book 12? The answer, I think, has to do with a portion of Augustine's audience about which he expresses continual concern: the so-called "little ones" (*parvuli*), those good and decent Christians like his mother Monica who have faith but who lack the benefit of either a liberal arts education or that intellectual conversion which liberates the mind from thinking materialistically. For such folk, a careless exposure to classical pagan texts could be disastrous, as indeed it was for the young Augustine. Better, then, to make the dangers of such works frighteningly clear, and only later on to speak in hushed tones, as it were, to one's more advanced readers about their more constructive potential. Augustine's reserve thus acts as a self-screening process, for the only readers who will recognize the silent re-use of these texts are those who are already familiar with them. Like the Academic art of concealment, which Augustine claims earlier in his life to imitate (Ep. 1.1), and like the scriptural polysemy which Augustine wishes he could imitate, the *Confessions* is able to sustain substantially different audiences, providing each with a knowledge proportionate to their ability to use it well.[43] This, in turn, reminds us of the care we must take when exposing our students to new ideas that are easy to misinterpret or misappropriate.

Michael P. Foley

References

Aristotle 1938. *The Organon*. Trans. Harold P. Cooke. Cambridge, Mass.: Harvard University Press, 1938.

Augustine, St. 2006. *St. Augustine's Confessions*, Trans. F.J. Sheed. Ed. Michael P. Foley. Indianapolis, Indiana: Hackett Publishing.

——— 1962. *Confessions*. Trans. A. Solignac. Paris: Desclée de Brouwer.

Bagley, Paul 1992. "On the Practice of Esotericism," *Journal of the History of Ideas* 53, no. 2: 231–47.

Bennett, Camille 1988. "The Conversion of Vergil: The *Aeneid* in Augustine's *Confessions*," *Revue des Études Augustiniennes* 34: 47–69.

Cleary, John J. 2002. *Aristotle on the Many Senses of Priority*. South Bend, Ind.: St. Augustine's Press.

Crosson, Frederick 1990. "Structure and Meaning in St. Augustine's *Confessions*," in *The Ethics of Having Children: Proceedings of the American Catholic Philosophical Association*. Vol. LXIII. Ed. Lawrence P. Schrenk. Washington, DC: ACPA. 86–97.

——— 2005. "Esoteric Versus Latent Teaching," *Review of Metaphysics* 59, no. 1: 73-93.

Foley, Michael P. 2003. "Augustine, Aristotle, and the *Confessions*," *The Thomist* 67, no. 4: 607–22.

——— 1999. "Cicero, Augustine, and the Philosophical Roots of the Cassiciacum Dialogues," *Revue des Études Augustiniennes* 45, no. 1: 51–77.

Hagendahl, Harald 1967. *Augustine and the Latin Classics* Goteborg: Elanders Boktryckeri Aktiebolg.

Marrou, H.-I. 1938. *S. augustin et la fin de la culture antique*. Paris: Boccard.

——— 1949. *S. augustin et la fin de la culture antique*. Paris: Boccard.

O'Donnell, James J. 1992. *Augustine Confessions*. Vol. 2. Oxford: Clarendon Press.

——— 1992. *Augustine Confessions*. Vol. 3. Oxford: Clarendon Press.

O'Meara, J.J. 1963. "Augustine the Artist and the *Aeneid*," in *Melanges Offerts a Mademoiselle Christine Mohrmann*. Utrecht: Spectrum Editeurs. 252–61.

Stephany, William A. 1989. "Thematic Structure in Augustine's *Confessions*," *Augustinian Studies* 20: 129–42.

Strauss, Leo 1952. *Persecution and the Art of Writing*. Glencoe: Free Press.

——— 1989. "Exoteric Teaching," in *The Rebirth of Classical Political Rationalism: An Introduction to the Thought of Leo Strauss*. Ed. Thomas L. Pangle. Chicago: University of Chicago Press. 63–71.

——— 1959. "On a Forgotten Kind of Writing," in *What is Political Philosophy?* Glencoe: Free Press. 221–32.

Marie de France
Lais

Utter mystery surrounds the woman we call Marie de France. Scholars generally attribute to her four works: (1) the *Lais* (a collection of twelve short narrative poems, composed ca. 1165, and intended to be recited in public with musical accompaniment, such as the strumming of a harp); (2) a collection of Aesopic *Fables* (ca. 1167–89); (3) the *Purgatory of Saint Patrick* (ca. 1190), derived from a Latin text composed by Henry of Saltrey; and (4) the early thirteenth-century *Life of Saint Audree*, adapted from the Latin *Vita* of Saint Etheldreda. Because a "Marie" names herself in each of these works and because all the poems bear notable similarities in style, we assume them to be composed by the same author. Taking inspiration from a line from the Epilogue to the *Fables* (Marie de France 1898) – "My name is Marie and I come from France" ("*Marie ai num, si sui de France*") – the sixteenth-century French historian Claude Fauchet elected to call this mysterious poetess "Marie de France," or "Marie from France" (Fauchet 1581).

Marie's corpus is well known to French scholars and medievalists, but less familiar to students of world and British literatures. More often than not, the *Lais* are viewed as archaic yet entertaining fairytales that bear witness to the literary tastes of the court of Eleanor of Aquitaine, the wife of King Henry II of England. In all fairness, as we shall see, Marie implies that the poems she composes are complex and "obscure" (Marie 1999, 41). Modern students and teachers face the challenge of refining their sensibilities so as to develop eyes and ears to apprehend the rich web of references Marie weaves into the *Lais* in response to classical, vernacular, biblical, and theological traditions. Consequently, an introduction to Marie de France – the earliest French (and British) woman poet of record – is also an induction into thinking and seeing the world as Marie and her contemporaries did.

In the present chapter, I draw upon my own teaching experience as well as current research to suggest some fruitful entry points into the *Lais*, especially for undergraduate seminars. There are many ways to approach the poems, and the interpretations I advance here are not the only plausible ones; Marie is famous for her ambiguity. But the selected tales – *Guigemar*, *Laüstic*, *Fresne*, and *Eliduc* – provide a useful introduction to the most prevalent themes and questions raised by the collection as a whole.

Thinking about Context

Before diving into the text, it can be useful to pause and consider the cultural context in which the *Lais* came into being. Today, we can run out to the local bookstore or go online to purchase a nicely packaged paperback edition of Marie's work. That many undergraduates read a modern English or French translation (preferably with reference to the Old French text) is not the only thing that distinguishes them from Marie's contemporaries. To state the obvious, twelfth-century audiences and readers had no concept of the printing press, although they did have a very acute sense of the importance of books.

The second half of the twelfth century finds us in the midst of the period Charles H. Haskins (1927) called the Renaissance of the Twelfth Century. Students in Anglo-Norman England and on the Continent read avidly, annotating and copying the works they inherited from Greco-Roman author(itie)s (or *auctores*) like Virgil and Ovid. Such emphasis on the transmission and interpretation of the classics (*translatio studii*) is in no small part due to the popularity of Plato's *Timaeus* (Murray 2008, 3–47), which circulated widely in the partial Latin translation and commentary by Calcidius, a fourth-century Iberian monk.

In the beginning of Plato's dialogue, Critias narrates the Myth of Atlantis (Calcidius 1972, 12–19). He explains how the great Athenian lawgiver Solon traveled to Egypt long ago. There, he marveled at the civilization of the Egyptians. It seemed to him that they were a much older civilization than Athens because they were so learned. Imagine Solon's surprise when an Egyptian priest informs him the same goddess (Athena) founded Athens one thousand years before Egypt!

The Athenians don't remember any of this because they never wrote down the story. To emphasize that point, the Egyptian priest recounts to Solon how the power-hungry civilization of Atlantis rose up and sought to conquer the entire European continent. The Greeks fought bravely against the tyrants and pushed them back to Atlantis, but in the midst of the night, an enormous tidal wave swept over the entire island and all of the soldiers – Greeks and Atlantians alike – died. No one lived to tell the story.

The Egyptians somehow got wind of the cataclysm; perhaps someone watched the island sink from the coast. What Plato's myth makes clear, in any case, is that the Egyptian priests preserved the details of the event on scrolls of papyrus, or, perhaps, carved in hieroglyphs along the walls of their temples. "Ah Solon," the priest exclaims, "you Greeks are only children! You have no concept of tradition, no knowledge hoary with age." The implication – our "take-away lesson" from the Myth of Atlantis – is clear: without books, without reading, without writing, we can aspire only to a limited understanding of the world in which we live or our place in the intellectual tradition. In many ways, Plato was the first advocate of a great texts curriculum: without books we, too, are only children.

The topos of *translatio studii* (inherited, I think, in large part from Plato's *Timaeus*) is developed by many of Marie's near contemporaries. For example, in the Prologue to the *Roman de Troie* (*Romance of Troy*), Benoit de Sainte-Maure adds that without the "great books" (*granz livres*) of the past, we would live not only as children, as the *Timaeus* suggests, but "as beasts" (Benoît de Sainte Maure 1904–12, v. 14). Chrétien de Troyes is equally famous for the description he gives in *Cligés* of the locus of learning shifting from Greece, to Rome, and finally, to France – where, he tells us, it will remain by the grace of God whereas "God had [only] lent it to the others" (Chrétien de Troyes 1994, v. 40, my trans.).

The emphasis Chrétien places on the Christian nature of twelfth-century learning is important. Like Dante, Marie de France lived in a deeply spiritual time when a single book – the Bible – provided the key basis for understanding the human experience. In fact, the bulk of twelfth-century Anglo-Norman literature surviving from this period is devotional and religious in theme. It therefore makes sense that recent scholarship on Marie de France has begun to reconsider the influence Marie's overt Christian identity exerts on her work and, consequently, on our interpretations of it.[1]

Saint Augustine (who had also read the *Timaeus*, but in another partial Latin translation by Cicero) provided what has become arguably the most famous articulation of the relationship of Christian readers to pagan authors in *On Christian Doctrine*. According to Augustine, the medieval Christian reader can find truth within the works of Plato and Virgil because all truth is, ultimately, the Christian God's truth. He explains this through the example of the Israelites who, fleeing from Egypt, salvaged the golden idols of the Egyptians and later put the precious metal to better use by creating the Ark of the Covenant (Augustine 1995). In this same vein, John of Salisbury reports how the famous twelfth-century teacher Bernard of Chartres compared the medieval reader and author to a puny "dwarf" (John of Salisbury 1955, 1.24). The Ancients, meanwhile, are like great "giants." But the medieval dwarf can see further than the giant because he stands on the latter's great shoulders, and, Bernard implies, because of his Christian faith. It is for this very reason that Virgil can only go so far in Dante's *Divine Comedy*, although this limitation does not undercut how important the Roman poet is to setting in motion Dante's spiritual journey: "You are my master and author!" Dante exclaims when he first meets Virgil in canto one of the *Inferno* (Dante 2002, 1.85, my trans.).

In order to climb up on those gigantesque shoulders, twelfth-century students engaged in exercises of close reading and commentary (*commentatio*), and, in turn, imitated the style of Virgil, Ovid, and others by composing their own poems, first in Latin and then in Old French (a process known as *imitatio*). Few major literary works, however, were composed in Old French prior to the twelfth century.[2]

And yet, by the time Marie composes the *Lais* the use of the vernacular as a written and literary medium has become prolific. In Anglo-Norman England, translations of the Psalter and saints' *Lives* (e.g., the Anglo-Norman *Voyage of Saint Brendan*, based on an early eighth-century text composed by an Irish monk living on the Continent) flourish alongside vernacular romances like the Oxford *Tristan*. Continental scholars make numerous adaptations of classical works, including, for example, the "antique" romances like the *Eneas* (translated from Virgil's *Aeneid*, ca. 1150) and *Romance of Troy*, as well as *lais* adapted from Ovid's *Metamorphoses* (such as the anonymous *Narcissus and Dané* or *Piramus and Tisbé*, or the *Philomela* by Chrétien de Troyes). Arthurian romance, reworkings of the Celtic *Tristan* legends, and Jean de Meun's great poetic summum, the *Romance of the Rose*, appear shortly thereafter.

Finally, while adulterous liaisons are prevalent in many twelfth-century romances (and the *Lais* are no exception), readers will do well to keep in mind that Marie's contemporaries had no concept of the so-called "courtly love" motif invented by the nineteenth-century philologist Gaston Paris (1883). They were, however, heavily influenced by the lyric poetry of the itinerant troubadours and *trouvères* (see for example Mora-Lebrun 1986). Very often, such works describe the poet's affection for an unattainable and in all likelihood married lady he woos from afar. The *amor de lohn* ("love from far away") and *fin'amors* ("refined love") he bears her ennobles him in some way; perhaps he wins more tournaments because of his admiration for the lady; perhaps he writes better poetry as an attempt to bridge the gap between himself and the object of desire. Marie plays with such themes considerably throughout her *Lais. However,* we ought not assume from this that she celebrates the adulterous lovers. As Andreas Capellanus's *De Amore* (*About Love*) clearly attests, twelfth-century authors were also quick to critique and ridicule the excesses of *fin'amors*.

An Invitation to the Text: The General Prologue

Five manuscripts containing one or more of Marie's twelve *Lais* have survived. Only one of them, Harley 978 in the British Library in London, contains all of the stories together, and they are preceded in the manuscript by a fifty-six-line introduction known as the General Prologue. In this much-discussed passage,[3] Marie explains the genesis of her project and sets the ethical framework for her poems.

Marie builds upon two biblical parables to define the responsibilities of twelfth-century authors and readers. Echoing the Parable of the Talents (Fitz

1975), she states that "anyone who has received from God the gift of knowledge and true eloquence has a duty not to remain silent: rather should one be happy to reveal such talent" (Marie 1999, 41). Marie composes poems because she conceives of her ability to write as a gift bestowed upon her by God. And, therefore, it demands a whole-hearted response. Embodying the teaching of Matthew 10:8 ("Freely you have received, freely give"), she creates the *Lais* and offers them up as an earthly gift to a "noble king" – probably Henry II, although one cannot help but wonder if she is not also offering up her poems to God, as the Psalmist David did.

The second parable to which Marie alludes is that of the Sower. For good seed to flourish, it must fall on well-prepared ground. Only then can it mature and bear fruit. Marie adopts organic, vegetative imagery to enhance our understanding of the process whereby knowledge spreads and fructifies: "when a truly good thing is heard by many people, it then blooms for the first time; and when it is praised by many, then its flowers are in full bloom."[4] It is not enough to read books; the reader of great texts must go out and share that knowledge with his or her fellow human beings. In this way, to prolong Marie's metaphor, we tend to the soil and the plants we inherit from the past and, in turn, plant the new seeds we collect from them.

The process plays out over centuries of reading, interpretation, and writing. With the passing of time, Marie presumes that our body of knowledge also increases and that we are better placed to interpret more subtly the texts we inherit. (The implication is that we, too, will one day be surpassed by future generations of readers.) Hence the ancients, like "Priscian," wrote "obscurely" so that later readers could "gloss the letter" (*gloser la lettre*) and put the "surplus" or "finishing touches" (*surplus*) to the meaning. Marie's charge to contemporary readers is to be like the glossators of medieval manuscripts, who elucidated complicated passages and words by scribbling notes in the margins and between the lines of the codices they were reading. Hence, the task of the reader (medieval or modern) is not to pin whatever interpretation we choose on a text but, rather, to shed light on the meaning hidden beneath its surface (Foulet Uitti 1981).

Diligent textual study serves an ethical purpose, too. According to Marie, the study of ancient writings can "ward off great suffering" and "guard against vice."[5] This is another reason why so many of her peers, including the brave soul who translated the whole of Virgil's *Aeneid* into Old French ca. 1150, worked so diligently to make the masterpieces of Latin and Greek antiquity available to their contemporaries. Modern traditions of storytelling have their place in this debate, too; at least that's what Marie tells us. Rather than translating something from Latin into Old French, she has chosen to preserve in writing (for the first time, we presume) the oral traditions she has heard in the British Isles and Armorican Brittany. The statement is a bold one: twelfth-century oral storytelling traditions from the Atlantic seaboard have just as much to teach (and can entertain just as effectively) as the writings of the highly respected *auctores*. Consequently, these Celtic *lais* are as worthy of preservation and transmission as the more prestigious matter of Rome. Marie's studious dedication mirrors that of the interpreters of classical texts, and the image of her sitting hard at work in her study calls to mind the nightly vigils of Martianus Capella's philology (Martianus Capella 1977) and the intellectual activity to which Boethius's philosophy exhorts her devotees (Boethius 1973). Furthermore, because she is a woman and her name is Marie, one would be hard pressed not to associate this feminine studiousness with the Virgin Mary, who is typically depicted in medieval painting and manuscript illumination hard at work in her study, or, at the very least, reading the Bible, at the moment of the Annunciation.

The interplay of Christian narrative and pagan traditions inherited from the Atlantic and Mediterranean worlds permeates the General Prologue to the *Lais*; and it infuses the rest of the Harley collection.

Marie and Ovid: The Example of Guigemar

The first story in the Harley manuscript, *Guigemar*, provides an opportunity for students to explore Marie's relationship to Ovid. Although she tells us in the General Prologue that she will avoid translating from Latin into Old French, allusions to ancient literature fill the *Lais*. In *Guigemar*, for example, Marie responds to the tale of Narcissus in Book Three of Ovid's *Metamorphoses* (Ovid 1984; see Gertz 2002, 75–77).[6]

Like Narcissus, Marie's protagonist goes hunting in a forest and strays from his companions; in both poems the main action is set in motion by a curse. The curse in Marie's *lai* – that Guigemar shall not be cured until a lady suffers for him in love as much as he suffers for her – recalls the plea of the spurned suitor to the goddess Rhamnusia in the *Metamorphoses* ("So may he himself love, and not gain the thing he loves" 3.405), although in the Anglo-Norman *lai* it is delivered by a marvelous androgynous white hind (see Pickens 1996).

Guigemar does not fall in love with his own reflection in a pool of water, but the arrow with which he wounds the hind bounces back to strike him in the thigh, thereby mimicking the play on reflections in Ovid. The very literal and material arrow in the *lai* also recalls the metaphorical arrow of love that pierces the eyes of unfortunate Ovidian protagonists before they become sick with love. Furthermore, the androgynous hind, which is female but has antlers characteristic of a stag, recalls the ambivalent sexual identity of the prophet Tiresias, who narrates the story in Ovid's book. To this we can add that Marie's Guigemar, like Narcissus, rejects love (Marie 1999, 44).

The Anglo-Norman *lai* departs significantly from its classical antecedent as soon as the hind delivers the curse. Desperate to find the woman who will cure him, Guigemar boards a marvelous, crewless boat that carries him to an undetermined place far away and over the ocean, a sort of Celtic otherworld. There, he is discovered by a *malmariée* (an 'ill-married lady'), confined to a tower by her jealous and elderly husband. With the help of her female servant, she nurses Guigemar back to health.

The lady's husband appears to have commissioned a mural for his wife to contemplate as she goes about her daily business (see Whalen 2008, 96–101). It depicts Venus casting into the fire "Ovid's book in which he teaches how each of us can control love" (Marie 1999, 46).[7] Scholars generally agree the mural is intended to incite the lady to give in to her husband's desire for her (e.g., Mickel 1974) – a rather odd situation since the two are, after all, married. Ironically, when we finally see her giving in to the kind of passion to which Venus exhorts her devotees, it is not directed towards the husband at all; instead, Marie's lady engages in a passionate adulterous affair with Guigemar. What are we to make of all this?

Clearly, Marie de France does not outright condemn extramarital love in this *lai*; without the lady's love, Guigemar would, we assume, die. It is not surprising, then, that the painting of Venus typically has been interpreted as a symbol of the triumph of the love that heals Guigemar as he spends over a year and a half in amorous dalliance with the lady. Readers cannot help but sympathize to some extent with the anonymous heroine, for her living conditions and marriage are far from ideal; her husband locks her up like a piece of property. But Guigemar's so-called healing exhibits the characteristic features of Ovidian love-sickness. Passion strikes like an arrow and love burns within the protagonists like fire (Marie 1999, 48). Drawing on Ovid, Marie explains that frustrated *eros* is "an invisible wound" and "long-lasting ill" (Marie 1999, 49). Sick with love, Guigemar no longer feels the pain in his thigh. The suggestion is that he is no longer impotent, but he does not seem to have warded off the kind of suffering against which Marie warns us in the General Prologue. We now understand that the flames into which Venus casts Ovid's book eerily invoke the image of a funeral pyre not unlike the one upon which Virgil's Dido, driven insane by fraught *eros*, threw herself when Aeneas sailed away from Carthage – a passage well-known to twelfth-century audiences thanks to the popular *Roman d'Enéas*. Like Aeneas, Guigemar has arrived at the lady's castle via the ocean, and his sojourn in the foreign land is destined to be temporary; moreover, Marie's lady, mimicking Dido, attempts to commit suicide when she thinks she has lost Guigemar. Thus, in the mural, the flames in which Venus intends to destroy the book that teaches how to control and suppress unbridled passion alert the attentive reader to the consequences of excessive erotic desire and furnish a thinly veiled allusion to the Pauline injunction that "it is better to marry than to burn" (1 Cor. 7:9).[8]

The painting of Venus does more than set up an explicitly Ovidian context and tone for Marie's story: it problematizes the tension between *eros*, embodied by Venus (the kind of passion that leads to Dido's demise) and sacrificial Christian love, or *caritas*, exemplified by the Christian God and commemorated during the daily offices in the chapel located at the entrance to the lady's chambers. This contrast enables the reader to come to terms with the ambiguous ending of the *lai*.

Eventually, the jealous husband discovers the lovers. (And, ironically, his jealousy is now justified.) Rather than killing Guigemar, though, the husband allows his wife's lover to sail away on the marvelous boat that is still docked at the sea front (we presume it has waited for Guigemar all this time). The husband then places the lady in a new tower and she spends the next two years lamenting her fate. It is rather odd that Guigemar never comes back for her nor does he make any attempt to find her. Maybe he cannot remember how to get back to her land, or perhaps he has simply given up on her altogether. After all, the lady has shown far more initiative throughout the story than Guigemar: she is the one who devises the means by which the lovers will recognize one another if they are ever reunited by tying a special knot in his shirt. Although Guigemar pledges faithfulness to her, it is also the lady who girds her own loins with the chastity belt. The lady is pro-active in ensuring the future of their relationship; Guigemar simply goes along with her plan.

What, then, are we to make of the fact that one day, after two years, the lady walks up to the door of her tower and realizes not only that it is unlocked but also that she found "no key or bolt" (Marie 1999, 52)?[9] Are we to interpret this detail as the sign a miracle has occurred? Or has the door been unlocked all this time? If the second scenario is true (this seems to be the case because the narrator makes very little fuss about the unlocked door) then Marie suggests the lady has been imprisoned all of this time by her own misery. Her disposition recalls Boethius at the beginning of the *Consolation of Philosophy*. Longing only for her lover, absorbed by grief and self-pity, she is completely blind to the fact that she could go to the door and walk out of the tower. Of course, her husband does not expect her to find the magical boat docked at the seafront, since he watched Guigemar sail away on it. And yet, that is precisely what she does find, and so she assumes her lover is dead. Intent on drowning herself in the same spot, the lady climbs aboard, but faints, presumably on the very bed upon which Guigemar fell unconscious earlier in the story.

Guigemar does not find the lady when the boat docks; another knight, Meriaduc, discovers her. Marie's use of language implies that he takes possession of the lady as he would a material object: "Taking her by the mantle, the lord took her off to his castle, delighted by his discovery, as the lady was extremely beautiful."[10] Time goes by and there is still no sign of Guigemar. Since Meriaduc has heard of Guigemar's knotted shirt, it is logical to assume that news of the arrival of a mysterious fairy-like lady on an enchanted boat, and wearing a unique chastity belt, has spread throughout the land. Still, Guigemar makes no attempt to locate her. Is he imprisoned by grief just as the lady was when she failed to notice the door to the tower was unlocked? Whatever the case may be, it is eventually Meriaduc who sends for Guigemar. When he arrives at court, the lady recognizes her lover without difficulty. Guigemar, however, hesitates, thinking that all women look the same. (Just how many fairy-like beauties has he encountered during his lifetime?) Even when the lady undoes the knot in his shirt, Guigemar "was not completely convinced" of her identity – not until he sees and unties the chastity belt. At that point, he actively attempts to free her, by proposing to serve Meriaduc loyally in exchange for her freedom. Meriaduc refuses, insisting on his ownership of the lady: "I found her and I shall keep her and defend her against you."[11] Note how nobody – not even, at this point, the reader – is prone to recall that a husband is waiting for the lady at home. Her anonymity contributes to her objectification; no one pays attention to her desires or needs.

On the surface, the conclusion of the *lai* is utterly logical. When Meriaduc refuses to release Guigemar's beloved, the latter enlists the help of one of Meriaduc's neighboring opponents and wages battle. The whole situation bears remarkable similarities to the war at Troy: the conflict centers on a woman who is the object of male desire; it results in a lengthy period of siege; and thousands of innocent people die. Although most readers will, at this point, be sympathetic to the lovers' plight, one cannot fail to reflect upon the details upon which Marie brings her *lai* to conclusion: the image of "Guigemar beseig[ing] the town" and "starv[ing] all those inside" (Marie 1999, 54). After capturing Meriaduc's city, Guigemar shows no mercy (unlike the lady's husband, who let him sail away when he discovered the lovers). The contrast between the suffering of Meriaduc's people and Guigemar's *joie* ("joy"; Marie 1999, 55) is remarkable. Of the lady, meanwhile, we hear only that Guigemar takes her away. Marie insists that "his tribulations were over," but we hear nothing of the anonymous heroine's future, and it is not clear that she will fare better with Guigemar than she has to date. At the end of the *lai*, only one thing is certain: the rivalry between Meriaduc and Guigemar, fueled by Ovidian desire, has brought down and destroyed a whole country. Thus the story leaves us with a sense of dissatisfaction – and a hefty warning against the excesses of *cupiditas*.

Biblical Allusions in Laüstic

The nature of romantic love and, more specifically, of destructive *eros*, continues to dominate most of the *lais*. In addition to Ovidian materials, the Christian Bible provides an important context for understanding this dimension of Marie de France's work. In *Equitan,* for example, Marie plays humorously with the tale of David and Bathsheba in the Old Testament.[12] For Marie, those who – like Equitan and his mistress – give in to the sway of the passions inevitably fall into sin. And in *Laüstic*, she continues to explore this idea by carefully blending Ovidian and Christian motifs.

Only 160 verse lines long, *Laüstic* is the second shortest of the *Lais* (after *Chevrefoil*). Marie provides the title in the opening lines and then diligently translates it into English ("nightingale") and French ("rossignol"). The little bird and its death constitute the focal point of the narrative. Provençal poets often link the nightingale to the cult of *fin' amors* and so it is not surprising that readings of Marie's poem have tended to focus on this association. Recent scholarship has gone so far as to suggest that this particular *lai* provides one of the most perfect expressions of the "secret and courtly love" Marie portrays throughout her collection (Bloch 2003, 67). Alas, to read *Laüstic* as a celebration and vindication of *fin' amors* is, I think, to miss Marie's point. This becomes clear when we interpret the *lai* in light of the Ovidian and Christian backdrops woven into the story.[13]

I find it useful, when teaching *Laüstic*, to assign the tale of *Philomela* in Ovid's *Metamorphoses* (and, when time permits, Chrétien de Troyes's twelfth-century version, composed around the same time as Marie's *lai*). Marie was no doubt familiar with the origin of the nightingale in Ovid's book, an episode that focuses on the tragic destiny of Philomela and her sister, Procne (see e.g., Cottrell 1968 and Rothschild 2005).

When Procne marries Tereus of Thrace, she is saddened to be parted from her sister. Shortly after the wedding, Tereus returns to Athens and asks his father-in-law to allow him to take Philomela to visit Procne. When he sees Philomela, Ovidian *eros* kindles within him a vicious desire for her and, after taking her away, he brutally rapes her again and again. To prevent his sister-in-law from revealing this sordid abuse, he cuts out her tongue and locks her up.

Philomela is (like many of Marie's heroines) quite resourceful; she weaves a message into a tapestry and sends it to her sister. Outraged, Procne comes to free Philomela and, together, the women plot their revenge. Their plan centers on Itys, Procne and Tereus's son. In a horrific scene, Philomela and Procne slit Itys's throat, cut him into tiny pieces, and make a stew that they feed to Tereus for dinner. After the meal, Philomela appears clutching Itys's bloody head and hurls it at Tereus. Enraged, he chases the two women and all three of Ovid's protagonists turn into birds: Tereus into a hoopoe, Procne into a swallow, and Philomela into a nightingale. Both the swallow and the nightingale, Ovid notes, bear red marks of shame on their chests in memory of their brutal and horrifying murder of the innocent child (Ovid 1984, 6.669–70).

Ovid's narrative undergirds much of Marie's *lai*, which begins peacefully but degenerates into images of violence and death. Like Itys, Marie's eponymous nightingale is entirely innocent and yet it is brutally murdered by the male protagonist. The manner in which the lady wraps the bird's corpse in rich cloth and sends it as a message to her lover, so as to announce the end of their affair, further recalls Philomela's sending the tapestry as a message to her sister (see McCash 2005). And, when the husband throws the dead bird at his wife, the red blood that stains her chest recalls the mark of shame borne by Philomela and Procne after their metamorphosis into birds. The lady is responsible for the nightingale's death: by lying to cover her seemingly innocuous exchanges with the knight who lives next door, she sets in motion the events that lead to the bird's demise. In *Laüstic*, the red blood mark on the lady's chest does not point to her breaking heart; nor does it suggest that Marie's sympathies lie with the lovers. By playing against passages of the Old and New Testaments, Marie de France sets an explicitly Judeo-Christian context in which we are invited to recognize the moral shortcomings of each of her protagonists.

To understand all of this, we must return to the beginning of the *lai*, which opens with a detailed presentation of the two men and woman. Marie explains that the two men are knights of equally fair and generous disposition, of like power and wealth, and that they live next door to each other in very similar homes. The only difference between them is that one is "a bachelor" (or "young man") whereas the other "had taken a wife," who at least appears to be "elegant, courtly, and wise" (Marie 1999, 94). And yet, as is often the case in Marie's *lais*, appearances are deceptive and misleading. Thus, although the narrator describes the bachelor knight as "a young man who was well known amongst his peers for his prowess and great valor [and] performed honorable deeds gladly and attended many tournaments, spending freely and giving generously whatever he had," we learn shortly thereafter that "he loved his neighbor's wife."[14] Such an explicit reference to one of the Ten Commandments ("Thou shalt not desire [or love] thy neighbor's wife," Exodus 20:17) would not have been lost on Marie's Christian audience, and it sets the tone for her critique of covetous and destructive love portrayed in the *lai*. The knight's devotion to his married neighbor, which explicitly transgresses the Commandment, is not in keeping with his worldly reputation. Although he wins tournaments and bestows generosity on his peers, his attitude towards the lady's husband (who is, literally, his neighbor) is far from honorable, generous, or full of valor.

The narrator's silence regarding the actions of the female protagonist is equally revealing. Marie hints at no mitigating circumstances for the lady's betrayal of her marital vows: her husband does not lock her up and, until he suspects the affair, we never see him mistreat her.

Even the affair itself is described in frivolous terms. To all intents and purposes, the lady falls in love with a man who is the exact double of her husband (they even own similar adjoining homes). Moreover, her affection for the knight who lives next door is purely superficial. As Marie puts it, she loves him "both for the good she had heard about him and because he lived close by."[15] The emphasis placed on the close proximity of the two homes is particularly humorous and witty: everything about the love affair mocks and subverts the Gospel commandment to "love thy neighbor" (Matthew 22:39).

Of course, one might object that the lady's relationship with the neighboring knight is harmless. The two never have sex, and only rarely find time to be alone together. (They are reduced to tossing, in a rather ridiculous fashion, presents back and forth over the wall that separates their homes.) They do, however, delight in seeing one another (*veer*, v. 77) – and here is our clue to interpreting the situation. Within a Judeo-Christian context, the emphasis Marie places on sight reminds us that the lovers are adulterous, whether or not they consummate the affair, for "whosoever looketh on a woman to lust after her hath committed adultery with her already in his heart" (Matt. 5:28).

In response to his wife's affair, the husband becomes jealous. Like the seneschal in *Equitan*, he succumbs to wrath, another of the deadly sins: "But so frequently did she stand there [at the window] and so frequently leave her bed that her husband became angry and asked her repeatedly why she got up and where she went."[16] The husband's anger is situated exactly at the midpoint of the *lai* (v. 80), a strategic position in romance narratives of the twelfth century where some kind of revelation occurs. Notice how the lady responds to her husband's questions with a lie, thus transgressing the ninth commandment (Exod. 20:16). She blames the nightingale's song for her sleeplessness, as many Provençal poets do, but there is actually no indication in the text that the lady ever hears a real *laüstic* sing. This, in turn, causes her husband's anger to intensify. Filled with wrath (*ire*) and spite (*maltalent*), he devises a plan to ensnare the innocent bird. The midpoint of the *lai* thus centers on a chain of sin begetting sin: from the adultery of the wife, to the wrath of the husband, to the wife's lie and, ultimately, the intensification of her husband's anger. This chain of events at the center of Marie's story closely parallels the message of James's Epistle, namely that "lust when it hath conceived beareth sin, and the sin, when it is full grown, bringeth forth death" (James 1:14–15). The death of the nightingale is aptly foreshadowed – as is the spiritual wasteland in which the three human protagonists find themselves at the end of the story.

The lady's reaction to her husband's anger is revealing. When she takes the dead bird's body in her hands, she does not weep out of repentance or sympathy for the nightingale; nor, even, for the pain she has caused her neighbors. She focuses solely on her own grief: "'Alas,' she said, 'misfortune is upon me. Never again can I get up at night or go to stand at the window where I used to see my beloved'" (Marie 1999, 95).[17] Full of self-pity, she blames others, failing to recognize her own responsibility in setting the "trap and snare" for the bird. When she sends the corpse to her lover, it is only out of fear that he will consider her to be fainthearted, and that her reputation as a devoted lover will be put into question.

The knight's reaction to her message strikes the reader as strange, to say the least. It is perhaps the most ambiguous turn of events in Marie's *lai*: he orders that a portable shrine be constructed for the martyred bird, so that he may keep the memory of his lady close to him at all times, as one would a precious relic. (The shrine constructed for the bird resembles the reliquaries that were commissioned during the Middle Ages to preserve the bodily remains of Christian saints; see Tudor 1993.)

Scholars have concluded that the act of preserving the bird affirms the lovers' undying affection. Robert Cottrell (1968, 404–05) has even suggested that it signifies the metamorphosis of their love from a lustful, earthly plane, to a more spiritual dimension: he continues to love the lady, despite the fact that they can never be together physically (nor can they even continue to visit at night on either side of the wall that separates their homes). Given the emphasis placed throughout the *lai* on Judeo-Christian ethics, I believe a much less benevolent reading is more in keeping with the tenor of Marie's story. In sending him the dead bird, the lady, who focuses solely on her own self-centered need to tell the knight that the affair is over, condemns him to love her always: "the lover carries around with him always the agonizing memory of his lost love" (Mickel 1971, 55). The lover in *Laüstic* willingly submits to a perverted form of love that can never be fruitful. Like Dante's Paolo and Francesca in canto 5 of Dante's *Inferno*, Marie's lovers are bound together in an unproductive relationship predicated on frustrated lust. In this way, the enshrined nightingale, that the knight prizes above all other things, becomes an idol. As C. S. Lewis puts it, "love, having become a god, becomes a demon" (Lewis 1960, 56).

At the end of the story, we presume the lady's marriage is ruined, that she will never see her lover again, and that the close friendship between the two knights has been fractured – no doubt to the cost of the whole city. It is hard to construe this as a happy ending. In *Laüstic*, and throughout the *Lais*, Marie de France reminds Christian readers and auditors that anything undertaken in this world with an eye to self-gratification is doomed to failure.

Charity and Resolution in Fresne and Eliduc

In contrast to the selfish, self-serving nature of the lovers' relationship in *Laüstic*, *Fresne* and *Eliduc* portray two examples of deeply meaningful, sacrificial, Christian love (or "charity").

The setting of *Fresne*[18] is quite similar to *Laüstic*: "there once lived in Brittany two knights who were neighbors, powerful and wealthy men, worthy and valiant knights from the same region" (Marie 1999, 61).[19] This time, however, the two men are married.

In the first part of the story, Marie draws attention to the dangerous consequences of another deadly sin: envy.[20] When her neighbor gives birth to twin sons, the other lady, who is "deceitful and arrogant, prone to slander and envy,"[21] publicly declares that no woman can conceive twins unless she has had sex with two men. Although the vicious rumor is unfounded, it has disastrous effects for the young mother. People gossip about her throughout the land and her husband keeps her in custody (Marie 1999, 62).

There is no indication that the envious lady thinks about the consequences of her actions until one year later, when she conceives and delivers twin girls. The words she utters out of dismay and self-pity – "whoever slanders and lies about others does not know what retributions await him"[22] – ring true; but her application of the statement is shortsighted and selfish. The lady is concerned here only with her reputation in the mortal world and the fact that her hurtful declaration is coming back to haunt her: she does not repent in any meaningful way for the ill she has done. Furthermore, her response to the crisis at hand is quite shocking. Rather than be found out, she concludes that she will "have to murder one of the children."[23] Through this extraordinary set of circumstances, Marie shows how the sinfulness of the protagonist leads, as it did in *Equitan*, to the intent to transgress one of the Judeo-Christian Commandments ("Thou shalt not kill," Exodus 20:13) – and, as was the case in *Laüstic*, the victim is entirely innocent. Yet again, Marie's *lai* turns Christian ethics upside down. This is all the more striking (and amusing!) when the lady demonstrates a total lack of understanding of repentance and grace by declaring "I would rather make amends with God [later, for killing my child] than shame and dishonor myself [right now in this earthly world]."[24] Her concerns are centered on the earthly, material world; she erroneously anticipates that forgiveness can be obtained by bartering with God, regardless of her motives and intentions.

The response of the lady's attendant is just as interesting. To some degree, we are relieved that she prevents the lady from murdering the baby girl. Nonetheless, her solution is far from ideal. She proposes, instead, to abandon the child somewhere in the forest, preferably near a church, in the hope that someone will find her and care for her. This proposal feigns to relieve the lady and her attendant of responsibility. The baby's survival now hinges ironically on some stranger's having the Christian virtue her mother has failed to exhibit: charity.

At this point, readers cannot fail to be disconcerted. Why does no one tell the truth? The situation could be resolved quickly if the lady admitted that she has lied and slandered her neighbor. Instead, she is determined to find some way to conceal her sinfulness. To the Christian reader, it comes as no surprise, then, that the path the attendant takes through the forest with the child is a "wide" (Marie 1999, 63) one, "for wide is the gate and broad is the road that leads to destruction" (Matt. 7:13). Muttering a (no doubt heartfelt, but, given the circumstances, highly ironic) prayer to God to keep the child from perishing, the attendant abandons her in a large ash tree (Old French *fresne*). When the porter and abbess of the local abbey find her there, they appropriately name her after the ash (Marie 1999, 64). Fresne is in fact the first of only three female protagonists (along with the heroines of *Eliduc*) to be named by Marie in the *Lais*.

The young woman grows up and a local nobleman falls in love with her. Even in the context of their liaison, Marie's critique of hypocritical actions and intentionality continues to drive the story forward. So that he may spend more time with Fresne, Gurun gives the abbey much of his wealth and establishes a residence there. When the knight further proposes that Fresne run away with him, the reader gets the hint that he enjoys far more than her good company and conversation, for he insists the abbess "would be most aggrieved and extremely angry if [Fresne] became pregnant in her house."[25] In any case, when she leaves the abbey, Fresne takes with her the brocade and the ring with which she was found. We understand these objects to be precious to her: paralleling the knight in *Laüstic*, she places them "in a casket which she carried with her, for she did not want to leave or forget it."[26] Both the ring and the cloth are gifts from Fresne's mother, and the items (symbols, perhaps, of the most meager form of motherly love the lady exhibits toward her daughter prior to abandoning her) are the only clues Fresne possesses to her noble origin. They play a crucial part in the second half of the story.

Fresne and Gurun appear to be happy together, but trouble surfaces when the landed knights reproach their lord for neglecting his sovereign duties. Gurun has not married Fresne (she is his "concubine"), no doubt because her birth rank is unknown (Marie 1999, 65). His vassals counsel him to marry a young woman known as La Codre ("the hazel tree") – who happens to be Fresne's sister (although nobody knows that). Fresne's reaction to news of Gurun's wedding stands in stark contrast to the behavior of her mother at the beginning of the story: she remains loyal to her beloved. Her mother, who remains unaware of Fresne's identity, does not appear to have changed. Fearful that Gurun's love for Fresne will interfere with La Codre's marriage, she devises a plan to kick Fresne out of the house. It is when Fresne selflessly prepares the marriage bed that the true miracle of the story occurs: she places her brocade over the bed so as "to honor" Gurun (Marie 1999, 66). This act of utterly selfless love, or charity, brings about a profound change in Fresne's mother, who recognizes her daughter and humbly repents, confessing her sins publicly (we assume) for the first time:

> Once, in my great wickedness, I slandered my neighbor. I spoke ill of her two children, but in fact I did myself harm. The truth is that I became with child and had two daughters, one of whom I hid. I had

> her abandoned at a church and sent with her our brocade and the ring you gave me when you first spoke with me. It can be hidden from you no longer. I have found the cloth and the ring, and have recognized here our daughter whom I had lost by my folly. This is the damsel, so worth, wise and fair, whom the knight loved and whose sister he has married! (Marie 1999, 67)[27]

Accepting God 's grace and goodness, the man forgives his wife, declaring "God has given us great joy rather than allowing the sin to be doubled." Everyone decides to request that the archbishop un-marry Gurun and La Codre the next morning, so that he can be rightfully married to Fresne, with her family in attendance. (This detail is important, as twelfth-century ecclesiastical law did not allow for someone to marry a man or woman if he or she had had carnal knowledge of one of their family members.) Through this odd turn of events, set in motion by Fresne's selfless love for Gurun (and enabled by the material gifts given to her by her mother), Marie de France exhibits how "it is a more blessed thing to give, rather than to receive" (Acts 20:35). In keeping with the General Prologue, we see that "when a truly beneficial thing is heard [or seen] by many people, it then enjoys its first blossom, but if it is widely praised its flowers are in full bloom" (Marie 1999, 41).[28] The unmistakably happy ending of *Fresne* thus stands in stark contrast to the tragic conclusion of *Laüstic*.[29]

The resolution of the central crisis in Marie de France's *Eliduc* is also brought about by a selfless act of charitable love. *Eliduc* is the last *lai* in the Harley manuscript. At over 1180 verse lines, it is also the longest.[30] The *lai* is typically known by the name of the male protagonist. However, Marie insists from the outset that it would be more fitting to adopt the names of the women – *Guildeluëc and Guilliadun* (Marie 1999, 111) (See Prior 1998).

Carrying over a theme from *Fresne* and the Prologue to *Guigemar*, Eliduc falls out of favor with his king due to the slander and accusation of envious peers. Until things cool down, he decides to cross the sea to the kingdom of Logres. He takes leave from his wife, Guildeluëc, and promises to remain faithful to her (Marie 1999, 112).

Upon his arrival in Britain, Eliduc exhibits much prowess in battle and attracts the interest of Guilliadun, the daughter of the local king (Marie 1999, 114). Venus strikes swiftly: "Love dispatched its messenger who summoned her to love him. It made her go pale and sigh . . . " (Marie 1999, 115).[31] Eliduc becomes anxious and, sensing that he is developing feelings for the maiden, repents "for he remembered his wife, and how he had assured her that he would be faithful and behave loyally."[32] Eliduc is conscious that engaging in an affair would transgress his duties and responsibilities as a husband – and yet, he tells Guilliadun nothing of his marriage to Guildelüec. His silence enables the princess to become increasingly infatuated with him. He, meanwhile, accepts two gifts from Guilliadun (a ring and a girdle), leading her to assume that he returns her love. Soon, Eliduc exhibits the telltale signs of Ovidian *eros* – "he ha[s] no joy or pleasure, except when thinking of her" (Marie 1999, 117) – but the joy he experiences in spending time with Guilliadun intermingles with guilt. Once again, he remembers the promise he made to his wife before his departure.[33] Marie takes pains to emphasize that Eliduc knows that the path he is about to choose is morally problematic.

Note how the narrator presents Eliduc as a victim, "trapped" by the clutches of Ovidian desire and who ostensibly cannot refrain from acting on impulse (Marie 1999, 117). Yet again, we recognize a similar situation in canto 5 of Dante's *Inferno*, where Francesca declares that love made her and Paolo act upon the physical attraction they felt for one another (Dante 2002). Although Francesca presents the lovers as powerless victims, the reader understands why they are condemned to Hell: they have failed to take responsibility and repent for their actions. Through her choice of phrasing, Marie de France makes Eliduc's moral weakness explicit and causes us to recognize his responsibility in the situation at hand: endowed with free will (and, therefore, not bound by the laws of Ovid's storybook world), he makes a conscious decision to begin the affair with Guilliadun. And, although he does not sleep with her, Eliduc's decision has consequences both for himself and those around him.

Messengers from Eliduc's liege-lord in Brittany arrive to summon him home. Like the lady in *Laüstic*, he focuses on his own sorrow. And, recalling the mother in *Fresne*, he seems to claim responsibility for his actions – "'Alas,' he said, 'I have behaved badly!'" (Marie 1999, 119)[34] – when in fact he laments the untenable situation in which he now finds himself (and for which, we might add, he is entirely to blame):

> "I have been too long in this country. Alas that I ever saw it! Here I have deeply loved a girl, Guilliadun, the king's daughter, and she has loved me. If I must leave her thus, one of us will have to die, or perhaps even both. But nevertheless I must go, for my lord has summoned me in a letter and required me by oath, and my wife as well. Now I must take care. I can remain no longer and must leave." (Marie 1999, 119)[35]

Eliduc has serious problems. He owes his allegiance to two earthly lords, and his heart is promised to two women. In fact, he seems to give primacy to his girlfriend over his wife and by declaring: "if I were to marry my beloved, the Christian religion would not accept it."[36] Eliduc's self-identification as a Christian is particularly ironic. One wonders how he gets the impression that Christianity accepts adultery any more than it does polygamy – or how transgressing the Commandment not to lie (e.g., by remaining silent about his marital status) sits with his faith. Eliduc is effectively trapped – not by Ovidian love-sickness, but by his own lies and deceit. As he puts it, "things are going badly in all respects!" Dramatic irony reaches an all-time high when he commits always "to do right by [his] beloved." Setting aside the obvious question (what about doing right by his wife?), the reader might expect Eliduc finally to tell Guilliadun the truth, but he does nothing of the sort. Instead, he promises to return and visit her very soon and sets sail for home.

After a brief sojourn in Brittany, Eliduc comes back for his mistress. He continues to maintain silence about his marriage. During the return boat trip, a great storm arises and one of the sailors proposes to throw Guilliadun overboard in order to appease the wrath of God.[37] This episode begs to be read in light of the story of Jonah in the Old Testament (Fitz 1974). By playing off the biblical narrative, Marie de France further problematizes Eliduc's continued attempts to avoid his marital obligations. As is her habit, she humorously turns the biblical narrative on its head.

The sailor in *Eliduc* correctly identifies the actions that have offended God: "'You have a loyal wife and now with this other woman you offend God and His law, righteousness and the faith'" (Marie 1999, 121).[38] However, the conclusion he reaches is completely illogical. Instead of casting Eliduc (the transgressive, Jonah character) overboard, he proposes, instead, to throw Guilliadun into the sea: "'Let us cast her into the sea and we shall soon arrive safely!'"[39] Marie's *lai* thus marks a radical departure from the Book of Jonah, where the guilty man confesses his refusal to do God's will and instructs the innocent sailors to throw him overboard so that their lives will be spared (Jon. 1:8–15). We know Guilliadun is innocent because, when she first hears of Eliduc's wife, the news shocks her so badly that she faints (Marie 1999, 122).[40] Everyone on the boat believes her to be dead.

Eliduc's reaction to Guilliadun's death, when read in light of the biblical motif, highlights his own corruption. Instead of admitting his guilt and accepting responsibility for misleading the young woman, he becomes angry and viciously murders his servant by striking him with an oar and throwing him overboard (Marie 1999, 122). Like the seneschal in *Equitan*, Eliduc takes vengeance and judgment into his own hands – in this case, to cover up his own sinfulness.[41] As we now understand, the whole storm scene gravitates around the theme of selfishness: self-interest of the sailor, who proposes to drown Guilliadun in order to save himself; selfishness of Eliduc, who avoids (like Jonah) facing the truth, and who commits murder instead of acknowledging his own shortcomings. By emphasizing the self-serving nature of all the characters on board (with the exception Guilliadun), Marie de France has set the stage for the self-sacrifice that constitutes the focal point of the final scene of *Eliduc*.

When he lands the boat in Brittany, Eliduc takes Guilliadun's body to a chapel in the forest, where he intends to bury her "with great honor and with a fine service in a consecrated cemetery, for she was a king's daughter and had a right to this" (Marie 1999, 122).[42] He also intends to donate significant portions of his land to establish an abbey nearby, where "monks, nuns or canons . . . would always pray for her." Unfortunately, the holy hermit who tends the chapel is dead. (Eliduc discovers his newly dug grave on the premises.) The timeframe of the hermit's death, which, the narrator informs us, occurred eight days ago, is significant: in medieval numerology, eight is the number of resurrection and regeneration. In Marie's *lai*, the eight days that have passed signal an important shift in the focus of the narrative and announce the process of regeneration and resurrection set in motion by the charitable and selfless love of Eliduc's wife, Guildelüec.

To most modern readers, the ending of *Eliduc* is shocking. Concerned by her husband's melancholic disposition, Guildelüec has him followed and discovers Guilliadun's body lying in the chapel. Instead of becoming angry, she pities the young woman and grieves for her husband's loss (Marie 1999, 124). Moreover, when the opportunity arises, she does everything in her power to bring Guilliadun back to life. Observing a weasel that resuscitates its mate by feeding it a small, bright red flower from the woods, Guildelüec manages to knock the blossom from the animal's mouth and feeds it to Guilliadun. The princess regains consciousness immediately.

Everything about the scene echoes the celebration of the Eucharist: Guilliadun is lying in a chapel; the small flower, placed in Guilliadun's mouth, functions like the communion bread (or body of Christ); because it is red, the flower is also suggestive of the wine or blood; and, when she ingests it, Guilliadun is effectively brought back to life. Her physical awakening anticipates the spiritual renewal soon to follow.

One would be hard pressed to imagine a greater example of charitable love: Guildelüec has brought back to life her husband's lover (see Lochrie 2003). Although she is not a priest (of course, as a woman she could not be), through the administration of the Eucharist-like flower, Marie identifies Guildelüec as a person who is holy.[43]

Even if we doubt that, under similar circumstances, we would have the strength to imitate Guildelüec, modern readers can admire her decision to save Guilliadun. Few, however, will understand at all her decision to "set [Eliduc] free completely and take the veil" (Marie 1999, 125)[44] so that he can marry his mistress. I find it helpful to read this extraordinary turn of events in light of the more or less contemporary theological writings of St. Bernard of Clairvaux.

In *De Diligendo Deo* (or *On Loving God*), St. Bernard speaks of the transformative powers of love – even lust. The love of the flesh is but the first of four degrees of love (summarized in Chapter Fifteen), and it must be reshaped and remolded until it is directed selflessly toward God: "Because we are born of the flesh, so too must our love begin in the flesh. . . . But it must find its consummation in the spirit" (Bernard of Clairvaux 2005).[45] The first step on this path of transformation is to direct one's love outside of one's self, as Guildelüec does when she feeds the red flower to Guilliadun.

Guildelüec's decision to take the veil makes little sense to modern readers because it is not supposed to make sense. Her decision is not reached through human reason, but through faith. Focused only on her love of God, Guildelüec forsakes all earthly ties, including her marriage to Eliduc. In place of her earthly spouse, she achieves a (vastly superior) heavenly one. With time – and, no doubt, because of the prayers she says for them – Guilliadun and even Eliduc follow her example.

The final *lai* in the Harley manuscript resolves all worldly tensions (political, marital, societal) by having the major characters take the Holy Orders and submit themselves to a life of service to God . In so doing, they exemplify the fourth of St. Bernard's degrees of love – the love of self for God's sake – and achieve a degree of peace and reconciliation to which none of Marie's other characters (with, perhaps, the exception of Fresne) can aspire. The point here is not that we should all get "to a nunnery" (Shakespeare 1992 Act 3, sc. 1). The conclusion of *Eliduc* is idealistic and unlikely to happen in this world. (Indeed, Bernard acknowledges that it is highly unusual to attain the fourth degree of love during the mortal life; the final stage appears to be reserved for saints.) The point of *Eliduc*, however, seems to be that most earthly challenges and difficulties, including those portrayed in Marie's other tales, are linked to misguided or misdirected affections. The final *lai* in the Harley manuscript transcends the impediments of lust, envy, lies, and betrayal as it shifts away from a selfishness that leads to destruction towards an attainable model of selflessness and community founded on the charitable love of one's neighbor. In this way, the exemplum of spiritual love portrayed in *Eliduc* transcends all other examples of human love and desire in the *Lais*.

All of this does not negate the fact that Marie de France's *Lais* are entertaining; and indeed, the stories do bear witness to the literary tastes of the Plantagenet court, especially the female entourage of Eleanor of Aquitaine; moreover, they certainly do confront the reader with numerous cases of extramarital love. But to reduce Marie's *Lais* to such themes is to see, in lieu of universals, only the particulars.

Each of the stories preserved in the Harley manuscript speaks to some degree about human frailty. Like Geoffrey Chaucer's *Canterbury Tales*, the *Lais* invite medieval Christian auditors and readers to look beyond the limitations of the mortal world. For all of these reasons, Marie de France is one of the most intriguing Neo-Platonic Christian authors of the twelfth century. The moral and ethical questions she weaves throughout her *Lais* make them particularly well suited for analysis and discussion in the Great Texts seminar, where students and professors are still in the business of "glossing the letter."

References

Archibald, Elizabeth 2000. "*Lai le Freine*: The Female Foundling and the Problem of Romance Genre" in *The Spirit of Medieval English Popular Romance*. Ed. Ad Putter and Jane Gilbert. Longman Medieval and Renaissance Library. Harlow: Longman.

Benoit de Sainte-Maure 1904–12. *Le Roman de Troie*. Ed. Leopold Constans. Paris: Firmin Didot.

Bernard of Clairvaux 2005. *On Loving God*. Trans. Emero Stiegman. Cistercian Fathers Series. Kalamazoo, Mich.: Cistercian Publications.

Bloch, Howard 2003. *The Anonymous Marie de France*. New Haven: Yale University Press.

Boethius 1973. *Consolation of Philosophy. Theological Tractates and the Consolation of Philosophy.* Trans. By H. F. Stewart, E. K. Rand, and S. J. Tester. Loeb Classical Library. Cambridge: Harvard University Press.

Brumlik, Joan 1997. "Secondary Characters in *Equitan and Eliduc*." *The Court and Cultural Diversity*. Cambridge: D. S. Brewer. 189–95.

Burgess, Glyn 1977. *Marie de France: An Annotated Critical Bibliography*. London: Grant and Cutler. Supplement no. 1, 1986, Supplement no. 2, 1997, Supplement no. 3, 2007.

Calcidius 1972. *Timaeus: A Calcidio translatus commentarioque instructus*. Ed. Jan H. Waszink. London: Warburg Institute.

Callahan, A. 1999–2000. "*En remembrance et en mémoire:* Grief, Memory and Memorialization in the *Lais* of Marie de France." *Romance Notes* 40: 259–70.

Chrétien de Troyes. 1994. *Oeuvres Completes*. Ed. Peter F. Dembowski, Philippe Walter, Karl D. Uitti, Daniel Poirion, and Anne Berthelot. Bibliothèque de la Pléiade. Paris: Gallimard.

Cottrell, Robert 1968. "*Le lai du Laüstic*: From Physicality to Spirituality." *Philological Quarterly* 47.4: 499–505.

Dante Alighieri 2002. *Inferno*. Ed. and trans. Anthony Esolen. Modern Library. New York: Random House.

Denis, Françoise 2002. "Religion et héroïsme féminine au XIIe siècle: variations narratives et manipulations d'auteurs." *Féminités et masculinités dans le texte narratif avant 1800: la question du 'gender.' Actes du XIVe colloque de la SATOR (Amsterdam/Leyde, 2000)*. Louvain: Peeters. 271–81.

Fauchet, Claude 1581. *Recueil de l'origine de la langue et poésie françoise.*

Fitz, Brewster E. 1974. "The Storm Episode and the Weasel Episode: Sacrificial Casuistry in Marie de France's *Eliduc*," *Modern Language Notes* 89.4 (1974): 542–49.

——— 1975. "The Prologue to the *Lais* of Marie de France and the Parable of the Talents: Gloss and Monetary Metaphor." *Modern Language Notes* 90: 558–596.

Foulet, Alfred, and Karl D. Uitti 1981. "The Prologue to the *Lais* of Marie de France: A Reconsideration." *Romance Philology* 35.1: 242–49.

Paris, Gaston 1883. "Études sur les romans de la Table Ronde: *Lancelot du Lac*." *Romania* 12:459–534.

Gertz, Sun Hee 2002. *Echoes and Reflections*. Amsterdam: Rodopi.

Glendinning, Robert 1986. "*Pyramus and Thisbe* in the Medieval Classroom." *Speculum* 61.1: 51–78.

Haskins, Charles H. 1927. *The Renaissance of the Twelfth Century*. Cambridge: Harvard University Press.

Hourihane, Colum. 2002. *King David in the Index of Christian Art*. Princeton: Princeton University Press.

John of Salisbury 1955. *Metalogicon*. Trans. Daniel McGarry. Berkeley and Los Angeles: University of California Press.

Lewis, C. S. 1960. *The Four Loves*. New York: Harcourt.

Lochrie, Karma 2003. "Between Women," *The Cambridge Companion to Medieval Women's Writing*, ed. Carolyn Dinshaw and David Wallace. Cambridge: Cambridge University Press, 2003. 82–84.

Marie de France. 1898. *Fables. Die Fabeln der Marie de France.* Ed. Karl Warnke. Halle: Niemeyer.

——— 1925. *Die Lais der Marie de France*. Ed. Karl Warnke. Third edition. Halle: Niemeyer.

——— 1987. *Marie de France: Fables*. Ed. and trans. Harriett Spiegel. Toronto: University of Toronto Press.

——— 1999. *Lais*. Trans. Keith Busby and Glyn Burgess. London: Penguin.

Martianus Capella 1977. *The Marriage of Mercury and Philology*. Trans. William H. Stahl and Richard Johnson. Vol. 2 of *Martianus Capella and the Seven Liberal Arts*. New York: Columbia University Press.

McCash, June Hall 1997. "*Amor* in Marie de France's *Equitan* and *Fresne*: The Failure of the Courtly Ideal." in *The Court and Cultural Diversity*. Cambridge: D. S. Brewer. 179–88.

——— 2005. "Philomela's Window: Issues of Intertextuality and Influence in the Works by Marie de France and Chrétien de Troyes." In *De sens rassis: Essays in Honor of Rupert T. Pickens*. Ed. Keith Busby, Bernard Guidot, and

Logan E. Whalen. Amsterdam: Rodopi. 415–30.

McCreesh, Bernardine 1999. "Translation and Adaptation in *Lay le Freine*." *Forum for Modern Language Studies* 35: 386–95.

Mickel, Emmanuel J. 1971. "A Reconsideration of the Lais of Marie de France," *Speculum* 46.1: 39–65.

——— 1974. *Marie de France.* New York: Twayne.

Mora-Lebrun, Francine 1986. "Marie de France héritière de la lyrique des troubadours: l'exemple de *Chaitivel*." *Traveaux de linguistique et de littérature* 24.2: 19–30.

Murray, K. Sarah-Jane 2008. *From Plato to Lancelot: A Preface to Chrétien de Troyes*. Syracuse: Syracuse University Press.

——— 2011. "Marie de France, Ethicist? Questioning 'Courtly Love' in *Laüstic*." *Modern Philology* 109.1

Murray, K. Sarah-Jane and Preston Yancey 2010 (forthcoming). "Of Burning Books and Scalding Bathtubs: *Guigemar* and *Equitan* in Counterpart." *Le Cygne. Journal of the International Marie de France Society.*

Ovid 1984. *Metamorphoses*. 2 vols. Ed. G. P. Goold and trans. Frank Justus
Miller. Loeb Classical Library. Cambridge: Harvard University Press.

Pickens, Rupert T. 1996. "Marie de France and the Body Poetic." *Gender and Text in the Later Middle Ages*. Ed. Jane Chance. Gainesville: University Press of Florida. 135–71.

Prior, Sandra P. 1998. "*Kar des dames est avenu/ L'aventure*: Displacing the Chivalric Hero in Marie de France's *Eliduc*" in *Desiring Discourse: The Literature of Love, Ovid through Chaucer*, ed. James J. Paxson and Cynthia A. Gravlee. Selinsgrove, Penn: Susquehanna University Press. 123–39.

Shakespeare 1992. *Hamlet*. Ed. Barbara A. Mowat. The New Folger
Shakespeare. New York: Washington Square Press.

Rothschild, Judith 2005. "The Brutish World of Marie de France: Death and Violence in the *Lais*," *Le Cygne* 3: 23–34.

Tudor, Adrian 1993. "The Religious Symbolism of the Reliquary of Love in 'Laüstic,'" *French Studies Bulletin* 46: 1–3.

Whalen, Logan 2008. *Marie de France and the Poetics of Memory*. Washington, D.C.: Catholic University of America Press.

Virdiz, Maurizio 1993. "La tempesta e il mancato naufragio nell'*Eliduc* di Marie de France." *Naufragi: Atti del Convegno di Studi, Cagliari, 8–10 aprile 1992*. Ed. Sannia Nowé and Maurizio Verdis. Rome: Bulzoni Editore. 77–91. Reprinted in *Gloser la lettre*. 85–97.

Thomas Aquinas
On Evil

If Socrates were advising university professors today, to the Delphic maxim "Know yourself" he surely would add "and get to know your students." The fears and dreams they bring to the classroom are quite different from those that motivated their parents and grandparents. Back when I was an undergraduate during the Vietnam War years, the desire for personal freedom and a cynical appraisal of institutions were all the rage. Ethics classes grooved on what we called "existentialism" – a heady mixture of decontextualized snippets from Jean Paul Sartre, Albert Camus, and Friedrich Nietzsche swirled together to be "relevant" to our sophomoric hankering for safe rebelliousness and personal crankiness. Christian professors threw in their (unintentional) misreading of Søren Kierkegaard to demonstrate that smarter-than-thou disciples could be "existentialists" too. What formative influence did that curriculum have on our characters? Perhaps some future intellectual historian, weighing the Baby Boomer generation's contributions to culture, will tell us.

The Boomers' children and grandchildren who are filling university classes these days have different dreams. Some of them are overly career-oriented, but many share a youthful idealism quite distinct from their elders' hopes and dreams. With a longing for what has gone missing in their lives, they are not searching so much for personal freedom, individuality, and rebellion, as for personal commitment, community, and critical appropriation of tradition. They hunger for deep-rootedness and, consequently, the curriculum that fed the Boomer generation will no longer satisfy.

I do not raise this important contrast between the textures of youthful idealism in the current generation and my own because I think teachers must tailor their choice of texts to students' interests. After all, this anthology is about teaching *great texts*, whose value for guiding critical inquiry in the academy and informing students' character can stand the test of time and transcend many societal changes. Nevertheless, the enduring greatness of a text and the merit of studying it carefully with undergraduates can be more apparent at some times and places than others. I call attention to the distinctive features of the current generation's idealism because it leads me to a greater appreciation of Thomas Aquinas's *On Evil* (*Quaestiones disputatae de malo*).

Robert Pasnau thinks this is "Aquinas's finest work in moral philosophy," for it shows him "at his very best, arguing in careful and extended detail for a wide range of theses surrounding the ethical questions that he cared so deeply about" (Pasnau 2004, 599). In both its form and content, *On Evil* is remarkably suited to help the current generation articulate their yearning for commitment, community, and tradition. This work is a private disputation (*disputatio privata*), a "family affair" between Thomas Aquinas (1224/6–1274) and his students, in which they critically probe the Christian tradition of the capital vices, or "deadly sins."[1] These seven dispositions – vainglory, envy, spiritual apathy (*acedia*), anger, avarice, gluttony, and lust – are, on Aquinas's analysis, the inceptive deformations of the human self that partly have their origin, and their destructive outworking, in the distorted relationships and institutions of the wider society.

Idealistic students encounter a kindred spirit in Thomas Aquinas, who as a young man defied the desires of his privileged family to embrace the new intentional communities formed by Saint Dominic Guzman, the indefatigable reformer of thirteenth-century church and political life. Overly career-oriented students discover in this work an alternative vision that may "wake them from their dogmatic slumbers." My students' evaluations of *On Evil* are telling. In the semester-end reviews, they invariably rank it as the most difficult and least enjoyable text to read, but the most valuable and recommended to use again in an ethics course. "When we finally caught on to how to read *On Evil*, we learned so much from it" is a typical comment. I will never forget, however, when in mid-semester a young man in the front row blurted out, "This is the most *depressing* course I have ever taken!" That is not the sort of criticism a teacher can ignore, or put off with the usual "Let's talk about that problem later." Why was he so depressed? I asked, and he replied, "Because Aquinas is basically right."

I will return to address key points these comments raise about the text's *form* (a disputation format that my students struggle to interpret) and *content* (an unremitting gaze at the vices that distort the human self). But first I will sketch the Christian tradition that Aquinas and his students critically probe in *On Evil* – the rich moral psychology of the capital vices.

The Rich Tradition of the Capital Vices

The prototype of Aquinas's list of capital vices emerged as an instrument for spiritual self-examination and cultural critique among the fourth-century desert Christians. This motley group of disciples – many were peasants, but a few were highly educated and from privileged families – stepped away from the decaying Roman Empire and created intentional communities in the wilderness areas of Egypt, Palestine, and Syria.[2] Their ultimate goal was to restore the proper functioning of the mind (*nous*) to know God fully and to love God and one another unselfishly.

One of their leading theoreticians, Evagrius Ponticus (c.345–399), deploys an original schema of vices to characterize the adversaries they encountered in the struggle (*askêsis*) to become spiritually disentangled from the destructive wider culture.[3] In a number of works written to guide monastics in the Egyptian desert, Evagrius carefully analyzes eight dispositions that inhibit knowledge and love, and organizes them around corrupted human appetites (gluttony and lust), desires (greed and vainglory), and emotions (anger, restless spiritual apathy [*akêdia*], sadness, and pride); occasionally he adds a ninth disposition, envy. He generally characterizes these adversaries as evil thoughts (*logismoi*) and passions (*pathê*) because they are shaped by a person's free choices grounded in false conceptions and distorted desires. For each disposition he recognizes a corresponding demon (*daimôn*) or spirit (*pneuma*), a non-human rational agent who jealously attacks monastics through the psychological state in order to undermine their loving intimacy with one another and with God. With this fluid terminology Evagrius balances the individual's culpability for engendering the dispositions (or, at least, not trying enough to resist their formation) with due consideration of external influences that constantly threaten to distort the human self.[4]

Evagrius was a noted clinician who held conferences for his fellow monks in which he would diagnose their symptoms of spiritual decay and encourage remedial practices. "The brothers would gather around him on Saturday and Sunday, discussing their thoughts with him throughout the night, listening to his words of encouragement until sunrise. And thus they would leave rejoicing and glorifying God, for Evagrius's teaching was very sweet," Palladius (c.368–c.461) records in *The Life of Evagrius*. "Furthermore, he was so hospitable that his cell never lacked five or six visitors a day who had come from foreign lands to listen to his teaching, his intellect, and his ascetic practice" (Palladius 2004, 83–84).

While Evagrius's teachings had a profound, albeit dissimulated, impact on Eastern Christian ascetical theology,[5] they would have remained unknown in the Latin West were it not for the influential writings of his disciple, John Cassian (c.360–c.430). In *The Institutes* (*De coenobiorum institutis*), the Evagrian schema of eight vices becomes the heart of Cassian's guidance for creating intentional Christian communities in southern Gaul. After the five introductory chapters on prayer, Cassian devotes a chapter to each vice, diagnosing its symptomatic presentation and destructive potential before commending appropriate spiritual remedies. A few years later in his masterwork *The Conferences* (*Collationes*), Cassian summarizes the Evagrian model in the fifth conference, "On the Eight Principal Vices." Cassian prudently avoids the theological controversy that swirled around Evagrius by not mentioning his mentor's name at all, and wherever Evagrius's technical terminology might invite misunderstanding, Cassian substitutes a more acceptable scriptural phrase with no sacrifice of meaning.[6]

Aquinas undoubtedly discovered the tradition of the vices through *The Institutes* and *Conferences*, for these treatises were required reading (by Benedict's *Regula monachorum* 42.3 and 73.5) in the Benedictine community of Monte Cassino where he lived and studied for about eight years. Yet he cites these books only sparingly in *On Evil*. His primary source for interpreting the vices is Gregory's creative development of the tradition in *Morals on the Book of Job* (*Moralia in Job*).[7] Pope Gregory the Great (c.540–604) was the first monk to become pope, and in this work – a rambling, verse-by-verse, moral interpretation of the biblical book of Job – he frequently draws from his Benedictine training on the vices. In a remarkable commentary on Job 39:25, Gregory introduces the concept of seven principal vices (*septem principalibus vitiis*) and reshapes the tradition in two essential ways: he streamlines and reorders the list of vices to the seven that are the template for Aquinas's reflection,[8] but more importantly he articulates the notion that these are *principal* vices, or (what Aquinas calls) *capital* vices.

Gregory believes that wherever human beings sincerely desire to live virtuous lives together in community, they soon will encounter a spiritual struggle within themselves, an "invisible contest" to be free to love one another as they should. In this "spiritual battle of our liberation" (Gregory 1844–1850, XXXI, 45, n. 87) human beings are not defenseless, but they may be dangerously naïve, not even recognizing the advancing enemies of their love before it is too late. For this reason, they must cooperate with one another, through God's grace, to sharpen their capacities for self-reflection and self-concern. The increased vigilance they require, Gregory says, is prefigured in Job 39:25 in the heightened senses divinely bestowed on the warhorse:

> When the trumpet sounds, it says "Aha!"
> From a distance it smells the battle,
> the thunder of the captains, and the shouting.[9]

Giving a moral interpretation of this verse, Gregory warns that when persons progress in virtue, they will be attacked first by pride. If they accept pride's lie that they are self-made in their goodness, even their highest virtues may be twisted into vices. Their learning may give rise to arrogance, righteous zeal to uncontrolled anger, concern for justice to cruelty, and tenderness toward wrongdoers to moral carelessness (*Moralia*, XXXI, 45, n. 86). Only when they become self-righteous in this way will the seven vices assail them next. Gregory says these seven vices are principal, or leading, vices in two senses: they are *first in order of attack* after pride and, like thundering "captains," they *lead armies* of other vices that destroy persons' love for one another and God. In themselves, then, the seven vices are no more destructive of human agency, damaging to other people and the wider creation, or abhorrently wicked than many other traits. For example, a total loss of self-respect will undermine one's human freedom more than gluttony and the rest. Likewise, a murderer's sadism will maim one's body and a tyrant's cruelty will deform one's life more than the seven. Their prominence, for Gregory, is not due to their egregious violations of deontological limits or low scores on a utilitarian calculus. Rather they are harbingers of destruction. Noticing the first signs of their approach is an "early warning system" essential to awaking persons into resistance against all the vices that can destroy the human self and undermine human communities.

The Private Disputation Format

These writings on the capital vices in late antiquity are apothegmatic in form. Evagrius and Cassian thematically arrange pithy sayings, illustrative stories, and brief scriptural exegeses according to the schema of the eight thoughts, and Gregory discusses the principal vices in isolated passages in his commentaries, sermons, and a manual for pastors. These writers could assume that readers – usually priests in training or monastics – would relate the apothegms to one another and interpret them in "conferences," or teaching sessions, led by spiritual directors in intentional communities. This pattern of education continued for hundreds of years.[10] However, with the creation of medieval universities in the eleventh and twelfth centuries, the training of top church leaders shifted to classroom instruction. Aquinas's *On Evil* is the most thorough, systematic investigation of the capital vices written for use in the new universities.

On Evil is organized around fifteen major themes, or "questions," each one subdivided into one to fifteen more specific topics, or "articles." The first seven questions deal with foundational issues about the nature of evil, sin, the human self, and freedom. Gregory's account of the pivotal nature of the capital vices and their relation to pride is the topic of the eighth question. The remaining seven questions take up the capital vices one by one, beginning with vainglory and concluding with lust. A separate treatise on demonology is appended as a sixteenth question. However, since it was not included in the original manuscript and does not engage the tradition of the capital vices, I do not discuss it when I teach *On Evil*.[11]

Medieval university masters, or professors, often gave lectures on a major text and later published "commentaries" based on their lecture notes. But sometimes they offered more advanced courses in a discussion format and then wrote "disputations" that reproduced the give-and-take of classroom debate. *On Evil* seems to be based on a "private disputation," a form of seminar in which the master designed a series of questions to be debated through the semester. In each class meeting, students and bachelors (graduate students training to be masters) offered arguments on either side of an assigned question and a secretary recorded the proceedings. In the following period, the master answered the question and left no stone unturned, responding to every student's argument that ran counter to the master's considered view. Then the process began again. Aquinas famously mimics this format in *Summa Theologiae* and *Summa Contra Gentiles*, where he begins each article by stating a handful of opposing views before he articulates his own position and responds to the imagined opponents. In a disputation like *On Evil*, however, we sense a less polished and more real debate. Each article opens with ten to twenty thematically organized objections. Many of these objections inform Aquinas's answer to the question, and he concludes by responding to every one of them, sometimes at length.

Presumably the private disputation format used in *On Evil* was familiar and engaging to his medieval readers, but it is baffling for students today. Some of them mistake the opening objections (which may run to several pages in length) for Aquinas's own arguments, and thus conclude he is contradicting himself. Others understand how the format works, but think it wastes too much time getting to the point. To "catch onto" Aquinas today, students need to *understand* and *appreciate* how he presents his arguments.

To help my students *understand* the disputation format, I encourage them to read each article "backwards." They should start by studying Aquinas's answer to the question. Then they should read the most important replies to objections – the replies that break new ground by clarifying or extending Aquinas's argument in the answer. Often these important replies are the longer ones, but I tell students which ones I think are most significant. Finally, they should go back and read the initial objections that Aquinas has answered at length.[12]

To help them *appreciate* the disputation format, I explain how it represents a serious attempt by Aquinas to engage competing interpretations of texts and experiential insights. These interpretations and insights are offered, of course, not only by the students in his Paris classroom but also, through their citations of the literature, by various authorities in the philosophical and theological traditions they share. Through this sophisticated text, I assure them, Aquinas is inviting us to join a multi-layered intellectual community.

Evil, Sin, and Moral Wrongdoing

Today, when we categorize bad behavior in the most general way we usually describe it as morally wrong. Aquinas deploys a much richer conceptual scheme: he speaks of evil and sin as well as moral wrongness. This is why I ask students to begin reading *On Evil* at Question II, article 2, where Aquinas defines these basic concepts.

In response to the question "Does sin consist solely of the will's act?" Aquinas notes that "sin" (*peccatum*) has several meanings in ordinary usage. When we decry *the sin* that exists in the world, we refer to a condition of *sinfulness* – brokenness, "deformity," or "privation of form" – in ourselves or other things. When we complain that a person has committed *a sin*, we call attention instead to a particular *sinful act*. The act's sinful feature might be located in the person's disordered choosing to do it (which Aquinas calls the "internal act" or "will's act"), the damaging thing the person does or produces (the "external act"), or both.

To make sense of this, Aquinas distinguishes evil (*malum*), sin (*peccatum*) in a technical sense, and moral wrong (*culpa*) as nested categories.[13] In this conceptual scheme, evil is a "deformity," the condition of a thing that is not the way it is supposed to be; sin is "any disordered act" (voluntary or not) that expresses or reveals an underlying deformity; and moral wrong is a sin that "is voluntary…[for] the act is within the person's power" (Aquinas 2003, Q II, a 2). His examples of evil and sin are a crooked leg (a deformity) and limping on it (a disordered action that reveals the deformity).[14] To extend this example, intentionally breaking a leg, or failing to care for an injured leg (provided one could do so without too much trouble), would be morally wrong.

Many people use "sin" and "moral wrong" interchangeably, Aquinas admits, but he insists on giving "sin" a technical meaning to name a more general category of disordered actions than moral wrongdoing. Why would he do this? Throughout *On Evil*, Aquinas is alive to the fact that though the vices (*vitia*) are evil (*malum*) dispositions of distorted thinking, perceiving, and feeling, they can lead people to bad behavior (*peccatum*) in many ways. Sometimes people voluntarily choose the act (that turns out distorted) and are morally wrong (*culpa*), but other times they find themselves acting very carelessly, or even impulsively (as though by a spiritual addiction). In every case the actions are distorted, but the agents may not be fully blameworthy.

Analyses of the Vices

Aquinas turns in Questions IX through XV to provide conceptual analyses of the individual vices. These questions share a framework of three articles that investigate whether the disposition is a sin (*peccatum*), a mortal sin (*peccatum mortale*), and a capital vice (*vitium capitale*). In the first two questions, on vainglory and envy, Aquinas does not go beyond this basic outline; in the other questions he includes more articles to treat thorny issues raised by his analysis of a vice. Can the disposition toward anger ever be morally good, he wonders, and if so, how is it distinguished from hatred and envy, which are surely evil? Is the institution of usury (lending at interest) a societal expression of avarice? Is gluttony as complex a phenomenon as Gregory thinks? And, in regard to lust, what additional moral problems attend the variety of disordered sexual acts?

Because these seven questions are independent of one another, they are easy to reorder for classroom discussion. Sometimes I assign them in reverse (i.e., Evagrian) order beginning with gluttony and concluding with vainglory, or regroup them to highlight certain features of the vices.[15] I encourage students to compare Aquinas's conceptual analyses with other interpretations on offer – in significant texts from late antiquity through the renaissance,[16] contemporary writings that develop the tradition and deploy it for cultural critique[17] or personal examination,[18] treatments that are dismissive of the tradition and attempt to redefine the vices,[19] or rich exemplifications of the vices (and countervailing virtues) in art and literature.[20] In every case, they discover that Aquinas more than holds his own as a moral psychologist.

These analyses of the vices are the material in *On Evil* that some of my students, like the young man mentioned in the introduction, find "depressing." They become discouraged about themselves, their relationships, and the prospects for society for several reasons. On the one hand, Aquinas does not commend practices to resist the vices and to remediate the spiritual and social damage they cause. For completely neglecting this facet of the early tradition of reflection on the vices, he can be faulted. This significant shift in emphasis began historically as the social context of reflection on this material drifted away from spiritual conferences in intentional communities and moved into university classrooms. When students today become discouraged for this reason, they are recognizing that modern classrooms lack the requisite spiritual and intellectual community for a full and accurate interpretation of this complex tradition. I take this opportunity to reflect with them on the sort of community that could "handle" the unremitting gaze on human vice, and to consider the resources they might find in their families, friendships, student organizations, and religious congregations for spiritual examination, confession, and redemptive encouragement. We sample the remedies commended by Evagrius, Cassian, Gregory, and other writers in the early tradition. And we search for viable patterns of community in the central writings on friendship by ancient and medieval philosophers. No modern ethics class can be such a community, I admit to them, but it can provide them a framework to evaluate and treasure the relationships they will need in order to get at the truth about these vices. In Christian universities like Baylor, where I teach, practices of mutual discernment and accountability flourish in many university-sponsored venues – corporate prayer, worship, and Bible study groups in residential-learning centers; reflective service among the poor in the city or on short-term mission trips; and the spiritual friendships among faculty, staff, and students. Local congregations and parachurch organizations sponsor similar programs in most university communities. I encourage students to participate in these opportunities for spiritual correction and growth in virtue.

Another source of discouragement for students is that Aquinas does not analyze countervailing virtues, or dispositions that would enhance the proper functioning of the human capacities for love which these seven vices so badly disfigure. For this neglect, however, he should not be faulted. The tradition of the capital vices does not lend itself to this treatment. From the beginning it was an "early warning system" designed by and intended for people who are living together in community and find themselves in a spiritual battle with the distorting influences of the wider society. It was never intended to point toward a full account of human virtue.[21]

A colleague who teaches at Calvin College, Rebecca Konyndyk DeYoung, has an interesting response to this source of discouragement. Professor DeYoung introduces students to Aquinas's reflection on the capital vices through his analyses in *Summa Theologiae* II.II which are well integrated into his explication of the cardinal and theological virtues. While the *Summa* analyses run parallel to those in *On Evil* (Aquinas probably composed the two works simultaneously), they are shorter, not as fully developed, and tend to get lost among discussions of the many other vices that are opposed to the fundamental virtues.[22] For these reasons, I continue to commend *On Evil* to students and help them look for good news about the human condition in this text. That good news is lurking, ironically, within Aquinas's explanation of the "deadliness" and centrality of the seven vices.

Deadly Sins

For centuries the capital vices have been called "deadly sins" in more popular accounts. This description induces some interpreters to make wild speculations about their "deadliness" – that these vices will physically destroy those who have them, will cause them to kill others, are equally heinous traits, are worse traits than any other vices, will undermine their victim's moral autonomy, are unforgivable by God, and so on. In Aquinas, at least, we find none of this.

From the early Christian tradition, Aquinas inherited a complex distinction between mortal and venial sin that cuts across all sorts of distorted acts – not just the ones symptomatic of a capital vice. That is why "Is it a mortal (deadly) sin?" remains an open question that he must address when he delineates the actions characteristic of each capital vice.[23]

In Question VII, article 1, Aquinas sifts the tradition to find the essential difference between mortal and venial sin. Mortal sin, it is commonly said, deserves eternal punishment, while venial sin deserves only temporal punishment. Likewise, mortal sin deprives one of grace, while venial sin does not. These traditional elements are reflected in the etymology of "venial" from *venia* (Latin for "pardon"). Yet neither element can be the essential difference he is seeking, because whether actions are pardonable in this way must be grounded in something deeper in their nature. Some theologians trace the difference to human capacities involved: venial sin, they say, reflects a distortion in sense appetites only, while mortal sin involves reason and will. Aquinas rejects this approach too, arguing that venial sin can flow from a distorted human reason and will.

Aquinas construes sin and pardon relationally, on analogy with a disease (of the soul) and its cure by a physician. He writes, "Therefore, as there are some curable diseases and some incurable diseases, which we may call mortal, so there are some quasi-curable sins, which we call venial, and some sins of themselves incurable, which we call mortal, *although God can cure them*" (Aquinas 2003, Q VII, a 1, emphasis added). Just as incurable bodily diseases destroy the life of the body, so mortal sin – the deadly disease of the soul – destroys the spiritual "life principle," the very thing that defines human existence. Drawing now from the Christian theological tradition, Aquinas describes the spiritual "life principle," the *telos* human beings seek in all that they do, as a loving relationship with God and one another. Here, then, is the essential difference: mortal sin involves a turning of the human self away from God and neighbor, while venial sin does not.

To articulate further this essential difference between mortal and venial sin, Aquinas shifts to a different analogy in Question VII, article 11. Human love, he says, is similar to bodily heaviness (as understood in ancient physics). Consider how something heavy, say a rock in your hand, "desires" to continue down unless some other thing, like your hand, prevents it. If you move your hand away, of course, the rock will continue toward its goal until it "rests" on the ground. The rock is still "restless," for if you dig a deep hole in the ground, it will continue until it reaches the bottom, and so on. The ancient physicist would say the rock is restlessly seeking the center of everything, which happens to be at the center of the earth (because the earth is composed of all the rocks and other heavy stuff that beat your rock to the center of everything). Augustine had employed this beautiful analogy of human love to heaviness when he opened his *Confessions* with this prayer: "Man, a piece of your creation, desires to praise you…. You stir man to take pleasure in praising you, because you have made us for yourself, and our heart is restless until it rests in you" (Augustine 1991, Book I, Chapter 1). God, Augustine and Aquinas are saying, is the object of our desire for happiness, the very center of every personal relationship and community we seek, even if we do not realize this. Nothing else can explain our natural and undistorted movements toward any good person, place, or thing.

Now "both mortal and venial sin prevent perfect happiness, mortal sin in one way, venial sin in another way," Aquinas continues. "Just so, something heavy can be prevented from moving downward either because it has lost its heaviness [cf. mortal sin], or because there arises an impediment that prevents its movement from attaining its natural end [cf. venial sin]" (Aquinas 2003, Q VII, a 11). Venial sin is related to a person's perfect happiness, through fulfilling love for God and neighbor, the way your hand is related to the rock you are holding: the rock still desires to move on to its goal, but your hand is an "impediment." Venial sin distorts the human self in a similar way: though persons desire to love God and one another, they are not good at it because distorted thoughts about sex, money, personal status, or resentment get in the way. Mortal sin is much worse: it is as though the human self just hovers, no longer welcoming healthy personal relationship and true community with God and others. It has become focused on itself and lost its taste for the other.

The other differences between mortal and venial sin flow from this essential difference. In time and with God's help, every impediment to love can be cleaned away. This was the project of the desert Christians. If one rejects God's love, however, there is no other source of love, no other physician of the human self.

So here is the first bit of good news lurking in *On Evil*: the happiness that draws us, the goal of the moral life, is a personal God, rich in mercy and steadfast in love. The deprivation of grace, the eternal separation, and the total loss of desire for others that we rightly fear are all due to our unfaithfulness. On God's side there is only empowering grace: "*God can cure them*."

Capital Vices

Recall that Gregory says the capital vices are like "captains" who lead armies of vices that destroy persons' love for one another and God. And he takes names: "For from vainglory there arise disobedience, boasting, hypocrisy, contentions, obstinacies, discords, and the presumptions of novelties. From envy there spring hatred, whispering, detraction, exultation at the misfortunes of a neighbor, and affliction at his prosperity," and so on. How exactly do the capital vices lead their followers? "The first vices force themselves into the deluded mind as if under a kind of reason," Gregory says. They change how we think about ourselves and other people. Vainglory, for example, exhorts the "conquered" self, "You ought to aim at greater things…[so that] you may be able to benefit many other people." A fully reasonable person will see through this petty charade and laugh it off, but a vain person who is rather pleased with himself will be taken in "as if under a kind of reason" (Gregory 1844–1850, XXXI, 45, n. 88). Envy instructs the "conquered" self to think this way: "You think that fellow is better than you in some way? Why not refocus on this other quality or relationship, where you are clearly better than he? Base your self-worth on what you can do that he cannot! See, he has no reason to act so superior, or even equal, to your glorious self." It would sound so trite and unreasonable, if the person were not already captured by envy.

Aquinas analyzes the leadership style of capital vices in Question VIII, article 1. Each capital vice, from the word *caput* (Latin for "head"), directs the self into some twisted thinking and "deploys his army to attain his objective." This is a type of *formal* causation: the capital vice introduces a new end, or goal, at which the subordinate vices aim. It cannot invent a new goal *ex nihilo*, so it must "simulate happiness." That is, through deception and misdirection it makes one think its sham goal is really good. Vainglory, for example, in its little speech above, "aims to attain a good of the soul…namely the excellence of honor and glory" (Aquinas 2003, Q VIII, a 1). Gluttony and lust twist one's thinking about real goods of the body, and avarice distorts one's view of an external good.

That, at least, is the official theory Aquinas offers to articulate Gregory's rich metaphor of the commanding "captains." He deploys it successfully to explain the subordinate vices that Gregory associates with vainglory, envy, spiritual apathy, anger, and avarice, where he can show, "the other sins are oriented from [the capital vice], ordained to its end" (*alia vitia ex se oriuntur, ordinata ad finem eius*) (Aquinas 2003, Q IX, a 3). However, he admits that this official theory cannot explain the subordinate vices that Gregory associates with gluttony and lust. For example, Aquinas notes that the subordinate vices of gluttony on Gregory's list – sexual impurity, dulled senses, garrulousness, and rude gestures – "result from" (*consequi possunt*) the capital vice (Q XIV, a 4). In other words, Gregory is merely identifying bodily conditions (impurities, impairments, and obnoxious behaviors) that he thinks are caused by eating or drinking too much. Excessive consumption is the physiological cause of the subordinate vices, but there is no psychological connection of the sort the official theory predicts – that is, there is no false goal suggested by "immoderate pleasure in food and drink" that a person pursues via the vices on Gregory's list.

This is a significant fault in Aquinas's analysis. He misses an opportunity to correct Gregory's work and develop the tradition creatively. Surely there are vices – failures of hospitality, mistaken social policy priorities, false entitlements, and damaging social constructions of desire – that beset the glutton whose thinking has been "conquered" by the inordinate pleasures and ready availability of the preferred foods and drinks. Gregory and Aquinas's official doctrine could provide helpful insight here, but they fail to give it a chance in the cases of gluttony and lust.

And here is a second bit of good news in *On Evil*: even the destructiveness of the vices, Aquinas claims, is grounded in human nature being oriented toward the good. It follows that the personal relationship and community our students seek – even though they often pursue them in distorted ways including casual sex, fascination with social networking technologies, shallow engagement with social causes, and constructing their identities through consumer products – are true echoes of what human beings were created for. Likewise even the sophomoric rebellion against institutions by my generation is a deformed mask of a natural human longing for freedom – a desire to be free from all external coercion that might keep us from loving the good we were created to enjoy. The true, undistorted longings of every generation require no rejection or overcoming of human capacities, only their restoration and enhancement. The poet John Greenleaf Whittier gets it exactly right in his prayer:

> Dear Lord and Father of mankind,
> forgive our foolish ways;
> reclothe us in our rightful mind,
> in purer lives thy service find,
> in deeper reverence, praise.[24]

Conclusion

From the very beginning, unfettered love – or "to love as God loves," as Roberta Bondi puts it – was the *telos* of the self-examination and cultural critique grounded in the capital vices. The goal was to be freed by God's grace from dispositions that impede human beings from loving God and one another.[25] "Do not be conformed to this world," the Apostle Paul had urged the Christians in the capital of the Roman Empire, "but be transformed by the renewing of your minds (*nous*), so that you may discern what is the will of God – what is good and acceptable and perfect" (Rom. 12:2, NRSV), and the desert Christians took this injunction literally. They watched in one another for the thoughts, emotions, and actions symptomatic of the vices attacking those who were serious about restoring personal relationship and community, and traced these back into the surrounding disordered society. The gift they left behind for others who shared their dream is the rich tradition of the capital vices. In *On Evil*, Aquinas brings to philosophical articulation their framework for naming the distortions of love.

Robert B. Kruschwitz

References

Aquinas 1995. *On Evil.* Trans. John A. Oesterle and Jean T. Oesterle. Notre Dame: IN: University of Notre Dame Press.

Aquinas 2003. *On Evil.* Trans. Richard Regan. New York: Oxford University Press.

Augustine 1991. *Confessions*. Trans. Henry Chadwick. New York: Oxford University Press.

Bondi, Roberta C. 1987. *To Love as God Loves: Conversations with the Early Church*. Minneapolis, MN: Augsburg Fortress Press.

Born, Daniel, Mike Levine, and Don Whitfield, eds. 2007. *The Seven Deadly Sins Sampler*. Chicago, IL: The Great Books Foundation.

Born, Daniel, Molly Benningfield, Judith McCue, Abigail Mitchell, Lindsay Tigue, and Donald Whitfield, eds. *Even Deadlier*. Chicago, IL: The Great Books Foundation.

DeYoung, Rebecca Konyndyk 2009. *Glittering Vices: A New Look at the Seven Deadly Sins and Their Remedies*. Grand Rapids, MI: Brazos Press.

Dorotheos of Gaza 1977. *Discourses and Sayings*. Trans. Eric P. Wheeler, O.S.B. Kalamzoo, MI: Cistercian Publications.

Driscoll, O.S.B., Jeremy 1999. "*Apatheia* and Purity of Heart in Evagrius Ponticus." *Purity of Heart in Early Ascetic and Monastic Literature*. Eds. Harriet A. Luckman and Linda Kulzer. Collegeville, MN: Liturgical Press. 141–160.

Evagrius 2003. *Evagrius of Pontus: The Greek Ascetic Corpus,* Oxford Early Christian Studies. Trans. Robert E. Sinkewicz. New York: Oxford University Press.

Fairlie, Henry 1978, 1995. *The Seven Deadly Sins Today*. Notre Dame, IN: University of Notre Dame Press.

Funk, Mary Margaret 1999. *Thoughts Matter: The Practice of the Spiritual Life*. New York: Continuum.

Gregory 1844–1850. *Morals on the Book of Job*. Oxford: John Henry Parker.

Harmless, S.J., William 2004. *Desert Christians: An Introduction to the Literature of Early Monasticism*. New York: Oxford University Press.

Harmless, S.J., William 2008. "Monasticism." *The Oxford Handbook of Early Christian Studies*. Eds. Susan Amstrong Harvey and David C. Hunter. New York: Oxford University Press. 493–517.

Kent, Bonnie 2003. "The Moral Life." *The Cambridge Companion to Medieval Philosophy*. Ed. A. S. McGrade. New York: Cambridge University Press. 231–253.

Kreeft, Peter 1986, 1992. *Back to Virtue.* Ft Collins, CO: Ignatius Press.

Paladius 2004. *Four Desert Fathers: Pambo, Evagrius, Macarius of Egypt, and Macarius of Alexandria: Coptic Texts Relating To The Lausiac History Of Palladius*. Trans. Tim Vivian. Crestwood, NY: St. Vladimir's Seminary Press.

Pasnau, Robert 2004. "St. Thomas Aquinas, *On Evil* [book review]." *The Review of Metaphysics* 57, no. 2: 599–601.

Schimmel, Solomon 1997. *The Seven Deadly Sins: Jewish, Christian, and Classical Reflections on Human Psychology*. New York: Oxford University Press.

Solomon, Robert, ed. *Wicked Pleasures: Meditations on the Seven "Deadly" Sins.* Lanham, MD: Rowman and Littlefield.

Stewart, O.S.B., Columba 2005. "Evagrius Ponticus and the 'Eight Generic *Logismoi*.'" *In the Garden of Evil: The Vices and Culture in the Middle Ages*. Ed. Richard Newhauser. Toronto, ON: Pontifical Institute of Mediaeval Studies. 3–34.

Taylor, Gabriele 2006. *Deadly Vices.* New York: Oxford University Press.

Torrell, O.P., Jean-Pierre 1966. *Saint Thomas Aquinas: The Person and His Work*. Trans. Robert Royal. Washington, DC: The Catholic University of America Press.

Willimon, William H. 2005. *Sinning Like a Christian*. Nashville, TN: Abingdon Press.

Dante
The Divine Comedy[1]

Dante, it is sometimes said, is the most Christian of poets. Certainly, his dominant themes, from his works on interpretation ("Letter to Can Grande della Scala"; *Convivio*) through his *Vita Nuova*, a work which unites the genesis of inspiration in the poet with a lyricism born of human love which leads to the Source of Love, would be classics of Christian poetic reflection even if he had written nothing else. But he did write something else, above all his great *Commedia*, still universally regarded as the greatest epic work by a Christian, surpassing even as it predates Milton's *Paradise Lost*. What is most striking to a reader of the great texts of western tradition, however, is just how much of the pagan world is still present in Dante, and not merely as a foil for his Christianity. In fact, in this great poem, a *tour de force* of craftsmanship, encyclopedic in its learning, what may most strike the modern reader is just how powerful is the presence of the pre-Christian, Greek and Roman, literary past in Dante's medieval epic.

For a balanced reading by a student of great texts of this seminal and universal author it is essential that the *frisson* in his text between the glory that was Rome and the glory of human salvation in Christ be appreciated as just that—a fruitful tension in which the nobility of the one and the merciful charity of the other are mutually reinforcing. Virgilian *pietas* is not Christian piety, but one is better understood in terms of the other; Roman love for the city at the heart of the world (*amor/roma/amor*) is not the believer's yearning love for the celestial Jerusalem, but Dante's representation of love for one's true *patria* in either instance enriches both. For numerous intellectual topics, from the question of meaning in history to the formation of personal identity in terms of the larger meaning of human life, the relation of the highest good to the quest for the common good, of personal virtue to public virtue, Dante's poem extends rather than rejects, redeems rather than refutes, the great insights of the ancient poets and philosophers. In fact, for him these writers offer an important foundation for the truth of holy scripture and the writings of the fathers. His poem is thus a *locus classicus* for reflection on humanism and liberal learning in western culture.

The poem begins, however, with the persona Dante, stumbling about in the midst of a shadowed uncertainty regarding most of these things, having lost his way, *nel mezzo del camino da nostra vita*. The phrase makes it grammatically clear that he speaks not only for himself, but for a would-be Christian, would-be Roman culture that has also lost its way. In the internecine conflicts of the city from which he has been exiled, the power-grabbing, fragmentation and licentious sinfulness for which both the church and civil authorities had become notorious, it was clear enough to his immediate readers that their culture itself had lost its way—not just Dante's persona. Many people scarcely knew what to believe, or what to love.

Dante wrote the *Commedia* from exile in Ravenna, a small but beautiful city with the feel of a mausoleum, full of beautiful churches with gorgeous mosaic domes reflecting in their golden colors the splendor of a time that may have seemed less disordered by comparison. (It was not.) He reveals later in his poem that he has set the beginning of his representative spiritual exile on Good Friday, associating it both with the fall of Adam and the beginning of the decisive acts in history of human redemption. Dante the Easter pilgrim will journey down into Hell, back up through Purgatory, till he is able to see for himself what at the outset he is unable really to imagine, let alone believe—a glimpse, as Aquinas put it, of that vision of God in his essence which is the true object of every authentic quest for meaning, the goal to which the right use of faith and reason, poetry and history, would direct us.

For our purpose in this volume, we may learn much about how Dante effects his relation of pagan and Christian wisdom regarding the quest for ultimate meaning by beginning our examination, as for an epic is fitting, *in medias res*.

It is Easter morning, and the deep sapphire of the twilight sky has given way to the broad morning light. Dante and his guide Virgil are climbing up the lowest slopes of the mountain of Purgatory. For a time they are facing westward, when Dante glances to the ground, sees only one shadow there, and panics. "I thought I'd been abandoned," he says. When he turns round, Virgil meets his gaze and reads his thoughts. It is a moment of profound sadness.

Before I recount Virgil's words to Dante—words which I believe are among the most poignant and most significant in the *Divine Comedy,* and which speak to us directly as we heirs of rationalism attempt to read or to teach the sacred poem—I should like to recall what marvels Virgil has witnessed on this morning. At the seashore, it was Virgil, not the Christian Dante, who first perceived that the approaching glow upon the waters was an angel pilot speeding his boat to the mountain. Virgil has heard what he has never heard before: a communion of souls, singing a Latin hymn that unites them as a people more tightly knit than were the patriots of old Rome. That is because what unites them is not a nation or a way of life, but "quello Dio," as the heartbreaking Italian of *Inferno* had rendered it, "che tu non conoscesti," the God whom Virgil never knew:

> "*When from the land of Egypt Israel came,*"
> they sang together in a single voice,
> with all the verses written in that psalm. (2.46–48)

"So hard it was to found the Roman state," wrote Virgil, thinking of the hardships that his pious hero Aeneas had to face, hardships placed in his path by fate or by hostile gods. But these souls, made one in their faith, know nothing now of hardship and toil. "In the beginning there is always a gift," as Joseph Pieper (2009, 36) has said, and it is of the essence of their liberation from the bondage of sin that they receive the promised land as a gift, a Sabbath of milk and honey.

The angel then blesses the souls with the sign of the Cross, they disembark, and are free to proceed up the freedom-making mountain. But when they come upon our pilgrim poets and notice that Dante is breathing, they jostle up to him to behold the wonder, like townsmen who hear the tidings of peace. Dante's metaphor is apt, because these "spirits blessed by fate," these "happy souls," are a foreshadowing of the city of God, the city of peace. And sure enough, one of those childlike souls recognizes Dante and bursts into a gesture of spontaneous love:

> And one of them in pressing forward came
> to take me in his arms with love so warm,
> he moved me in return to do the same.
> Oh empty shadows, solid though you seem!
> Three times behind his back I clasped my hands,
> returning empty to my breast each time. (76–81)

The newly arrived soul, whom Dante has not yet even recognized, is his old friend from Florence, a singer and musician named Casella. The old annotators tell us that Casella had set Dante's youthful love poems to music, and indeed Dante will soon turn to Casella to ask him to sing one of those old songs to soothe his soul. It is the first time in the *Divine Comedy* that Dante will have turned to someone besides Virgil for consolation. He turns to his friend, to the youth they enjoyed in one another's company, and, implicitly, to Beatrice who inspired the love songs in the first place. It is a holiday moment that does more than commemorate the dead and gone: it brings it back to life with all its playful fervor.

No such holiday feeling can be found in the *Aeneid,* not even with its occasional quaint etiologies of Roman feasts. That already marks a great divide between the sacred poem and the Roman epic. But there is more. For Dante's Virgil is given to us, by a miracle of poetic insight, as a man, and as a man he too is made for praising God, nor will his heart rest unless it rests in God. So let us behold the man in this picture. All this time Virgil has but watched and listened, appreciating the friendship from without. He has in fact seen a moment from his own *Aeneid,* played out again in the major keys of faith, and hope, and charity. The moment is the failed embrace. For Aeneas had to make his way down to the underworld to learn from his father Anchises what he must do to settle his refugee people in Italy, and what the future would be of that city, Rome, which his descendants would found. Anchises is the most important human being in Aeneas's life; he is the "best of fathers," says Aeneas. Recall that paradigmatic emblem of piety sculpted so tenderly by Bernini: Aeneas, carrying his crippled father on his shoulders, a lion skin thrown about for the old man to rest upon, while the elder carries the figurines of the ancestral gods, and the younger takes by the hand his little boy, the future of the Trojan race. This best of fathers, then, long awaiting his son, greets him with joy when he meets him in the Elysian fields below. Aeneas tries to embrace him, but that desire will never again be fulfilled. His arms pass through the shadow of his father. He will never know the touch of the old man's hand again.

Now what makes Dante's meeting with Casella comic, rather than tragic? It is simply this. Casella has been saved, and Dante will be saved likewise. They will belong to the city above. At the resurrection of the flesh, they will see one another in the flesh again, and press the flesh, united by Christ, who took flesh of the Virgin, and died and rose again in the flesh. They will be invited to celebrate the wedding feast of the Lamb. For the moment, the two Italian friends know embarrassment and wonder and happy expectation. And Virgil looks on kindly, silently. It could not be borne upon him more forcefully that he who wrote about that body called Rome is not of the body; he who penned the scene between Aeneas and Anchises could not know the full meaning of that scene. That is because he lacked the faith. He is with Dante, then, and not with Dante. He is happy for Dante, but happy for a blessing he will never share, for at the resurrection of the flesh, he will be on the rim of hell, where perhaps a hand upon the shoulder of a fellow poet or philosopher will be the best he will know of such communion.

We know what faith it is that Virgil lacked. He was not Christian. But it is important to specify why Dante has made such a point of it, and what it has to do with the end of man as a being fulfilled, with all his fellows among the blessed, in the loving vision of the transcendent *Thou*—as Gabriel Marcel calls that God who is Himself a relationship of love. Dante was prescient in this regard, as one who has set his contemplation upon the eternal will always be. Many critics will call Dante the first modern, the first poet with a complete vision of a secular world. If he was such, I wish to assert that he was also and consequently the first man to reject the modern. That is, in his final masterpiece, while not disparaging the value of and the need for the city of man, Dante shows that what we call "secular humanism" is a contradiction in terms.[2] It is impossible; for what is fully secular can never be fully human.

Not that it was always clear that Dante would come to that conclusion. In his *Convivio,* as Etienne Gilson discusses in *Dante the Philosopher,* our poet shouldered metaphysics aside from its primacy among philosophical studies and replaced it with ethics, specifically political ethics (see Gilson 1948). In doing so he departed from his two great masters, Aristotle and Thomas Aquinas. More to the point, he took up a suggestion from Thomas, that a just and wise life in a well-ordered state would fulfill the yearnings of man's nature—for heavenly beatitude, says Thomas, is an elevation of man beyond himself; it is a supernatural good, over and above all of man's natural longings (Thomas Aquinas 1957, Book 3, Part II, chapters 25–51). Since reason could provide this natural and secular good on its own—so goes Dante's thinking in the *Convivio*—there ought to be a severe separation of philosophy and theology, just as there ought to be a separation between the powers of the pope and those of the emperor. Linked with this line of argument is a latent rapprochement to the work of the Arab commentator on Aristotle, Averroës. I hope I do not sacrifice too much subtlety here for conciseness, but Averroës denied the survival of the individual person, arguing that whatever we possess of active understanding we possess by participating in a great and impersonal and ectoplasmic Agent Intellect, into which our portions of intellect are reabsorbed at our death. There is a cryptic materialism, then, in Averroës. We are not agents in our own right, not persons whose souls are *capax universi,* but the sufferers of actions that impinge upon us from without. The sacred Qur'an is but a tissue of quaint poetical allegories to satisfy those minds that cannot ascend to—or I should say that refuse to surrender to—this doctrine.

I am not saying here that Dante had ever lost his Christian faith, or that in the *Divine Comedy* Dante has rejected his insistence that Empire and Papacy ought to mind their own business. His greatest invectives, against Boniface VIII and Philip the Fair, attack what he saw as transgressions of the spiritual authority upon the secular and of the secular authority upon the spiritual. But I do say that he has tried the way of the *Convivio* and found it wanting. That he finds it so, can be seen in the person of Virgil. For if anyone could stand for the man supremely wise in the natural virtues, and wholly devoted to the good of an earthly community, that would be Virgil. But it is Virgil, as wise and devoted as he is, who shows us that the earthly city is as nothing compared with the city we truly long to enter.

It is an odd paradox. Precisely because Dante holds reason, by which he means principally moral reason, in such high esteem, he gives us a Virgil whose only sin is that of omission: he did not "give God homage as [he] ought" (*Inf.* 4.38). As a consequence Dante could not allow Virgil to enter Paradise: that would breach the separation of intellectual disciplines upon which he founds his politics, and which allows him to grant so high a dignity to reason. All this would be fine and clear, *except* that by the time Dante writes the *Comedy* he has committed himself once again to the love of his youth, that mysterious love of the young lady named Beatrice, who comes to be for Dante a sacramental means for encountering the love of Christ. It is that transcendent love for which he longs, which no earthly empire no matter how grand can fathom or contain, and which he now cannot help but confess is the God-ordained end for man – and therefore for man's reason.

So then, we return to that moment on the mountain, when Dante wheels about in a panic, and sees that Virgil is beside him after all. Virgil's words suggest that again he, not Dante, was the first to notice something. He has seen the single shadow there. It has made him recall already the body that he left above, and that other body, the city called Rome, which once inspired his song. Yet his words to Dante bespeak a man for whom that communion, with its limited vision, is not enough:

> And then my strength, my comfort, said to me:
> "Even now, such little faith? Don't you believe
> that I am with you, and will guide your way?
> The evening falls already by that tomb
> where lies the body that once cast my shadow,
> for Naples took it from Brundisium.
> Thus if no shadow follows where I go,
> it's no more wondrous than that heavenly light
> shines unencumbered by the spheres below.
> To suffer the tormenting fire and ice
> the Power assigns us bodies that are like,
> but never wills to show us how He does,
> For, trusting to man's reason, mad is he
> who hopes to plumb the endless ways of those
> three Persons in substantial unity.
> Be satisfied with '*So it is*,' O Man,
> for if you could have known the whole design,
> Mary would not have had to bear a son;
> And you've seen men desire in vain before,
> whose intellects might well have calmed the yearning
> that now is made their sorrow evermore:
> I speak of Aristotle and of Plato
> and many others," and he bowed his head,
> troubled, and did not say another word. (3.22–45)

All Virgil needs to say here, one would think, should be, "Don't you remember that I have no real body?" But the insubstantiality of Virgil's body should strike us as puzzling. After all, Virgil has led Dante by the hand. He will help pull him up tough passages on the mountain. He held him tight when in Hell they descended upon Geryon's back down to the pouches of the fraudulent. He turned him around fast lest he look upon the Medusa, and covered his eyes with his hands. His affection for Dante has been expressed with warm physicality.

A poet of far less genius than Dante would have averted the contradiction. We must conclude then that Dante intends the contradiction, and, given that it is Dante we are talking about, that he means something surprising by it. Virgil's words suggest more than that reason cannot find out everything. Dante had already conceded as much in the *Convivio. They suggest that reason cannot find out everything that reason would:* that reason is not only limited, but unfulfilled, pointing towards something beyond itself, something that might have "calmed the yearning" of the greatest minds of the past, those of Aristotle and Plato. But there is still more here. For the question of the moment has to do with bodies, and we can never think of those in Dante without thinking also of families, cities, and states, communities of virtue and love. Indeed Virgil thinks first, wistfully, of his own body, of how he died while waiting to set sail from Brundisium, and of how Augustus Caesar, in tribute to his friend, had the bones removed to Naples, where they were nobly entombed. It was a good thing for Augustus to do, but it was still only an entombment, and not even within Rome itself. In short, it is not simply that reason cannot speak of the deepest truths of God. It is that even in the things that concern us most upon earth, for instance our common life in the body, reason falls short. It gives us no cause for hope, and none for hope's object, which is love.

If I am right, Dante has seen that reason severed from faith must end in a terrible distortion or constriction of our desires, *and that no really thriving community can be built upon it.* That is a point illustrated by the materialist heretics in Hell. They and their comrades in heresy dwell within tombs, like with like. Dante seems to have chosen the tomb as punishment to correspond with the particular heresy he highlights, that of materialism. Says Virgil:

> These will be bolted on the day of doom
> when from the Valley of Jehosophat
> the souls bring back their bodies to the tomb.
> On this side, in his cemetery, lies
> that Epicurus with his followers who
> put it that spirit dies when body dies. (*Inf.* 10.10–15)

Now Dante will meet exactly two spirits in this ring: the grand and impressive Farinata, with his great chest and great brow, "surging as if he held all Hell in scorn" (36), and the timid, plaintive Cavalcante de' Cavalcanti, father of Dante's best friend and fellow poet Guido Cavalcante, who rests his chin on the edge of the tomb and longs to know where his son Guido is. These two spirits personify two ways in which Dante himself might have gone wrong: by believing, like Farinata, that only the material fortunes of his family and party were worth living for; or by believing like Cavalcante, that the height of human glory is to be found in artistic achievement. Both are men of ardor—yet ardor that is curiously trammeled up in the self. Both are in for a cruel disappointment here. Farinata, the political strongman, whose family was exiled from Florence because of their part in the massacre of Montaperti, will hear from Dante that that family has not yet returned to the city, nor is their return likely. Cavalcante, the doting father, will *think* he hears from Dante that his son Guido is dead. Farinata remains unreconciled with Florence, and irreconcilable; Cavalcante fears he will never see his son again. It seems not to matter to him that Guido would have to go down to Hell for that.

Farinata loved Florence, and though he was a leader in that massacre, yet he stood up for her when his victorious party wanted to destroy her. Says he:

> But when each man agreed to wipe away
> Florence from off the earth, I was alone,
> her sole defender in the sight of all. (91–93)

He loves in vain; he cannot amend the wrong he did. He is a failed patriot; and I believe we must see his failure as inextricable from his narrow materialist vision. As Cavalcante is a failed father. When the old man asks Dante why Guido is not with him, he makes a curious, even bizarre assumption—bizarre for someone who should know by now that there are powers beyond that of the human mind. He assumes that it is "genius at its height" that is leading Dante along the tracks of Hell, a powerful intellect working by itself. But Dante replies with cautious modesty:

> "I haven't come here on my own.
> He who stands waiting leads me through this place,
> for one your Guido, maybe, held in scorn." (61–63)

The old man will hear only one word—"held," and only really the past tense of it, crying in despair that Guido therefore must be dead, and somehow not understanding that if Guido is dead and is *not* in Hell, that would be a good thing for him. But Dante's words, as I read them, suggest that Guido, maybe, held in scorn the one to whom Virgil submits in leading Dante through Hell. That one would be Beatrice, and the one to whom Beatrice ever directs our gaze, Christ. *If* Guido did hold Beatrice in scorn (and Dante leaves open the possibility that his Averroist friend and love poet died repentant), then the fault is in part Cavalcante's—or Dante's own. What might have happened to Guido is what would have happened to Dante, had not Virgil come to rescue him from the dark wood of error.[3]

Now that is an odd thing, too: Virgil, apparently the embodiment of the best that human reason alone can do, Virgil the poet and patriot, comes to rescue Dante from what Gilson called "philosophism." I might call it more particularly the wood of rationalist or positivist error, the error of believing that the earthly city is enough, or that you can even have a genuine communion on earth without its being a shadow of, or participation in, the communion of saints above. As Virgil refers to Farinata with great respect, but does not speak to him, so genuine reason keeps rationalism at a distance; they are not the same thing, because reason loves what rationalism does not grasp, and what rationalism does grasp, it mishandles and loves badly. So when Farinata foretells that Dante himself will be a victim of exile from Florence, Virgil soothes his friend not with a counter-prophecy about the city, but with a promise that someone else, someone beautiful, will bring him both knowledge and comfort:

When you shall come before the radiance
of that sweet soul whose lovely eye sees all,
from her you'll learn the journey of your life. (130–32)

For Virgil is a man of love. Since he does not have the faith, he will not enjoy the fulfillment of his love; but as reason is oriented towards the beauty it cannot explain, so Virgil is moved not by calculation but by love. The reader is meant to recall that after Virgil told Dante that he could not escape from the dark wood except by undertaking a journey to behold the damned, our poet got cold feet. He did not want to go. Indeed he thought it might be "folle" to go, mad, unreasonable. At which point Virgil did not give him a lesson in philosophy. He did not lay before him a kind of Pascal's wager: if you stay here in the wood, you shall certainly be lost, but if you come with me, you stand half a chance. Instead he told him a story of courtly love:

I was among the souls in Limbo when
so lovely and blest a lady called to me,
I asked her for the grace of a command.
Her eyes where flashing brighter than the stars,
and she addressed me with an angel's voice,
sweetly and softly, in such words as these:
"O kind and gracious soul of Mantua,
whom the world still renowns and ever shall,
whose fame will last as long as earth endures,
The friend I love—and not a fortune-friend—
has been so checked along his journey up
the desert slope, he has turned back for dread,
And from what I have heard of him in Heaven
I fear he may have wandered so far wrong

my rising for his help may come too late.
Go then, and with the beauty of your words,
and any skill you have to set him free,
help him, that I may be consoled. I am
The blessed Beatrice who bid you go;
love makes me speak, and bade me hasten from
the place that stirs my longing to return.
When I shall stand before my Lord, I vow
often to speak to Him in praise of you." (2.52–74)

It is a tale of astonishing beauty, and surprise. Virgil's courtly submission is heartfelt and immediate. He disposes himself entirely to Beatrice, asking her "for the grace of a command" even before he knows who she is and what she wants. It is the right and reasonable thing for him to do. The first stars Virgil sees after his death are the eyes of Beatrice, who breaches the limits of Hell for love. Then Virgil's friendship with Dante is born here, in his prior love for Beatrice; but beyond even that, in the whole communion of love that Paradise is, the divine love that has spurred Beatrice to leave Heaven, and that stirs her "longing to return." We will indeed learn that Beatrice's act of love has been preceded by the love of Mary and Saint Lucy, who encourage her to help the lost poet. Virgil hears all of this, and wondrously becomes a part of it, a crucial part, in the grace and providence of God. He will even hear that at least in praise, he will be a part of the communion of saints, when Beatrice speaks to God about his goodness.

Then perhaps we understand Virgil's role in the poem best not as thinker, but as teacher and friend, in whom the conclusions of reason are not to be severed from love, and, moreover, whose love yearns beyond the bounds of reason. There is instilled in Virgil, mysteriously, a love that walks to the threshold of faith and that somehow, by the grace of God, glimpses beyond. Virgil *sees Beatrice;* that in itself is remarkable. When he and Dante approach the wall of fire that separates every soul in Purgatory from Earthly Paradise at the summit of the mountain, he must again persuade the poet to overcome his fears. Initially he tries arguments from reason and experience, even from empirical evidence—begging Dante to test the fire by holding the hem of his tunic to it, to see that in fact it will not burn. But Dante is immovable. Whereupon the reasonable man sees that it is time to appeal to love. Says Virgil, again a little troubled, "Son, look now, / what's keeping you from Beatrice is this wall" (*Purg.* 27.35–36). And even as they walk through that fire—so hot, Dante says, that to cool off he would have leapt into boiling glass—Virgil encourages his friend with a vision of the beautiful beloved: "I think I can already see her eyes" (54).

They pass through the fire, and although Virgil bravely acknowledges that he has reached the limit of his instruction, and that Dante is to take not his own reason but his own *pleasure* for his leader now, yet he remains awhile, walking with the younger poet through the grass and the flowers of Eden, beholding the pageant of the Old and New Testaments led by the griffin, the eagle-lion symbol of Christ Himself, and seeing, veiled atop her chariot, Beatrice, embodiment of the faith he did not have. It is the last time in the poem that he shows himself quicker to understand than Dante is, for when Dante, overcome by the power of love that penetrates the veil and sees before the eyes and the mind can see, turns to Virgil with words from the man's own *Aeneid,* to say, "I know the traces of the ancient flame!" (30.48), Virgil has

> deprived us of his light,
> Virgil the sweetest father, Virgil, he
> in whom I trusted that I might be healed. (49–51)

It is also his last act of love, graciously to give way, to allow Dante to meet the new teacher, the beloved, who yet will utter both men's names with a stern but motherly tenderness:

> Dante, because Virgil has gone away,
> do not weep now, now's not the time to weep;
> another sword must make you cry today. (55–57)

For the briefest moment the three are together—almost. Then Virgil will return to the shadowy fragments of community to be found among the best of those who had not the faith. They speak little, down there. What, finally, would there be to speak about?

I will not here discuss the possibility of salvation for such people as Virgil. Thomas Aquinas had left the door ajar, and so does Dante, I believe, when he discusses the presence of the pagans Trajan and Ripheus in the circle of the just rulers, in Paradise. Instead I wish to affirm that just as the reasonable thing for reason to do is to fall in love, so the entire theology of Dante's *Divine Comedy* overleaps itself, so to speak, ever pitching headlong into the joy of communion. Reason stands trembling at the threshold of love; speech stammers before it bursts into song.

And the *Paradiso* is that love song. We have, for instance, the beautiful nun Piccarda, in the lowest of the heavenly spheres, smiling "like a girl in the gleaming of first love," giving Dante what looks at first like a theology lesson, when he asks whether she and her companions desire a higher place. "Recall," she says, "that heaven is / to live in loving, necessarily." But her reply soon swings into a hymn of love:

> For it is of the essence of this bliss
> to hold one's dwelling in the divine Will,
> who makes our single wills the same, and His,

So that, although we dwell from sill to sill
throughout this kingdom, that is as we please,
as it delights the King in whose desire
We find our own. In His will is our peace." (*Par*. 3.7–85)

Ne la sua volontade e nostra pace, says she. She loves to be where she is, and to see what she sees, because she is wholly in love with the One who gives her and her fellows their place. Or we might recall the magnificent conclusion to Canto 10, after Thomas Aquinas—of all people, that titan of an intellectual—has cheerfully named himself and the eleven other souls in the garland of the theologians. It is an image of reason ordered to love:

Then like a tower clock that tolls the hour
when the bride of the Lord rises to sing
morningsong to her Spouse, to win His love,
Sounding so sweet a knelling of ting ting
as all the gears within it push and pull,
a soul that's well disposed must hear the ring
And swell with love: so now I saw that wheel
rendering voice to voice in harmony,
and in sweet temper that no man can feel
If not where joy is for eternity. (10.139–48)

But most of all I here recall the scene wherein Dante, like a bachelor about to take his oral examinations in theology, is grilled by Saints Peter, James, and John on faith, hope, and charity. Beatrice appeals to this "brotherhood elected for the great / feast of the blessed Lamb" (24.1–2), and like dancers they descend, one of them "turning in three turns round Beatrice," singing a hymn whose words Dante cannot comprehend. When finally he can make out the words, it is Peter, exclaiming:

"My holy sister! So devotedly
do you beseech, so ardent is your will,
it has unbound me from that lovely sphere." (24.28–30)

It is in *this* context of loving brotherhood that, I believe, we are called to define faith; not the solipsistic motion of a proud mind attempting to understand all things, but the happy submission of a humble mind to those truths given to the communion of the Church.

In other words, faith by its very nature partakes of the mystery of song. And that is hard for us in our tuneless age to conceive. When God said, "Let there be light," he uttered no conclusion of an argument, but rather by love brought something into existence which need not have been. Saint Augustine, that other titan of an intellectual, is reputed to have said, "He who sings prays twice," and "Singing is what the lover does." Indeed, because song is playfully extra, gratuitous, exuberant, free. God did not need to create, and the grateful singer does not need to sing, but God creates out of love, and man responds with hymns of praise. Virgil did not merely speak about Rome, but, as Dante affirms with just precision, *sang of it,* and sang of the just man Aeneas and his wanderings. He was a singer, and therefore a lover, for singing is what the lover does. So too what the believer does, as his heart yearns to behold Him who is even here, now, nearer to us than we are to ourselves, yet hidden, as behooves the object of a desire that is God-given and godlike.

And so we see this permeation of faith by ardent song all through the examination that Peter administers. Peter asks Dante to define the virtue, and Dante gives us its classic formulation from Saint Paul (though Hebrews [11:1] is not now thought to be by Paul, it was then), but not before he tells us what Peter and Paul were to one another and to Rome:

"Father, as it was written by the true pen
of your beloved brother Paul, who joined
your work in setting Rome on the good line,
Faith is the substance of things hoped for and
the argument of things not come to light.
This is its essence, as I understand." (61–66)

And what do we hope for? Dante will answer that question, asked by Saint James, in the next canto, with a surprise: "to be robed with a double robe," body and soul, "in our true land, this land of Paradise." Again, it is not a solipsistic engulfing, but life in a country, body and soul, where the blest can once again behold the faces of

their mammas,
their fathers, and the others they held dear,
before they had become eternal flames. (14.64–66)

But the examination with Peter continues: Whence do you derive your belief? What makes it reasonable? Why should you trust the testimony of scripture? Once Dante has dispatched all these questions, master and pupil reach the climax of it all, when Dante must profess what he in fact believes. And again we find reasoning overleaping itself into love—as does faith itself, for it was faith that caused Peter to outrace John to reach the tomb, says Dante. At last, echoing both the great *Summa* of Thomas *and* the love poetry of his youth, Dante begins:

E io rispondo: Io credo in uno Dio
solo ed etterno, che tutto 'l ciel move,
non moto, con amore e con disio.

And I respond: I believe in one God,
sole and eternal, who was never moved
but moves all Heaven with love and with desire. (24.130–32)

And, after affirming the doctrine of the Trinity, that fundamental communion of love, Dante describes what the faith means to his heart:

This is the spark, this is the principle
that spills out into such a living flame
it glitters like a star within my soul. (145–47)

At which noble Saint Peter, he of the massy keys, dances for welcome and for joy:

When a lord listens to what pleases him,
soon as his servant finishes he'll fling
his arms around him for the happy news—
So did he bless me now, so did he sing
three times encircling me with happy light,
that apostolic lamp at whose command
I'd spoken what had brought him such delight! (148–154)

It is a gladness that reason can see from afar. Good reasons there are to believe, but the sweetest reason is the inebriating laughter of the blessed, the joy of love. For where there are nations and just laws, they and their laws will pass away; and where there are philosophers speaking in tongues stranger than those heard in the ruins of Babel upon the plains of Shinar, those tongues shall fall silent. For we long not to see truth as the conclusion of a syllogism, but to know Truth, even as we are known. We long to know Him in the flesh, to see Him face to face, Him who unites us in one flock, one body. We long to utter praises to Him that the spoken word cannot rein in from singing. Therefore these three remain, faith, hope and love, and the greatest of these, the one that moves the sun and the other stars, is Love.

Anthony Esolen

References

Auerbach, Erich 1974. *Mimesis: The Representation of Reality in Western Literature*. Trans. Willard R. Trask. Princeton: Princeton University Press.

de Lubac, Henry 1995. *The Drama of Atheist Humanism*. San Francisco: Ignatius.

Gilson, Etienne 1948. *Dante the Philosopher*, trans. David Moore. London: Sheed and Ward.

Pieper, Joseph 2009. *Leisure: The Basis of Culture*. Trans. Alexander Dru. San Francisco: Ignatius Press.

Thomas Aquinas 1955–1957. *Summa Contra Gentiles*. Trans. Anton Pegis, Anderson, Bourke and O'Neil as *The Truth of the Catholic Faith,* 5 vols. New York: Doubleday.

SUGGESTED FURTHER READING

Freccero, John 1986. *Dante: The Poetics of Conversion*, ed. Rachel Jacoff. Cambridge: Harvard University Press, 1986.

Hollander, Robert 1996. "Dante's Deployment of *Convivio* in the *Comedy*." *Electronic Bulletin of the Dante Society of America*. October 7.

——— 1993. "Le opere di Virgilio nella *Commedia* di Dante" in *Dante e la 'bella scola' della poesia: Autorità e sfida poetica*. Ed. A. A. Iannucci. Ravenna: Longo. 247–343.

Mastrobuono, Antonio C 1990. *Dante's Journey of Sanctification*. Washington, D.C.: Regnery Gateway.

Mazzotta, Giuseppe 1993. *Dante's Vision and the Circle of Knowledge*. Princeton: Princeton University Press.

Moore, Edward 1969. *Scripture and Classical Authors in Dante*. Oxford: Clarendon Press.

Singleton, Charles 1960. "In exitu Israel de Aegypto." *Annual Report of the Dante Society* 78: 1–24.

Catherine of Siena
The Dialogue

On October 4, 1970, Catherine of Siena (1347–1380), together with Teresa of Avila, was honored with the title of doctor of the church (and was the youngest at the time of her death to be so recognized).[1] A Dominican tertiary, her writings reflect a contemplative's devotion to prayer combined with an active life of service to the church, especially to the sick and poor. In her book *The Dialogue* Catherine reminded her readers that the women and men with whom they share this world are not just objects or even primarily subjects of their own thoughts and feelings, but signs of God's intentions for creation, and thus they help to mark the way of union with God. According to Catherine, God says to the soul:

> I ask you to love me with the same love with which I love you. But for me you cannot do this, for I loved you without being loved. Whatever love you have for me you owe me, so you love me not gratuitously but out of duty, while I love you not out of duty but gratuitously. So you cannot give me the kind of love I ask of you. This is why I have put you among your neighbors: so that you can do for them what you cannot do for me – that is, love them without any concern for thanks and without looking for any profit for yourself. And whatever you do for them I will consider done for me. (Catherine 1980, 121; see 165)

According to her biographer, Raymond of Capua, she insisted that the commands to love God and neighbor were the two feet on which we must walk in the way of Christ, which is indeed the way of wisdom.[2]

In addition to her exemplary spiritual life and writings, Catherine wielded a tremendous amount of social influence during her short lifetime. She was frequently called upon to serve as a mediator in disputes between the prominent families of Italy, and traveled to Pisa, Lucca and Florence on diplomatic missions. In 1376 she went to Avignon, where she met with Pope Gregory XI in an attempt to make peace between the papacy and the Florentines, urging the pontiff to return to Rome (which he eventually did, though he died shortly thereafter). Unfortunately, her many attempts at reforming and unifying the church eventually came to naught.[3]

Catherine's book brings new and intriguing issues to the present conversation about the reading of great texts, above all, the impact of medieval mysticism upon the quest for wisdom. In this important work she fashioned a compelling picture of a human life well lived, holding together what may seem to us to be contrary tendencies: contemplation and the active life, prayer and corporeal works of mercy, reason and revelation, the acquisition of virtue and absolute dependence on God's grace, the life of the mind and the life of the affections, the importance of ascetic discipline and the inclusion of the laity who walk the ordinary way of love. As a lay member of the Dominican order, she commended neither the cloistered existence of the convent nor the solitary life of her contemporary Francesco Petrarch as the proper context for the pursuit of wisdom, but lived fully in the world. She did not marry as was expected of women outside the convent, but lived an ascetic life in the midst of the world, both the rich and powerful, and the poor and dying.

The Dialogue, the only book that Catherine produced, also provides insight into important developments in the first few centuries of the second millennium in the way Christians had come to understand the beginning and end of human life. It therefore merits serious consideration for its place within the unfolding tradition of medieval theology and spiritual formation, especially in light of the emergence of women authors such as Gertrude the Great, Mechthild of Hackeborn, Bridget of Sweden and Marguerite d'Oignt in the late thirteenth and fourteenth centuries.[4] In what follows I shall first engage in a close and charitable (though altogether too brief) reading of its plain sense, following its depictions and descriptions, injunctions and narrations as traditionally done within its primary interpretive context (in this case, medieval Catholic theology and spirituality). We might describe this mode of reading as embarking on a journey of sorts, with Catherine's text as itinerary or guide. This image is particularly appropriate for this work, given its subject matter. In a manner not unlike that of Bonaventure (and of course many others), Catherine's primary concern is to direct the soul to union with God.

I shall then examine *The Dialogue* as we would any important text, with all the critical tools at our disposal, and specifically, as set within the larger "text" of theology and spiritual formation in the Middle Ages (which in turn forms a substantial section in the even larger text that is a great texts curriculum). This tradition, extended in time and embodied in particular social groupings, can be parsed into three dimensions – the social-historical, the literary-rhetorical, and the philosophical-theological. These dimensions are inextricably connected and therefore cannot be treated reductively. Careful consideration of these dimensions is invaluable for any great texts curriculum that has wisdom for its end.

Instances of the interconnections between these dimensions abound in *The Dialogue*. For our purposes perhaps the most significant begins with an analysis of the literary dimension, which is structured around a dialogue between God and "the soul." Catherine's selection of genre raises a question as to its theological meaning as well as its historical and social setting. Is she essentially recounting so-called "mystical experiences" in the book, as some believe (including some of her most devout proponents), so that her third-person references to the soul are largely circumlocutions for her own private, ecstatic encounters with the divine? This reading presupposes, in an entirely anachronistic fashion, a conception of human knowledge that depicts the knowing subject as an isolated individual unencumbered by particular times, places and traditions. Both the activity of knowing and the justification of knowledge are thus defined from a first-person perspective: How can *I* be sure that *my* beliefs, *my* perceptions, *my* experiences connect reliably with the external world? (MacIntyre 1990, 12; cf. Taylor 1995, 1–8). Problems of knowledge, and *mutatis mutandis* of spirituality, are thus conceived under the image of an engineering project, seeking to determine the best way to build a reliable bridge across that "space" that separates the disembodied subject from the "external" world (or God).[5] If this is the case, then to misquote Alfred North Whitehead, religion really is something that principally happens to individuals in their own solitude (Whitehead 1926, 16).

However, if we associate Catherine more closely within her social and historical setting, we will read her dialogue within the context of a rhetorical tradition that dates back to antiquity, and which typically treats moral, spiritual and epistemic questions from a third-person, communal standpoint. From this context a person's soul is but one of many, and her or his intellectual, moral and spiritual pilgrimage can only be rightly understood in terms of a teleological account of souls as such. According to this conception, a soul is said to know something, not when it has successfully spanned the "ditch" between it and the external world, but when it has progressed along a path that culminates with it becoming formally identical with its proper object, in this case, union with God (MacIntyre 1990, 12; Taylor 1995, 3). The best example of this approach is the conversation that Augustine recounts in his *Confessions* between himself and his mother Monica shortly before her death. Together they seek to discover, in light of present truth, the Truth that is God. As they lift their gaze upwards, they leave behind all creatures, including the sun, moon and stars, ascending by inward thought and wondering discourse on the divine works. They arrive at the summit of the human mind, which they then also transcend, not by setting it aside and turning to the affections, but as the culmination of an ascent that took place within the intellect. They finally attain "to the region of abundance that never fails, in which you feed Israel forever upon the food of truth, and where life is that Wisdom by which all these things are made, both which have been and which are to be" (Augustine 1960, IX.10.24).[6] It is clear from the fact that this was something that Augustine and Monica shared that the ascent of their minds was not a "'mystical' equivalent to sense experience" (Turner 1995, 262).

When Catherine is read from this standpoint, the exchange she narrates between God and the soul functions like a Socratic dialogue, in the words of Pierre Hadot, as "a kind of communal spiritual exercise." According to Hadot, Socrates' interlocutors were invited to participate in this exercise as an examination of conscience and attention to oneself in keeping with the ancient dictum, "know thyself." Though the original meaning of this dictum is unclear, says Hadot, it surely "invites us to establish a relationship of the self to the self . . . to know oneself *qua* non-sage: that is, not as a *sophos*, but as a *philosophos*, someone *on the way toward* wisdom" (Hadot 1995, 90). Like Socrates, Catherine places great importance on the need for self-knowledge, stating at the very outset of *The Dialogue* that every perfection and virtue comes from charity, and to attain charity one must dwell constantly in the cell of self-knowledge (Catherine 1980, 25, cf. 118).

The implications for critically discerning the correct interpretive context are enormous, not just for understanding Catherine, but ultimately also for what it means to read great texts with an eye toward wisdom. With respect to *The Dialogue* it means that, in Catherine's estimation, women and men cannot finally attain true wisdom, i.e., spiritual union with God, apart from the discipline of prayer, worship, study and works of mercy that constitute a fully Christian existence perfected in friendship and filial love (Catherine 1980, 118). Though she recounts many ecstatic visions, and thus is often identified as a "mystic," she does not posit any sort of private experiential consciousness as the foundation for attaining wisdom and the union with God typically associated with mysticism. Instead, wisdom comes with the acquisition of virtue (divine charity above all) and self-knowledge (grounded in humility).

With respect to the larger question, the need to establish through careful use of all the critical tools at our disposal the proper context in which to read a work such as Catherine's suggests that the search for wisdom that is at the heart of a program of reading great texts cannot simply be juxtaposed to the quest for knowledge that is the hallmark of the contemporary university. At the same time, the way we take up that critical task will resist the temptation to be content with technical expertise, because in this context it is not an end in itself, but has as its primary aim the moral, intellectual and spiritual formation of our students. In other words, a great texts program guided by Christian virtues both takes advantage of, and relativizes the kinds of knowledge that form the warp and woof of the modern (and now postmodern) academy.

Important Motifs in Catherine's The Dialogue

The Dialogue can be a difficult work to read for those who are more familiar with, say, Aquinas's *Summa Theologiae*. Catherine did not provide a closely reasoned progression through the various topics of theology. She was not formally trained in the scholastic theology of the day, though she certainly imbibed its insights.[7] The structure of the work may be favorably compared with the "sonata allegro" form in classical music, in which thematic and harmonic materials are first heard in an initial, typically quite brief exposition (often repeated immediately), then elaborated and contrasted in a development section, and then resolved both harmonically and thematically in a recapitulation. Catherine, in like fashion, introduces a theme, develops it for a time, then moves to another. She typically returns to these themes later in the book, but now in new contexts and with additional insights and connections. In this way she arranges an incredibly large number of ideas and images into a richly textured, polyphonic work (which is not to say that the book is not repetitive and at times even redundant).[8]

Of the many ideas and images that Catherine weaves together in *The Dialogue*, none is more central than that of the bridge that takes the soul over the pleasures and conditions of this world to union with God. She introduces this image in connection with God's response to the third of four petitions she offers at the beginning of the work.[9] These petitions are 1) for herself, 2) for the reform of holy church, 3) for the whole world in general, and in particular for the peace of Christians who are rebelling against holy church, and 4) for "a certain case" that had arisen (the nature of which is unknown). This bridge, which is nothing other than God's only-begotten Son, makes it possible for the soul to cross over the river of the world's disordered loves and desires (Catherine 1980, 26). Students who come to Catherine's *Dialogue* after having encountered Augustine, Aquinas and Dante will find a further development to the medieval understanding of the soul's journey to God.

The bridge has three stairs, two of which were built on the wood of the cross, and the third as he drank the gall and vinegar. The first is the feet of Jesus, and signifies the affections, which carry the soul just as the feet carry the body. Once the soul climbs this stair it reaches the Son's opened heart, where she begins to experience the consummate and unspeakable love of the crucified one in her own heart. This is the second stair, when the soul, recognizing how much she is loved, overflows with love. The final stair is the Son's mouth, where she discovers peace from the war she has waged owing to her sins. The soul is thus stripped of her sin at the first stair (presumably in self-knowledge), dressed in love for virtue at the second, and tastes peace on the third (Catherine 1980, 64–5).

The bridge is a symbol for the incarnation, says Catherine, for even as the body of the Son was raised up high on the cross, his divinity was not cut off from the lowly earth of the soul's humanity. When he was raised up the Son drew all things to himself (the allusion to the Fourth Gospel is readily apparent), he drew the human heart by his love, along with its rational powers of memory, understanding, and will. When these powers are harmoniously united in Christ's name, all that the soul does will be drawn in union with God in peace through the movement of love (Catherine 1980, 65).

The bridge has walls of stone built of true solid virtue and fashioned on the cross with the mortar of his blood. All virtues are perfected in him and thus draw their life from him. These walls protect pilgrims from the rain of divine justice, "sheltered by the mercy that came down from heaven through the incarnation of this Son of mine." The gate that leads to the bridge (indeed, which is one with the bridge) was unlocked with the Son's blood. Located at the bridge is the hostelry of holy church to serve the bread of life and the blood to the pilgrims, who otherwise would grow weary and faint on the way. The Son is the Way, the Truth and the Life, and if you follow this truth you will never die of hunger, because the Word himself has become your food (Catherine 1980, 66–7).

With the ascension of the Son to the right hand of the Father forty days after his resurrection, this bridge was raised high above the earth. In his place God sent the Teacher, the Holy Spirit, who, being one with the Father, bears the Father's power, the Son's wisdom and his own mercy. Though the Son's (bodily) presence is no longer with the soul,[10] his teaching remains, as do his virtues. In addition, the Way he taught and the road of his Truth is verified by the apostles, proclaimed in the blood of the martyrs, enlightened by the doctors, attested to by the confessors, and preserved in the pages of holy writ by the evangelists. His teaching is like a boat ready to be boarded by souls to save them from the stormy sea and convey them to the port of salvation (Catherine 1980, 68–70).

Those who climb the three stairs, make their way across the bridge, and escape the river are assured of God's presence on the journey by grace. This crossing is not made alone, however, but as Jesus taught, only where "two or three are gathered in my name" (Matt. 18:20). God says to the soul, "You must be thirsty, then, and you must gather together, as he said, either two or three or more." The isolated traveler is excluded from God's companionship because God "cannot be 'in the midst' of someone who has no companion." Those who are wrapped up in selfish love are alone and thus mere nothings, thereby cutting themselves off from God's grace and charity for their neighbors. Deprived of both God and neighbor they turn to nothingness, "for I [God] alone am who I am" (Catherine 1980, 107).[11]

For Catherine, following in the tradition of Origen, Ambrose, Augustine and Pseudo-Dionysius, union with God in this life occurs within the life, liturgy, and discipline of the church. It is important to remember that there was no such thing as a purely private or strictly personal vision for these esteemed teachers of the church. In the words of Bernard McGinn, "Whatever gift of divine presence we are given here below can be realized only in and through our bond in the Body of Christ" (McGinn 1992, 251). There is little in *The*

Dialogue, then, that resembles Plotinus' mystical "flight of the alone to the alone" in the *Enneads*.

The wicked, invited into the water of death by the devil, choose to travel beneath the bridge, where they are blinded by the pleasures and honors of the world and then drown (Catherine 1980, 89–90). When they first step into the water they conceive sin in their hearts and become weak, then give birth to that sin and lose the life of grace, along with the powers of the soul. They become like the dead because they cannot move save for being picked up by others: "Because they are dead they remember nothing of my mercy. Their minds neither see nor know my truth (for their sensitivity is dead, and they see nothing but themselves, and that with the dead love of selfish sensuality[12]). And so their wills also are dead to my will, for they love nothing but what is dead." They have become trees of death, rooted in the height of pride and nourished by their sensual selfishness. Impatient, they lack all discernment, thus completing the four chief vices that kill the soul. Everything they do is thus dead as far as grace is concerned (Catherine 1980, 73).

A related theme concerns the relationship between the commandments (also known as precepts), which all Christians are obligated to keep, and the evangelical counsels, which are reserved for those who would be perfect. As was common in the literature of the time, Catherine distinguished between those who follow what she also refers to as the way of ordinary love from those who would travel the road to perfection, who take up Christ's injunction to the rich young ruler that to be perfect he must sell all that he has and give it to the poor (Matt. 19:16–22). She did not, however, draw a bright line between those who follow these two ways: "For all things are good and perfect, since they were made by me, and I am supreme Goodness. I made them and gave them to you not for you to use them to embrace death, but that you might have life through them" (Catherine 1980, 110). Those who travel the way of ordinary love must therefore keep the commandments in the spirit of the counsels, because they are ultimately bound up with each other. Regarding property, for example, God says to the souls that travel this path: "Though they may possess the riches of the world, they must own them humbly, not with pride, as things lent to them rather [than] as their own – for in my generosity I give you these things for your use." Those who treat their material possessions in this manner, cutting themselves off from the sting of disordered love, will keep the commandments and merit eternal life (Catherine 1980, 96–7).[13]

For those who would journey along the way of perfection, Catherine identifies three stages on the way: the imperfect, the perfect, and the most perfect. She likens the first of these to the work of a mercenary, the second to a faithful servant and the third to the child who loves God with no regard for self-interest. The imperfect are those who have arisen from the "vomit" of deadly sin due to slavish fear, reacting to the penalty that follows upon their sin, gathering together the three powers of soul: memory to recall their vices, understanding to see the punishment that awaits them, and the will to hate the sin. By itself, however, fear will not merit the soul eternal life, which is the Old Law given to Moses. Fear must be joined to love, on which the New Law is built. Catherine exhorts those at the first stage to consider not only the punishment but also the reward of virtue and the love that God has for them, for then they will climb to the second stair of the bridge, "with the feet of their affections stripped of slavish fear," becoming faithful instead of faithless servants (Catherine 1980, 113).

The faithful servants serve God with love, but only imperfectly, because they do so for their own profit, or for the delight and pleasure they find in God. The imperfection in their love is revealed when God removes his spiritual comfort from them. God does this "to bring them to perfect knowledge of themselves, so that they will know that of themselves they have neither existence nor any grace." But those at this second stage are not strong enough to endure to the end; they grow lax and doubt whether the exercises are worth the effort when deprived of God's spiritual comfort. They also lack the kind of intimacy with God given to those who make their way to the third stage: "If you love me the way a servant loves a master, I as your master will give you what you have earned, but I will not show myself to you, for secrets are shared only with a friend who has become one with oneself" (Catherine 1980, 115).

If, however, such servants act on this knowledge of themselves, and learn to have contempt for their imperfection, together with love of virtue, they can use hatred to judge themselves so that the slavish fear and mercenary love in their hearts can be corrected in the light of faith. Those who persevere and do not cease in holy prayer and other good works, then, will eventually come to the third stage, that of filial love. God will then show himself to them, and they will become one with God: "This is how it is with very dear friends. Their loving affection makes them two bodies with one soul, because love transforms one into what one loves" (Catherine 1980, 60).[14] The soul completes its journey by moving from the perfection of friendship to filial love, which is the most perfect. Becoming a child of God thus proceeds from a holy charity that is nourished by humility, which in turn is the result of knowledge and holy hatred of one's selfish sensuality (Catherine 1980, 118).

Reading The Dialogue in Context

The Dialogue is indeed a remarkable text in its own right, but its place within the canon of great texts becomes more apparent when it is read in connection with the dynamic intellectual tradition of medieval Europe. Momentous social and political changes interacted with theological, liturgical and moral developments in the years leading up to Catherine's time to fashion one of the most dynamic and volatile periods in the history of Western Christendom. If *The*

Dialogue is in fact a form of spiritual exercise grounded in prayer and the works of mercy, then these changes form the communal background against which Catherine's work should be read, for in some ways she mirrored these shifts, but in others she resisted the tendencies of the times.

In his classic summary of trends in theology and spirituality that developed during the eleventh and twelfth centuries, Colin Morris notes that, with respect to patterns of spiritual formation, patristic descriptions of Christ's cosmic triumph over death, the devil, and sin were gradually supplanted by a preoccupation with the pains of Christ in his passion, accompanied by a shift in focus for spirituality from the gathering together of all things in Christ to the fate of the individual after death (Morris 1972, 70–75, 139–52). Spiritual formation from the time of the New Testament to the early Middle Ages had found its occasion and significance in the radical restructuring of bodily life and language brought about by the intrusion of God's messianic regime into a fallen world. To borrow from the title of Timothy Weber's book about American millennialism, the early Christians lived in the shadow of the second coming (Weber 1979; cf. McGinn 1998, xviii). In Paul's epistles the adjective *pneumatikos* moved within the semantic orbit of *to pneuma*, the Spirit who the apostles proclaimed was in Jesus and who was also the gift of the risen Christ to his followers. Spiritual persons were women and men whose whole way of acting in and relating to the world was under the influence of the Holy Spirit, and thus those who, in and through their bodies, manifested the presence of the Spirit in the world. Spirituality accordingly did not refer principally to a property that an individual possessed or a discrete facet of one's private inner life, but to a pattern of personal growth and maturation that took place within the community of those who had been gathered together by the risen Lord "to be a kingdom and priests serving our God" (Rev. 5:10a).

The concern with eschatology prevailed in the church through the start of the second millennium, as both great and ordinary ordered their lives in anticipation of the Second Coming and the world to come. Gregory the Great, for example, in his letter to new convert Ethelbert of Kent, states that, "We also wish Your Majesty to know, as we have learned from the words of Almighty God in holy Scripture, that the end of the present age is already drawing near and that the unending kingdom of the saints is approaching."[15] Paradoxically, says McGinn, "the formation of a distinctive Western European culture was the product of leaders whose hopes were not centered on building a new society but on the expectation of the end of all human effort in the Last Judgment" (McGinn 1995, 58). The eschaton in light of which the early church judged and evaluated the world, says Alexander Schmemann, did not involve a denial of the world but "a certain way of looking at it and experiencing it." The church's "ultimate content and term of reference was not the world but the Kingdom of God, and thus rather than being 'anti-world' it was a 'pro-

Kingdom' attitude in which it differed from eschatologies that developed later." The eschatological reign of Israel's God, "announced, inaugurated and given by and in Christ," permeated the early church's mode of practice and governed its antinomical relationship with the world (Schmemann 1979, 28).

Though eschatological reflection certainly did not cease after 1000 (indeed, in some ways it intensified, given the threat posed by Islamic forces who challenged both Eastern and Western Europe), it did become increasingly disconnected from matters of spiritual formation. The pilgrimage of the elect through history toward God's eternal city, for which the church serves as both sacrament and vehicle, became divorced from the *itinerarium mentis in deum* – the journey of the mind to God. Henri de Lubac frames the matter well: "collective eschatology and the expectation of the final resurrection, which once enjoyed such a high profile, were fading out of the picture. In a framework that remained ecclesial, the focus was no longer primarily on the destiny of the Church but on the destiny of each of the faithful." As a result, says de Lubac, "a certain spiritualism was being established on the ruins of its ancient forms" (de Lubac 2006, 286–87). As personal teleology was separated from cosmic eschatology, the fate of the individual believer after death, depicted so poignantly by Dante in the *Divine Comedy*, gradually took center-stage.

Where then did Catherine stand with respect to these christological and eschatological shifts, and how did they shape her understanding of the acquisition of wisdom? As already noted, *The Dialogue* had a pronounced christological focus, reiterating time and again that the sole basis for the union of the soul with God is the incarnation. The bridge of God's only-begotten Son stretches from heaven to earth, thus "joining the earth of your humanity with the greatness of the Godhead. This is what I [God] mean when I say it stretches from heaven to earth – through my union with humanity" (59). It is also clear that her understanding of the incarnation reflected the medieval emphasis on Christ's passion, with numerous references throughout to the soul's redemption through the blood of the Son, again in connection with the image of the bridge. The first two stairs that lead over the flood of the world's disordered loves, in which the wicked drown and come to eternal damnation (109–110), are built on the wood of the holy cross, specifically, his nailed feet and opened heart. The last stair is his mouth that "tasted the great bitterness of the gall and vinegar they gave him to drink" (64). Of the souls that united to the Son, God thus says that, "when they are suffering, when I allow them many troubles, they rejoice to see themselves in the suffering and shame of Christ crucified. Therefore, if it were possible for them to have virtue without weariness, they would not want it, for they would rather delight in the cross with Christ and acquire virtue with suffering than to gain eternal life in any other way. Why? Because they are enflamed and submerged in the blood, where they find my burning charity" (155).

The themes of the return of Christ and the day of judgment are also present in *The Dialogue*, but again they have principally to do with the fate of the individual soul on the last day. God says to the soul, "I have told you of the good the glorified body will have in the glorified humanity of my only-begotten Son, and this is the guarantee of your own resurrection." The souls of the just thus wait for divine judgment with gladness and not fear, for they are assured that the face of the Son upon his return will be not terrifying or hateful, having finished their lives in charity, and delighting in God and exhibiting good will toward their neighbors. As for the unrighteous, "When that terrifying voice says to them, 'Arise, you dead, and come to judgment!' their souls will return with their bodies. The bodies of the just will be glorified. But the bodies of the damned will be forever tortured, and the sight of my Truth and of all the blessed will be for them a great shame and reproach" (85–6).

The influence of developments in the medieval church can also be seen in Catherine's eucharistic reflections. In the years leading up to the fourteenth century, the focus of eucharistic observance had been shifting from a communal context to a mode of devotion that increasingly emphasized the inner experience of the individual (Morris 1972, 12). In patristic and early medieval texts, the Eucharist was typically described in terms of a threefold articulation of "the body of Christ" found in the Pauline epistles: the historical body of the man Jesus of Nazareth; the sacramental body (*corpus mysticum*, mystical body); and the ecclesial body (*corpus verum*, true body). The sacramental body and the ecclesial body were closely linked in these early writings, with a temporal *caesura* or gap between them and the historical body (de Lubac 2006, 13–36). This gap separated the life, death and resurrection of Jesus (the original founding event) from the manifestation of its effects, seen in both the liturgical complex of a visible community and secret action or "mystery" (de Certeau 1992, 82–3). The gathered community (*communio*) and the invisible action of the sacrament thus forged the essential unity between the past event of Christ's life, death, and resurrection and the present community which understands itself as "the body of Christ." As William Cavanaugh notes, "The 'mystical', then, is that which 'insures the unity between the two times', and brings the Christ event into present historical time in the church body, the *corpus verum*" (Cavanaugh 1998, 212). Together the Eucharist and the church constitute the contemporary performance of the historical body, the unique event of Jesus.

In the later medieval period, due at least in part to heated debates concerning real presence, the historical and sacramental bodies were conjoined, and a synchronic gap opened between them and the ecclesial body. The consecrated bread and wine were designated as the true body of Christ, and the liturgical emphasis shifted from incorporation into Christ's body and mission to awed contemplation of a sacred object venerated in the midst of grand spectacle.

Severing the connection between the Eucharist and the church's offering of itself as the true body of Christ resulted in "a greatly diminished sense of the essentially social implications of the Christ's eucharistic presence" (Schindler 1998, xiii).

With the eclipse of the corporate and social implications, combined with the introduction of new practices such as the elevation of the host, the celebration of the Eucharist was redirected towards the subjective devotional life of the individual in the isolation of her own thoughts and affections (Morris 1972, 12). "The emphasis," writes Sarah Beckwith, "was increasingly on watching Christ's body rather than being incorporated in it" (Beckwith 1993, 36). According to Dom Gregory Dix, it did not stop with mere watching: "The part of the individual layman . . . had long ago been reduced from 'doing' to 'seeing' and 'hearing'. Now it is retreating within himself to 'thinking' and 'feeling'. He is even beginning to think that over-much 'seeing' (ceremonial) and 'hearing' (music) are detrimental to proper 'thinking' and 'feeling'" (Dix 1982, 599). Nothing "inessential" could be allowed to intrude upon an individual's private encounter with the divine. This proscription could conceivably extend to the sacramental elements themselves.

There is no doubt that Catherine held to the real presence of Christ, both divine and human, in the Eucharist. But her emphasis, in discussing the sacrament, which constitutes spiritual food to strengthen individual pilgrims traveling across the bridge of Christ, lay almost exclusively in the spiritual discernment of Christ: "You know that all your eyes see is this white bit of bread; this is all your hand can touch and all your tongue can taste, so that your dull bodily senses are deceived. . . . What tastes and sees and touches this sacrament? The soul's sensitivity. How does she see it? With her mind's eye, so long as it has the pupil of holy faith." What one sees, touches and tastes in the sacrament, then, comes from one's inner life: the spiritual eye of the mind, the hand of charity, and the tongue of holy desire: "The body tastes only the flavor of bread, but the soul tastes me, God and human" (Catherine 1980, 209–11). Though she did not say it (and would have been horrified to have it attributed to her), one could almost hear her say that over-much "tasting" could be detrimental to eucharistic devotion.

We see Catherine beginning to diverge from dominant trends of the fourteenth century in her descriptions of the connections between spirituality, theology and the body. In the early church, research, study, argument, and reflection on God and his ways with the world had found "their source and their completion only in prayer" (Torrell 1996, 157).[16] In the words of the fourth century desert father Evagrius of Pontus, "If you are a theologian, you will pray truly; and if you pray truly, you will be a theologian" (Evagrius 2003, 199). Rigorous theological inquiry, rightly conceived, comprised "an aspect of the mystical journey by means of which God is leading creatures back into unity with the divine life. Theology is the attempt to notice how this is happening, to articulate the stages of the community's journey, to point ahead to the One who alone could mystically arouse the uplifting ecstasy that always leads beyond" (McIntosh 1998, 6–7, 56). Spirituality thus pertained to the impression made by the encounter with God that took place within the new network of communal relationship and perception that was provided by the church as the embodied fellowship of the Spirit.

Beginning around the twelfth century, however, the idea of *spiritualitas* began to take on new connotations and shed old ones. Scholastic theologians started to use the term in a more specialized sense, designating what pertains to the soul as part of a sharper distinction between "spirit" and "matter" or "body." The adjective *spiritualis* was likewise used to designate intelligent creatures (i.e., human beings) as opposed to non-rational beings, with the effect of vacating its Pauline eschatological sense in favor of a meaning "more radically opposed to corporeality" (Sheldrake 1995, 43). Though for a time this new sense stood side by side with its former meaning, says McGinn, scholasticism unwittingly helped to give birth to "conceptions of spirituality which willy-nilly used it as the reason for giving the physical world and especially the human body a largely negative role in what they conceived of as authentic Christian life" (McGinn 1993, 3).

This privatizing tendency in the practice of spirituality gained momentum, with increasing emphasis placed on the interior state of the soul, and especially on how one achieved ever more refined stages of inner purity and exaltation (McIntosh 1998, 7). Confessional practices accordingly began to stress the importance of self-examination, with a marked distinction between public penance and the inner sorrow that marked true repentance, the latter being that which God most valued.[17] A new interest in and study of the detailed inner workings of the soul thus emerged during this time, with an awareness of the degree to which a variety of motivations, affections and appetites were involved in an individual's spiritual progress (Morris 1972, 76–86).[18]

To be sure, evidence of a keen interest in the interior state of the soul can be found in *The Dialogue* in numerous admonitions of God to the soul that it is true, heartfelt, or perfect contrition and sorrow that atone for sin (Catherine 1980, 3–4, 6, 12, 14, 23, 37, 45, 66, 68, 75, 83, 110, 116, 128–9, 133, 143, 155, 166). Catherine's division of the way of perfection into three stages, again with an emphasis on the soul's inner state, also reflects, to a certain extent, the shift in medieval spirituality that emphasized inner sorrow as the mark of true repentance and that which God most valued. These emphases are counterbalanced in *The Dialogue*, however, by the stress that she placed on the acquisition of virtue and the active life on behalf of the neighbor, and by her own life of service to the poor and the dying.

Her distinctiveness with respect to her time and place becomes more apparent when we look at the way she viewed the relationship of spirituality to theology. For many in the years leading up to the fourteenth century, as *spiritualitas* became restricted to a person's private, interior life, it also was divorced from the intellectual concerns of theology, so that fewer and fewer persons were competent to integrate spirituality and the other aspects of theology in their own lives (McIntosh 1998, 63). "How few of them are saints," complains Denys the Carthusian in the fifteenth century, "Thomas [Aquinas] and but few others."[19] A deep wedge was being driven between the intellective and the affective aspects of the soul. As Denys Turner says of this development, it was becoming more widely accepted in Catherine's day that "if we are to enter into the true 'mystical' darkness of the divine, then the intellectual knowledge of the philosopher has to be set aside in order to leave room for the God of faith, known, it is said, not by intellect, but by love. For *amor ipse notitia est*, love is itself a kind of knowing, of which intellect can know nothing" (Turner 2004, 77–8).[20]

For Catherine, however, there was no separation of spirituality from theology. The union of the soul with God involved both the intellect and the affections, with the Augustinian triad of memory, understanding and will prominently featured throughout the work. In addition, she gives little or no indication that at some point the soul on its journey to God must transcend the intellect so that love takes over. "First Truth" (*prima Verità*) and "Gentle First Truth" (*prima dolce Verità*) are among her favorite names for God (Catherine 1980, 27, n. 9). On the contrary, when the memory finds itself filled with God, the understanding is lifted up as it gazes into the Truth of God, and the will, "which always follows the understanding, loves and unites itself with what the eye of understanding sees" (148).

A Final Assessment

We find in Catherine's book the wisdom of one who was deeply interested in the reform of the church, which, in addition to the reform of the clergy and return of the pope to Rome, involved efforts to mitigate the two-tiered system of piety (religious and lay) by extending participation in communal spiritual exercise and discipline to those who followed "the ordinary path of love." She insisted that every state of life is pleasing and acceptable to God "if it is held to with a good and holy will" (Catherine 1980, 110). In Catherine we also find an author actively engaged by her own time and circumstances. She exemplified the conceptions and interests of later medieval theology and spirituality, not in slavish imitation, but as one capable of improvising on motifs and themes first formulated by others. And though as a woman she was denied formal scholastic training, Catherine displayed keen theological instincts and a profound ability to grasp vital insights of theologians such as Augustine,

Anselm and Aquinas. The result, among other things, was a depiction of the unity of the affections and the intellect that is unsurpassed by any author, before or since.

How we should assess the eclipse of eschatology from spirituality as reflected in *The Dialogue* is a question that must be addressed in the context of reading medieval texts in historical sequence. Hadot notes that a Socratic dialogue may best be understood as an invitation to know oneself, not as a *sophos*, but as a *philo-sophos*, someone on the way toward wisdom. But is it only individuals that embark on this path? Or is the personal quest embedded within another pilgrimage, one that the whole world has undertaken (regardless of whether it knows it or not)? If the latter is the case, what happens to the personal quest for wisdom when it is divorced for long from the ecclesial journey to the *civitas dei*?

In conclusion I would like to take up a question that I posed at the beginning but have only alluded to through the essay: was Catherine a mystic, and should *The Dialogue* be seen as a mystical text? Part of the difficulty in answering these questions is that the meaning of "mysticism" has mutated over the centuries. Over the last century or so the notion of mysticism has been used to talk about the cultivation and achievement of a transcultural, unmediated encounter with the divine by an individual. In this way of viewing the matter, the mystic's understanding or consciousness is analogous to sense experiences characterized by extraordinary inner sensations, pronounced states of ecstasy and raptures. As a result of this experientialist configuring of the term, it is now common to talk about individuals practicing "mysticism" as such, and that these "mystics" share something that crosses religious, ethnic and cultural lines.

In this sense of the term, Catherine was not a mystic. But Rowan Williams contends that if the notion of mysticism is worth salvaging, it cannot be to designate "a cross-cultural, supra-credal specific experience, but a jumble of attempts to perceive how consciousness is drastically 'reconditioned' by the living-out in depth of a particular religious commitment; 'Christian mysticism' is therefore the cluster of such attempts which assembles around the central symbols of Christian speech and action" (Williams 1984, 209).[21] If this is the sense of the term that we employ, then Catherine was most definitely a mystic. But as Turner observes, if this is the case, "then theology in so far as it is theology is 'mystical' and in so far as it is 'mystical' it is theology" (Turner 1995, 265). We should add that for Catherine true wisdom is rooted in the mystical ascent to God, which cannot be made apart from the passion of the incarnate Son of God.

Barry Harvey

References

Augustine 1960. *The Confessions of St. Augustine*. Trans. John K. Ryan. Garden City: Image.

Beckwith, Sarah 1993. *Christ's Body: Identity, Culture, and Society in Late Medieval Writings*. New York: Routledge.

Catherine of Siena 1980. *Catherine of Siena: The Dialogue*. Trans. Suzanne Noffke, O. P. New York: Paulist.

Cavallini, Giuliana O. P., 1998. *Catherine of Siena*. London: Geoffrey Chapman.

Cavanaugh, William 1998. *Torture and Eucharist: Theology, Politics, and the Body of Christ*. Malden, MA: Blackwell.

Coakley, Sarah 2002. *Powers and Submissions: Spirituality, Philosophy and Gender*. Malden, MA: Blackwell.

de Certeau, Michel 1992. *The Mystic Fable*, Volume One. Trans. Michael B. Smith. Chicago: University of Chicago Press.

de Lubac, Henri, S.J. 2006. *Corpus Mysticum: The Eucharist and the Church in the Middle Ages*. Trans. Gemma Simmonds, C.J. Notre Dame: University of Notre Dame Press.

Dix, Dom Gregory 1982. *The Shape of the Liturgy*, with additional notes by Paul V. Marshall. New York: Seabury.

Evagrius of Pontus 2003. *Evagrius of Pontus: the Greek Ascetic Corpus*. Ed. Robert E. Sinkewicz. New York: Oxford University Press.

Hadot, Pierre 1995. *Philosophy as a Way of Life*. Ed. Arnold I. Davidson. Malden, MA: Blackwell.

MacIntyre, Alasdair, 1984. *After Virtue*, Second edition. Notre Dame, IN: University of Notre Dame Press.

———. 1990. *First Principles, Final Ends and Contemporary Philosophical Issues*. Milwaukee: Marquette University Press.

McGinn, Bernard 1993. "The Letter and the Spirit: Spirituality as an Academic Discipline," *Christian Spirituality Bulletin* 1: 1, 3–10.

———. 1987. "Love, Knowledge, and Mystical Union in Western Christianity: Twelfth to Sixteenth Centuries," *Church History* 56: 7–24.

——— 1992. *The Presence of God*, Volume One, *The Foundations of Mysticism*. New York: Crossroads.

——— 1998. *Visions of the End: Apocalyptic Traditions in the Middle Ages*. New York: Columbia University Press.

McIntosh, Mark A., 1998. *Mystical Theology: The Integrity of Spirituality and Theology*. Malden, MA: Blackwell.

Morris, Colin, 1972. *The Discovery of the Individual 1050–1200*. New York: Harper & Row.

Noffke, Suzanne, O.P., 2003. "Catherine of Siena, Justly Doctor of the Church?" *Theology Today* 60: 49–62.

O'Driscoll, Mary, O.P., ed. 1993. *Catherine of Siena – Passion for the Truth, Compassion for Humanity: Selected Spiritual Writings*. New York: New City Press.

Schmemann, Alexander 1979. *Church, World, Mission*. Crestwood, NY: St. Vladimir's Seminary Press.

Sheldrake, Philip 1995. *Spirituality and History: Questions of Interpretation and Method*, rev. ed. London: SPCK.

Schindler, David L., 1998. Introduction to *The Mystery of the Supernatural* by Henri de Lubac, S.J. Trans. Rosemary Sheed. New York: Crossroad.

Taylor, Charles 1995. *Philosophical Arguments*. Cambridge, MA: Harvard University Press.

Torrell, Jean-Pierre, O.P., 1996. *Saint Thomas Aquinas*, Volume One, *The Person and His Work*. Trans. Robert Royal. Washington, D.C.: The Catholic University of America Press.

Turner, Denys 2004. *Faith, Reason and the Existence of God*. New York: Cambridge University Press.

——— 1995. *The Darkness of God: Negativity in Christian Mysticism*. New York: Cambridge University Press.

Tylus, Jane 2009. *Reclaiming Catherine of Siena: Literacy, Literature and the Signs of Others*. Chicago: The University of Chicago press.

von Balthasar, Hans Urs 1989. *Explorations in Theology*, Volume One, *The Word Made Flesh*. Trans. A. V. Littledale and Alexander Dru. San Francisco: Ignatius.

Weber, Timothy P., 1979. *Living in the Shadow of the Second Coming: American Premillenialism (1875–1925)*. New York: Oxford University Press.

Whitehead, Alfred North 1926. *Religion in the Making*. New York: Macmillan.

Williams, Rowan 1984. "Butler's *Western Mysticism*: Toward an Assessment." *Downside Review* 102: 197–215.

Chaucer
The Canterbury Tales

From the late nineteenth century almost until the present, Chaucer study has been shaped more by the influence of romanticized Victorian "medievalism" than by knowledge of medieval literary conventions and Chaucer's own context. It is still more common for students to encounter highly selective textual presentations of a poet whose place in the curriculum owes more to sniggering appreciation of his light-hearted sexual jokes and anti-clerical disdain than to the guiding themes and architectonic unity of his major works. One consequence has been that the tales best known by students are those whose plots and narrative inflection are the most lascivious: the Miller's Tale, the Wife of Bath's Tale, and the Franklin's Tale. Even when Chaucer's *Canterbury Tales* have been offered as translated texts it has frequently been the practice to leave out the philosophical tale Chaucer assigned to himself as a pilgrim narrator, the Tale of Melibee, and astonishingly, the concluding Parson's Tale and Chaucer's own final word, his confessional and self-examining Retractions. The argument that these are inferior and prose tales containing boring religious material only highlights the distortion in typical selections. To be sure, Melibee is a kind of moral treatise on the virtue of forgiveness and the Parson's Tale is a sermon on repentance, but their placement in the overall *Canterbury Tales* is such as to make absolutely clear that the heart of Chaucer's narrative architecture and the ultimate social vision he projects are hardly to be sufficiently grasped in revelry over the "moustache kiss." Moreover, these pivotal tales, and other neglected tales with them, show that Chaucer himself is a sophisticated reader of the great books, and that the Christian worldview he projects is symbolically profound and his poetics semantically rich and artfully polysemous. Those who choose to read him merely for a belly laugh have not really read Chaucer in anything like enough maturity of understanding. As a consequence, they actually miss many of his finest jokes. The reader who reads without an ear for Chaucer's Christian moral and theological nuance is likely, in fact, to laugh at all the wrong places. This ignorance is not to be encountered only in regard to Chaucer; it extends to readings of other medieval texts and also to our understanding of paintings, sculpture, and architecture of the period.

Analogies can be helpful here pedagogically. Art historians distinguish between three broad approaches to the study of the visual arts in a way that has analogous value for those of us whose object is the study of literary art. One approach is *formalist,* which is to say the study of style, media, and forms of expression as they change according to innovations in technique or material media. The second broad approach is *iconographic*, a study of the visual vocabulary of an art, such as may become evident in symbol, motif, color, and gesture, with attention to how these vary from artist to artist, culture to culture, and change over time. The third approach that many associate with the study of works of art in their broader intellectual context (including their religious context) is called *iconological.* It draws on the insights of both of the other approaches, but in such a way as to connect understanding of the "vocabulary" of a given work of art to evolving ideas about such elements in the broader oeuvre of the artist or artistic movement in the fuller culture of which the artist (and indeed patrons of the art) are situated. The element common to all three approaches, it will be obvious, is an appreciation of change over time.

The utility of approaching works of art in the light of their place in an evolving intellectual, as well as art-technical, history is that we become more aware of cultural difference, of the perpetual tension between the creativity of change and the intelligibility of continuity, and thus can strive to appreciate a given work in respect to at least two horizons of perception, the "then" of the production of the work of art and the "now" of our own attempt at a richer appreciation of the value of the work. Great pictorial art, like great literary art, retains in this way something of its value as "other" in our present conversation; it speaks to us from *without* and thus *to* our own taste and capacity for perception, broadening and deepening our understanding of human nature rather than being made to serve merely as an imperfect mirror for our present, personal horizons of taste.

Iconological Methodology

It is a version of the iconological approach (again, broadly speaking) that most properly commends itself in a Great Texts approach to major literary texts of the late Middle Ages and Renaissance. This is not least because in its greater comprehensiveness of synthesis it inscribes a diachronic rather than merely synchronic pursuit of understanding in the contemporary reader. As a first step, situating a text historically allows us more fully to appreciate the "otherness" of a centuries-old work. To take one example, Ovid's telling in his *Metamorphoses* (Book 1) of the myth of Daphne and Apollo, each struck by opposing arrows from Cupid's bow, may sensibly be read in the original as an attempt to comprehend the meaning of erotic desire more fundamentally; here is a tale that enables us, cognitively as well as emotionally, to see more fully into the paradoxes of such desire, even the antimonies of love and mortal limit. In the *Ovide Moralisé*, an enormously influential retelling of Ovid (with allegorizations) of the late thirteenth century, the figures of Apollo (in this Old French text, Phebus) and Daphne (Dané) are read as a suggestive parable of wisdom in pursuit of love, and of the frustration that arises from the failure of these virtues to consummate in a fruitful union (de Boer 1920, 1.3116–71). Or, in "un autre sentence," says the anonymous French poet, we may read the text as an allegory of right- versus- wrong ways to cherish virginity, in the fashion suggested also by the parable of the wise and foolish virgins who await the coming of the bridegroom in Jesus' parable (Matt. 25:1–13). Or, we may imagine this myth as unwittingly implying a Christian allegory, in which Daphne suggests the Virgin Mary – and so on (de Boer 120, 1.3215–3412). In several of these medieval readings the original Ovidian frisson between *eros* and *thanatos* is muted, in others it is heightened.

The ultimate psychic register of Ovid's myth is captured with exquisitely poignant beauty in Bernini's sculpture of "Daphne and Apollo." When we look at Bernini's magnificent work in the light not only of Ovid's text, but of intervening reflections on the myth by medieval and Renaissance poets, we may sense that his arrest of the tension between flight and fixedness, between desire and resistance to closure, has been shaped into a polyvalent perception of the anguish sometimes occasioned by great beauty, stirring up reflection about the asymptotic character of all art, the inevitable frustration of artistic desire to capture Beauty itself. The artist will always, in effect, be an Apollo to some fleeing Daphne. Yet his primal yearning remains unrequited. In the pagan myth even a god must settle for less, and in the poem, though aspiring touch may reach even to the bosom of desire's occasion, may sense under fingertips a trembling pulse – as Ovid has it, that heart under the bark still beating – such ecstasy is not consummated but rather exquisitely tantalized in the successful work of art. It is no accident that the poet's laurel should be woven from Daphne's laurel leaves, for, in the sad ending of the myth, these memorials to her eternal beauty nod only ever so slightly in the direction of Apollo's reaching hands, consenting to not more than a gesture, a hint at his dream of reciprocation.

Ovid has many stories of this sort, and they fascinated medieval and Renaissance imaginations. Such striking insights as they occasion for these later writers typically arise by way of a confluence of (textual) memory and present desire, by a living "intertextuality" which acquaints an experienced and attentive reader at several levels with the unavoidable tension in all the arts between continuity and change. To jump forward for another example: when we read the poetic commentary on this same Ovidian text by Thomas Carew, a seventeenth-century English poet, we can hardly avoid recognizing how polyvalent may be the resonance that informs and, in a meaningful sense, transfigures both Ovid's poem and, as it may be, our appreciation of Bernini's sculpture:

> *Daphne* hath broke her barke, and that swift foot,
> Which th'angry Gods had fastned with a root

To the fixt earth, doth now unfetter'd run,
To meet th'embraces of the youthfull Sun.
("A Rapture," 1640 [Dunlap 1949, 49–53])

This is, of course, ironic reversal, and, as the title of Carew's poem suggests, another metamorphosis. That is, under Carew's hands one *mythos* is transformed by another, yet its very newness and beauty, even its own notion of the true, the good, and the beautiful, depend upon continuity with the old, familiar story. Recollecting the Ovidian poem first on its own most poignant terms, Carew then achieves his striking turn of expectation by drawing down the infused light of another story, opening a new horizon, extending the possibility of meaning and insight in respect of the original. This shows how the poignancy of irresolution or insight framed in an original text, such as here, Ovid's famous myth, may well be plumbed to some order of satisfaction by playful misdirection in a later reading. Consider Carew's suddenly unfettered Daphne – running, astonishingly, to meet the Sun from whom she had originally fled. Or Andrew Marvell's ironic juxtaposition: "The gods that mortal beauty chase, / Still in a tree did end their race" ("The Garden"). It is for such surprising confluences of story with story – as well as hopes of intimate disclosure in the original – that we strive to preserve the "otherness" of Great Texts. This pedagogical aim ought to be a conscious motive, I think, even and perhaps most particularly as we strive to deepen our understanding of a great text in light of the whole tradition of "readings," the "intertextuality" of which it forms a part.

Chaucer as a Reader of Great Texts

To read the Chaucer of *The Canterbury Tales* in this light, as I am recommending here, is to read him as a reader not only of Ovid (which most evidently in many of his tales he was) but of many "great texts," and of intervening transformations of such stories in interaction with foundational texts from both the classical and the biblical libraries. For Chaucer's greatness as a poet resides above all in his determination to read, inwardly digest, and then retell old stories in such a way as to reconstitute their counsel for his own time. Nowhere is this more evident than in his *Canterbury Tales*, which is a staged retelling of many tales, old and new, in such a learned and yet creative way as both to reveal their own inherent wisdom and, simultaneously, to draw attention to the tendency of "interested" re-tellers to pervert or misconstrue such wisdom. It will be clear that not all of Chaucer's narrators are reliable. In fact, it is central to his larger purpose to show that some readers are "misconstruers," usually through their own self-serving preoccupations; they insist on reading in terms of "what it means to me" instead of reading other texts (or hearing other voices) in their own terms. This is a point at which

Chaucer becomes particularly pertinent for the larger rationale of a Great Texts curriculum.

Pilgrimage and Conversational Structure

It is accordingly critical for our appreciation of Chaucer's project that we recognize in *The Canterbury Tales*, structurally and synchronically, philosophically and diachronically, the poet's determination upon a conversation. His method is dialogic, not monologic, and the modern reader, as much as the fourteenth-century hearers of Chaucer's work in the court of Richard II, is skillfully invited into this "conversation," a symposium that will inevitably reflect a multiplicity of points of view, past and present. Just as any of the tales may now be told "in sondry wyse/ of sondry folk," so too with present understanding: "diverse folk diversely they seyde" (Chaucer 1992, Prologue to the Reeve's Tale, 3857; tail-link to The Tale of Sir Thopas, 941–2). Now at the literal level the idea of horseback narration is, of course, entirely unrealistic: twenty-nine or thirty people cannot hear each other if all are riding along a well- traveled road. But even this element of artifice in his fiction serves Chaucer's larger historiographical purpose: there is for him a sense in which all human stories are already part of a larger story and an unfolding history. That history may well begin in a familiar place haphazardly (or so it seems) but it is likely to end in quite another place, a place we think we know but which may be revealed in the end to be decisively different from what we imagined.

The first structural element with which we are to conjure, then, is evident in the title of the work. This is to be a pilgrimage from a notoriously disrespectable suburb of London to Canterbury, seat of the Church Catholic in England. To anyone familiar with the dominant form of grand narrative in western literature, this is then a "tale of two cities," in its proposed narrative of a journey from one to the other implying already some notion of a progression in understanding. Such a reader may well think of Virgil's *Aeneid*, a tale of two cities whose narrative serves to attribute transcendent significance to the triumph of secular power. But this same reader will, one hopes, be prepared to juxtapose Virgil's epic with its most famous commentary, that in Augustine's *City of God*. Augustine's tale of two cities, on a biblical analogy with Babylon and Jerusalem, sees Rome in another light: the city of the World and the City of God co-exist in time, but secular power is no longer the governing issue. Spiritually, those for whom the "kingdom of God" is within, as Augustine says (quoting Heb. 11:13–16) in his introduction, are strangers and pilgrims en route to "a better city" to which, by faith, they have undertaken to make their way.

Invocations of such reiterated patterns are typically tacit. Chaucer's General Prologue opens with a translation of the opening lines of Guido delle

Colonne's *Historia destructionis Troiae,* implying to those who recognize such paroemia (meaningful borrowing from another text) that the worldly city from which the pilgrims set out may in some sense not be their true home. Contemporary political criticism of the ineffective Richard II, moreover, often drew on the mythographic history of England (such as one finds in Geoffrey of Monmouth)[1] to refer to England in decline as a second Troy, London as *Novum Trinovantum* or New Troy, and even to King Richard II as Troilus. None of this is particularly flattering to the "City of the World."

Chaucer also makes it clear that pilgrimage to Canterbury has a specific association with the tomb of St. Thomas à Becket, martyr to one of England's most famous conflicts between church and state. Thomas was a saint especially to be appealed to when secular power was disordered. But the authority of the Church was in Chaucer's time also in grave disorder. What has been called the "Babylonian Captivity" of the papacy, with removal of the pope to Avignon and eventually a conflict between rival popes, one in France and one back in Rome, had created among many the conviction that these were apocalyptic times.[2] Many fourteenth-century writers betray their sense that "the world is not our home." A general sense of cultural demise had heightened the desire of many that Christ's kingdom in all its reality would come, his will be done, "on earth even as in heaven." We, who do not live daily with the words of Scripture and the prayers of the liturgy echoing in our minds, and who are still less aware of the historical context in which a text like *The Canterbury Tales* was written, can scarcely without attunement hope to catch all of the allusions that Chaucer could depend upon being understood by his fourteenth-century audience. But when, with just a little exposition and reflection on the signposts, even as modern readers we come at last to the walls of the symbolic "city of God" in the Parson's Prologue, we should not be surprised that there our poet makes explicit his analogy between the Canterbury pilgrimage and another, "To shewe you the wey, in this viage,/ Of thilke parfit glorious pilgrimage/ That highte Jerusalem celestial" (Chaucer 1992, Parson's Prologue 49–51).[3] For his immediate audience the analogy has been there all along, even as has their recognition that typically such earthly pilgrimages were assigned as a form of penance during Lent, preparatory to personal confession, reconciliation, and a return to Holy Communion at Easter.

Personal confession is thus also a tacit context for "telling one's story" in *The Canterbury Tales*. Just as in penitential confession, purity of intention in the teller is critical to efficaciousness, so here literarily, Chaucer is concerned with motive in the teller of each tale – motive for choice of the tales to be told, and motive for the "editing" and personal reshaping of each text. I have suggested elsewhere that, as in a motet or fugue, there are three broad movements or groupings of tales in *The Canterbury Tales* as we have them, and that these movements succeed each other in a development of definition of "*entente*" as reflexive preconception, as more or less thoughtful presupposition, and finally as a deliberative declaration of the will as purpose (Jeffrey 1996, 191–207). Between the General Prologue, with its iconographically rich description of the twenty-nine pilgrims at the Tabard Inn, and the final group or manuscript unit, including the Parson's Prologue and Sermon and Chaucer's Retraction – all presented as if in the precincts of Canterbury Cathedral – we find what appears to be a characteristically three-fold medieval pattern: three groups of seven tales each. One way to read development in the tales is as a *scala* or progress of purgation or clarification of the will with both self-justifying autobiography (e.g., the Wife of Bath's Prologue) and selective representation of pre-existent literary texts (e.g., Man of Law's Tale, Manciple's Tale) offering workshops or exemplars at each stage. This way of reading the *Tales*, nominally incomplete as they are, credits the poet with having intended them – as his structure so clearly suggests – as a progression of ideas (rather than just as one entertaining thing after another).

But this is not the only way to read *The Canterbury Tales*. Nor is it the only way to appreciate the pilgrim journey as a progress. I would like to suggest two other congruent yet distinct ways to characterize Chaucer's narrative pedagogy, each of which can be demonstrated in a context where reading three tales, one from each seven-fold group, is practicable. (In either case the "frames" – General Prologue, Parson's Prologue and Tale, and Chaucer's Retractions – are indispensable.) The first of the following approaches directs attention to the perfection or maturation of knowledge, not merely in the narrow technical sense of justified true belief favored by contemporary epistemology, but in the richer dimensions of personal knowledge and sapiential teaching as medieval Christians understood it. The second approach would be by way of reflection on the development of virtues, specifically the three theological virtues of faith, hope, and charity. That these two approaches are indeed congruous, and in fact harmonious with the progression of the will mentioned above, will become clear enough; no one of these emphases need exclude the others. I think each offers certain pedagogical advantages, depending on the texts and thematic emphases that students have been previously met with in the syllabus.[4] For students to profit from these approaches, however, it will be necessary for them to be introduced to some rudiments of medieval theology and psychology.

Toward Wisdom

In his famous homily on the Sermon on the Mount, Augustine distinguishes three elements in the processes of human perception: an ordered progress of understanding which he locates in the universal human experience first as individual sense perception (*sensus*); after a perception occurs it is followed by *scientia* or the systematizing knowledge of material things; and *sapientia*, that higher and synthetic function by which both sense and reason are circumscribed in respect of the highest principle. For Augustine even this highest principle is derivative from the divine mind, and while, as with St. Paul and the Psalmist he thinks all mortal beings have glimpses of such wisdom through natural revelation, he believes that for its fullness man is dependent on the revelation of Christ in sacred Scripture.[5] Unfortunately, this *scala* or ladder of knowing is conditioned by the fallen human organism in which it is embodied; hence, Augustine is at pains to show that any acquisition of knowledge that seeks to bypass the synthetic principle corrupts. It inverts the hierarchy by which sense impression should refer itself for understanding to cognitive ordering, and cognition to sapiential judgment before action, so it is by definition contrary to health. Thus his allegory of the Fall: the serpent's presentation of the forbidden fruit is *sensus*, a sensual "phantasm" offered to Eve (*scientia*), whose "knowledge" ought then to have been referred to Adam (*sapientia*) before action, and then Adam's sapiential judgment ought finally to have been determined by what God has already commanded. At the moment when Eve decides to eat the apple and tell Adam later, the proper order of knowing has been fundamentally compromised. When the serpent rather than God prescribes the outcome, in fact, everything is, as the Wife of Bath puts it, "up-so-doun." Not only is the admixtured "knowledge of good and evil" something of an intellectual mess, each successive yielding to sensuality makes things messier. Stopping merely at rational cognition without reference to wisdom informed by revelation produces at best immaturity; at worst, the sophomoric flounderings of partial knowledge, when taken as sufficient, lead to a destructive idolatry of reason.

One can readily see how the first tale in each of the three "movements" of Chaucer's composition both announces the taxonomy and exemplifies its manner of operation. The Knight's Tale, told by an admirable character apparently possessed of the right sort of affections,[6] introduces us to a world in which the wisdom of Athens has theoretically subsumed unbridled passion (Ypolita had been queen of the fabled Amazons) to civic order. The tale opens, moreover, with Duke Theseus rectifying civic disorder by dispatching Creon, King of Thebes, rescinding Creon's cruel post-battle ban, and thus permitting the grieving women to bury their dead. When Theseus chooses not to participate in the scandalous practice of holding noble survivors for ransom, instead putting Palamon and Arcite into a rather comfortable prison, he nonetheless sets in motion a demonstration that his prisoners are unrepentant Thebans (in medieval terms the lineage of Thebes is identified with sensual oblivion). From their tower window Palamon and Arcite look out and spy a woman they have never met and who, not incidentally for the point of this tale, is entirely unaware of their interest. Immediately, they fall "in lust" with her. She is at this point simply a phantasm for the senses (Palamon claims to have been stuck by

Cupid's arrow through his eye into the heart – an adaptation of the Ovidian figure made familiar in the French *Roman de la Rose*), and their confusion of passion with reason (they begin to throw miscontextualized citations of Boethius's *Consolation of Philosophy* at each other) is hilarious but ultimately fratricidal. The elaborate symmetrical recensions of the plot are framed and ordered by the prayers of each lover characterizing their ruling passion in a different temple (Emelye goes to the temple of Diana, in which the Ovidian art unsurprisingly includes "Dane, yturned til a tree" [Knight's Tale, 2062]). The ambiguously answered prayers are followed by a tournament, funeral, and final marriage of Palamon and Emelye ordered by Theseus, even though marriage, strictly speaking, is not what either of them wants.

Philosophically, the narrative is guided by subsequent, more witting quotations from Boethius expressing such conceptions of wisdom and civic order as the metaphor of marriage (as opposed to rampant lust) itself signifies. Symphonically, these elements unite the plot and its initial theme or predicament with the tales that follow. To be brief, the Miller, Reeve, Wife of Bath, Man of Law, Friar, and Summoner all reveal in their prologues as well as their tales that they are extremely carnally minded, that they are hardened against reason, oblivious to wisdom, and in consequence predictably inclined to distort everything they "read" toward merely sensual indulgence. This provides much merriment for any reader who has read some of the texts they mangle (in the case of the Wife of Bath, for example, the Bible; in the case of the Summoner's Friar, the Franciscan Rule), but our recognition that sensual preoccupation is a form of arrested cognitive development in these characters – precluding sensible reading – is basic to the first group of tales taken as a whole.

The second movement begins with the Clerk's Tale. The Clerk, or Oxford student, is described in such a way that contemporary students should be able to identify him as something of an intelligent nerd. He is, for example, willing to starve himself so as to save up for a complete set of Aristotle's works, beautifully bound; medieval readers would recognize such an aspiration as wildly unrealistic (the cost would be far more than any such person could earn in a lifetime). Yet they would also see, as we might not, that in his faithfulness in prayer on behalf of those who have been funding his education he reveals sincere spiritual affections (301–2). This is consistent with his love for learning for the sake of understanding, rather than, as is the case with the Physician in the General Prologue, as something to be pursued merely for monetary gain (297–300). And his effort to make his speech both wise and virtuous signifies an intellectual journey that might one day make him a worthy teacher (303–8). That he is not perhaps quite yet where he aspires to be may be deduced from his tale.

In a rather lengthy disquisition the Clerk acknowledges that his contribution is a retelling of a text by Francis Petrarch, poet laureate of Italy and archdeacon at Padua. In the mouth of his Clerk, Chaucer makes it plain that he will adapt it to his own English circumstance (Clerk's Prologue, 21–56) and that he has found it in a version retold by another worthy scholar of Padua, recently deceased. We enter here upon the complexity of textual transmission, both its desirability and its uncertainties. The tale as the Clerk tells it becomes a political parable for England under Norman rule, with the imperious duke Walter abusing his Saxon-seeming wife Grisilde in their marriage, subjecting her to torments and testing of her fidelity both unreasonable and cruel. In fact, Chaucer intensifies the cruelty,[7] whereby it seems that the progeny of their union will be preserved even as Grisilde is ignominiously reduced again to the servitude from which she came. Grisilde is here, iconographically, the virtuous handmaiden of her lord, but Walter is a lord who abuses her trust. There is a further allegory here – an allegory in which the rule of reason over flesh, with nothing to temper it, is seen as insufficient to health either in the individual or the community. The Clerk stresses that his tale is not to be received as some sort of literal counsel to wives (he can imagine abuse of the paradigm, cf. lines 1139–63); in fact, in his final song (in some MSS attributed to Chaucer as an *envoi*) he urges wives *not* to be patient like Grisilde, but to fight back and even overmaster their husbands (1177–1212) as the Wife of Bath had recommended. This *envoi* effectively runs contrary to the burden of the tale as he tells it, even as it does to Petrarch's original, alerting readers that while the Clerk may have some conciliar texts at his disposal, either he is too insecure to draw fully upon their wisdom or he is being evasively ironic. Tales which follow in this group accord with the failing: the Merchant's overtly Ovidian tale has a foreshortened view of the proper rationale for Christian marriage, and is further complicated by the Merchant's strictly literalistic version of the *hortus conclusus* from the Song of Songs. This text had already been parodically invoked in the lewd Miller's Tale from the first group, in which the *quia amore langueo* passage typically interpreted allegorically in contexts more chaste (such as the hymns of St. Bernard) is here burlesqued to satirize the disordered affections of faithless clerics. In the case of one of these upstart sons of the Church, appropriately named Absalon, disordered desire is sealed, so to speak, with that decidedly anti-erotic "moustache" kiss. Likewise, in the Merchant's Tale, improperly referenced textual understanding leads to a disastrously comic burlesque in which adulterous lovers end their "race" in a tree while Ovid's equally adulterous Pluto and Proserpine look on; thus is the lust-blinded Januarie made most definitively a fool in a mock-Solomonic garden of his own fantasies. The Squire's foppery portends accurately his own jejune romanticism; the Franklin's tale offers a phony notion of "courtly love" vows and their keeping; and the Pardoner, Shipman and Prioress all tell tales which in their right context might have some of reason's virtues but which here, deprived of wise application, are entirely insufficient in themselves to turn vice to virtue in their tellers.

So we come to the final movement, in several ways unsatisfied. Appropriately enough, this series is to be begun by the master narrator, Geoffrey himself as "pilgrim." This is one of those points in *The Canterbury Tales* at which we can readily note Chaucer's careful and integratively useful distinctions between himself as actual "auctor," his pilgrim persona as fictive author, the many other pilgrims as similarly fictive authors, and the tales of those earlier authors which they respectively adduce – all as "readers" in a great tradition. We see here part of the elaborate framing device of *The Canterbury Tales* refocused for us: the General Prologue, head-links and tale prologues, tail-links and recensions (including Chaucer's own Retractions), all serve to keep us mindful that before us there are texts and there are readers, and that *each* requires of us an act of thoughtful interpretation.

Chaucer heightens our appreciation, nevertheless, that not all texts are equally worthy of interpretation by having his fictive "Chaucer," self-deprecatingly introduced, attempt to tell a sort of medieval romance. The plot is obscure, to say the least, and the verse truly miserable doggerel. Even the evidently obtuse "judge" of the tales, Harry Bailey the Host, is exasperated. Harry cuts "Chaucer" off, saying "Namoore of this, for Goddes dignitee," calling pilgrim Chaucer's pointless narrative a "verray lewednesse" and "drasty speche" (919–24), lacking either "murthe" or "doctrine."[8] Chaucer can then, his persona having been fictively "reprimanded" for rhymed drivel, commence upon a meatier prose narrative. This new tale, he now says, on the example of the unity-in-diversity of the four gospel accounts concerning Christ, will be his signature narrative (Melibee, 2133–56). Despite its different "manner," he assures both his fictive and actual readers that the meaning of this new tale will be entirely consistent with what he says in *The Canterbury Tales* overall. In short, the Tale of Melibee which he retells (from a text attributed to Albertanus of Brescia) will, in its compounded wisdom drawn from both biblical and classical literature, provide a synecdoche for the "sentence" of the whole work of which it is a part.

Although the Tale of Melibee introduces the third, sapiential movement of *The Canterbury Tales* and is Chaucer's "own," so to speak, it (along with the Parson's Sermon and the Retractions which conclude this great work) is seldom taught or represented in modernized versions of Chaucer. (This is literarily egregious, and in some cases it seems, ultimately, an attempt to edit out Chaucer's Christian worldview and authorial purpose.)[9] But it is critical to understanding Chaucer's overall *intentio auctoris*, obviously, that both this tale and Chaucer's formal *explicit* be reckoned with responsibly in a Great Texts curriculum. For a close reading of the Tale of Melibee one might profitably consider Proverbs 31 and the influential figure of the *mulier fortis* so strikingly contrasted in the Wife of Bath, though the text reads reasonably perspicuously on its own. Basically it is an allegory about the conditions of right judgment and "right reading." It begins with a nominally good man, Melibee, whose capacities for a life of virtue have been dulled by a surfeit of rich living. His estate is broken into by three foes (implicitly, the "three foes of man" in the medieval children's primer, namely the flesh, the world, and the devil) and they wound his daughter with "fyve mortal wounds in fyve sundry places." Melibee wants revenge as a means of justice, but his wife Prudence resists his angry impulse and characterizes his temper as a failure of mature judgment. She urges him, patiently, to consider more than his natural outrage and an instinct to use his martial knowledge to exact "justice." Rather, beginning with Ovid's *Remedia Amoris* and St. Paul's Epistle to the Romans, she adduces both classical and biblical counsels of wisdom in terms of which he might consider that he cannot, without first coming to healing wisdom himself, even begin to comprehend the situation, let alone address it profitably. This text is, of course, explicitly a species of court counsel for a time in which reflexive impetus to self-justification has repeatedly propelled the court into savage and unprofitable conflict at home and abroad. But it anchors also Chaucer's overall thesis in *The Canterbury Tales*, in which, as six centuries later with G.K. Chesterton, the correct answer to the question "What's wrong with the world?" is "Me." The counsel of wisdom from the great texts which Prudence gathers and patiently teaches to Melibee has at last its desired effect; he comes to see that justice tempered with mercy and forgiveness is the very wisdom of God and that this wisdom alone can change the world. Grasping the "trewe entente" (2664) of his faithful wife Prudence, Melibee "conformed hym anon," thanking God for this wisdom, and then he forgives his enemies. The tale concludes with an explicit reminder of the teaching of Jesus, that our own forgiveness is conditional upon our forgiveness of others, and with a prayer for such forgiveness. This is a point for reflection which Chaucer will return to explicitly in his own final confession, or Retractions, as he invites his readers to pray for God's forgiveness for his own errors and misjudgments, including his readerly and writerly misjudgments. Several of the tales that follow show what ensues when sound knowledge – including biblical knowledge – is left incomplete through a failure to apply it in the light of that ultimate wisdom, the wisdom made known in Christ Jesus (e.g., Monk's Tale, Nun's Priest's Tale, even the Manciple's Tale, with its Ovidian tale interrupted in such a way as actually to heighten the desire for expected closure; see Jeffrey 2011). Yet here we find tales also of transformation of the sort that Melibee exemplifies (Second Nun's Tale, Canon Yeoman's Tale). The intent of this series seems clearly to induce in us as readers a sense of our need of a knowledge transformed by higher wisdom, and of a metamorphosis of our desires that anticipates and illustrates the regeneration of souls by repentance and conversion, the ultimate *metanoia* that is the Parson's theologically rich subject and Chaucer's own conclusion.

Faith, Hope, and Love

And so, inevitably, we return to the subject of love itself. Though fully as important, and in one sense the fruit of the reader's pilgrimage from sensual self-absorption through knowledge to wisdom, the simultaneous overtones of a journey by faith through hope to love are concordant enough that they may be indicated here in briefer notation. Here, suffice it to say, Chaucer's medieval irony, by which one teaches a virtue in part by considering the consequences of its opposing vices, makes it possible for the teacher of *The Canterbury Tales* to employ any number of tales from each of the three movements to good and pedagogically sound effect. There is one additional advantage: teaching *The Canterbury Tales* in the light of the theological virtues, though perhaps less illuminating of Chaucer's extraordinarily rich intellectual and intertextual tapestry, requires somewhat less theological knowledge. This approach, I would suggest, can be facilitated by Dante's *Commedia* having already appeared in the syllabus, and even more naturally so if the *Commedia* has been read in the light of Augustine's *Confessions* and Dante's *La Vita Nuova.*

In the first movement of tales we are given a sequence of tellers – and tales – in which the predominant occasion of plot conflict is a species of infidelity, a breach of one or another type of covenant. In the Miller's, Reeve's, and Wife of Bath's tales this lack of faith (or as we might now say, absence of "good faith") becomes overt infidelity or faithlessness. Here it pertains to the institution of marriage at the domestic, literal level. In the narrative obfuscation of the Man of Law and the grotesque infidelity to their vows (poverty, chastity, obedience) of the Friar and Summoner, we are dealing with "marriage" at the spiritual level and faithlessness in that analogous context. Carnally induced blindness to the truth of such necessarily self-transcending obedience to covenantal *feodas* in their sources is an index of a related faithlessness in the teller. That faithlessness is likely to produce a certain self-willed blindness in figures such as the Wife of Bath in her prologue, or the rapist knight at the end of her tale, is made apparent to the reader through misunderstood allusions to the texts that they adduce and confound. The dramatic irony thus occasioned is a source of delightful humor for the witting reader, but on occasion the dark seriousness of such misprisions reveals simultaneously the moral seriousness in our actual author. For example, in the Friar's vengeful tale about a summoner who consorts with the devil, ultimately committing himself to a *pactum diaboli* which results in his being carried off to hell, the reader sees that the devil has a knowledge of theology considerably more perfect than his clerical victim. As with the demons in the gospels, who are aware both of the true identity of Jesus and of the ultimate consequences of their war against him and all those he would redeem, so here: this horseback devil, for example, has theological discernment sufficient to distinguish between words as spoken and true "entente" (Friar's Tale, 1539–68), a distinction to which the tale's carnally corrupted summoner is utterly obtuse. Though the devil tells him that he may only snatch away those who abandon the means of their salvation, and that in the end a devil's torments may even serve as "Goddes instruments" to turn men from the ultimate consequences of their faithlessness, "Al be it that was not oure entente" (Friar's Tale, 1474–1503), the summoner fails to take the point. In all of these tales, the virtue of "faith unfeigned" (1 Tim. 1:5; cf. 2 Tim. 1:5) is highlighted contrastively; in the context the result is a kind of chiaroscuro that reveals the needed virtue by the shadow of its terrible contrary.

In the second movement we have a variety of explorations of the frustrations of hope. This is evident in the Clerk's Tale, in which patient Grisilde is deprived of the grounds of hope by her cruel husband, yet resists despair. The Merchant January places his false hope in the delights of his "paradys terrestre," though sure enough, as his wise counselor Justinus predicts, his young bride May becomes at best his "purgatorie," betraying him in the pleasure garden with his own servant in a manner artfully reminiscent of the tale's Ovidian prototypes. The Squire's and Franklin's tales elaborate the theme: hope dependent on amorous or "courtly" love for its object is doomed to end in despair and foolishness, even ignominy. The Physician's and Pardoner's Tales both reveal characters despairing of hope and are about the death of hope, *wanhope*, or hopelessness. The latter of these is a parody of the Mass in which the revelers eat and drink to their own damnation (to invoke St. Paul), while the Shipman's Tale is about a wife despairing of sexual love and a corrupt monk who takes advantage of the fact. The Prioress's Tale is of a type forbidden by Pope Gregory precisely because its cruelty and sentimentality occlude the proper grounds of Christian hope.[10] Indeed, even without knowing this, an astute reader is more than likely to sense in this whole group of tales a pervasive "hopelessness," in all the usual modern senses of the word. The proper remedy, Christian hope, is more than optimism; it has a transcendent object. My own choices for a representative tale illustrating this theme in the movement would be either the Merchant's or the Franklin's Tale.

The third grouping begins, as we have seen, with the Tale of Melibee, told by Chaucer the pilgrim, and it commences a series in which the tales show both the consequences of disordered love and the benefits of love rightly ordered toward God and neighbor. The Monk's dark telling of myriad stories of tragic downfall illustrates the manifold consequences of disordered loves, but by denying to each exemplum its possibility of a better ending he fails to indicate love's remedy. After he is rebuked by the Host for this defect, it is the turn of the Nun's Priest. This modest chaplain tells a fable about the obsessive passions of a rooster named Chauntecleer for his flock of hens, especially his favorite, Pertelote. Chauntecleer's cupidity blinds him to all the sources of wisdom available to him, even prophetic dreams of special revelation, and if at the last possible moment he is able to escape the devilish fox to whom in the garden he has fallen prey, it is only by cleverly appealing to the fox's own cupidity and pride. The Second Nun's Tale that follows is a classic tale of Christian transformation, a metamorphosis of natural love by Christian charity and chastity which leads in consequence to martyrdom – but also to conversions. The Canon's Yeoman's Tale is about the consequences of cupidity, a false love for gold and the deceptions that attend it, yet here, unlike in the Pardoner's Tale in which the topic (*radix malorum cupiditas est*) was introduced, the teller himself is transformed as he tells his story through candid confession of the truth about his own concupiscence and his admission that "swich a lucre is in this lusty game, / A mannes myrthe it wol turn unto grame [grief]" (Canon's Yeoman's Tale, 1402-3). His confession is the price of admission; he joins the pilgrim community, swelling its number now to thirty.

Yet there is one more, penultimate retelling before the Parson's conclusion. The Manciple's Tale has its Ovidian source in the second book of the *Metamorphoses*, and recalls another of the unsuccessful amours of Phebus Apollo, this time as mediated specifically by Christian allegory in the *Ovide Moralisé*. In its artfully attenuated telling the Manciple's version highlights the terrible judgment of Phebus Apollo, "semelieste man/ That is or was, sith that the world bigan" (Manciple's Tale 119–20) upon the adulterous cupidity of the "wyf/ Which that he lovede moore than his lyf" (139–40), reminding Chaucer's audience that the consequences of disordered love can include both infamy and death. Once again, however, the original tale is cut short, denied its redemptive conclusion. Here again the knowledgeable reader is made keen for the health of a more charitable and merciful love through its deliberate denial. In this fashion Chaucer piques his readers' desire for more than an ephemeral love, so preparing us for the fulsome analysis of rightly ordered faith, hope, and charity in the Parson's Sermon. In this final movement, both the Nun's Priest's Tale and the Second Nun's Tale offer particular advantages for exploration of Chaucer's reflection on charitable love as the greatest of the theological virtues.

Making An End

We know that Chaucer did not complete the project he set himself in the General Prologue of *The Canterbury Tales*; that would have required two tales per pilgrim each way, for either 116 or 120 tales, depending on how we might calculate the obligations of the Canon's Yeoman, the thirtieth pilgrim, after he joins the group almost at the end of the journey to Canterbury. But whether Chaucer intended this massive quantum or not (he died shortly after the

Retractions were complete at the end of his own holograph manuscript of *The Canterbury Tales*), it is clear that he crafted – perhaps sensing time's immanent foreclosure – an *explicit* end to the Tales such as by then were written. This conclusion bears the firm imprint of an intellectual program and artistic design.

The Parson's Prologue provides important keys to our understanding of the larger work. By echoing in the sun's descent to twenty-nine degrees and the moon's uprising in Libra (the scales of justice) the opening General Prologue with its twenty-nine pilgrims and a call for final judgment on the best story, Chaucer both reminds us of the outer frame of his grand narrative and raises the reader's still unanswered questions. Moreover, when the narrator measures the shadow cast from himself to the ground as a ratio of six (since Augustine, the number of the soul) to eleven (the number, short of twelve, for individual short-comings and sin), and speaks solely from his own point of view, Chaucer subtly shifts our reflection from the noisy "many-ness" of the *Tales*' opening scenes to a quieter singleness of focus on the weighty matters now before us as individual readers. The Host declares that, in fact, only one story is lacking, and he calls accordingly upon the Parson to "knytte up wel a greet mateere" (Parson's Prologue, 28). In his disclaimer the Parson is entirely self-effacing; since he is no poet, he will (like Chaucer in Melibee) tell his "myrie tale in prose":

> To knytte up al this feeste, and make an ende.
> And Jhesu, for his grace, wit me sende
> To shewe yow the way, in this viage,
> Of thilke parfit glorious pilgrymage
> That highte Jerusalem celestial.
> (47–51)

Averring that he is open to all learned criticism, since he is "nat textual" (not learned), he commences upon what is effectively a detailed exposition of the vices and virtues, organized under an exposition of penitence, the means of contrition, confession, and satisfaction; the fruit of these, he will go on to say, is the theological virtues, and their ultimate fulfillment, through grace, in heaven. While perhaps not every teacher will be able to guide students through this frankly catechetical conclusion to *The Canterbury Tales*, one of the rewards for those who do will be myriad recognizable comments on individual tales, and a sense of their ingathering as to meaning and final purpose. This, or something very like this, is surely what Chaucer intended.

As with all of *The Canterbury Tales*, the Parson's sermon is replete with the citation of previous great texts, in this case, as we would expect, from Scripture and the Fathers. That is, the Parson's wisdom is the wisdom of a faithful reader, and it might even seem that against all odds he is the one who should be judged to have told the tale "of best sentence and moost solaas"

(General Prologue, 798), and thus be granted "a sopre at oure aller cost" (799). We know that medieval readers loved such games; Chaucer's actual audience must have had their literary appetites whetted to see who the Host would declare the winner. But such an announcement never comes. Rather, in the silence following the Parson's conclusion, as his medieval readers ineluctably imagine the scene of pilgrims dismounting and filing into Canterbury Cathedral to make their confession, thus to prepare for Holy Communion, we, as readers, are left each alone to our own reflective self-examination in silence – and perhaps then to experience a sudden, momentous recognition. Together, on their knees before the altar, the pilgrims will feel the competitiveness of their own, often self-justifying tales fade away in the candlelight. Their boisterous worldly host has here given way to another Host; judgment is now to be tempered with divine mercy to those who are penitent. Thus, full closure in *The Canterbury Tales* comes less as a sense of masterful resolution of contestation on the author's part than as unexpected grace – a grace beyond the reach of art. No other tale than one qualifies. Our unfinished business is not about which pilgrim gets a supper paid for at the cost of all, but rather a matter of accepting – or not – a joyous communal partaking of a Supper for all that has been paid for at the cost of One.

Temporal endings, as teachers of Great Texts well know, are not always synchronous with the real sense of closure that a great work of art can provide. In Christian art, to experience such closure sometimes implies, in effect, participation in the means of grace, and thus openness to having everything in our own favorite story changed, our view of life itself transformed. Readers in any era may find this a risky business. In Chaucer's text the ultimate metamorphosis for each mortal story comes from without; internalized, it creates an ironic reversal in the dominant passions of one who will receive the gift, or, to put this more literarily, it transforms every teller who will receive it by induced participation in the One true story. Chaucer's long and patient artfulness seems calculated to obtain his readers' sudden realization, in the twinkling of an eye, that only in this final metamorphosis may our own incomplete, fragmented stories at last achieve *their* closure, their persistent, yearning desire for meaning then at last be fulfilled.

David Lyle Jeffrey

References

Beichner, Paul E., C.S.C. 1961. "The Grain of Paradise," *Speculum* 36, no. 2: 302–7.

Chaucer, Geoffrey, 1992. *The Canterbury Tales*. Ed. A.C. Cawley. New York and Toronto: Alfred Knopf/Everyman.

de Boer, C., ed. 1920. *Ovide Moralisé*, 2 vols. Amsterdam: Muller.

Dunlap, Rhodes, ed. 1949. *The Poems of Thomas Carew*. Oxford: Oxford University Press.

Gaylord, Alan T. 1962. "The Unconquered Tale of the Prioress," *Papers of the Michigan Academy* 47: 613–36.

Jeffrey, David Lyle 1996. *People of the Book: Christian Identity and Literary Culture.* Grand Rapids and Cambridge: Eerdmans.

——— 2011. "Trying to Get to Canterbury: Closure in the Manciple's Tale" in *The Ignatius Critical Chaucer.* Ed. David Williams. Fort Collins: Ignatius Press. 78–97.

McCall, John P. 1962. "The Trojan Scene in Chaucer's *Troilus*," *English Literary History* 29, no. 3: 263–75.

Peck, Russell A. 1967. "Number Symbolism in the Prologue to the Parson's Tale," *English Studies* 48: 205–15.

Severs, J. Burke 1942. *The Literary Relationships of Chaucer's Clerk's Tale.* New Haven: Yale University Press.

Williams, David, ed. 2011. *The Ignatius Critical Chaucer.* Fort Collins: Ignatius Press.

Wyclif, John 1886. *De Ecclesia*. Ed. J. Loserth (London: Wyclif Society, 1886).

Teresa of Ávila
Las Moradas (The Interior Castle)

For a number of years, I have read Teresa of Ávila's classic, *Las Moradas*, with my students, both undergraduates and seminarians. While they take exception to Teresa's often self-deprecating remarks about women, they respond positively to her emphasis on the spiritual life as an interior journey traveling into the deep recesses of one's soul. When Teresa refers to the soul and to "interior matters" (Teresa 1961, 7), my students easily assume that Teresa is describing a highly privatized spirituality. In our late modern context, in fact, it is easy to read Teresa as advocating an internal, *unmediated* quest for God, one in which such "externals" as the sacraments, Holy Scripture, and the body called "church" have all receded far into the background.

This essay argues that such a reading of Teresa is distorting, and obscures the scriptural and ecclesial wisdom that she offers. Teresa ought not be read as an early modern figure withdrawing into the inner world of the self. She is not advocating an "adventure of interiority . . . of the soul that goes to find itself"[1] in a gnostic kind of inner exploration.[2] Rather, she narrates a scriptural pilgrimage that aims for unity in the visible body of Christ. In fact, the title of her work, *Las Moradas*, does not mean "interior castle," as the standard translation suggests, but "the dwellings" or "the abodes." As I will display more fully, Teresa uses "dwellings" in a profoundly scriptural way to refer to how the triune God dwells in and with creation. I argue then that *Las Moradas* does not describe a gnostic journey into the self, but rather an ecclesial, scriptural, and sacramental journey with and toward Christ, a transformative journey toward being Christ's body for the world.

Teresa and modernity

Before examining this claim more fully, however, it will be helpful to consider modern misreadings of Teresa, all of which isolate Teresa's writings from scripture, sacrament, and church. Those who know little else about Teresa of Ávila have often seen Giovani Lorenzo Bernini's famous sculpture, "The Ecstasy of Saint Teresa" (1647–1652), located in the Santa Maria de la Vittoria Church in Rome. The sculpture appears, at least to most modern viewers, to be deeply erotic, an impression confirmed when they read the words from Teresa's autobiography on which the sculpture is based:

> I saw in his hands a large golden dart and at the end of the iron tip there appeared to be a little fire. It seemed to me this angel plunged the dart several times into my heart and that it reached deep within me. When he drew it out, I thought he was carrying off with him the deepest part of me; and he left me all on fire with great love of God. The pain was so great that it made me moan, and the sweetness this greatest pain caused me was so superabundant that there is no desire capable of taking it away; nor is the soul content with less than God (Teresa 1995, 200).

Modern viewers understandably question this so-called ecstasy. Is this really about God or is it about Teresa's own unfulfilled sexuality, as one might expect from a celibate nun? And indeed, this is how some popular anti-Catholic works, such as Dan Brown's *Angels and Demons,* describe it.[3] This typically modern reading assumes that "religion" inevitably serves as a mask for Freudian psychological-erotic projection, the projected joy of a repressed nun for a lover/spouse, much as the disciples' joy in the resurrection can become a projected desire not to be abandoned by a father-figure.

In contrast to this "sophisticated" reaction to Teresa as unenlightened and self-deceived, by far the most popular interpretation of Teresa (the one my students are most drawn to) has been to embrace her as a "mystic for *our* time." From this perspective, *Las Moradas* narrates the enlightened inward journey of a soul making its way to God, without the crutch or impediment of religious dogma. Teresa's "interior castle" thus shows people how "to find life's answers deep within their own souls."[4] Some passages in *Las Moradas* may seem to lend support to this kind of reading. For example, Teresa famously begins *Las Moradas* with a vivid description of the soul as a diamond castle with many mansions, "and in the centre and midst of them all is the chiefest mansion where the most secret things pass between God and the soul" (Teresa 1961, 5). Does not this kind of emphasis on the soul and God suggest that Teresa's spirituality is, in the final analysis, a private one? Are not Word or sacrament *irrelevant* in her account? Some have said so, concluding that Teresa's "mysticism" is not bound by the particularities of time, place, and tradition. On the contrary, her spirituality is universal because everyone can find God within. Barbara Mujica reflects this interpretation of Teresa:

> Her spirituality is an *interior* spirituality that doesn't hang on ritual but rather teaches people to find God *within*. And in this time of sectarianism, Teresa is a person who reaches across cultures and religions. She speaks to everyone.[5]

Teresa can speak across cultures and religions, according to Mujica, because she locates God within the inner recesses of the self. No external rituals, dogmas, or "sectarian" practices need inhibit Teresa's spirituality. She speaks to everyone precisely because she is *not* confined by the church which, for these authors, is either invisible in Teresa's work, or appears in opposition to Teresa (as an inquisitorial force, for example).[6] In this view, Teresa is an enlightened, modern mystic not bound "by self-incurred tutelage."[7] Our students, who are deeply formed by late modernity, will naturally tend to read Teresa in this light.

Ecclesial interiority

The reading of Teresa as an enlightened, universal mystic, though misguided, nonetheless raises important questions: how is "interiority" to be understood within *Las Moradas*? More broadly, how ought Christians to think about "interiority" vis-à-vis doctrine and the church, or about the relation between the self and the community, or between personal experience and tradition? As I intend to show more fully, Teresa's performance of scripture disallows these kinds of stark, modern dualisms. For her, the church is the condition of the possibility for spirituality because all Christian experiences of God are structured by ecclesial practices, which are themselves grounded in God's Word.[8]

This means that there is no such thing as an inner generic or universal "spirituality" apart from specific stories, traditions, and practices that make such spirituality possible. Within the Christian story, as Teresa understood and embodied it, "interiority" is not an inward, invisible realization of the soul, but rather a *transformation* of the person in Christ and so also into the visible body of Christ. "Do you know when people really become spiritual?" she writes. "It is when they become the slaves of God and are branded with His sign, which is the sign of the Cross, in token that they have given Him their freedom" (Teresa 1961, 234). Thus, pilgrims are journeying faithfully to the extent that they become like Christ, not in the robotic sense of repeating Christ's life exactly (which, since Christ is the divine Son, is impossible), but in the improvisational sense of learning to live faithfully in communion with Christ, which is itself true freedom.

We can see this reliance on an ecclesially conditioned "interiority" in Teresa's autobiography where she writes of her encounter with Augustine.

> As I began to read the *Confessions*, it seemed to me I saw myself in them. When I came to the passage where he speaks about his conversion and read how he heard that voice in the garden, it only seemed to me, according to what I felt in my heart, that it was I the Lord called (Teresa 1995, 9.8, 51).

In this famous scene to which Teresa refers, Augustine hears a child singing, "Pick it up and read, pick it up and read," and hears in these words God's own word telling him to open the Book. He picks up his "book of the Apostle's letters" and reads Rom. 13:13–14, part of which states "put on the Lord Jesus Christ, and make no provision for the flesh or the gratification of your desires." Realizing that the grace of Christ will transform his disordered life, Augustine writes that "the light of certainty flooded my heart and all dark shades of doubt fled away" (Augustine 1997, 10.6.8). When Teresa herself reads this account, she too undergoes a transformation, "I remained for a long time totally dissolved in tears and feeling within myself utter distress and weariness" (Teresa 1995, 9.8, 51). While the reception of God's Word by Augustine and Teresa differs to some extent, Teresa like Augustine is "pierced" by the Word of God.[9] Like Augustine, her senses are opened to God's gifts and desires, so that she can later gladly exclaim not only about the Word but also about the Eucharist, "Your delight is to be with the children of the earth."[10] For Teresa, the gifts and love of God are mediated through the Word, the Eucharist, and the communion of saints, especially in this instance Augustine, St. Paul, and the Augustinian nuns of Our Lady of Grace.[11] This Word is not already inside Teresa, but is rather mediated to her through a vast communion and through traditional practices (reading scripture). Augustine does say that he was without, trying to find order in his life, while God was *within*.[12] And Teresa develops a key image of "His Majesty," Christ, as already dwelling *inside* the soul: "for the soul's capacity is much greater that we can realize, and this Sun, Which is in the palace, reaches every part of it" (Teresa 1961, 13). These passages, however, need to be read in light of God's dwelling with humanity through Christ, not as though persons already have a gnostic inner light that circumvents or denies the goodness and reconciliation of creation through God's Word given to the church on behalf of the world.

"I am a daughter of the church"

As I have been arguing, then, *Las Moradas* is best read not as a modern gnostic journey into the self but rather an ecclesial and scriptural journey. In fact, *Las Moradas* offers a commentary on scripture. Most surprising for the contemporary student, however, will be the fact that Teresa did not have access to the whole Bible. Sections of the Bible translated into Spanish were available to her in anthologies, but the modern practice of having an entire Bible to read from was unknown to Teresa. But this did not prevent her from claiming, "I would die a thousand deaths for the faith or for any truth of Sacred Scripture" (Teresa 1995, 235). In saying this, Teresa is not staking her life on the Word alone (*scriptura nuda*, as it has been called). She had no such concept.

To see how Teresa was willing to stake her life on scripture, we must note that she inhabited a deeply liturgical world, where time was marked by praying the daily office; where making confession was as common for her as watching TV is for us; where the year was measured by frequent feast and fast days; and where the celebration of the Mass was the high point of all time. As Eamon Duffy describes this world,

> Within the liturgy, birth, copulation, and death, journeying and home-coming, guilt and forgiveness, the blessing of homely things and the call to pass beyond them were all located, tested and sanctioned. In the liturgy and in the sacramental celebrations which were its central moments, medieval people found the key to the meaning and purpose of their lives. (Duffy 1992, 11)

The daily rhythm of frequent prayer, the celebration of the Eucharist, the oral reading of scripture, sermons, confessions, and the singing of scripture would have all shaped Teresa, enabling her to absorb scripture mediated through these various practices of the church. On her deathbed, in fact, eyewitnesses report that Teresa said many times over, "Finally, Lord, I am a daughter of the church."

Such strong confidence in the church does not mean Teresa is unaware of the church's sins and weaknesses. In *Las Moradas*, she laments how she has had to suffer from the ignorance of some of her male confessors. She acknowledges the trials of living in community with her sisters. Teresa herself leads a reformation of her monastic order, establishing seventeen foundations of discalced Carmelites. Finally, as we see in *Las Moradas*, Teresa is deeply aware of her own sinfulness. In spite of this sinfulness, or better *because* of it, Teresa relies upon Christ's grace as mediated through his body.

We are now in a better position to see that *Las Moradas* ought to be read as a kind of commentary on scripture that is deeply shaped by the liturgy and the church broadly understood (as a fellowship of saints, that included brothers such as Augustine, across time). By calling Teresa a commentator on scripture, I do not mean that she systematically comments verse by verse on particular books.[13] In fact she sometimes quotes from scripture without remembering the location of the verse (as we might expect from someone who does not have the text before her). *Las Moradas* is rather a commentary that extends and illumines the contours of the Christian story. Teresa's confessor, Fr. Gratian, no doubt had this kind of illumination in mind when he charged Teresa to "put down the *doctrine* in a general way without naming the one to whom the things you mentioned happened" (cited by Kavanaugh 1980, 263, my emphasis).[14] Her response was *Las Moradas*. Let us now turn more fully to how *Las Moradas* provides scriptural commentary.

Teresa as Expositor of Scripture

As practitioners of scriptural reasoning have recently emphasized, to use scripture wisely is, ironically, not simply to *use* scripture, but rather to be nurtured and healed by it.[15] And healing is the goal of Teresa's journey. The seventh and final dwelling, for example, is marked by unity with Christ in the Body of Christ. Mary (sitting at the feet of Jesus) and Martha (feeding Jesus and bringing him souls) together, according to Teresa, embody the kind of love that Christ both desires and gives (Teresa 1961, 236). To dwell in this Mary/Martha pattern is to receive healing from the Word. Teresa would agree with Augustine that "whoever, then, thinks that he understands the Holy scriptures, or any part of them, but puts such an interpretation upon them as does not tend to build up this twofold love of God and our neighbor, does not yet understand them" (Augustine 1977, 1.36.40).

Teresa is at her best, in my view, when she uses certain scriptural figures (such as *moradas* or dwellings, marriage, journey) creatively to understand her own time and place in scriptural terms. A figurative reading of scripture can be said to transport "the historical events of the past into the present and future; it also sees the future in the past and present as a way to interpret scripture in terms of the divine economy."[16] On this reading, *Las Moradas* is not an individual journey, but rather encompasses a broader scriptural reality: the creation of Israel, its wandering in the desert, and its entry into the promised land. The church as a figure of Israel repeats this journey, which is ultimately fulfilled by and in Christ. Consider first Teresa's key figure¯the castle¯to see more fully how Teresa's classic displays an outworking of this scriptural form.

Teresa begins *Interior Castle* with a reference to the Gospel of John: "In my Father's House are many rooms; if it were not so, would I have told you that I go to prepare a place for you?" (John 14:2), a passage which she relates to the *imago dei*: "for, as he himself says, he created us in his image and likeness" (Teresa 1961, 2). Teresa interprets the passage from John as not only about life after death; it describes our current condition. To be in the image of God is already to be¯in a sense¯in "my Father's house." This is not a large stately mansion, such as the ones Teresa no doubt saw across her Castilian landscape. Teresa rather uses the Spanish words *moradas*, *piezas* and *aposentos* to refer to more humble dwelling places, though dwellings of great beauty (Kavanaugh 1980, 484). Through the resurrection, alluded to already in the John passage, Christ is in the castle and thus *already* dwells where we are. For Teresa, to be in God's image is not a quality that humanity possesses, but a relation between humanity and God. That is, just as humans are already a diamond castle (albeit a castle covered in darkness) so also are they already inside a relation with God (even if it is unacknowledged). Teresa laments, though, that many people, including her own sisters, do not fully know who they are. "It is a shame and unfortunate," Teresa writes, "that through our own fault we don't understand ourselves or know who we are" (Teresa 1961, 2). By "through our own fault," Teresa means that we fail to confess sin and thus to accept Christ's forgiveness; we fail to receive what God desires to give us; we fail to pray; we fail truly to love.

Even so, the castle is beautiful. As is well known, Teresa describes the castle as carved out of a single diamond with seven mansions, each with an abundance of expansive rooms through which souls can wander and move as they journey toward the center: Christ, "His Majesty." Teresa is so struck by the sheer beauty of the dwelling that she writes:

> I can find nothing with which to compare the great beauty of a soul and its great capacity . . . there is no point in fatiguing ourselves by attempting to comprehend the beauty of this castle; for, though it is His creature, and there is therefore as much difference between it and God as between creature and Creator, the very fact that His Majesty says it is made in His image means that we can hardly form any conception of the soul's great dignity and beauty. (Teresa 1961, 4)

While the castle is itself stunning, the beauty can be diminished or left undiscovered. One can remain in the outer courtyard; fear, anxiety, sin and so forth are all "ways of 'being' in a place" (Teresa 1961, 6) that can obscure the castle's beauty. But the beauty cannot be *erased* because the word of God is constant and faithful, dwelling at the center.

Now, we can examine more fully how this castle is a scriptural figure. The figure of dwelling¯of God dwelling with a people – is a key scriptural form. Zion, the holy mountain in Jerusalem, is God's dwelling place. The Psalmist, using language similar to Teresa's, describes it as "the perfection of beauty" (Ps. 50:2). Zion is beautiful because it is identified with the City of David, the Israelites, God's chosen ones with whom God dwells.

In the book of Revelation, there is again a holy city made of beautiful jewels like Teresa's castle: jasper, and gold, clear as glass (Rev. 21:18). A voice from the throne repeats what was said about Zion, "See, the home (or tabernacle) of God is among mortals. He will dwell with them as their God; they will be his peoples, and God himself will be with them; . . . " (Rev. 21:3–4). Though this is about a future hope, it is also a hope and an abode already present; God already dwells with us. As Teresa reflects, God resides in a house with many dwellings. *Las Moradas*, as Teresa envisions it, is not a gnostic reality but a cosmic one. God dwells with all of creation through Christ and his body.

Finally, the scriptural figure of dwellings comes into focus most fully in the Word that "became flesh and lived ('tabernacled') among us" (John 1:14). This Word is not "mere" speech, but the agent of all creation, through whom "all things came into being" (John 1:3), who at the same time "pitches his tent" among us. John's Gospel adds, "No one has ever seen God. It is God the only Son, who is in the bosom of the Father, he has made him known" (1:18). Eamon R. Carroll S.T.D. states that words similar to these, such as what Philip said at the last supper, "'who sees me sees the Father' (John 14:9), were axiomatic in Teresa's life" (Carroll 1984, 135). Christ dwells in the flesh, enabling believers through the Spirit to see and share in the Son's communion with the Father. It is through these particular scriptural prisms of God dwelling with humanity‾Zion, Jerusalem, and most fully, Jesus‾that one sees God dwelling with all of creation. Since Christ "tabernacled" in the flesh, Christ continues to tabernacle in the flesh now, disclosing through the Spirit the fullness of all creation. From this perspective, creation itself, for Teresa, has a triune imprint.[17]

But is Teresa saying that Christ already dwells *in* everyone? If the answer is "yes," this seems to short circuit human agency. Doesn't one need to have faith or take the sacraments or do good works to have Jesus inside?

New Testament theologian Douglas Harink sheds light on this point in his discussion of 2 Corinthians 5, which he translates: "For the love of Christ urges us on, because we are convinced that one has died for all; therefore all have died. . . . From now on, therefore, we regard no one from a human point of view. . . . So if anyone is in Christ, there is a new creation: everything old has passed away; see, everything has become new!" (2 Cor. 5:14, 16, 17). Harink notes that these verses have often been interpreted as being about the state of the individual. He argues, however, that

> the new creation being asserted here is not a claim about the state of the Christian; it is a claim about how the world and in particular the other human being, must be acknowledged as new creation by the Christian, who knows that the old creation has been invaded, challenged and judged, in the death of Christ. . . . The other who stands before me is already cosharer in that new creation; the task of the Christian in the face of this other is to call attention to that fact. (Harink 2003, 252–253)

In Teresa's depiction of persons as diamond castles, she is stating that all persons are already sharers in Christ's new creation. This is not to say that all are Christians, but rather to emphasize the renewal of all creation in and through Christ who has "invaded" the old creation through death and resurrection. God uniting himself to creation in Christ exposes sin and death in their defeat as well as the magnificent *beauty* of new creation. As contemporary theologian David B. Hart states,

> . . . Christians are bidden to see in Christ at once the true form of God and *the true shape of humanity*, and to believe that the Father sees with pleasure his own very likeness in Jesus of Nazareth, even him crucified, and furthermore, consents to view *all of humanity as gathered into the beauty of his Son*. (Hart 2003, 336)[18]

Teresa's diamond castle is a way of describing the true shape of humanity.

One hardly needs to point out that humanity, in many ways, is not beautiful. Wars, hatreds, jealousies and innumerable petty sins can make talk of beauty seem almost obscene. Teresa registers this fact in her own way when she describes those who have grown so accustomed "to living all the time with reptiles and other creatures to be found in the outer court of the castle that they have almost become like them" (Teresa 1961, 7). In her account, reptiles are ominous figures related to Teresa's own vivid sense of the "dark depths of the demonic world."[19] The soul, says Teresa, separates itself from God by preferring to give pleasure to the devil; "and, as the devil is darkness itself, the poor soul becomes darkness itself likewise…producing nothing but misery and filth" (Teresa 1961, 10). This terrible darkness, however, does not negate God's dwelling in the castle: God's presence to and with each creature. God's faithful presence may, however, come in different forms: as judgment, offense, consolation, forgiveness, and so forth.

Journey to the promised land

The second figure from *Las Moradas* that I want to consider is that of a journey. Though "His Majesty" dwells in the center of the castle, he can be seen to some degree from all places in the castle.

> Think of a palmito, which has many outer rinds surrounding the savory part within, all of which must be taken away before the centre can be eaten. Just as around this central room are many more, so there also are above it . . . and this Sun, Which is in the palace, reaches every part of it. (Teresa 1961, 13)

Teresa's image captures the Psalmist's description, "Whither shall I go from thy Spirit? Or whither shall I flee from thy presence? If I ascend to heaven, thou art there! If I make my bed in Sheol, thou art there" (Ps. 139: 7–8). For Teresa, however, it is the journey that enables us to see that we are already inside a relation with God.

The journey through the castle is the journey of the Israelites. The Exodus is relevant to Teresa's time and place because God is still leading people from slavery to freedom, from captivity to salvation. *Las Moradas* thus describes an exodus from the outer court, from concerns about "honor" and reputation, and even from a zeal for "perfection." The journey requires humility, which Teresa relates to self-knowledge, but the only way travelers can gain self-knowledge is through seeking to know God: "we shall never succeed in knowing ourselves unless we seek to know God" (Teresa 1961, 14). The Hebrew people discover their identity (and even that they are "a people") through their obedience as God leads them to the Promised Land; the same is true also for the travelers through the castle. Applied to our context, we could say that the point of truthful self-knowledge is to become free from the autonomous "self," and therefore free to see ourselves in communion with God. The alternative, notes Teresa, is to be bound by our fears and by the "slough of cowardice . . . . We shall always be glancing around and saying: 'Are people looking at me or not?' . . . 'Will people think better of me if I refrain from following the crowd?'" (Teresa 1961, 15). Such words echo Moses' own response to God's call to lead the Hebrews out of slavery: "But suppose [the Israelites] do not believe me or listen to me, but say, 'The Lord did not appear to you'" (Exod. 4:1).

Teresa's journey involves wandering, like the Israelites, in the wilderness or dry land. In the third mansions, Teresa tells her sisters to move through times of "aridity" and not "at a snail's pace" (Teresa 1961, 39). They pass through waters and manna rains down. In the fourth mansions, Teresa describes God's consolations as different kinds of fresh and refreshing waters. Like the waters of salvation (passing through the Red Sea), God opens up a way forward where previously none existed, moving those gathered toward the Promised Land. In the fifth mansions, the wanderers receive the commandments, particularly the commandments to love of God and neighbor (Teresa 1961, 103). Finally, in the seventh and final mansions, they enter into the Promised Land, which is a life lived in communion with God and others, described in terms of Teresa's monastic context.

The reader can see that Teresa herself is a Moses figure, who encounters God in dramatic burning bush-like ways (through locutions and visions), and leads her hearers to the Promised Land. Teresa does not describe herself in these terms. Like Moses, she voices self-doubt and sometimes makes belittling statements about herself and about being a woman. But the point is that the reader, perhaps even more than Teresa herself, can see biblical patterns in Teresa's life and writings.

Teresa's journey through the dwellings is also liturgical. There is an entrance, confession of sin and listening to sermons (second mansions). The waters associated with prayer that Teresa describes so vividly (fourth mansions), like the waters of baptism, make possible a dying and rising with Christ: a new life heretofore unimaginable. In the sixth and seventh dwellings, Teresa describes betrothal and marriage to God, using language that reflects an intimacy and friendship between God and his people. But this union is not "spiritual" as opposed to "material." Rather, it is thoroughly eucharistic. As Augustine famously notes, the Eucharist reverses the normal pattern of food consumption. "Other food is digested by Christian believers, but the Eucharist as a heavenly food digests its own communicants, making them immortal and giving them a share in resurrection life."[20] For Teresa, to dwell with Christ is to live eucharistically. In being "consumed" by Christ, we become the body of Christ for the world. Thus Teresa can state, "The surest sign we are keeping the two commandments (love for His Majesty and love for our neighbor) is, I think, that we should really be loving our neighbor; for we cannot be sure if we are loving God, although we may have good reasons for believing that we are, but we can know quite well if we are loving our neighbor" (Teresa 1961, 103).

From this perspective, *Las Moradas* is about not only hearing the Word, but also being consumed by it. Teresa's sisters are apparently concerned that they cannot offer much to God, like the apostles or other great teachers. Teresa counters that the Son takes whatever we can offer, and unites our offering, however meager, with his offering to the Father, "so it may have the value won for it by our will, even though our actions in themselves may be trivial" (Teresa 1961, 238). Such convictions rest upon and are formed by eucharistic practice where Christ joins our offering, sacrifice and praise to his own making possible our communion with the Father. As Geoffrey Wainwright says about worship more broadly, "The classical movement of Christian worship has always meant a participatory entrance into Christ's self-offering to the Father and correlatively being filled with divine life" (Wainwright 1980, 23). In this sense, *Las Moradas* is a liturgical book, in which the movement of the creature to God is "no independent human movement, but belongs within the movement from God to God by which the Spirit adds a new song to the love between the Father and the Son" (Rogers 2005, 193).

Far, then, from being a journey into the invisible world of the interior soul, *Las Moradas*, read as commentary on scripture, describes a journey that makes the body of Christ more visible for the world. For Teresa, the beauty of this life is seen not in the majestic castles that marked the Spanish countryside, but in the eucharistic way of life marked by humility, grace, and love capable of honoring and serving Christ.

Wounds on the Body

Teresa writes *Las Moradas* as a kind of epistle to the Carmelite communities that she has founded and reformed, and through which she seeks healing for the whole church. In *The Way of Perfection*, Teresa tells about the pain she feels over troubles in the church in Europe. In her *Foundations*, she writes of her deep concern for those millions who have never heard of Jesus Christ. In both her writing and her life, Teresa is attending to the wounds on the body of Christ, one of the deepest of which was growing division within the church. This is not to say that Teresa had first-hand knowledge of the divisions taking place in the church in the sixteenth century. For example, like many Spaniards, Teresa uses "Lutherans" to refer to the French Calvinist Huguenots. Even so, Teresa participated (and continues to participate through the communion of saints) in "that continual reformation of which [the Church] always has need" (Pope John Paul II 1995, paragraph 16).

One particular scene in her life gives insight into how Teresa's theological wisdom provides healing for Christ's body. The episode took place during Lent, 1554, when Teresa was thirty-nine years old. As she tells it, she came upon a figure of Christ crucified, and was struck by the figure of Jesus in his moment of isolation, above all in Gethsemane. What astounds her is the realization that Christ, in his woundedness, *needs* her. If it is true that Christ cannot be separated from his body (understood as the church), then this scene can be "read" as also about the wounds of the church and the church's need for Teresa and her gifts. Archbishop Rowan Williams, in his discussion of this scene, notes that Teresa "had allowed herself to be hampered and controlled by anxiety about acceptability" (Williams 1991, 70). In her day, acceptability was related to honor, and in sixteenth century Castile, honor involved a complex set of qualities: pure blood, reputation and the attainment of certain social graces. These ranked above wealth, though money could, to some extent, buy honor though "not necessarily full social acceptance" (Bilinkoff 1989, 110).

In what ways had this anxiety about social acceptance and honor also constrained the life of the church? We know that Teresa's own order had in part allowed itself to be seduced by concern with social class and distorted concepts of honor. Yet Teresa eventually replaces this conventional acceptability and honor based on blood and class with an honor and acceptability derived from Christ alone. In reflecting on how Christ enriches us, Teresa asks, "how can anyone benefit and share [her] gifts lavishly if [she] doesn't understand that [she] is rich?" (Teresa 1995, 55). Before the wounded Christ, Teresa sees herself and others more fully in the light of the gifts God gives for the purpose of attending to Christ's wounds and serving him in the world. In so doing, one both receives honor from Christ and extends it to him. *Las Moradas* rests finally on the conviction that receiving and honoring Christ enables the community to become more transparent before the world (so that Christ is seen), and vulnerable to the world (serving Christ there as well). Such transparency not only offers freedom from false self-understandings but also allows the beauty of the diamond dwelling to become visible.

Even in Teresa's own day, Cervantes' *Don Quixote* debunks the illusions and follies of honor associated with chivalry. Peter Berger argues that honor, as it was understood in Teresa's time, has today become an obsolete concept for the most part. He says, "Modern man is Don Quixote on his deathbed, denuded of the multicolored banners that previously enveloped the self and revealed to be *nothing but a man*: 'I was mad, but I am now in my senses. I was once Don Quixote de la Mancha'" (Berger 1984, 152). Replacing this honor, according to Berger, is the "solitary self that modern consciousness has perceived as the bearer of human dignity and of inalienable human rights" (Berger 1984, 153). Whether the empire's "honor" or "inalienable rights" protected by the nation-state, politics is identified with the public arena of rulers, presidents, governments, and, finally, the powerful in society. The good or *telos* of such politics is the maintenance, if not the expansion, of a particular set of geographical boundaries, patrolled ultimately by those willing to use violence.

The politics of Teresa's castle

Throughout *Las Moradas* the most common language that Teresa uses to refer to Christ is "His Majesty," language that might seem antiquated to the modern reader, but was a title reserved for the highest nobility in her society. "King" invokes the politics of the Spanish monarchy, just as "President" implies the politics of democracy. To describe Christ as king therefore implies a *politics*. If "Christ became one of us, then he (like us) was embodied; and if Christ is king, then his kingdom is embodied as well."[21] For Teresa, the politics of "his Majesty" is not defined by geographical boundaries, social approval, or "pure" blood, nor is her understanding of the Christian life apolitical. She rather envisions and lives a political alternative to the dominant politics of her day.

Another story from her life is particularly revealing. In 1570, Teresa attempted to found a convent in Toledo (where her grandfather had lived). This initiative met with considerable opposition because of the *converso* (Jewish converts) background of many of her backers and the current prejudice in Spain that Jewish blood was shameful. In the midst of this controversy, she writes: "While I was at the monastery in Toledo and some were advising me that I shouldn't give a burying-place to anyone who had not belonged to the nobility the Lord said to me, 'You will grow very foolish, daughter, if you look to the world's laws. Fix your eyes on me, poor and despised by the world. Will the great ones of the world, perhaps, be great before me? Or, are you to be esteemed for lineage, or for virtue?'" (Cited in Bilinkoff 1989, 130). Teresa challenges anti-Jewish animosity by reimagining honor, and so also the politics that sustained this whole system. Her grandfather, like all *conversos*, had been considered unclean and without honor.[22] Yet Teresa sees that Jesus does not have these qualities: pure blood (lineage), reputation or wealth. Rather he is poor and despised. And yet, Jesus is precisely the one she and her sisters are to honor. Teresa places purity, class and wealth on a different "map," so to speak. Purity has to do not with lineage but with virtue (and virtue for Teresa can best be described as living a life habituated to God's grace). Wealth and class have to do not with family inheritance or business, but with an abundance that comes from God.[23] Thus Teresa can conclude, "True poverty brings with it overwhelming honor."

The politics that Teresa describes and embodies is one in which Christ is honored in all things. This is not the politics of the grand or important gesture, where one is always at the mercy of a system of power and reward, but rather a politics of small gestures. Teresa is well known for her saying, "the Lord also walks among the pots and pans." At the end of *Las Moradas*, Teresa imagines her sisters saying back to her, "[we] are unable to teach and preach like the Apostles." A current version of this might be, "we cannot change society," or "we do not have the great gifts of the saints." With irony, Teresa counsels, "instead of setting our hand to the work which lies nearest to us, and thus serving Our Lord in ways within our power, we may rest content with having desired the impossible" (Teresa 1961, 237). For Teresa, politics is not a system, a party, or something other people do. It is rather a community living in friendship with God, willing to live a *cruciform* life in response to God's love. In this alternative politics, it does not matter if one does "great" things. It requires rather a willingness to do the small thing that lies in front of us, but with great love. Such politics is grounded finally not in human effort, but in the divine king who heals not through violence but through the cross. Such a politics is formed and embodied not by trying to rule the world, but by the practices of prayer, worship, Eucharist and humble service, all of which make the body of Christ visible in a way it cannot be when other political arrangements dominate.[24]

Conclusion

Reading Teresa as an interpreter of the Word enables readers to see that *Las Moradas* is not a privatized spiritual quest for the autonomous individual. In describing the dwellings, Teresa is rather narrating an ecclesial way of life oriented, ultimately, around the goodness of God in Christ who through the Spirit gives us what we need to be faithful. This includes a transformation such that one sees Christ more clearly, and thus also the diamond that she and others are because of Christ's reconciliation and recreation of human flesh. At the same time, however, Teresa acknowledges how the body of Christ is wounded and weak. Toward the end of her work, she cites Paul's well-known words to the Philippians, "For to me, to live is Christ, and to die is gain" (Teresa 1961, 217). To live in Christ is not only to share in Christ's recreation; it is also to share in Christ's wounds, to be willing to die to and for the world so that it might be healed. For Teresa, this is the life that all Christians are baptized into, a life of dying and rising with Christ.

In this light, it is significant that Teresa, after long years of debate, received the title *doctor ecclesiae* (doctor of the church) in 1970, the first woman in the Catholic Church to be so designated.[25] From early on, *doctor ecclesiae* has referred to theologians who interpret and illumine scripture for the whole church. The title "has its roots in the Latin Bible's widespread use of the Latin word *doctor* for teacher" (Egan 1981, 154). (*Doctrina* in Latin means the act of teaching.) To be a "doctor of the church" is not simply to be "learned," however. As it developed in the West, to be declared *doctor ecclesiae* required illumination of scripture along with outstanding sanctity and an affirmation by the church. In this essay, I have sought to show how Teresa's *Las Moradas* illumines scripture and so also our lives.

On a final note, if one has to select portions of *Las Moradas* to teach, I would recommend reading all of the first three mansions. Each is relatively short, and the student will read about Teresa's key image (the diamond castle) as well as how she narrates the beginning of the Christian pilgrimage, the difficulties faced and the overarching theme of God desiring our companionship, however flawed and minimal it might be. In the fourth mansions and following, Teresa begins to describe how God's grace and abundance flow and become more deeply internalized and transformative in the lives of the faithful. I recommend the following selections. In the fourth mansions, I recommend chapters 2 and 3, where Teresa begins to discuss different kinds of waters and includes her well-known description of Christ as shepherd. In the fifth mansions, I suggest chapters 2 and 3, which include Teresa's vivid discussion of the silkworm. From the sixth mansions, which is the longest section, I recommend chapters 2, 3 and 7, in which Teresa describes more fully how, at times, God draws persons to himself in strange ways. Here the student can engage Teresa's criteria for evaluating "experiences" of the Spirit. Finally, I recommend reading all of the seventh mansions, which is relatively brief, and which will give the student a fuller sense of the aim and final end of the Christian pilgrimage, as Teresa understands it.

Elizabeth Newman

References

Augustine 1997. *The Confessions*. Trans. Maria Boulding, O.S.B. Hyde Park: New City Press.

——— 1977. *On Christian Doctrine* in *The Nicene and Post-Nicene Fathers of the Christian Church*. Ed. Philip Schaff. Grand Rapids: Wm. B. Eerdmans.

Berger, Peter 1984. "On the Obsolescence of the Concept of Honor" in *Liberalism and Its Critics*. Ed. Michael Sandel. New York: New York University Press.

Bilinkoff, Jodi 1989. *The Avila of Teresa*. Ithaca: Cornell University Press.

Brown, Dan 2000. *Angels and Demons*. New York: Pocket Star Books.

Carroll, Eamon R., S.T.D. 1984. "The Saving Role of the Human Christ for St Teresa," in *Carmelite Studies, Centenary of Saint Teresa*. Ed. John Sullivan, OCD. Washington, D.C.: ISC Publications.

Cavanaugh, William 2008. *Being Consumed*. Grand Rapids: Wm. B. Eerdmans.

De Lubac, Henri 1959. *Medieval Exegesis: The Four Senses of Scripture, Volume 1*. Grand Rapids: Wm. B. Eerdmans.

Du Boulay, Shirley 2004. *Teresa of Avila, An Extraordinary Life.* New York: BlueBridge.

Duffy, Eamon 1992. *The Stripping of the Altars, Tradition Religion in England 1400–1580*. New Haven: Yale University Press.

Egan, Keith 1981. "The Significance for Theology of the Doctor of the Church: Teresa of Avila," in *The Pedagogy of God's Image, Essays on Symbol and the Religious Imagination, The Annual Publication of the College Theology Society*. Ed. Robert Masson. Chico: Scholars Press.

———1984. "Teresa of Jesus: Daughter of the Church and Woman of the Reformation" in *Carmelite Studies, Centenary of Saint Teresa*. Ed. John Sullivan, OCD. Washington, D.C.: ISC Publications.

Fowl, Stephen 2005. "Theological and Ideological Strategies of Biblical Interpretation" in *Scripture, An Ecumenical Introduction to the Bible and Its Interpretation*. Ed. Michael J. Gorman. Peabody, MA: Hendrickson Publishers. 163–175.

Goodson, Jacob no date. "A Baptist Theology of Mary?: Reading Paul, Remembering Mary." Unpublished.

Harink, Douglas 2003. *Paul among the Postliberals, Pauline Theology Beyond Christendom and Modernity*. Grand Rapids: Brazos Press.

Hart, David Bentley 2003. *The Beauty of the Infinite, The Aesthetics of Christian Truth*. Grand Rapids: Wm. B. Eerdmans.

Hauerwas, Stanley and Michael Baxter, C.S.C. 1995. "Why Freedom of 'Belief' Is Not Enough," *In Good Company, The Church as Polis*. Notre Dame: University of Notre Dame.

Kant, Immanuel 1959. "What is Enlightenment?" in *Foundations for the Metaphysics of Moral and What is Enlightenment?* Indianapolis: Bobbs-Merrill Educational Publishing.

Kavanaugh, Kieran, O.C.D. and Otilio Rodriguez, O.C.D. trans. 1980. *The Collected Works of St. Teresa of Avila*, Volume Two. Washington, D.C.: Institute of Carmelite Studies.

Martens, Peter W. 2008. "Revisiting the Allegory/Typology Distinction: The Case of Origin," *Journal of Early Christian Studies* 16, no 3: 283–317.

McGinn, Bernard 1999. *The Doctors of the Church*. New York: Crossroad.

Pope John Paul II 1995. *Ut Unum Sint*.

Radner, Ephraim 2004. *Hope Among the Fragments, The Broken Church and Its Engagement of Scripture*. Grand Rapids: Brazos Press.

Shlumpf, Heidi 2007 (1/24). "A Mystic for Our Times," Religion Bookline, Publishers Weekly Online.

Rogers, Eugene F. Jr. 2005, *After the Spirit, A Constructive Pneumatology from Resources Outside the Modern West*. Grand Rapids: Wm. B. Eerdmans.

Steinmetz, David 1988. *Memory and Mission*. Nashville: Abingdon.

Teresa of Ávila 1995. *The Book of Her Life*, Trans. Kieran Kavanaugh, O.C.D. and Otilio Rodriguez, O.C.D. Indianapolis: Hackett Publishing.

——— 1980. *The Collected Words of St. Teresa of Avila, Vo*l. 2. Trans. Kieran Kavanaugh, O.C.D. and Otilio Rodriguez, O.C.D. Washington, D.C.: Institute of Carmelite Studies.

——— 1961. *Interior Castle.* Trans. E. Allison Peers. New York: Image.

Wainwright, Geoffrey. 1980. *Doxology: The Praise of God in Worship, Doctrine, and Life*. New York: Oxford University Press.

——— 2007. *Embracing Purpose, Essays on God, the World and the Church*. Great Britain: Epworth.

Williams, Rowan. 1991. *Teresa of Avila*. New York: Continuum.

Wittgenstein, Ludwig. 1953. *Philosophical Investigations*. New York: Macmillan Publishing.

William Shakespeare
King Lear

In the early morning hours of a November day decades ago, my mother called from a hospital in the suburbs of Chicago to tell my father and me that eighteen-year-old Gordon, my only brother and their only other child, had died in her arms just moments earlier. The news stunned us, because it came at a time when we thought Gordy had turned a corner in his recuperation from surgery to remove a ruptured appendix.

I was a sophomore in high school then, and in the darkness of that November dawn, I made two inexplicable decisions. The first was to go to school that day and the second was to act as though nothing had happened by refusing to tell anyone, teachers and friends alike, of the devastating news we had just received.

Of that day at school, I remember nothing specific but only a general feeling. As I kept the secret of my brother's death, I was shocked that life went on around me as though nothing had happened. "How," I asked when I saw guys and girls jostling in the halls, janitors sweeping the floors, and cafeteria workers scooping out portions of food, "how can you go on acting as though everything was normal, when the most important person in the world to me has died?" My life had changed forever, overnight, and to my addled adolescent mind, everyone else seemed to be living in a carefree world without end.

To a boy of fifteen, the loss of an only brother served as a singular event, and I had no way to prepare for the waves of grief that washed over me and my family in the days and years that followed. I desperately began to search for a context to anchor my experience, and finding none of substance in my home, on the streets, or in the popular culture of the day, I turned to the books I was reading in school, particularly those assigned in my English classes. In those difficult years, what Henry David Thoreau had written more than a century earlier proved true for me as well: "How many a man has dated a new era in his life from the reading of a book . . . . The at present unutterable things we may find somewhere uttered" (Thoreau 1985, 408–9).

It would be three years before I was to find the unutterable experience of Gordy's death uttered, when I read William Shakespeare's *King Lear* as a college freshman. The whole of this astonishing play gripped me, but one particular speech spoke to the anguish I had felt on that dreadful November day.

Given in the last scene of the play, the speech belongs to King Lear, as he, a spent and broken father, hovers over the lifeless body of his daughter Cordelia. In this agonizing lament, a great king gave voice to the inarticulate grief of a broken-hearted boy:

> And my poor fool is hanged: no, no, no life?
> Why should a dog, a horse, a rat, have life,
> And thou no breath at all? Thou'lt come no more,
> Never, never, never, never, never. (V.3.306–9)

"Questions always bring out the undetermined possibilities of a thing," writes Hans-George Gadamer in *Truth and Method,* his incomparable study of human understanding (Gadamer 1989, 375). Gadamer is describing the essential, productive role that a reader's questions play in the process of enabling a work of art to speak with power and authority to its audience. Our questions open the work to our understanding without determining what it will say or how we may be transformed as a result of the encounter. For more than thirty years, *King Lear* has responded to countless questions I have posed to it. Many of those questions have emerged from the crucible of the classroom, some have surfaced in my research into intellectual and cultural history, while others have arisen from my experience of playing the multiple roles of son, husband, and father.

These personal contexts and the questions they provoke are crucial, yet they are only part of the story, when it comes to comprehending a work of art as sweeping and enduring as *King Lear.* Even as I read the play for the first time as a college freshman, I yearned to understand the larger context of the particular trauma that had drawn me to it in the first place. The appalling grief that battered my mother, father, and me had driven us into our separate selves and apart from one another, and I wanted to know whether there might be any greater story that could be told to make sense of our sorrow.

I searched with some urgency, because that sorrow only seemed to confirm the adolescent judgments I had been forming about the nature of the world and the nature of the God or gods who might rule over it. As an unchurched boy trained in the public schools of an industrial city, I tried as best I could to puzzle out the cosmic conclusions I might draw from the private contexts of my life. To me, life seemed ruled by an uncanny mix of accident and necessity. Things, sometimes terrible things, simply happened – the neighbor's infant daughter killed by a bucket of scalding bath water, my never-to-be known older sister strangled in the birth canal by her umbilical cord, and my sweet-spirited aunt struck down in her prime by the ravages of multiple sclerosis. These events seemed either to be random – that is, they didn't fit into any discernible pattern – or to be the workings of a divine power so distant and indifferent that the thought of submitting to its dictates or of enduring what it still had in store for me was unbearable. If I had read them at the time, the following lines from Czeslaw Milosz's "Either-Or" would have made perfect sense to me:

> If what is proclaimed by Christianity is a fiction
> And what we are taught in schools,
> In newspapers and TV is true:
> That the evolution of life is an accident,
> As is an accident the existence of man,
> And that his history goes from nowhere to nowhere,
> Our duty is to draw conclusions
> From our thinking . . . . (Milosz 2001, 540)

This was the context for my first reading of King Lear as a freshman at Wheaton College. I was a seeker on the way to faith, and the key questions of my life, along with my understanding of Christian truth, were hammered out in the reading of several remarkable books in the spring semester of that year. In Beatrice Batson's teaching of King Lear and Fyodor Dostoevsky's The Brothers Karamazov and in Arthur Holmes's discussions of Friedrich Nietzsche's Beyond Good and Evil, I found a way to set my private anguish and aspirations within a dramatic framework of God's covenantal faithfulness and reconciling love. The journey that had begun on that bleak November morning had led me to Lear and through him, at last, to the cross and the empty tomb.

King Lear and the Intimate Universal

My purpose in speaking of *King Lear* this way is not primarily autobiographical. My real interest is in the way great works of art often gain access to our lives through our most intimate concerns and then place those concerns within a broad understanding of history and the human condition. This move from the intimate to the universal seems particularly pertinent to Shakespeare's play. Written in the opening years of the seventeenth century, *King Lear* is poised on the pivot of vast historical changes. The play is set sometime in the eighth or ninth century before Christ, but it often seems to read as though it had been written just weeks ago. Paraphrasing A. D. Nuttall, Harold Bloom argues that "Shakespeare is out ahead of us, illuminating our latest intellectual fashions more sharply than they can illuminate him, and Shakespeare enables us to see realities that may already have been there but that we would not find it possible to see without him" (Bloom 1998, 487).

I would add that Shakespeare is not only out "ahead of us" but far behind us as well, as he manages within the scope of a single play to carry us back to the pagan ages and their mythical time and forward to the moral and political landscape of our own day. This unusual mix of a sense of timelessness and changes leads, I believe, to the uncanny way that *King Lear* imparts a *figural* cast to the whole of history and human experience. By *figural interpretation* I have in mind what Erich Auerbach describes in his brilliant treatment of interpretive practices in the history of Jewish and Christian interpretation. Figural interpretation works by establishing "a connection between two events or persons in such a way that the first signifies not only itself but also the second, while the second involves or fulfills the first." The poles of a figure are separated in time, but they are both "within temporality. They are both contained in the flowing stream which is historical life, and only the comprehension, the *intellectus spiritualis*, of their interdependence is a spiritual act" (Auerbach 1953, 73).

There is, of course, an element missing in Shakespeare's play that is crucial to the Christian practice of figural interpretation. It is the clear confidence in "Divine Providence" that, according to Auerbach, secures the figural connections in Jewish and Christian practice. This connection "between two events which are linked neither temporally nor causally . . . is impossible to establish by reason in the horizontal dimension." Instead, "it can be established only if both occurrences are vertically linked to Divine Providence, which alone is able to devise such a plan of history and supply the key to its understanding" (Auerbach 1953, 73–74). *Lear* provides no such linkage.

Still, while I recognize the absence of that linkage in *Lear* and while I resist speaking of Shakespeare as though he were a godlike creator, I nevertheless think of the Christian interpretation of literature in general and works of *King Lear's* magnitude in particular as having a great *figural* potential. Like the incarnation itself, a Christian reading of *Lear* may drive us deep into the particularities of its language, its dramatic unfolding, and its historically situated production. Yet at the same time it has the power to carry us far beyond those details to see a wider significance and trace a rich, intricate course of historical development and connection.

In this sense, I feel profoundly privileged to have first encountered *King Lear* in the context of the deeply considered and generously held Christian humanism that marked a Wheaton College education several decades ago. That training in reading encouraged me to focus closely on the particularities of texts, even as I was being taught to develop a universal historical and theological context for the intimate details of those works and the intimate realities of my life.

One useful way of mapping the course these figural connections run in *King Lear* is to chart the subtle and evocative use of certain key words in the play. As we track these words on their way through the play, we find that they are not fixed in time by their dictionary definition for 1605. Instead, each of the four words that we will explore – *nature, bond, nothing,* and *cause* – is like a vibrant human life itself, in that it bears the indelible and tangled imprint of the endless generations that have led up to it even as it sparks the myriad possibilities of the future that will follow upon it.

Nature's Nature

We begin with *nature,* a word at the heart of a great divide in *King Lear.* It surfaces in the central arguments of the play's devastating first scene. The aging King, weary of the responsibilities of his crown and wary of the dangers of a son-less succession, has decided to divide his kingdom among his three daughters. To guide his choice, he devises a test of love that his daughters must pass: "Tell me, my daughters . . . / Which of you shall we say doth love us most,/ That we our largest bounty may extend/ Where nature doth with merit challenge" (I.1.48, 51–53).

Faced with this challenge, Goneril and Regan play their parts to perfection. They flatter their father with praise and receive from him the promise of an abundant inheritance in return. His response to them also makes them realize that even at his best, their father has been a "rash" leader and parent; they confide to each other that his behavior is likely to be marked increasingly by an "unruly waywardness." So, Goneril and Regan tell him what he wants to hear even as they plot to strip him of his powers and his dignity (I.1.284–306).[1]

Lear obviously has no idea of what they plan, for in his vanity and vulnerability, he hears only the words of lavish praise they utter and detects nothing of the calculating undertone of irony that marks what they say. So it is that when he turns to Cordelia, his youngest and most beloved child, Lear expects to hear something even richer, louder, and even more elaborate than what her sisters have already offered.

LEAR: Now, our joy, . . .
　　What can you say to draw
　　A third more opulent than your sisters? Speak.
CORDELIA: Nothing, my lord.
LEAR: Nothing?
CORDELIA Nothing.
LEAR: Nothing will come of nothing. Speak again.
CORDELIA: Unhappy that I am, I cannot heave
　　My heart into my mouth. I love your Majesty
　　According to my bond, no more nor less. (I.1.82, 85–93)

Lear's stunned response to Cordelia is swift and brutal. He disowns her as a daughter and banishes her as a subject, relinquishing her to the care of the King of France, the only suitor who will still have her. He does advise France to consider turning his "liking a more worthier way/ Than on a wretch whom Nature is ashamed/ Almost t' acknowledge hers" (I.1.211–13). But when France insists on pledging his love to Cordelia, Lear vows never to see "that face of hers again," as he sends the betrothed couple on their way "without our grace, our love, our benison" (I.1.263–65). They all then depart, leaving

Goneril and Regan to offer their blunt assessment of their "wayward" father and to vow, "we must do something, and i' th' heat" (I.1.306).

So ends *King Lear's* first scene, which has been marked by a remarkable economy of language and which has unfolded at a breathless pace. In fewer than 300 lines, a kingdom has been divided, a family has been torn asunder, and a host of ominous forces and possibilities have been unleashed. Much of the import of what has unfolded is this scene is bound up in three of our four key words: *nature*, *nothing*, and *bond*.

Behind the first two uses of "nature" in *King Lear* – in an angry exchange Lear has with the Earl of Kent and in the rebuke of Cordelia that the king offers to France – lie centuries of use and assumption in the English language and the cultures of Europe. The predominant sense of "nature" as Lear uses the word can be traced back to the ancient Greeks, particularly to Aristotle. In his study of the word's history, C. S. Lewis explains that for Aristotle nature represented the "real character (the *phusis* or what-sortedness)" of a thing; we have "learned from Aristotle that the *phusis* of anything is 'what it is like when its process of coming to be is complete'" (Lewis 1967, 55–56).

In this context, for a person, a pattern of behavior, or a state of affairs to be *natural* means for it to fulfill the appointed end for which it has been created. And for human beings, the pursuit of those ends can only take place within the intricate practices of social and cultural life. For King Lear and his daughters, whether we are considering them in their eighth century BC context or as emblems at the end of the Elizabethan age, the meaning of what was *natural* would have had a certain clarity to it. It was *natural* for children to honor their parents and for subjects to respect and pay deference to their king. As a result, in this fundamental sense, even though we may feel there is something profoundly unsettling or even offensive in the way that Lear turns so violently and completely upon his daughter, there was nothing *unnatural* about his angry claim that *nature* herself might be ashamed to claim Cordelia as her own.

In an illuminating discussion of the play, Northrop Frye says that for Shakespeare's audience, there would have been four operative levels in the hierarchy that governed thought about nature. At the top would have been Heaven, symbolized by the sun and stars and the home of God beyond them, and at the bottom or at the brink would have been the demonic world and its final, fixed form of Hell. In between Heaven and Hell would have stood the realms of *nature* as early seventeenth-century people would have known them. There is the "higher or human order of nature," which is "the level on which man is intended to live as continuously as possible with the aid of religion, morality and the civilized arts." The second, lower level is that of "physical nature, our present environment, a world seemingly indifferent to man and his concerns." The spiritually astute person, however, can still detect in this lower order of nature traces of its original splendor (Frye 1986, 106).

Frye's "higher" sense of the word *nature* reverberates throughout *King Lear.* Not surprisingly, the king himself employs it most fully and forcefully, as he struggles to comprehend the *unnatural* orientation, first of Cordelia and then, more devastatingly, of Goneril and Regan. When those two sisters are about to turn him out into the stormy night at the end of the play's second act, Lear tells Regan, "thou better know'st/ The offices of nature, bond of childhood,/ Effects of courtesy, dues of gratitude" (II.4.172–74). This meaning of the term also surfaces, albeit ironically, in the deceptive claims and false proclamations of affection and loyalty that the dastardly characters put forward. Gloucester's scheming son Edmund, for example, prates on and on throughout the play about the "unnatural" actions of his brother Edgar, while Regan's husband Cornwall tells Edmund himself that "natures of such deep trust we shall much need;/ You we first seize on" (II.1.115–16).

To us, on the shores of the twenty-first century, this use of *nature* looks like the ebb tide retreating far beyond our sight. From where we stand, we can barely spy the horizon of a time when human behavior and social practices might conceivably have been thought of as being either *natural* or *unnatural.* Yet the other sense of *nature* that we discover in *King Lear* is not an ebb tide but a storm surge that batters our contemporary coasts and floods our modern valleys. And at the beginning of the second scene of the play, just after Goneril and Regan have departed the stage, we can already spot the swells forming far out from land:

> EDMUND: Thou, Nature, art my goddess; to thy law
> My services are bound. Wherefore should I
> Stand in the plague of custom, and permit
> The curiosity of nations to deprive me,
> For that I am some twelve or fourteen moonshines
> Lag of a brother? Why bastard? Wherefore base,
> When my dimensions are as well compact,
> My mind as generous, and my shape as true,
> As honest madam's issue? Why brand they us
> With base? with baseness? Bastardy base? Base?
> Who, in the lusty stealth of nature, take
> More composition and fierce quality
> Than doth within a dull, stale, tirèd bed
> Go to th' creating a whole tribe of fops
> Got 'tween asleep and wake? Well then,
> Legitimate Edgar, I must have your land.
> Our father's love is to the bastard Edmund
> As to th' legitimate. Fine word, 'legitimate.'
> Well, my legitimate, if this letter speed,

And my invention thrive, Edmund the base
Shall top th' legitimate. I grow, I prosper.
Now, gods, stand up for bastards. (I.2.1–22)

In the early seventeenth century this is the *nature* that the men and women of the future will come to know. This is nature seen as an amoral realm where desiring, acquiring selves meet and compete free of social restraint and cultural precedent – "the curiosity of nations" and "the plague of custom." In Edmund's vision, all the labored talk about *natural* and *unnatural* actions and dispositions shrinks to nothing in an instant. The nuances of social, cultural, and religious status, the legal and moral judgments surrounding human sexuality, family life, and inheritance, and the complex network of taboos and restraints that covered everything from the lending of money to the burial of the dead – all these things scud into the past, driven by the gales of goddess nature.

Shakespeare's famous contemporary, Francis Bacon, spoke of putting nature to the question in order to force her, Proteus-like, to yield her secrets to our mastering minds and technological powers. The goal was an ostensibly noble one, Keith Thomas notes in *Religion and the Decline of Magic:* "Francis Bacon listed as *desiderata* the prolongation of life, the restitution of youth, the curing of incurable diseases, the mitigation of pain, the speeding up of natural processes, the discovery of new sources of food, the control of the weather, and the enhancement of the pleasures of the senses" (Thomas 1971, 661).

But for all she has yielded in the way of advancements and ameliorations, goddess nature has exacted a heavy price from her human partners. In the swift and brutal actions and reactions of the play, Lear begins to gauge the costs immediately. Born of an unspeakably desperate need to be loved without reservation and with ostentation, his decision to test his daughters has propelled him and his kingdom into a moral revolution and has led to a vertiginous reordering of standards. When Cordelia tells him she has *nothing* to offer in the way of effusive praise, he warns her: "Nothing will come of nothing. Speak again" (I.1.90). She refuses, and her single word "has a resonance beyond its immediate conversational context," A. D. Nuttall cogently observes. "A black hole opens in the fabric of the play. Lear falls through the hole into a dark counter-world of continuing subtraction, a reduction now authorized by the moral movement of the drama itself." Lear quickly moves from being the robed and furred king to the agonized man of the "uncovered body" who is desperately trying to understand the worth of the "poor, bare, forked animal" that lies beneath the layers (III.4.97, 102). Lear "passes from the upper-class England of the map – good hunting here, good fishing there . . . to an under-nation of wretched poverty and madness" (Nuttall 2007, 305).

The Loosening of Bonds in a Natural World

There are moral and tragic dimensions to Lear's descent, and we will return to them shortly. For now, however, our focus remains on the human price exacted by the new order of nature and society in *King Lear*. The king discovers with alarming speed that *nothing* has indeed come of the "nothing" that Cordelia refused to add beyond the *bond* of a daughter's love and the honor of a subject's devotion. In the movement of the play, it takes but a matter of moments for the key elements of Lear's identity to melt away from him. "I have perceived a most faint neglect of late," he complains and then is insulted by Goneril's servant, who calls him not the "King" but "my lady's father" (I.4.65, 76). Lear's own Fool calls him a "fool" and says he does so because "all thy other titles thou hast given away; that thou wast born with" (I.4.142–43). Then, in short order, because he has a privileged status with his lord and master, the Fool is able to riddle Lear with a series of barbs, all of which point to his drastically reduced state. For having forsaken the responsibilities of authority while trying to retain its symbols, Lear has been left with the "two crowns of the egg" whose "meat" in the middle has been eaten up; Lear is a "0 without a figure" and a "shealed peascod" (shelled pea-pod); and the Fool can only lament to Lear, "I am better than thou art now: I am a fool, thou art nothing" (I.4.151–52, 183–85, 190).

The terrifying drama that swirls around the language of "bond" and "nothing" reaches its peak in a confrontation at the end of the second act. It involves the bargain Lear had struck with Goneril and Regan concerning their care for him after his abdication of authority. They had agreed that he would share his time between them, travelling from one to the other accompanied by a retinue of one hundred knights. The daughters are quickly put off – perhaps understandably so – by the bother of it. The king's knights carouse and disrupt the lives of the sisters' households, and Goneril and Regan sense the lingering threat to their power that those knights represent. So, on the night of a terrible storm, the sisters stand hand in hand against their father and whittle away at the lingering symbols of significance their aging father and titular king clings to.

LEAR: Made you my guardians, my depositaries,
But kept a reservation to be followèd
With such a number. What, must I come to you
With five-and-twenty? Regan, said you so?
REGAN: And speak't again, my lord. No more with me.
LEAR: Those wicked creatures yet do look well-favored
When others are more wicked; not being the worst
Stands in some rank of praise.
(*To Goneril*): I'll go with thee.

Thy fifty yet doth double five-and-twenty,
And thou art twice her love.
GONERIL: Hear me, my lord.
What need you five-and-twenty? ten? or five?
To follow in a house where twice so many
Have a command to tend you?
REGAN: What need one?
LEAR: O, reason not the need! Our basest beggars
Are in the poorest thing superfluous.
Allow not nature more than nature needs,
Man's life is cheap as beast's. Thou art a lady:
If only to go warm were gorgeous,
Why, nature needs not what thou gorgeous wear'st,
Which scarcely keeps thee warm. But, for true need – (II.4.246–65)

The daughters and their husbands then turn King Lear out into the storm in the middle of the night, and for the next two acts, this wounded man is left to roam and rage his way across the heath. In the depths of his suffering and in the extremity of his condition, Lear for the first time sees himself and his kingdom as they are. "Thou art the thing itself," he tells Edgar, that "poor, bare, forked animal" lost in the midst of the howling storm (III.4.101–2). And of the suffering of the "poor naked wretches, wheresoe'r you are,/ That bide the pelting of this pitiless storm," King Lear can only lament: "O, I have ta'en/ Too little care of this" (III.4.28–29,32–33)!

Within the tragedy, all the values of the kingdom appear by this point to have been inverted as a result of Lear's monumental folly. His actions have led to the banishment of the loyal characters – Cordelia, Kent, and Edgar among them – who now can only serve him in secret, in disguise, or in absentia. In turn, his choices have led to power falling into the hands of self-serving men and women, with Goneril and Regan, Cornwall and Edmund in charge. In their world, *bonds* are at best temporary alliances of convenience, and a form of nihilistic *nothing*-ness has been unleashed. In this new order, there is no action so hideous, including the unspeakable blinding of Gloucester, that it cannot be deemed *natural* in that particular setting at that particular time. Having deceived both Gloucester his father and Edgar his brother, Edmund sums up tartly the new ethic unleashed in the world of *King Lear:*

A credulous father, and a brother noble,
Whose nature is so far from doing harms
That he suspects none; on whose foolish honesty
My practices ride easy. I see the business.
Let me, if not by birth, have lands by wit;
All with me's meet that I can fashion fit. (I.2.172–77)

If the world within *King Lear* seems disordered and charged with an uncertain energy lurching in an undetermined direction, how much more so does that appear to be true of the early seventeenth-century-world in which Shakespeare's great tragedy first appeared. We recall what Harold Bloom said about the playwright being "out ahead of us," and that seems especially the case with this play. Of the tragedies, only *Hamlet* can rival its blend of historical acuity and prophetic vision.

It is this mix of history and prophecy that opens *King Lear* most fully to a Christian interpretation of its significance, for the play maps the social, intellectual, and cultural terrain on which the Christian faith has played itself out over the past four centuries. At the heart of Christian efforts to practice and promulgate the faith in modernity we find dynamic, ongoing struggles to define the relationship of Christian belief (and believers) to nature and to history.

On these subjects, as on so many others, *King Lear* was there before us. Indeed, what Shakespeare sensed and exposed with characters such as Edmund was a dawning revolution in the human relationship to nature. Looking back from the twentieth century, for example, Paul Ricoeur understood this revolution to have begun in the early seventeenth century, although for him it was Descartes rather than Bacon who was the main actor in the drama. With its provocative meditations on the nature of symbols and its dramatic representation of the sudden reduction and dismissal of those symbols, *King Lear* deftly sketches the outline for a transformation that, according to Ricoeur, took for centuries to unfold fully.

Concerning the "symbols of the sacred," Ricoeur argues that "our modernity" is marked by an experience of "forgetfulness and restoration." It is a "forgetfulness of the signs of the sacred," and it entails a certain "loss of man himself insofar as he belongs to the sacred." Like Edmund binding his services to the "law of nature," modernity has bound itself to the mastery of those laws in its quest to realize the *desiderata* outlined by Francis Bacon in the early seventeenth century. "The forgetfulness, we know, is the counterpart of the great task of nourishing men, of satisfying their needs by mastering nature through a planetary technique." As a consequence of this "great task," we have developed in modernity two languages – one a precise, univocal, and technical discourse which ever enhances our power to predict and manipulate the processes of nature, and the other an increasingly intense and emotive vocabulary whose only dwelling place and destination are the lonely precincts of the human mind (Ricoeur 1969, 349).

Northrop Frye observes that when Lear is turned out into the storm after his symbol-laden argument with his daughters, he moves "into an order of nature that's indifferent to human affairs . . . . With his abdication, whatever links there may be between the civilized human world and the one above it have been severed" (Frye 1986, 108). The link that was severed in the play was, in turn, also broken in the history in which Shakespeare and his age were embedded, as the art of "mastering nature through a planetary technique" served to "create within the human spirit itself the silences of a spatialized universe" (Ong 1983, 318). As Lear stepped down from the throne and went out into the storm, the silence of the heavens began to descend upon the world of Shakespeare, Bacon, and Descartes – and *our* world – as well.

The history of this silencing and of its blessings and banes is a story that has been told often and well over the past century, by the likes of Martin Heidegger and Paul Ricoeur, Walter Ong and George Steiner. And in recent decades, Charles Taylor has covered this territory with astonishing thoroughness and clarity; his most recent study, *A Secular Age,* reads like an encyclopedia of our disenchanted modernity's delights and discontents.

Lear's Legacy: Nature, Persons, and the Substance of Christian Belief

There is no need to recount this history in a study of *King Lear* and its Christian implications, but two brief vignettes from modern literary history may bring into sharp relief the issues that concern us here. The first of these details what Henry Adams calls "the last lesson, – the sum and term of [his] education." In 1870, when his older sister, Louisa Catherine, contracted a case of tetanus after a cab accident, Adams rushed to Italy to be at her side. He was appalled by what he found. "Hour by hour the muscles grew rigid," he reported, "while the mind remained bright, until after ten days of fiendish torture she died in convulsions."

Confronted with this cruel power, Adams reported that, like Lear on the heath, "the human mind felt itself stripped naked, vibrating in a void of shapeless energies, with resistless mass, colliding, crushing, wasting and destroying what these same energies had created and labored from eternity to perfect." And just as the new sense of nature overturned the social order – that "plague of custom" and "curiosity of nations" – in *King Lear,* for Adams "society became fantastic, a vision of pantomime with a mechanical motion," as he watched his sister die. From this point on, "God might be, as the Church said, a Substance, but he could not be a Person" (Adams 1983, 982–83). Or, as Lear bellowed into the wind and rain three centuries before:

> Rumble thy bellyful. Spit, fire. Spout, rain.
> Nor rain, wind, thunder, fire are my daughters.
> I tax not you, you elements, with unkindness.
> I never gave you kingdom, called you children;
> You owe me no subscription. Then let fall
> Your horrible pleasure. Here I stand your slave,
> A poor, infirm, weak, and despised old man.

But yet I call you servile ministers
That will with two pernicious daughters join
Your high-engendered battles 'gainst a head
So old and white as this. O, ho! 'tis foul. (III.2.14–24)

Lear is a king and Henry Adams was the grandson and great-grandson of presidents, but the struggle they undertake with nature has hardly remained a matter of privilege or station in the modern world. Consider, for instance, the case of David Kern, a boy in his early teens who undergoes a mid-twentieth-century crisis of faith in John Updike's "Pigeon Feathers." Deeply troubled by a naturalistic account of the life of Jesus that he has read in H. G. Wells's *The Outline of History,* David finds his faith in God and confidence in life shaken deeply. To Wells, Jesus was little more than a "hobo" from a "minor colony of the Roman Empire," and twenty centuries of credulous Christian history had been set in motion by the "freakish" fact that Jesus had somehow survived his crucifixion and thus inspired his followers to found a religion. "Had Christ ever come to him, David Kern, and said, 'Here. Feel the wound in My side?' No." Indeed, the facts of nature and the incidents of history seem instead to have "proved the enemy's point: hope bases vast premises on foolish accidents, and reads a word where in fact only a scribble exists" (Updike 2003,14–15).

David then undergoes several more trials, including a terrifying vision of death and a dishearteningly awkward encounter with his unbelieving pastor. The latter confrontation unfolds during a Sunday afternoon catechetical class at the Lutheran church. They are discussing the third and final section of the Apostles' Creed, and David has a question for Pastor Dobson about the resurrection of the body. He wants to know, "are we conscious between the time when we die and the Day of Judgment?" In response, Dobson blinks, and "the faces of the other students went blank, as if an indiscretion had been committed." When Dobson says, "no," David shoots back, "well, where is our soul, then, in this gap?" As the sense grows of a "naughtiness occurring," with one girl giggling and others on edge, the pastor refuses to "repeat the words he said every Sunday morning." Instead he puts his heaven-denying, death-embracing point as bluntly as he can to David: "You might think of Heaven this way: as the way in which the goodness Abraham Lincoln did lives after him." When David counters with yet another question – "But is Lincoln conscious of it living on?" – Dobson closes off the conversation with "a coward's firmness": "I would have to say no. But I don't think it matters" (Updike 2003, 22–23).

"Pigeon Feathers" brings me back full circle to the devastating events I recounted at the beginning of this essay. In the story, David Kern is a year or two younger than I was when my brother died, and when I read this particular story at the age of twenty-one, it brought back memories of my own wrenching struggles. Yet by the time I read "Pigeon Feathers," I had come to be a professing Christian who had the benefit of four years of education in a Christian liberal arts college.

As a result, my reading of Updike's story differed quite significantly from my first encounter with *King Lear* several years before. When I had read *Lear*, its brazen presentation of cosmic injustice and the finality of death had seemed like salt being poured into the open wound of my unbelieving confusion. That wound had been sealed, however, and had begun to heal by the time I met David Kern. In classes on Christian doctrine and the history of philosophy, I had acquired a framework for understanding modern intellectual history and had found a context for situating Shakespeare and his tragedies at their pivotal point in early modernity. Out of the reading of St. Paul, St. Augustine, and Martin Luther, in particular, I had developed a Christian anthropology that enabled me to frame the actions of Lear, Cordelia, Edmund, and the others within an understanding of enduring human traits and complications.

And perhaps most important to my growing understanding of *King Lear* and the Christian faith were works of twentieth-century theology that spoke directly and boldly to the challenges that Edmund, Henry Adams, and Updike's unbelieving Reverend Dobson had posed. From Dietrich Bonhoeffer's *Letters and Papers from Prison* I learned how to read the history of modern secularity from a Christological point of view; Karl Barth opened up to me the healing possibilities of seeing the gracious condescension of God in Jesus Christ as a powerful response to the historical indifference of King Lear's stormy cosmos and Henry Adams's cruel, impersonal Substance; and in the work of Oscar Cullmann, I discovered dynamic and deeply satisfying treatments of the questions that had prompted great anxiety in David Kern, and in me, in the face of death.

Quite legitimately, one could provide a Christian reading of *King Lear* that focused on tensions between nature and grace in the play or delved into the relevance of the doctrine of original sin for the analysis of its characters. Or more specifically, there are plausible readings of the play that focus on Cordelia as a Christ-figure or the scene of Lear carrying her dead body in his arms as a gender-reversing depiction of the Pietà of Christian iconography.

These are solid and potentially praiseworthy approaches to a work as infinitely dense and inexhaustibly rich as *King Lear*. Nevertheless, this play also seems to cry out for a more expansive, contextualized reading of the kind I am suggesting here. And as I hint more than once along the trail of this essay's argument, such a reading can only issue, in the end, from a kind of communal practice. To get a bead on the vast transformations underway at the pivotal point of Shakespeare's age, and to acquire some sense of the manifold ways in which *King Lear* maps out of the challenges and possibilities facing Christian faith and practice in modernity, any one reader needs the help of a host of other eyes, a chorus of other voices. The rift that the play opens behind mind and *nature,* the disordering transformations of *bonds* that it anticipates and depicts, and the vertiginous sense of *nothing*-ness that suddenly opens like a chasm beneath the feet of Lear and at the heart of modernity – these powerful forces call for a robust interdisciplinary response that calls upon the scriptures, the history of the church, and the theology of the past century for aid and strength.

"No Cause, No Cause": Evil, Love, and the Freedom of God

Still, when all the historical developments have been elaborated, and all the theological points and philosophical counterpoints have been woven into the argument, *King Lear* remains a play about parents and children, siblings and spouses, the intimacy of the family and the intricacy of society. A Christian understanding of the play ought not to downplay these realities in favor of a more strictly theological or dogmatic interpretation of the tragedy. Instead, it should embrace these personal and social dimensions, because they provide an especially telling amplification of the larger theological themes.

This is the case, for example, with the subtle yet stunning use in *King Lear* of the final of our four words: *cause.* Unlike *nature, bond,* and *nothing,* which are foregrounded at the beginning of the play and weave their way throughout it, *cause* surfaces just several times in the middle acts. And the particular use I have in mind comes in two short speeches, both of which involve Lear and the subject of his daughters.

The first of these occurs in the sixth scene of the third act. Accompanied by his Fool and by Edgar masquerading as Tom o' Bedlam, Lear has decided to put Goneril and Regan on trial for their crimes against him. Tucked within a cottage during the howling storm, two joint-stools serve as the daughters in the dock, and Lear plays judge, jury, bailiff, and prosecuting attorney – the full array of authority – all in one. After he makes his case against Goneril, he turns his attention to her sister. "Then let them anatomize Regan. See what breeds about her heart," he pleads, and then he asks: "Is there any cause in nature that makes these hard hearts" (III.6.74–76)?

The question goes unanswered at this point, for Lear is weary, the storm rages, and the king must make his way to Dover to escape the forces pursuing him. The thread of the argument that is carried in Lear's question about *cause* does not get picked up again until he awakens at the end of the fourth act to find himself safely in the care of Cordelia, who has returned with France and his army to save her father's life and to restore his kingdom.

When the father first awakens to hear his daughter's voice, he gently chides her:

> You do me wrong to take me out o' th' grave.
> Thou art a soul in bliss; but I am bound
> Upon a wheel of fire, that mine own tears
> Do scald like molten lead. (IV.7.45–48)

After some gentle give-and-take that serves to bring Lear to a fully conscious state, the exchange between parent and child concludes:

LEAR: Pray, do not mock me.
I am a very foolish fond old man . . .
        Do not laugh at me;
For, as I am a man, I think this lady
To be my child Cordelia.
CORDELIA: And so I am! I am!
LEAR: Be your tears wet? Yes, faith, I pray weep not.
If you have poison for me, I will drink it.
I know you do not love me; for your sisters
Have (as I do remember) done me wrong.
You have some cause, they have not.
CORDELIA: No cause, no cause. (IV.7.59–60, 67–75)

With this simple repetition of this two-word phrase – "No cause, no cause" – Cordelia plumbs the depths of the fathomless mysteries of evil and of love. What Shakespeare's tragedy stands for steadfastly at modernity's dawn is what another great work – *The Brothers Karamazov* – reaffirms with equal force at its zenith. It is that when all the genetic, domestic, psychological, social, economic, and political forces and explanations have been taken into account, and all the mitigating factors and warping powers have been accounted for, there is, at last, *no cause* for the hardness of the human heart, *no cause* for the mystery of human love.

Cordelia's gentle use of this phrase is an act of affirmation and renunciation. She affirms Lear's judgment that regardless of his wayward treatment of Goneril and Regan, they had no justifiable reason to harm him as they did and to fail to love him as they should, and at the same time, she renounces any claim to anger or revenge on her own part. Love and evil, *King Lear* concludes, are drawn from wells whose depths we can never fully sound.

This is the mystery at the heart of *The Brothers Karamazov* as well. Here too we find a family at odds and a social order in disarray. Here too a foolish old father neglects and abuses his children, and here too one of his children plots his ruin while another devotes himself to acts of reconciliation and reunion. There are grand philosophical, religious, and political issues at stake, and in this novel they are elaborated in densely packed conversations rather than being delivered to us by means by potent images and compressed speech, as they are in *King Lear* as well.

But just as gestures and simple phrases carry great weight in Shakespeare's play, so do they encapsulate at certain points the much larger and longer arguments of Dostoevsky's novel. Consider two brief scenes, both involving one of the Karamazov brothers, Alyosha. The first of the two comes in the middle of a conversation he has with the complex and tormented Liza Khokhlakov. After she alludes to some of her fantasies of cruelty, she makes a confession of sorts to Alyosha, who asks her in turn for an explanation:

> "I just don't want to do good, I want to do evil, and illness has nothing to do with it."
> "Why do evil?"
> "So that there will be nothing left anywhere. Ah, how good it would be if there were nothing left!" (Dostoevsky 2002, 582)

"Nothing will come of nothing," indeed, and Alyosha's spiritual elder, Father Zosima, understands more clearly than any other figure in *The Brothers Karamazov,* with the possible exception of the Devil, who appears for an interview with the delusional Ivan Karamazov near the novel's close. Knowing the power of nothingness, the dying elder admonishes Alyosha and his other charges to embrace the *something* of God's creation. Why is there *something* rather than *nothing?* There may be no way of answering that question, Zosima understands, but there is a way of responding to it. "Kiss the earth and love it, tirelessly, insatiably," he urges them. "Water the earth with the tears of your joy, and love those tears." Alyosha does so days later when, at a point of exhaustion and in a state of confusion, he awakens from a dream, rushes outside, throws himself to the earth and longs "irresistibly to kiss it, to kiss all of it, but he was kissing it, weeping, sobbing, and watering it with his tears, and he vowed ecstatically to love it, to love it unto ages of ages" (Dostoevsky 2002, 322, 362).

Like the opening chapters of Genesis, like the psalmists and the prophets, like the apostle Paul, and like the Saints and theologians of the Church who have followed upon them – from Ambrose and Augustine to Bonhoeffer and Barth – *King Lear* and *The Brothers Karamazov* explore the wonder of the fact that the whole of our history is a drama having to do with the One who created the world in love and without cause and who entered it freely to suffer on behalf of the many who also without cause have turned their wills to the ways of *nothing*-ness, that *nihil* which lies at the heart of evil.

When King Lear asks, "why should a dog, a horse, a rat have life,/ And thou no breath at all?" Shakespeare does not provide an answer. Yet should that fact surprise us or disappoint us? To be sure, in posing the profound questions that it does – about the universal realities of parents and children, subjects and rulers, life and death, as well as about the meaning of the particular moment at which the play is poised at the dawn of modernity – *King Lear* offers extraordinary resources for a Christian exploration of the modern experience.

But Shakespeare's work remains, after all, a *play,* a response of human wonder and terror to the glory and sorrow of the multitudinous human experience. *King Lear* cannot tell us why there is something rather than nothing or why "the heart is deceitful above all things, and desperately wicked." Nor can this play or this playwright forgive sins or raise the dead. Only God can reveal those mysteries, only God can perform those miracles. Still, for showing us in incomparable language the mysteries we so restlessly pursue and the miracles we so desperately desire, may Shakespeare and *King Lear* be praised nonetheless.

Roger Lundin

References

Adams, Henry 1983. *The Education of Henry Adams, in Novels, Mont Saint Michel, The Education.* Ed. Ernest Samuels and Jayne N. Samuels. New York: Library of America.

Auerbach, Erich 1953. *Mimesis: The Representation of Reality in Western Literature.* Trans. Willard R. Trask. Princeton: Princeton University Press.

Bloom, Harold 1998. *Shakespeare: The Invention of the Human.* New York: Riverhead.

Dostoevsky, Fyodor 2002. *The Brothers Karamazov*. Trans. Richard Pevear and Larissa Volokhonsky. New York: Farrar.

Frye, Northrop 1986. *Northrop Frye on Shakespeare.* Ed. Robert Sandler. New Haven: Yale University Press.

Gadamer, Hans-Georg 1989. *Truth and Method,* 2nd rev. ed. Trans. Joel Weinsheimer and Donald G. Marshall. New York: Crossroad.

Lewis, C. S. 1967. *Studies in Words,* 2nd ed. Cambridge: Cambridge University Press.

Milosz, Czeslaw 2001. *New and Collected Poems, 1931–2001.* New York: Ecco.

Nuttall, A. D. *Shakespeare the Thinker.* New Haven: Yale University Press.

Ong, Walter, S.J. 1983. *Ramus, Method, and the Decay of Dialogue: From the Art of Discourse to the Art of Reason*. Cambridge, Mass.: Harvard University Press.

Ricoeur, Paul 1969. *The Symbolism of Evil.* Trans. Emerson Buchanan. Boston: Beacon.

Shakespeare, William 1970. *King Lear*. Ed. Alfred Harbage. New York: Penguin.

Thomas, Keith 1971. *Religion and the Decline of Magic.* New York: Scribner.

Thoreau, Henry David 1985. *Walden,* in *A Week on the Concord and Merrimack Rivers, Walden; or, Life in the Woods, The Maine Woods, Cape Cod.* Ed. Robert F. Sayre. New York: Library of America.

Updike, John 2003. *The Early Stories: 1953–1975.* New York: Knopf.

Milton
Paradise Lost

John Milton's *Paradise Lost* (1667) is a biblical epic written in the shadow of the English Civil War (1642–51). Although the poem arguably subsumes the entire epic tradition, it also offers a forward-looking intellectual engagement with modernity. Long before the full flowering of modern autonomous subjectivity among moral philosophers in the eighteenth century, the operations of such moral self-understanding had been vividly depicted by Milton a century earlier, in the character of Satan (Murdoch 1997, 365–366). Whether Milton intended readers to favor or reject the kind of self-identity depicted in Satan has long been a matter of debate.[1] Such debate is unavoidable because any interpretation of the poem requires readers, as a matter of course, to make judgments regarding the meaning, viability, and worth of the modern self-understandings dramatized by Milton's Satan. In a broader sense, however, much of the audacity of *Paradise Lost* arises from its ambition to imitate the very character of the entire cosmos, as a typological and dialectical reality imagined by Christian faith. One of the purposes of this essay is to show what "typological" and "dialectical" can mean in relation to *Paradise Lost*. But we should note from the outset that, by imagining a world in which characters are able to deny the justice of God, a world in which rational creatures can knowingly turn away from their own good and yet go on living in a movement toward redemption or judgment, Milton does nothing less than render in poetic terms a Christian understanding of the cosmos.

At the same time, such an undertaking of cosmic scope also implies Milton's belief in the poetic character of the world outside the poem – that is, the character of the cosmos as an aesthetic act of divine verbal making. The grandeur and psychological depth in Milton's portrayal of Satan led William Blake to say that Milton was "a true poet and of the Devil's party" (Blake 1982, 35). Such a statement fails to appreciate that Milton also understood God as the supreme "true poet," a poet within whose contingent verbal art (the cosmos) all rational creatures, including Satan at his creation, are able to act, love, make, sin, and suffer with real consequence. Nevertheless, Blake rightly appreciated that Milton understood himself first as "a poet." In keeping with Milton's understanding of the poetic quality of human and divine action, *Paradise Lost* emphatically takes the side of the poets in the "quarrel" between poetry and philosophy, a quarrel that Plato called "ancient" as early as the *Republic* (Plato 1992, 607b).[2] In due course, we shall consider Plato's characterization of "poetry" and "philosophy," as well as the "quarrel" between them. The argument here, however, unfolds in two stages: first, I outline some of the historical circumstances in which *Paradise Lost* was composed and the explicit elements of subject matter, genre, and purpose cited in the epic.[3] The second part of the argument suggests that the treatment of wisdom in *Paradise Lost* is framed, in part, as a response to the treatment of wisdom in Plato's *Republic* and specifically to the role of dialectic in the cultivation of wisdom. Ultimately, I contend that *Paradise Lost* aims not only to vindicate poetry in its "ancient quarrel" with philosophy but also to venture an account of divine revelation as intrinsic to human wisdom. In doing so, Milton presents a vision of wisdom that many of his contemporaries would view as politically dangerous.

Losing Paradise in Seventeenth-Century England

Despite the absence of direct references to seventeenth-century political events, *Paradise Lost* is obviously shaped by Milton's experiences in the English Civil War (1642–51), the subsequent failed experiments in republican government (1649–59), and the eventual Restoration of the English monarchy (1660). In the conflict between the English Parliament and the Crown, Milton had sided with Parliament and eventually served the parliamentary cause directly (beginning in 1649) as "Secretary for Foreign Tongues," composing diplomatic documents in Latin. Until the publication of *Paradise Lost*, Milton's primary *literary* reputation was based on his Latin writing. In *Pro Populo Anglicano Defensio* (1651) Milton defended, before all of Europe, the execution of Charles I and argued for the justice of those who had judged the ruler to be a tyrant worthy of execution. The Restoration of the monarchy in 1660 was the end of Milton's hope for English political liberty. For Milton, the return to monarchy was a political disaster rooted in a moral and spiritual failure. Writing just days before the Restoration, he compared the monarchy's formerly republican supporters to those ancient Israelites who preferred to go back to the slavery of Egypt, rather than endure the hardships of liberty (Milton 1953–82, 7:462). In the meantime, Milton's failing eyesight had left him completely blind by 1652, an event that some of his opponents interpreted as a sign of divine judgment (Milton 1953–82, 4:584–91). He had begun writing *Paradise Lost* by the late 1650s but did not complete it until the early 1660s, after narrowly escaping his own execution.[4] If the events of the Restoration fall in the middle of these years when he was writing *Paradise Lost*, we might reasonably ask, "What rhetorical purpose could be sought by an aging, blind, failed revolutionary, in retelling the story of Genesis 3 in the form of a classical epic?"

To begin answering this question requires that we consider one further important aspect of Milton's context: the debates regarding the public meaning of religious "enthusiasm." In the minds of many English leaders in Milton's time, the radical religious beliefs of those who had waged war against the Crown provided conclusive evidence that religious "enthusiasm" was a threat to the common good – a threat that warranted the use of civil force in order to suppress such religious fervor. The accusations aimed at such religious groups were ultimately concerned with the way in which people, often on the basis of intense emotional experience, believed themselves to be divinely inspired (Donnelly 2005, 236–38). There was also, however, a broad tradition of non-conformist teaching that viewed "Prophecy" as simply the exegetical preaching of scripture in conjunction with prayer.[5] Milton's position arguably comes closest to this latter sense of divine inspiration. As a result, although he was alert to the risks of deluded "enthusiasm," Milton insisted a person could be inspired by the Holy Spirit (Milton 1953–82, 7:242–44). In *Paradise Lost*, however, Milton goes further, as we shall see, and implies that true divine inspiration in response to the contingencies of human life is intrinsic to the common good. Thus, the direct and indirect treatments of divine inspiration in *Paradise Lost* also impinge directly on the political and moral dimensions of wisdom presented in the poem.

Paradise Lost foregrounds the sense of epic genre at the beginning of the narrative and throughout. Readers familiar with epic conventions might notice several features: the action beginning *in medias res*, the catalogue of military forces, the vast scale, the stylistic use of extended similes, the recounting of great deeds in battle, or the use of prophetic vision. The specific feature, however, to which I draw attention here is the invocation to the muse. Christian poets, such as Dante, Du Bartas, and others, had long established a tradition of using the names of pagan muse as figures for the Holy Spirit. Milton appreciated that the conventions of any given genre constitute a set of expectations that a writer might use, whether to fulfill, disappoint, or transform those expectations. The first invocation in *Paradise Lost* might appear customary for a biblical epic, in which the poetic voice links his own inspiration to that of Moses and the Creation story – the main verb in the first sentence is an imperative, "sing," addressed to the muse in prayer (Campbell 1992, 1.1–26).[6] Does *Paradise Lost* imply that Milton understood himself to be divinely inspired? Without presuming to answer such a question conclusively here, we can note how Milton appropriates and transforms the invocation as a feature of the epic genre. In the Book 3 invocation, the speaker implies that his audacity to narrate events at the throne of God is authorized by the spiritual vision which he, like the "prophets old," has been given in place of his lost physical sight (3.1–55). In the Book 7 invocation, the speaker calls upon the heavenly muse, Urania, specifying that he calls upon "the meaning, not the Name" and referring explicitly to "dangers" that seem similar to Milton's own circumstances in the Restoration (7.1–39). Finally, the invocation to Book 9 does not, strictly speaking, "invoke" at all, but merely acknowledges the poet's dependence on the muse "who brings [the poem] nightly to [his] Ear" (9.1–47). In this way, the invocations, when considered together, present the poet's relation to the muse, the Holy Spirit, in increasingly personal and intimate terms. The larger point to notice here is that, when *Paradise Lost* deploys what we recognize as an epic convention, we should ask three further questions: a) What are the antecedent epic contexts in which that convention is deployed? b) How do those contexts compare to the context here? c) How does the poem evoke and then redirect the expectations involved in that convention?

In one sense, the subject matter of *Paradise Lost* is simply the story of Genesis 3: the biblical account of how a serpent tempted the first humans to disobey their maker and thereby lose the enjoyment of paradise. In a further sense, however, *Paradise Lost* encompasses the entirety of biblical narrative, the central theme of which is redemption. This conjunction of local and large-scale engagement with biblical material is evident in the opening lines of the poem:

> Of Mans First Disobedience, and the Fruit
> Of that Forbidden Tree, whose mortal tast
> Brought Death into the World, and all our woe,
> With loss of *Eden*, till one greater Man
> Restore us, and regain the blissful Seat,
> Sing Heav'nly Muse . . . . (*PL* 1.1–6)

The first five lines present the object of the verb "sing." They are, in effect, a summary of what the "song" (poem) includes. As a result, even these few lines move from the fall of the first Adam to the coming of the second Adam, referred to here as the "greater Man" who will bring redemption. The most important feature to appreciate regarding Milton's biblicism is that, in dilating one biblical chapter into an epic narrative, he does not simply speculate about various details but characteristically weaves entire segments of biblical narrative back into the Genesis narrative (Donnelly 2009b, 79–81). Moreover, the very character of the biblical intertextuality that Milton deploys often draws upon and extends features of what is commonly referred to as "typology."

Typology was initially developed as a way for Christian interpreters to understand the narratives of the Hebrew Bible as finding fulfillment in Christ, the "one greater Man." Milton draws both form and content from such interpretive use of "types" that pre-figure later developments in a larger story. He does this on both a large scale and a small scale; here we can consider just one example of each. In terms of large-scale narrative structure, the most important re-working of biblical narrative is the way that Milton fills the gap between Genesis 2 and 3. Rather than merely speculate regarding what happened between Creation and the Fall, Milton presents adaptations of no less than four other biblical stories. He does this by introducing an angelic messenger, Raphael, who is sent to warn Adam and Eve about the coming temptation. During his visit, readers encounter inset adaptations of Psalm 2 (*PL* 5.577–907), Revelation 12 (*PL* 6), Genesis 1 (*PL* 7), and Genesis 2 (*PL* 8.250–520).[7] In this way, the material from other biblical texts provides the basis for understanding what happens between Creation and the Fall. Similarly, in the last two books of the epic, during the expulsion from Eden, Adam is given a revelation of the future that allows a recapitulation of the whole of biblical history. Such typological interpretation allows Milton to gesture toward an overarching story that, we should note, is specifically not a "metanarrative" in the modern sense: Milton's story assumes that created reality is a good gift rather than neutral matter for human disposing, and the purpose of the story is to foster the Christian virtues rather than to predict outcomes or master fortune (Donnelly 2009b, 169–187).

Milton also consistently weaves biblical intertextual connections into the small-scale details of his poem. The narrative action begins with Satan floating on the lake of fire, just after he and his companions are cast from heaven to hell. Once Satan stands on the shores of the fiery lake and summons his legions to rise, the narrator uses an extended simile so characteristic of epic. The fallen angels floating on the lake of fire are compared to:

> Scattered sedge
> Afloat, when with fierce winds Orion armed
> Hath vexed the Red Sea coast, whose waves o'erthrew
> Busiris and his Memphian chivalry
> While with perfidious hatred they pursued
> The sojourners of Goshen, who beheld
> From the safe shore their floating carcasses
> And broken chariot-wheels. (*PL* 1.304–311)

In effect, the simile answers the question, "Who is the serpent in Genesis 3?" by implying that the serpent is like the Pharoah in the Exodus story and is, in fact, the one whom Pharoah imitates. The ingenuity in Milton's elaboration of this narrative detail here, as elsewhere, lies in the way that he uses typology to infer an imagined "back-story," based on what the biblical text does say. As we have already noted, however, Milton also understood the Exodus story more generally as a movement from slavery to freedom, and he interpreted the Restoration of the English monarchy as a return to the slavery of Egypt, as a renunciation of a freedom given by God. In this sense, the interpretive dynamics of typology extend to include the world of the epic's readers.

In considering *Paradise Lost*'s relation to its biblical material, we should note one further crucial feature. In his 1644 tract, *Areopagitica*, Milton famously argues that, just as the exercise of moral virtue presumes the possibility of acting differently, so also growth in knowledge of truth requires an encounter with falsehood which he calls a "triall [sic]" "by what is contrary" (Milton 1953–82, 2:515). The crucial point to notice here is that Milton understood such a process of "triall" to be enacted by the biblical text which often "answers dubiously and darkly to the common reader" (2:517). In keeping with this view, *Paradise Lost* imitates the way that scripture takes readers through a trial "by what is contrary." As a given segment of narrative unfolds, readers are given opportunity to revise their initial beliefs, not by direct refutation but by questioning, qualifying, or revising their assumptions.

The epic treats various topics using this manner of "triall," but here are three examples that may suggest others. *Paradise Lost* begins by explicitly describing Satan and his companions as surpassing the highest examples of human heroic virtue in pagan and romance epic (*PL* 1.573–591). The typical seventeenth-century reader might initially be perplexed by the description of the well-known "Father of lies" in such honorific terms. This initial impression is later qualified, however, not by denying Satan's abilities as a warrior or by denying his courage, but by offering an alternative vision of what truly constitutes "heroic" deeds (see 9.13–41). Similarly, readers might begin Book 3 assuming that they understand what the "kingdom of God" means, only to discover in Book 5 that divine rule is most emphatically characterized by the scandalous action of giving authority away for the purpose of serving the good of those governed (5.603-610, 826-832; Donnelly 2009b, 101–23). Finally, readers might begin Book 4 of *Paradise Lost* assuming that they know the meaning of "patriarchy" (4.285–99), only to discover that the character of such rule (*arch?*) is most fully revealed in self-sacrifice (*PL* 10.211–17; Donnelly 2009b, 156–65).

In each of these cases, the reader is not simply drawn out and then reprimanded for holding false opinions;[8] rather, the narrative presents opportunities to make a series of distinctions (by contraries) all of which contribute to the very perception of divine justice – the topic that is central to the epic's explicitly stated purpose, as we shall see. For Milton, such a process of trial is central to authentic faith: without the internalization of truth that results from such a trial one becomes a mere "heretick in the truth" (1953–82, 2:543). The cultivation of wisdom, in Milton's account, can never be reduced to obtaining information or even intellectual clarity: rather, the process of trial enacts two essential aspects of growth in wisdom: 1) the ordering of affections – evoking desire for the right things in the right way; 2) habit-forming practice in discerning the divine voice regarding the contingencies in one's own life.

In uniting biblical matter with classical epic form, *Paradise Lost* also identifies its purpose, or final cause, as the attempt to "assert eternal

Providence / And justify the ways of God to men" (*PL* 1.25–26). The first crucial point to notice here is that these lines involve two verbs: "assert" and "justify." The passage makes it clear that the two actions are distinct and logically related. Secondly, the phrase "justify the ways of God" is not a synonym for "theodicy." Milton was familiar with the ancient arguments of Epicurus against "providence" (Milton 1953–82, 2:517) – that is, against the belief that God governs the cosmos for a good end. Epicurus advanced an ancient version of what is commonly referred to as "the problem of evil," which a "theodicy" argument aims to address. Although Milton is clearly concerned with divine justice, we shall misunderstand the epic's statement of purpose if we construe it primarily as a response to the "problem of evil." Epicurus argued against the existence of an all-powerful and completely good God (i.e., providence) by claiming that the existence of "evils" in the world necessarily refuted either God's goodness or God's power.[9] The arguments of Epicurus make two assumptions that Milton rejects: the assumption that "evil" is reducible to "pain" and the assumption that the relationship between God and the cosmos is a function of inexorable material necessity. By using the verb "assert," Milton indicates his recognition that belief in "eternal Providence" is not a topic that is very persuasively treated by direct logical argument. His choice of the verb "assert" arises from his appreciation that one may either believe in providence or not, but that attempts to prove or disprove it by appealing to incontrovertible "facts" will tend to appear circular.[10] By contrast, Milton's choice of the verb "justify," as in, "to show the justice of"[11] God's ways, indicates his recognition of what is at stake if one does indeed believe in providence. Those who deny providence have little interest in showing divine justice.

The logical connection between the two verbs, "assert" and "justify," is crucial: the stated purpose of the poem is to say, in effect, "If we grant (assert) that God governs the universe to a good end (Providence), how can divine justice be apparent to finite fallen humans?" For readers today, this might seem like a strange question: Milton, however, understood himself to be surrounded by people who denied precisely this central inference of his poem. For over a decade, Milton had been involved in political and ecclesiastical wrangling against Presbyterians and other Calvinists who believed in Providence but whose doctrine of predestination risked, in Milton's view, making God into a tyrant who sufficiently caused the Fall, or the entrance of evil into human history (Donnelly 2009a, 356–57). Such Presbyterians would have followed John Calvin's account of divine sovereignty, according to which God "arranged" the Fall of humanity.[12] Thus, the central explicit purpose of the epic is to show that belief in Providence – or divine governance of the cosmos to a good end – does not entail that God caused the entrance of evil into human history.

For many readers today, such matters might seem abstract or far removed from experience; for Milton, however, these doctrinal debates had direct practical consequences. In Milton's view, to say that human freedom, in causing the Fall, compromised God's governance was to mistake the very character of divine rule and to let God appear to human understanding as a tyrant. The crucial practical consequence that Milton appreciated about this absolutist view of divine sovereignty is the way that it correlated with support for religious coercion among Protestants. In effect, the willingness to let God appear to human understanding as a despot and the willingness to use civil force to compel religious uniformity among Protestants both assume that the only alternative to an arbitrary human "freedom" (reduced to randomness) is to insist on a compelled order based on sheer necessity (Donnelly 2009b, 11–20, 49–69). In other words, Milton understood the political consequences of a theology which failed to appreciate the aesthetic character of the relation between God and creation. By "aesthetic character" I mean simply that Milton understood the purpose of creation by analogy with a work of fine art.[13] In contrast to other arts (knowledge regarding making) that serve a use-function beyond themselves, fine arts find purpose in the delight that arises from the very being of the resulting artifacts. As such, the products of the fine arts do serve a purpose but not an extrinsic purpose beyond the evocation of delight; in the case of creation, that evocation of delight is divine glory (the beauty of God manifest in Creation). Such artistic works are not a function of external necessity; they arise freely. At the same time, however, such works have an internal order, an order that could be otherwise but is nevertheless an order which aims at a purpose that is intrinsic to its being. Understanding Creation by analogy with such artistic production enables Milton to suggest how the world can be ordered by God without implying that Creation is either a function of divine necessity or a contained sphere of random chance. Again, the political importance of this point for Milton is that those who argued for state-sponsored religious conformity were, in effect, assuming that the relation between God and Creation (including human creatures) is reducible to compulsion.

At this point, we can begin to discern how Milton's poetic deployment of "trial by what is contrary" also contributes to the epic's stated purpose. To show that the Fall resulted from a free action of the human will, the narrative takes readers through a series of episodes that entail distinguishing such an act of volition from other actions that may be similar or closely related in time but do not necessitate the Fall. Thus, readers encounter an angel, Uriel, who remains, in himself, flawless and unfallen but whose creaturely finitude leaves him susceptible to deception (*PL* 3.613–93). Similarly, Adam's interpretation of Eve's dream is based on ignorance regarding the actual causes of the dream as a contingent event. This event allows readers to notice that being mistaken about the circumstances in a given situation does not, in itself, cause the fall (5.95–128). Later, the narrator's observation that Eve remains "sinless"

(9.659) until the moment of choice emphasizes that neither her earlier temptation in her dream (5.30–135) nor her decision to disagree with Adam regarding the best way to approach their work in the garden (9.204–375) constitutes or sufficiently causes the Fall.[14] Thus, in narrating each of these actions, *Paradise Lost* offers an opportunity to make a series of distinctions in preparation for the climactic moment of temptation. At that moment, Eve, working alone, subject to deception, mistaken about the circumstances, and tempted, nevertheless remains free to obey if she so chooses. In this way, Milton's elaboration of the Genesis story unites the interplay between typological connections and these narrated distinctions (or contraries), specifically as they contribute to the elucidation of divine justice.

Cultivating Wisdom in Paradise Lost

Beyond the ways in which *Paradise Lost* evokes the epic genre and stories from classical myth, as well as biblical narratives and topics of theological debate, Milton's poem also engages philosophical texts. In particular, I suggest that *Paradise Lost* is in conversation with the central arguments of Plato's *Republic*.[15] Such a claim can be proposed here only as a hypothesis, but the initial directions for further investigation have been suggested elsewhere (Donnelly, 2007). Without denying that *Paradise Lost* engages a wide range of other texts, I suggest that there are obvious reasons for Milton to address specifically the *Republic*. On the one hand, Plato's dialogue offers the most influential account of justice in the western intellectual tradition; at the same time, the *Republic* also offers the most famous sustained attack on the idea that epic poetry could teach any moral virtue. Thus, an epic poem that takes divine justice as its explicit focus would do well to address Plato's dialogue. After some initial discussion of the aims and arrangement of the arguments in the *Republic*, we shall consider how the central educational episode in *Paradise Lost* offers points of engagement with Plato's dialogue. By considering the *Republic* as a context for Milton's epic, we shall answer one of the most immediate questions regarding the arrangement of events in *Paradise Lost*: given that Book 7 largely paraphrases Genesis 1 and the latter part of Book 8 dilates events recounted in Genesis 2, why does Milton place between these two episodes an inconclusive discussion of astronomy that seems to have no biblical antecedent? I contend that Milton's engagement with Plato answers that question but also foregrounds the account of wisdom that Milton posits in opposition to Plato's account.

The central explicit topic of the *Republic* is justice, understood as the supreme human virtue. The main argument attempts to show that justice is choiceworthy for its own sake rather than for some extrinsic benefit. As long as the benefits of justice are extrinsic to it, one needs only to appear just rather than to be just (362d–367e). The whole presentation of the kallipolis – or "good polis" – that occupies so much of the dialogue is ultimately to serve the two-fold purpose of discerning justice "writ large" in the polis so that the virtue can then be discerned in the soul, and then demonstrating that justice so defined is supremely choiceworthy in itself. In the course of defining justice, the argument also defines the virtues of temperance, courage, and wisdom, in the polis and the psyche. Two points are important here. First, the explicit purpose for Socrates forming the imagined kallipolis is to serve as an analogy for understanding virtues in the soul. Second, the central books of the *Republic*, the latter part of Book 5 through Book 7, explicitly focus on the education of those who must rule a city if it is to be just. In short, the just city must be ruled by those who have true knowledge regarding how to rule the entire city; such true knowledge of unchanging reality Socrates calls "wisdom" (428b–429a, 441e, 531a–540b). Socrates gives the name "dialectic" to the final stage of the process by which such knowledge is acquired (531a–540b), and this is the process which, I suggest, *Paradise Lost* aims not simply to reject but to transform.

In the final book of the *Republic*, Socrates mentions in passing an "ancient quarrel" between poetry and philosophy (607b). In the context of Plato's dialogue, Socrates is, at that moment, taking the side of philosophy in that quarrel, by arguing that poetry is three times removed from the reality that it purports to represent and, as such, involves a falsification of reality. Readers, however, may well be skeptical about the seriousness of this particular argument: after all, it depends explicitly on an extended simile which compares poetry to the making of images (600e–603c). Socrates' critique hinges on rejecting poetry as a mere similitude of a similitude – a rejection that applies no less to the similitudes in the central analogy by which he advances that critique (569b–603b). Given such ironies, we should not be surprised to find that, by the time Plato's texts are read in sixteenth- and seventeenth-century England, Plato was commonly recruited by those defending poetry. In effect, writers such as Philip Sidney, in his *Apologie for Poetrie,* inherited the Neoplatonist argument that poets can, in principle, base their fictive stories on direct knowledge of virtues rather than on the mere appearance of sensible experience (Sidney 1595, b2–c3).

Although Milton inherited such Neoplatonist arguments vindicating poetry, he appropriates them while holding in question Socrates' claims about the character of wisdom. By the term *poetica,* or "poetry," both Plato and Milton mean not simply writing in verse, or meter, but any imaginative use of language generally, whether in prose narrative, hymnody, or drama. Both writers would identify the most powerful "poets" of our present age as those who make our movies and our popular music. Likewise, we may take our initial understanding of "philosophy" from Socrates' characterization of it as a "love for wisdom." For Plato, the quest for wisdom proceeds specifically by the use of human reason (*logos*), rather than by the composition of imaginative narratives (*mythoi*) (474b–540b). To be sure, the philosophic quest, as Plato depicts it, often involves telling stories to those who lack real knowledge, and it often advances by means of reflection on shared stories, but Plato assumes that a soul's true growth in wisdom does not proceed by means of constructing new stories. In this particular regard, *Paradise Lost* proposes an alternative approach to the cultivation of wisdom, an approach that does not simply deny a place for dialectical reasoning but situates that process within a union of narrated action and divine revelation.

As any reader of Plato's *Republic* might appreciate, the specific sequence of topics in the dialogue is inseparable from the character of the argument. The most important example of this emphasis on the sequence of topics occurs at the beginning of Book 5, where Socrates is interrupted by his interlocutors. He has just finished describing the virtues as they would appear in his "city-in-speech" and is just about to describe the vices involved in the corruption of a city, when he is compelled to address three waves of objections to the very establishment of this imagined city. Socrates does not get back to his initial topic until Book 8. As a result, the intervening books 5–7 are taken up with what is, in effect, a digression from the discussion of the rise and fall of the kallipolis. The first two waves of objections are addressed in the early parts of Book 5, but from the latter part of book 5 through the end of book 7, the dialogue focuses on the third obstacle to the existence of the kallipolis: the requirement that wisdom lovers (philosophers) should rule, or rulers become wisdom lovers.

Eva Brann (2004) argues that this central episode (books 5–7) is part of a five-fold movement that informs the structure of the entire dialogue. Even if we reserve judgment on Brann's characterization of these central books, the episode is clearly set apart from the surrounding action and is explicitly concerned with the education of the philosophers who will be the guardians of the kallipolis. As Brann points out, however, there is also a symmetry to those books that surround this central "work" (*ergon*) of the dialogue: the preceding books (2–4) describe the establishment of the kallipolis, while the ensuing books (8–9) describe the decline of the kallipolis. Furthermore, Brann argues that Book 1 dramatically evokes, directly and indirectly, a mythical descent into Hades, while Books 9-10 similarly evoke an ascent from Hades. Brann describes this five-fold movement in chiastic terms, as a movement from *mythos* to *logos* to a central *ergon*, and then back, in reverse order, from *ergon* to *logos* to *mythos*. In short, Brann's description of the dialogue's movement looks like this:

1) Descent to Hades (Book 1) – *mythos*
2) Genesis of the kallipolis (Books 2–4) – *logos*

3) Education of the guardians (Books 5–7) – *ergon*
4) Degeneration of the kallipolis (Books 8–9) – logos
5) Ascent from Hades (Book 9–10) – mythos[16]

Brann's evidence and argumentation in support of this structure are detailed and subtle, but an evocation of this possible movement is sufficient for present purposes. First, readers of *Paradise Lost* should notice the obvious similarities in the overall movement in these two texts. The central inset narratives in *Paradise Lost* are framed explicitly in terms of sending the angel Raphael to educate Adam and Eve as the guardians of Eden (books 5–8). Similarly, the poem begins in Hell before moving on to describe the newly established Eden. Likewise, the decline of Eden is described only after the central educational digression. The epic then similarly describes events in Hell again before ascending back to recount events on earth.

The similarities between the two texts become even more notable when we consider the first version of *Paradise Lost,* which was arranged in ten books rather than twelve. In 1674 Milton divided what were initially books 7 and 10 of *Paradise Lost* into books 7–8, and 11–12, respectively. In doing this, he gave us the twelve-book version of the poem that most people read today.[17] We are not concerned here with Milton's possible reasons for this change.[18] We should note, however, that in the ten-book version of *Paradise Lost*, the central educational digression occupies exactly the same location as the central digression in Plato's *Republic*, from the latter part of book 5 through the end of book 7. Both of these educational digressions are concerned with the training of those who are guardians of the virtuous city. Furthermore, both of these episodes also peak in Book 6, with analogical accounts of "the Good" that informs all justice – Socrates presents an analogy between the sun and the form of the Good, while the angel Raphael deploys sun imagery to depict the Son of God in his chariot of paternal deity. In Book 7 of Plato's *Republic*, Socrates presents education in mathematics and dialectic as the means by which humans come to knowledge of the Good, which constitutes the highest kind of wisdom.

In light of this context, we can begin to see how, at one level, Book 7 of *Paradise Lost* implies that poetry informed by biblical narrative is a more reliable guide than Socratic dialectic regarding knowledge of the good. Ultimately, Milton does not simply privilege the wisdom of revealed biblical narrative over Socratic dialectic; *Paradise Lost* goes further by depicting a mode of divine revelation that is transformative specifically because of its dialectical character. In this way, *Paradise Lost* implies that even the most personal experience of divine revelation does not simply bypass the faculty of human reason or render it superfluous.

If we look at Book 7 in the ten-book version of *Paradise Lost* (now books

7 and 8), we might immediately ask how Milton ever imagined it as a single unit in the first place, given its large size and the wide range of topics that it treats. This part of Raphael's educational visit divides into six main segments:

1) Invocation to Urania (*PL* 7.1–69), describing a poet who has ascended to the "heaven of heavens" and must now descend to sing in "darkness with dangers compast round" (7.27).
2) Discussion between the angel Raphael and Adam regarding the purposes of Raphael's instruction (7.70–130).
3) Raphael's narration of the six days of Creation, paraphrasing Genesis 1 (7.131–640).
4) Discussion of astronomy – a kind of follow-up to the Creation narrative (8.1–178).
5) Adam's narration of his "celestial Colloquie sublime" (8.455) with God which leads to the creation of Eve, paraphrasing Genesis 2 (8.179–520).
6) Concluding discussion and final warning from Raphael (8.521–654).

We shall focus here on the 4th and 5th of these, the discussion of astronomy, followed by the "celestial Colloquie sublime"; however, we should first note that Book 7 of the *Republic* also falls into six segments that bear analogous internal relationships to one another:

1) The brief allegory of the cave (514a–517a) – depicts education as an ascent to light and a subsequent descent into darkness amid danger.
2) Explanation of the cave image with a view to the purpose of education – that is, in the first stage, to turn soul from changeable, sensible perceptions and toward unchanging, intelligible reality (517a–521d).
3) Discussion of the kinds of studies that are effective in turning the soul from the sensible to the intelligible – that is, mathematics and geometry (521d–528d).
4) Discussion of "astronomy" (three-dimensional geometry of motion) which dilates the preceding discussion of mathematical studies (528d–531d).
5) Description of dialectic's purpose as ascent to knowledge of eternal truth. In contrast to mathematics, which depends on hypothetical axioms that cannot be verified, dialectic ascends to knowledge of first principles without hypotheses (531d–534e).
6) Concluding discussion regarding who should be taught dialectic and how – final dialectical testing (535a–541b).

The most notable similarity between these two texts is that they both locate a discussion of astronomy just past the middle of Book 7 (in the 10-book version of *Paradise Lost*). To appreciate what the poem implies here, we need to notice the similar internal relation between two segments in each text. Just as Adam's questions about astronomy respond to Raphael's account of the six days of creation, so also Socrates' discussion of astronomy elaborates on the preceding discussion regarding the kind of studies that will prepare students for dialectical ascent. For Socrates, "astronomy" means three-dimensional geometry of motion; its primary benefit, as a subject of study, is to "turn the soul" from the sensible to the intelligible. Astronomy, like the other mathematical or geometrical arts, is not, strictly speaking, knowledge of eternal forms, but it does re-orient the soul. In this respect, Socrates' elaboration on the topic of astronomy is simply to clarify that its value as an area of study derives not from any empirical practice of watching sensible stars, but from the way in which the study of the three-dimensional geometry of motion is among those arts already described which serve the purpose of turning the soul from the sensible to the intelligible. This similarity provides one of the most important points of contrast between the *Republic* and Milton's poem.

In contrast to Socrates' emphasis on the unchanging character of eternal forms that constitute the only true objects of knowledge, Adam in *Paradise Lost*, after hearing the creation story, refers to Raphael as his "divine Historian" (8.6–7). Socrates emphasizes turning the soul from the contingent events of sense experience toward the kind of truth that is always necessarily true, whereas *Paradise Lost* emphasizes the contingent historical character of all Creation. Milton's placement of the creation story – a divinely revealed narration of a contingent historical action – implies that dialectic can never result in metaphysical knowledge because the cosmos, including the human knower, is simply not necessary. Thus, Raphael's account of the six days of creation involves three elements that are absent from the Socratic vision of what constitutes knowledge:

1) The inset creation story, as divine history, emphasizes that contingent historical events can be genuinely known in a manner that is appropriate to finite humans.
2) It emphasizes the need for divine revelation regarding those historical contingencies that, in this case, predate the creation of human beings.
3) It emphasizes the insufficiency of even unfallen human reason in understanding observed phenomena (in this case stars) without recourse to a divinely revealed history of this contingent universe.

Taken together, these three elements challenge the Socratic process of dialectic leading to knowledge. Although *Paradise Lost* obviously emphasizes the limits of unaided human reason, this does not mean, as we shall see, that the faculty of reason is simply replaced by divine revelation or left to atrophy.

If we consider also the two different accounts of astronomy that these texts present, we can see both an important similarity and an important difference.

Adam's question regarding whether the universe is heliocentric or geocentric (*PL* 8.5–38) gets a curious response from Raphael that is doubtful and circumspect (8.66–166), and which ultimately concludes, not by prohibiting such knowledge in absolute terms, but by emphasizing its irrelevance to Adam's immediate concerns in caring for Eden; he exhorts Adam to be "lowly wise" and to focus on what "concerns thee and thy being" (8.173–74). Many readers have recognized that this passage affords suggestive engagement with the controversy surrounding the cosmological arguments of Galileo Galilei. Exactly what point the epic seems to be making about that controversy, however, has been less apparent and has become the subject of a vast body of secondary literature (Lieb 2008; Danielson 2009). My argument does not deny the poem's obvious engagement with the astronomy of Milton's day. By considering the *Republic* as a further context for this episode, however, we can appreciate that Milton is also addressing the place of astronomy in the cultivation of wisdom.

Raphael's response is remarkably similar to the position of Socrates in one way: they both emphasize that definitive empirical knowledge regarding astronomy is not intrinsic to human happiness. This point, however, leads to a further contrast between the two texts: Socrates repeatedly insists that mathematical studies, such as "astronomy" rightly understood as three-dimensional geometry of motion, are not optional but are indeed required; such arts "must" be pursued, according to Socrates, for humans to begin the process (dialectic) that culminates in genuine knowledge of the Good. By contrast, because Raphael does not share Socrates' definition of "astronomy," *Paradise Lost* implies that, although human thriving will obviously include some use of mathematical abstraction and empirical observation, specific conclusions in such matters are not intrinsic to human moral virtue or happiness. More importantly, the thematic emphasis upon the goodness of sensible creation in *Paradise Lost* more generally makes Socrates' aims for such study irrelevant. Once again, for Socrates, the purpose of studying mathematics is to turn the soul from the sensible to the intelligible, whereas *Paradise Lost* emphasizes that the sensible universe participates in the intelligible and is capable, no less than angelic being, of revealing divine glory.

What about the ensuing narrative segment? Why does *Paradise Lost* present a dilation of Genesis 2 specifically at that point that corresponds to Socrates' description of the operations of dialectic? In effect, the conversation between Adam and God, which Adam calls a "celestial colloquie sublime," dilates a biblical narrative so as to model an alternative to Socratic dialectic. At the most basic level, the conversation enables Adam not simply to be told about his need for Eve but to go through a process of self-discovery regarding that need. At the end of the conversation, God refers to it as a "trial," the kind of trial that any reader of *Areopagitica* could recognize as a trial "by what is contrary." In this case, Adam is led to contrast his condition first with the condition of beasts and then with the unconditioned reality of God (*PL* 8.337–451). Adam's articulation of his need for a mate who can enjoy "all rational delight" (8.391) proceeds by contrast with the non-humans that surround him. The epic depicts a dialectical process that does not culminate in an ascent to a Form of the Good beyond all temporal becoming; rather, for Milton, the very process of discovery – the conversation – is a gift from the God who has already descended by crossing the division between Creator and Creation. There is, in *Paradise Lost,* a potential subsequent ethical ascent, which Raphael describes at the beginning of his visit (5.469–503), but such ascent is possible only because a divine descent has already happened (in the act of Creation). The dialectic in Book 7 of *Paradise Lost*, specifically as an adaptation of Genesis 2, thus culminates in the revelation that Edenic marriage provides an understanding, by analogy, of how the Form of the Good is communicative and oriented toward a particular other.

Ultimately, Milton presents these inset narrative adaptations of Genesis 1 and 2 specifically as positive alternatives to Socratic dialectic and the kind of wisdom it purports to give. At one level, *Paradise Lost* implies that dialectic, by itself, can never progress from reflection on created being to knowledge of necessary truth because the universe is itself a contingent aesthetic act. The epic implies that knowledge of such pre-human history is necessarily forensic – that is, a mode of rhetoric which depends on circumstantial evidence and testimony, or divine revelation. At a deeper level, however, the very form of the celestial colloquy, specifically as a conversation, is a form that Milton saw exemplified throughout the book of Genesis.[19] By presenting divine revelation in a conversational form here, Milton implies that, while divine revelation can include general principles and revealed narratives about past contingent events, it should not be reduced to these; rather, in order for divine revelation to be transformative – to induce wisdom in the full sense – the knowledge of principles and historical narratives must also include divine revelation specifically in conversational form: that is, divine revelation that speaks to the contingencies of a personal present but does not simply dispense information. Instead, this kind of divine revelation involves human participation which fulfills rather than supplants the faculty of reason. In this way, the epic depicts how divine inspiration can contribute to growth in wisdom and does not entail the corruptions of politically destructive enthusiasm.

Phillip J. Donnelly

References

Baldwin, Anna 1994. "Platonic Ascents and Descents in Milton" in *Platonism and the English Imagination.* Ed. Anna Baldwin and Sarah Hutton. Cambridge: Cambridge University Press, 151–62.

Blake, William 1982. "The Marriage of Heaven and Hell" in *The Complete Poetry and Prose of William Blake.* 2nd ed. Ed. David V. Erdman. Berkeley: University of California Press.

Brann, Eva 2004. "The Music of the *Republic*" in *The Music of the* Republic. Philadelphia: Paul Dry. 108–245.

Calvin, John 1989. *Institutes of the Christian Religion.* Trans. Henry Beveridge. Grand Rapids: Eerdmans.

Campbell, Gordon, ed. 1992. *John Milton: The Complete English Poems*. New York: Knopf, Everyman.

Corns, Thomas N. 2001. *Blackwell Companion to Milton*. Oxford: Blackwell.

Danielson, Dennis, ed. 1999. *The Cambridge Companion to Milton.* 2nd ed. Cambridge: Cambridge University Press.

——— 2009. "Astronomy." In Dobranski 2009. 213–25.

Dobranski, Stephen B., ed. 2009. *Milton in Context*. Cambridge: Cambridge University Press.

Donnelly, Phillip J. 2005. "Enthusiastic Poetry and Rationalized Christianity: The Poetic Theory of John Dennis." *Christianity and Literature* 54. 235–64.

——— 2007. "Poetic Justice: Plato's *Republic* in *Paradise Lost* (1667)" in "*Paradise Lost: A Poem Written in Ten Books"; Essays on the 1667 First Edition.* Ed. Michael Lieb and John T. Shawcross. Pittsburgh: Duquesne University Press. 159–81.

——— 2009a. "Logic." In Dobranski 2009. 349–60.

——— 2009b. *Milton's Scriptural Reasoning*. Cambridge: Cambridge University Press.

Fallon, Stephen M. 1991. *Milton Among the Philosophers*. Ithaca: Cornell University Press.

Fish, Stanley E. 1967. *Surprised by Sin: The Reader in* Paradise Lost. Berkeley: University of California Press.

Forsyth, Neil 2003. *The Satanic Epic*. Princeton: Princeton University Press.

Hart, David B. 2003. *The Beauty of the Infinite*. Grand Rapids: Eerdmans.

Jayne, Sears 1995. *Plato in Renaissance England*. Dordrecht; Boston: Kluwer Academic.

Lieb, Michael 2008. "Brotherhood of the Illuminati: Milton, Galileo, and the Poetics of Conspiracy." *Milton Studies* 47. 54–95.

McDowell, Nicholas and Nigel Smith, ed. 2009. *The Oxford Handbook of Milton.* Oxford: Oxford University Press.

Milton, John 1953–82. *The Complete Prose Works of John Milton.* 8 vols. Ed. Don M. Wolfe. New Haven: Yale University Press.

Murdoch, Iris 1997. "The Sovereignty of Good over other Concepts" in *Existentialists and Mystics*. New York: Penguin. 363–85.

Parker, William Riley 1996. *Milton: A Biography.* Revised edition. Ed. Gordon Campbell. Oxford: Oxford University Press.

Perkins, William 1607. *The Arte of Prophecying or, A treatise concerning the sacred and onely true manner and methode of preaching*. Trans. Thomas Tuke. London.

Plato 1992. *Republic.* Trans. G. M. A. Grube and C. D. C. Reeve. Indianapolis: Hackett.

Samuel, Irene 1947. *Plato and Milton*. Ithaca: Cornell University Press.

Shawcross, John T. and Michael Lieb, ed. 2007. *"Paradise Lost: A Poem Written in Ten Books"; An Authoritative Text of the 1667 First Edition*. Pittsburgh: Duquesne University Press.

Sidney, Philip 1595. *An Apologie for Poetrie*. London.

Rumrich, John P. 1996. *Milton Unbound*. Cambridge: Cambridge University Press.

von Maltzahn, Nicholas 1996. "The First Reception of *Paradise Lost* (1667)" in *Review of English Studies*, New Series 47, no. 188: 479-99.

Kant
Groundwork of the Metaphysics of Morals

Alone among the thinkers discussed in this volume, Immanuel Kant represents that significant era in the history of Western thought known as the Enlightenment.[1] Our conversation starts with ancient pre-Christian thinkers, dwells for a long while in a decidedly Christian epoch, and ends with those who write in a largely post-Christian world. The Enlightenment is often seen as the turning point from Christian to post-Christian context. Over one hundred years pass between Milton's *Paradise Lost* and Kant's *Groundwork.* During these years dramatic scientific advancement vastly increases humanity's understanding of the natural world. At the same time it casts long-accepted Aristotelian metaphysical views, and the Christian doctrines that have become allied with them, into doubt. When Dostoevsky writes *The Brothers Karamazov* another hundred years hence, doubt will dominate the reception of Christianity in many quarters. But that time has not yet fully arrived and Kant occupies a middle place.

The eighteenth century has also seen significant movements in political thought, movements that take freedom and autonomy as their watchwords and are working themselves out in the American and French revolutions even as Kant writes. No thinker gives these themes a more central place than does Kant. Concern with human freedom drives not only his political philosophy, but also his revolutionary treatments of metaphysics and epistemology, in which he is concerned to embrace the new scientific insights while maintaining a robust notion of freedom. And his moral philosophy, my focus here, places the notion of autonomy at its very core. This occupation with human autonomy has contributed to Christian thinkers' treatment of Kant as a villain, one who doesn't just stand at the turning point, but actively brings about the turn away from God and towards ourselves.[2] Both friends and foes of Kant's system have supposed that in his appeal to autonomy Kant decisively replaces God's authority with our own and so takes an important step away from a Christian worldview.

In my own intellectual development I experienced Kant's works, particularly *The Groundwork of the Metaphysics of Morals,* differently. With twelve years of Christian education behind me, I first encountered Kant in the setting of a secular university. There he appeared to me to be an ally, a thinker who stood against the relativism or nihilism that marked the moral outlook of many of my peers. I didn't encounter critical Christian treatments of Kant until later, and when I did I found that many relied on what seemed to me be to be misinterpretation or oversimplification. Frequently voiced concerns about Kant's high regard for human autonomy didn't address the complex concept that Kant has in mind. Undoubtedly, later thinkers deploy the idea of autonomy in decidedly un-Christian and even anti-Christian ways. Nietzsche, with his valorization of human power over against service to both God and neighbor, represents this trend.[3] But Nietzschean autonomy, which casts off the perceived limitations of morality, is largely alien to Kantian autonomy, which – as we will see – is realized only in subjection to the moral law.

While Kant departs from the Christian orthodoxy in which he was reared, Christian ideas nevertheless continue to mark his thought in profound ways. Christians will thus miss something important if we approach his work as that of either an unambiguous friend or an unambiguous adversary. We must keep in mind his middle place: by no means an orthodox Christian, but still far closer to Christianity than many who come after him, including some who appropriate his work. Careful and sympathetic reading reveals in Kant's thought resources that can help us develop wisdom, not merely by serving as a foil, but also in positive ways. Pointing to some of these resources will be my main purpose here.

I will make some reference to Kant's religious thought, but focus primarily on the *Groundwork of the Metaphysics of Morals,* long regarded as his most important text in moral philosophy. It is easy to find Christian themes here; in fact their presence is virtually assured by the method of the work. Kant takes as his starting point what he calls "common rational cognition," that is ordinary ideas about morality.[4] He aims first to systematize these, distilling them into a fundamental moral principle or law, and then to vindicate the authority of this principle. Since the "ordinary" thought that Kant addresses is that of a culture overwhelmingly shaped by Christianity, the law that he elicits reflects aspects of this outlook.[5] When teaching the text in a Christian classroom it will be helpful to identify these themes and investigate the ways in which Kant's treatment of them develops Christian thought on the one hand and departs from it on the other.

In what follows, I will provide an outline of this difficult text that brings out several of its affinities with a Christian worldview. I have already mentioned Kant's opposition to relativism and nihilism, and his affirmation of a reciprocal relationship between freedom and the moral life. In addition, Kant pointedly rejects the unconditional value of human happiness, understood as the satisfaction of whatever desires we may happen to have. He is alert to the difficulty of doing what is right and to some of our most characteristic vices. He is absolutely committed to the unique value and inviolability of every person. And he affirms our responsibility for what we do and what we are like. Finally, and perhaps surprisingly, Kant commends to us a moral humility, and ties this humility to our need for faith in God.

Does Kant Condemn the Lover of Virtue?
The Example of the Sympathetic Man

The *Groundwork* takes up the question that Roger Lundin, in his essay on *King Lear,* identifies as one of the central anxieties of modernity: where, in the mechanistic order of nature, can we find a place for ethics or moral requirements?[6] Kant takes this question to be equivalent to another: how can we have reason to act against our desires?[7] He embraces an approach to science that regards a human being and all her movements as natural phenomena. He argues that, nevertheless, we are free, responsible, and subject to obligations.[8] Kant executes this argument in two steps. In the first two sections of the book he is concerned to say what the moral law would have to be, if there is one. In the third and final section he aims to vindicate the authority of the principle that results.

The "common rational cognition" with which Kant begins is the idea of the good will, or virtuous person. He claims that virtue is the only thing that has *unconditional worth*, and defends this claim by reviewing and dismissing other plausible contenders (Kant 1997a, 4:393).[9] For each he produces counter-examples that are supposed to demonstrate that the value of the thing in question comes with conditions attached after all. Here, at the very outset of his text, Kant considers and rejects the thesis that human happiness is an unconditioned good. He asks us to consider the happiness of someone who is "graced with no feature of a pure and good will" (Kant 1997a, 4:393), believing that we will reject the claim that the happiness of such a person is good. This seems plausible, especially if we think of his happiness as somehow resulting from his misdeeds. Kant also points out that happiness, in the sense of complete satisfaction with one's condition, can be a precursor to the vice of arrogance. He concludes that we don't think that human happiness *per se* is good; rather we think that it is good when people are happy for the right reasons.[10] Kant holds that satisfaction of desire is valuable if, but only if, the desires in question are of the right sort.[11]

Having argued that only the good will is unconditionally good, Kant proceeds to elicit the principle on which it acts. His idea is that this will reveal what the moral law would have to be. But his characterization of the good will for these purposes invites confusion. In particular, one of his examples suggests the view, thus often attributed to him, that there is something suspect or non-ideal about fulfilling our moral duties willingly or joyfully. Since this example has been so influential in the reception of Kant's moral theory, it is worth pausing over it to make sure that we get it right.

Kant asks us to consider a sympathetic man who "find[s] an inner satisfaction in spreading joy around [him]" and claims that such a person's help for others has "no moral worth" (Kant 1997a, 4:398). The example continues: if the man later sinks into a sort of depression in which he can no longer take joy in benevolent action, yet continues to help others just out of a conviction that it is his duty to do so, then "the action first has its genuine moral worth." It is easy to see why someone would take the lesson to be that true virtue demands a dour demeanor. And, in light of this, it is unsurprising that many Christian readers contrast Kant's position unfavorably with Aristotle's account of virtue. For isn't Kant here denying that the wise person not only knows what is required of her, but also finds the good "beautiful, attractive, interesting, desirable" (Roberts [Introduction], 7)? Essays in this volume attribute this view not only to Aristotle, but also to Plato and Dostoevsky, among others. On what grounds could one disagree? In fact, Kant is not here dissenting from the consensus, but intends a very different lesson.

The problem Kant sees with the sympathetic person is not that he enjoys doing what he ought to do, but that he is – as Kant imagines him – regarding his enjoyment as providing the reason for doing these things. He helps others merely because he likes to help, and Kant is quite right to think that this is the wrong reason for helping. So, while the sympathetic man might still *act* rightly, he cannot serve as the exemplar of virtue. His will is not the good will.

Why exactly does the sympathetic man enjoy doing good? We can fill in the details in at least a couple of different ways each of which gives us insight into a variety of human vice. We could take Kant here to have his eye on the familiar form of human error that Aquinas calls vainglory. The vainglorious person too may do the right thing, at least in particular situations. But just such moral success can lead him to feel, as Kruschwitz describes, "rather pleased with himself" (Kruschwitz, 17). Kant's sympathetic man, as initially characterized, might be understood as this type: the person who acts well simply because it pleases him so to reflect on what a fine person he is. Alternatively, we might emphasize the man's literal sympathy: he tends to pick up the feelings of those around him, so by making others happy he creates happiness in himself as well.[12] Kant need not think that there is anything wrong with having such a disposition, but warns that making it the basis of one's assistance of others is unduly self-centered. The sympathetic person should help, not because doing so makes *him* feel good, but because others are in need and have a claim on his assistance.

The person of true good will, by contrast, may or may not enjoy any particular instance of doing the right thing. What distinguishes her is that she sees that, as far as what she ought to do goes, it doesn't matter whether she enjoys doing right. She sees that sometimes she ought to help whether she feels like doing so or not. Kant's sympathetic person fails to recognize this; he doesn't think that he would have reason to help others even if he did not enjoy doing so. It is because *this particular* man first recognizes this in the midst of his depression that *his* actions come to have moral worth only then. Because only then does *he* recognize the fact that something is required of him as providing him sufficient reason to do it, regardless of his feelings about the matter. Recognizing, and acting in light of, this conviction is what Kant means by acting on duty.[13]

Kant understands as well as anyone how very disordered human desire is apt to be. He thus commends the person who does what he ought to do in the face of countervailing temptation. This in no way rules out equal, or even greater, regard for someone who, while acknowledging that the fact that an action is morally required is sufficient reason to do it, also enjoys his virtuous activity. In fact, Kant affirms this model of virtue in another text. But in the *Groundwork,* his concern is with the content and authority of the moral law, rather than a theory of virtue, and he does not elaborate the latter here.[14]

Kant draws another lesson from the example: "an action from duty has its moral worth *not in the purpose* to be attained by it but in the maxim in accordance with which it is decided upon…" (Kant 1997a, 4:399). At the beginning of the book Kant observes that virtue is not characterized by what it accomplishes.[15] But now he claims something stronger. The sympathetic man has the same purpose both before and after his epiphany. His purpose in each case is to help others. If prior to his depression the man pursues this purpose for the wrong reason, and is criticizable on these grounds, then the example shows that virtue is not characterized even by what it *aims* to accomplish. I think that we have something to learn from this perhaps counter-intuitive feature of Kant's thought, and I return to it below.

The Categorical Imperative: Universal Law, Humanity, and Autonomy

Let's return now to the main thread of the argument. Recall that Kant is talking about the good will because he supposes that if we can identify the practical principle on which it acts we will have discovered the content of the moral principle. Kant has argued that the good will takes the fact that an action is morally required as sufficient reason for doing it, or acts on duty. Now he turns to the task of spelling out this motive into a principle of action. What follows are several, purportedly equivalent, formulations of his moral principle – at least three and as many as five, depending on how one counts.[16] First and most famous is the Formula of Universal Law: "Act only in accordance with that maxim through which you can at the same time will that it become a universal law" (Kant 1997a, 4:421). Scholars friendly to Kant have worked to show how this formal restriction on our principles of action can yield content, indeed content something like that of our pre-theoretical moral commitments.[17] We don't have space to examine these attempts here, but we ought to note that, whatever else it accomplishes, this formulation diagnoses and responds to our temptation to make exceptions for ourselves. We often want to allow ourselves to act in ways and for reasons that we would not allow others to act, and the Formula of the Universal Law highlights morality's opposition to this.

Next comes the Formula of Humanity as an End: "So act that you use humanity, whether in your own person or the person of any other, always at the same time as an end, never merely as a means" (Kant 1997a, 4:429). It is in his discussion of this way of understanding the moral principle that Kant most emphasizes his commitment to the value of each individual person. On his view, people have not only very great worth, but a special kind of worth, a kind that cannot appropriately be traded off against other values. Kant puts this by saying that the world contains two classes: *things,* which have price or an exchange value, and *persons,* which have dignity, a value beyond price.[18] On Kant's view dignity, in this sense of literally incomparable value, is a feature of each and every person: no person is worth more or less than any other.

Kant's commitment to the value and dignity of each person surely has Christian roots, and contrasts with both ancient and some contemporary moral outlooks. Ancient Greeks, including Aristotle, sorted human beings into types of greater and lesser worth.[19] Strands of this thinking resurface in Nietzsche and persist today. Contemporary ethical thought is also marked by a different tendency: that of treating *all* value as price, allowing or even requiring trade-offs that fail to respect the worth of individuals.[20] The Christian tradition affirms the equal worth and inviolability of each person as implications of the doctrine that each person bears God's image. We might ask whether Kant's treatment of the idea of dignity can help to illuminate the practical implications of the *imago Dei.*

Each of these formulae, as well as the next, the Formula of the Kingdom of Ends,[21] could provide the basis for much more fruitful reflection and discussion, but it is in his discussion of autonomy, if anywhere, that Kant arrogates to the individual moral agent authority that properly belongs only to God.[22] To see whether he is guilty of this charge, we must ask what motivates Kant's claim that we must legislate the moral law autonomously, what this claim comes to, what we might learn from it, and how far we should agree to it.

To be autonomous is, literally, to act according to a law that one gives one's self. Insofar as the emphasis falls on the authority of the self the view may seem a mere precursor to the lionization of human willfulness that we find in Nietzsche, among others. But, as Nietzsche himself well realizes, Kant's commitment to and emphasis on law resists this appropriation. The key to Kant's understanding of morality is the joining of freedom and law, the idea that true freedom can be realized only within the confines of the moral law.

This is a thesis that echoes themes in the Christian moral tradition, and Kant's rigorous treatment of this idea deserves careful consideration.

Kant's central claims about autonomy are two: First, human beings, being rational agents, *are* autonomous. Our autonomy is, in one sense, inescapable and the condition under which we inevitably act. Second, our own autonomy, in a different but related sense, is the only possible source of authority for the moral law. To understand and evaluate this second claim we must begin with the first. Kant is impressed by the fact that it is characteristic of rational agents that we not only act according to principles, but can consider the principles on which we act, and thus question whether we are justified in guiding ourselves by them (Kant 1997a, 4:412–413). Our interest in this question about justification is fundamentally practical: we raise it in the course of trying to figure out what we should do, and we can act on the answers that we reach.[23] Because we are capable of questioning in this practical way, whenever we act we at least implicitly claim that such action is justified, and in this way we put our own authority behind it. To act on any principle is then to give it the status of a law for one's self. In this sense we cannot do anything other than act on laws that we give ourselves, that is, act autonomously.[24]

This is Kant's first, descriptive, claim about autonomy. In the relevant sense we *are* autonomous. His second claim is normative, holding that in another sense we *ought to be* autonomous, and is undoubtedly much more difficult both to understand and to defend. So far we know that any principle that you act on will be, in one sense, one that you regard as law. You give such principles the status of laws for you. But what if you are committed to granting that status only to principles of action that really are fit to be laws, principles that are worthy of being regarded as having this authority? What principle or principles of action would you choose? Kant thinks that he has already provided the answer to this question: in his defense of the Universal Law formulation of the Categorical Imperative, he has shown that principles of action that can properly be willed as laws are just exactly the principles on which it is morally permissible to act.

When Kant claims that the only practical principles that do or could have authority for us are laws that we give ourselves, it may sound as if he thinks that I may do whatever I want to do. But his emphasis is on *laws*, not just *ourselves*. His ideal of autonomy turns out to be the very opposite of what it might appear: I have reason to act as I *want* to act only if I want to act in a morally permissible way. I can be autonomous only by acting from the moral law. In affirming the normative version of autonomy, Kant is claiming that the moral law sets the conditions on which my desires give me reason to act. Short of this, he does not think that my desires provide me with any reasons for action at all.[25]

Let's pause a moment to notice the attitude that Kant has here towards our desires. To my mind, he incorporates just the right level of suspicion. He recognizes that we may be – indeed will be – subject to the pull of desires to act in ways that we should not, but pointedly regards these desires as temptations, and indeed as indicators of our corruption.[26] We thus cannot regard our desire for something as sufficient to provide reason to pursue the thing, but rather ought to query desires for their fit with moral demands. On the other hand, Kant avoids a dualism that claims that all desires are evil and to be resisted. He believes, rather, that our desires can be fit bases for action. If I can act on it without violation of my obligations, a desire does give me reason to act. Here Kant provides a practical response to both the goodness and the corruption of our nature. We cannot trust our desires as they are given, but neither can we treat our desiring nature as foreign to what we ought to do.

Kant thinks that only those principles fit to be laws can be willed autonomously. Further he holds that these just are, in the first place, the moral principle, and derivatively the more particular ways of acting that the moral principle allows. It is only by limiting ourselves to morally permissible actions that we can be autonomous or, as he says elsewhere, free.[27] So Kant endorses and develops the important idea that sin and vice is a form of bondage, while freedom comes in doing what we ought to do. As he understands it, when we act against the moral law we succumb to the temptation of some desire that prompts us to act in a less than fully justified way. Wrongdoing, in this picture, always involves us in weakness, confusion or both.[28] To act wrongly is to be less than fully in control of one's self. By contrast the free agent directs herself by principles that she recognizes as laws. If this is right, then the free person and the moral person are one and the same (Kant 1997a, 4:447).[29]

Embedded in this development of the theme of autonomy, we find a surprising and striking call to humility.[30] Kant claims that all previous principles put forth as candidates for the moral law failed, and all for a common reason (Kant 1997a, 4:428, 4:432, 4:441–445). They were all what he calls "material principles," telling us to pursue a particular end or purpose. Though they varied in the purposes that they invoked, all failed because, as we have seen, a principle of action that designates a purpose to be realized is not of the right sort to be the moral law. The good will is not distinguished by what it aims to accomplish.[31]

Kant here diagnoses another characteristic human weakness: Love of what is good can tempt us to wrong. We can suppose, wrongly, that a good end justifies otherwise unacceptable means. As a corrective, Kant gives right action priority over good outcome.[32] The moral law commands absolutely and does not allow for exceptions in cases in which we think that violations would lead to a better outcome.[33] Accepting this demands a particularly difficult sort of humility, a willingness to do what is required of us, even when we cannot see that or how this will allow for things to turn out all right.

But this absolute commitment to the requirements of the moral law presents a problem, especially since the law itself does not direct us to realize a particular purpose. It may be true that we are sometimes tempted to do wrong in the service of producing outcomes that we value, and that such temptations ought to be resisted. But we are not capable of indifference to the outcome of our actions, and importantly such indifference would seem despicable rather than commendable. If the wise person loves the good, how can she love the moral life if it doesn't assure us of a good outcome?

Kant is fully aware of this problem, and raises it in his own voice, though not in the *Groundwork.* Instead he takes up the issue in his theological discussions in *Religion within the Bounds of Mere Reason* (Kant, 1998a, 6:3–6).[34] His answer is unacceptable to contemporary secular Kantians, but a familiar element of the Christian worldview: we can reconcile respect for the law with love of the good only through trust in God. We are to take responsibility only for what we are called to do. We can and must hope that God will direct the world so that the outcomes of our right actions are ultimately good. It is only faith in God, Kant thinks, that allows us to see the moral life as intelligible and worthwhile.

Autonomy and the Moral Authority of God

So far I have given a very brief overview of the argument of the *Groundwork,* suggesting along the way points at which this work might assist our development in wisdom. I have advocated for serious consideration of Kantian autonomy, claiming that it is more akin to a Christian view of freedom than to Nietzsche's opposition to limitations. And I have also explained how Kant's view not only allows for, but also demands, trust in God. But some may think that neither of these points of connection goes far enough in assuaging worries that the view is, in the end, in conflict with our recognition of God's moral authority. In this final section I consider this question, but what I have to say here is only speculative. If I had a class of Christian students, I would certainly use the study of Kant's *Groundwork* to reflect with them on what God's moral authority means for us, and how that authority is related to our own freedom and responsibility for what we do.

We can distinguish several questions here, and Kant is better positioned to answer some than others. First, could a Kantian acknowledge that God's will or command creates reasons for us? Kant sometimes claims that we need to understand all moral laws as God's command.[35] But in the biblical narrative God's commands to individuals often extend well beyond anything plausibly regarded as moral law. God is capable of giving us, through His will, reason to do things that we would otherwise have no reason to do.[36] Second, could a Kantian acknowledge that God can do this in a way distinct from, and capable of trumping, any human will? Finally, could it make sense, in a Kantian view, to trust and act on God's commands, even if they seem to us to command what is wrong? These three ideas present increasing levels of difficulty for a Kantian view, and I will discuss each in turn.

It might seem as though the requirement to act only on laws that we give ourselves rules out the possibility of taking another's will to create new reasons for us. But Kant himself is explicitly committed to the idea that *other* people's choices give me reason to act. In the *Groundwork* this is clearest in his discussion of the Formula of Humanity, which requires that we make others' ends our own (Kant 1997a, 4:430). This entails that others' choices give me reasons that I would not otherwise have had. If I encounter someone struggling to get a heavy stroller onto a bus, I have reason to make her end of loading the stroller my own, and so to offer assistance. I would not have had any reason to get the stroller on the bus had she not chosen to do so. Kant thinks that autonomy commits us to taking reasons like this seriously. If his view can be worked out, it shows not only the *compatibility* of my own autonomy with taking the choices or will of another as reason-giving, but its *incompatibility* with rejecting this.[37]

Kant himself will not countenance an easy extension of any such account to our relation to God. But his objection to doing so depends on epistemological views that commit him to think that we cannot know anything about God, and thus could not know of any particular purpose of God's. These commitments are arguably independent of the main lines of his moral philosophy.[38] And apart from them, we might think that what is true in the inter-human case should be all the more true in the God-human case. God, after all, never wills the impermissible or worthless projects that cause complications in the human case. By themselves, then, Kant's views about autonomy in the *Groundwork* don't raise trouble with the very idea that God's commands may create new reasons for us. Indeed, they might even help us to understand how such reason-giving is possible.

This provides at least the outline of an answer to our first question. It allows us to see how, when God tells Abram to leave his home and go to a place that God will show him, Kant can understand the command as having reason-giving force, even though Abram would otherwise have no reason to go (Gen. 12). We have also moved a step towards compatibility with the second aspect of God's authority, by invoking the assumption that God always wills both permissibly and not in a capricious or arbitrary way. This begins a story about why God's will trumps the reasons given by human wills: since God, unlike humans, is both perfectly good and omniscient, his will never fails to account for anyone's legitimate claims on us. Indeed, God's commands to us often direct us precisely to these claims. In the prophetic tradition's call for justice for the poor, we see God regarding such claims as more pressing than our conventional morality might have us believe.[39]

It is not clear, though, that any of this can speak to the third aspect of God's authority. This calls for a sort of moral trust different from what I discussed at the end of the last section, one that would allow for the possibility of cases in which what God requires me to do is not something that I can independently see as *right*. Suppose that the best answer I have for why I should do a certain thing is that God commands it. Can the Kantian countenance such an answer?[40]

Before answering, it is important to distinguish two kinds of cases. In one, God commands something that, apart from his command, seems nonsensical, a crazy scheme that one would never undertake on one's own. The command to Abram to leave his home is like this, and perhaps so too are God's commands to us to forgive and to love our enemies. I don't see that Kantians have reason to reject the *permissibility* of trust in these cases. If we suppose that the actions in question are, in any case, permissible, doing them because God told you to ought to be permissible as well. This will not yet vindicate the stronger claim that such trust is obligatory, but some of the considerations given above could be brought to bear here: God's will might be thought to trump my own in light of God's benevolence and wisdom.[41] So what would, in an inter-human interaction, merely create one reason among others, perhaps only a very trivial one, can in the God-human case create what amounts to an obligation.

But much more difficult is a second kind of case, in which God's perceived command doesn't merely supplement but actually violates our own best moral reasoning. Here God's command to Abraham that he sacrifice Isaac leaps to mind (Gen. 22). In his own discussion of the binding of Isaac, Kant avoids the claim that Abraham ought to have disobeyed God, saying instead that Abraham could not have been justified in attributing this command to God under any circumstances (Kant 1979, 7:62–65; 2000, 6:189–7). This response relies in part on the Kantian epistemology that I mentioned above, but Kant also appeals to the simpler idea that if one receives a command that is deeply in conflict with one's own best moral reasoning, one ought to conclude that it could not come from a loving and just God.[42] Kant is surely right that we should be exceedingly hesitant to engage in actions that otherwise violate our moral convictions, on account of a belief that doing so is God's will.[43] But he here goes beyond even an extreme principle of caution to rule out the very possibility of radical moral trust, at least trust as radical as Abraham's.[44]

No one should think that we can draw easy lessons from the story of Abraham and Isaac. But reflection on the story might prompt questions about Kant's confidence in human reason and judgment. Is he too confident that our reason gives us sufficient insight into what we ought to do? Though he allows that we may not be able to see the point or purpose of fulfilling our obligations, he believes that we can figure out on our own what those obligations are. Indeed, he is quite sanguine about such knowledge, certain that it is within anyone's reach.[45] Contrast this confidence with Dietrich Bonhoeffer, writing from prison after his arrest by the Nazis:

> The great masquerade of evil has played havoc with all our ethical concepts . . . . Who stands fast? Only the man whose final standard is not his reason, his principles, his conscience, his freedom, or his virtue, but who is ready to sacrifice all this when he is called to obedient and responsible action in faith and in exclusive allegiance to God – the responsible man, who tries to make his whole life an answer to the question and call of God. (Bonhoeffer 1998, 109–111)

In many ways, Kant takes a dim view of human nature,[46] but Bonhoeffer, faced with the enormity of human evil, expresses an even deeper pessimism about what we are able to accomplish without God. He believes not only that we are tempted not to *do* what is right, but that, relying on our own reason, we cannot even *know* what is right. We are, in Bonhoeffer's view, completely dependent on God's grace, in need of revelation in order even to know what we ought to do.[47]

It is a serious question which of these two views ought to guide us, or whether any reconciliation between them is possible. Kant's apparent optimism is largely a response to and warning against our tendency to rationalize and excuse wrongdoing by introducing unneeded complexity into our deliberations.[48] He believes that we often – perhaps even always – know perfectly well what we ought to do, and that claims that we do not usually serve to avoid the unpleasantness of doing it.[49] Surely we recognize ourselves in this diagnosis. The difficult commands – to love our enemy, to forgive, to be radical in our generosity – fall into the first category discussed above: they seem foolish by our human standards, rather than impermissible. About these, Kant seems right: we know what we ought to do; our difficulty is in doing it.

But something very different from this is at work in Bonhoeffer. Bonhoeffer is self-consciously responding to an extraordinary moral crisis, and claiming that (at least) in such situations our moral categories break down, our reason fails to guide us, and we must fall back on God's revelation to us, especially his revelation in Christ. He would not, I think, deny that even in such a time there is no escaping responsibility for acting on our own best judgments, and indeed he emphasizes responsibility here. Even the person who acts against her considered moral views, on the conviction that this is what God asks of her here and now, does what she finally judges she ought to do, and is answerable for this judgment. But there may come situations in which our judgment about what we ought to do is far from clear, and no appeal to moral principle can make it so. In such a situation confidence in our abilities to determine the right course of action by the force of reason might mislead us. Perhaps we will be blessed not to encounter the scale of moral crisis that drove

Bonhoeffer to these reflections. But it is possible that our moral confusion is only exposed, not brought about, by such situations, and that our need for revelation permeates even our mundane moral lives.

On the one hand, then, we have Kant's insight that we are prone to evade moral demands with purported confusion. On the other, Bonhoeffer's that misplaced confidence may obscure genuine moral confusion and dependence on revelation. We ought to acknowledge the truth in both of these claims. Our task, an appropriate one to undertake with our students, is to discern their implications for our own lives.

Conclusion

I began by commending an approach to Kant's texts that is simultaneously sympathetic and critical. In fact, this seems to me the right spirit in which to approach almost any great text: humbly open to its lessons and at the same time alert to its inevitable errors. I have tried to provide some more particular guidance about how to read Kant's moral philosophy, especially the *Groundwork,* in this spirit. I hope to have made good on my claim that his thought owes much and bears many affinities to a traditional Christian worldview, and the further claim that we have much to learn from his development of these themes. Kant's impressive moral system is a valuable resource, too much overlooked in the community of Christian scholars. His central claim that autonomy both grounds the authority of the moral law and also is realized only in deference to that law is one with which we ought to wrestle. We find ourselves surrounded by a culture that prizes individual autonomy, and often rejects the apparently countervailing claims of authority, community, and obligation. Perhaps Kant's paradoxical convictions about freedom can help us fashion the right response.

Kyla Ebels-Duggan

References

Adams, Robert Merihew 1999. *Finite and Infinite Goods.* New York: Oxford University Press.

Alison, Henry E. 1996. "The Reciprocity Thesis" in *Idealism and Freedom: Essays on Kant's Theoretical and Practical Philosophy.* New York: Cambridge University Press.

Aristotle 1984. *Politics* in *Complete Works of Aristotle.* Ed. Jonathan Barnes. Princeton: Princeton University Press. 1986–2129.

Bonhoeffer, Dietrich. *Dietrich Bonhoeffer.* Ed. Robert Coles. Maryknoll, NY: Orbis Books.

Chignell, Andrew 2007. "Belief in Kant," *Philosophical Review,* vol. 116, no. 3. 323-360.

Ebels-Duggan, Kyla 2009. "Moral Community: Escaping the Ethical State of Nature," *Philosophers' Imprint* vol. 9:8 (online journal).

Frierson, Patrick 2007. "Corruption, Non-ideal Theory, and Grace: A Reply to *Kant and the Ethics of Humility*, " *Philosophy and Phenomenological Research*. 75(3), 624–631.

Grenberg, Jeanine 2005. *Kant and the Ethics of Humility: A Story of Dependence, Corruption, and Virtue.* New York: Cambridge University Press.

Hare, John E 1996. *The Moral Gap: Kantian Ethics, Human Limits, and God's Assistance.* New York: Oxford University Press.

——— 2001. *God's Call: Moral Limits, God's Commands, and Human Autonomy.* Grand Rapids, MI: William B. Eerdmans.

——— 2007. *God and Morality: A Philosophical History.* Malden, MA: Oxford Blackwell.

Herman, Barbara 1993a. "On the Value of Acting from the Motive of Duty" in *The Practice of Moral Judgment.* Cambridge, MA: Harvard University Press. 1–22.

——— 1993b. "Mutual Aid and Respect for Persons" in *The Practice of Moral Judgment.* Cambridge, MA: Harvard University Press. 45–72.

——— 1993c. "Murder and Mayhem" in *The Practice of Moral Judgment.* Cambridge, MA: Harvard University Press. 113–131.

——— 1993d. "Moral Deliberation and the Derivation of Duties" in *The Practice of Moral Judgment.* Cambridge, MA: Harvard University Press. 132–158.

Kant, Immanuel 1979. *The Conflict of the Faculties.* Trans. Mary J. Gregor. New York: Albaris Books.

——— 1996a. *Metaphysics of Morals.* Trans. Mary Gregor. New York: Cambridge University Press.

——— 1996b. "On a Supposed Right to Lie from Philanthropy" in *Practical Philosophy.* Trans. Mary J. Gregor. New York: Cambridge University Press.

———1997a. *Groundwork of the Metaphysics of Morals.* Trans. Mary Gregor. New York: Cambridge University Press.

——— 1997b. *Critique of Practical Reason* Mary Gregor, trans. New York: Cambridge.

——— 1998a. *Religion within the Bounds of Mere Reason.* Trans. Allen Wood and George di Giovanni. New York: Cambridge University Press.

——— 1998b. *Critique of Pure Reason.* Trans. Paul Guyer and Allen Wood. New York, Cambridge University Press.

——— 2000. *Critique of the Power of Judgment.* Trans. Paul Guyer and Eric Matthews. New York: Cambridge University Press.

——— 2001. *Lectures on Ethics.* Ed. Peter Heath and J.B. Schneewind. Trans. Peter Heath. New York: Cambridge University Press.

Kierkegaard, Soren 1970. *Fear and Trembling and The Sickness Unto Death.* Trans. Walter B. Lowrie. Princeton: Princeton University Press.

Korsgaard, Christine M. 1996a. "Kant's Formula of Universal Law" in *Creating the Kingdom of Ends.* New York: Cambridge University Press. 77–105.

——— 1996b. "Morality as Freedom" in *Creating the Kingdom of Ends.* New York: Cambridge University Press. 159–187.

——— 1997. "Preface" in *Groundwork of the Metaphysics of Morals.* Trans. Mary Gregor. New York: Cambridge University Press.

Nietzsche, Frederick 1967. *On the Genealogy of Morals and Ecce Homo.* Trans. Walter Kaufmann. New York: Vintage Books.

O'Neill, Onora 1989. "Consistency in Action" in *Constructions of Reason,* New York: Cambridge University Press.

Taylor, Charles 1992. *The Ethics of Authenticity.* Cambridge, MA: Harvard University Press.

Wood, Allen 1999. *Kant's Ethical Thought.* New York: Cambridge University Press.

Dostoevsky
The Brothers Karamazov

Near the beginning of *The Brothers Karamazov*, on Alyosha's first day as a "monk in the world," in the gazebo, he stops and listens to his brother Dmitri's confession. In the beginning of their talk, Dmitri declares his doubt – and hope – that reading a beautiful work of literature can transform him, lift him from the pit of "Sodom," and closer to the aesthetic/ethical/religious ideal of the Madonna. Dmitri confesses to Alyosha: "I always read [Schiller's] poem about Ceres and man. Has it reformed me? Never!" (97).[1] Dmitri's confession raises a perennial question – one that, I have found, carries deep resonance for the students that I have taught in Church-related schools for the last twenty years – Notre Dame (Catholic), Valparaiso (Lutheran), and now Pepperdine (Church of Christ): *Can* reading a literary work ever re-form us, help us to become better; – more whole, more holy? In the first part of the essay, I will respond to that question by attending to what I call the "incarnational realism" of Dostoevsky's narrative art. In the second part, I will turn to Alyosha's encounter with Grushenka in "The Onion" chapter as illustrating Dostoevsky's incarnational realism.

"For All": The Precious Image of Christ

Certainly, Dostoevsky himself *sought* to inspire spiritual transformation in his readers. In his 1880 speech in praise of Pushkin, he affirms what he held to be exemplary in the poet's work: its transformational capacity. Pushkin had changed the life of Russia and Europe, for the better; he "gave us artistic types of Russian beauty that came directly from the Russian spirit that dwells in the People's truth"; "having diagnosed the ailment [of nineteenth-century Russia], he also gave us great hope" (Dostoevsky 1994, 1272). In his speech, Dostoevsky points specifically to one such image of hope, the "literary type" of the Russian monk that he had himself recently formed into the character of Father Zosima in *Brothers Karamazov*. The day before his speech, Dostoevsky had written a letter to his wife, describing to Anna the response he received by those who attended the Pushkin celebration – and had been reading the installments of *Brothers Karamazov* as it appeared in *The Russian Messenger*: "[C]rowds of men and women came backstage to shake my hand. As I walked across the hall during intermission, a host of people, youths and graybeards and ladies, rushed toward me exclaiming, 'You're our prophet. We've become better people since we read *The Karamazovs*.' (In brief, I realized how tremendously important *The Karamazovs* is.)" (Dostoevsky 1987, 504).

My argument is premised on the judgment that *The Brothers Karamazov is* a tremendously important book, and, moreover, one that may carry a unique potential to assist us in "becom[ing] better people" – better ethically, spiritually, and aesthetically to the extent that we are able to discern and reflect "the image of Christ" that the novel presents. Dostoevsky wanted to persuade his readers that a saintly Christian life was both real and possible for them. Of Book Six, "The Russian Monk," he wrote to his editor:

> If I can bring it off I will have accomplished something useful: *I will force them to admit* that a pure and ideal Christian is not an abstraction but a tangible, real possibility that can be contemplated with our own eyes and that it is in Christianity alone that the salvation of the Russian people lies. . . . It is for this theme that the entire novel is written, and I only hope that I will carry it off – that's what concerns me most now! (Dostoevsky 1987, 469–70).

Let us return to Dmitri's anguished confession: "I always read [Schiller's] poem about Ceres and man. Has it reformed me? Never!" (97). Dmitri's exclamation seems definitive, but, as Robert Louis Jackson observes, Dmitri continues to bow down to the divine, and that which mediates the divine, in veneration. Drawing on an image in a poem by Goethe, Mitya pleads: "Let me be vile and base, only let me kiss the hem of the veil in which my God is shrouded. Though I may be following the devil, I am Thy son, O Lord, and I love Thee, and I feel the joy without which the world cannot stand" (97).

At the precious least, the *beauty* of Schiller's poem moves Dmitri toward penitence. This is a crucial first step. As Robert Louis Jackson writes: "Precisely in his keenly felt sense of ignominy . . . in [Mitya's] moral despair at what he discovers in himself and in man, lies the measure of the possibility for change" (Jackson 1978, 64). In *On Beauty and Being Just*, Elaine Scarry similarly observes that beauty elicits in us a sense of our own error, and a consequent imperative that we change: "Homer was right: beauty is lifesaving (or life-creating as in Dante's title *La vita nuova),* or life-altering as in Rilke's imperative 'You must change your life' [from his poem "Archaic Torso of Apollo]" (Scarry 1999, 32).

As Jackson demonstrates, Dostoevsky continually sought beautiful form for and images in his novelistic art. He saw the paragon of beauty in Christ, compared with whom, as he wrote famously in 1854 to N. D. Fonvizina, he saw nothing more beautiful.[2] As Jackson writes,

> At the center of Dostoevsky's Christian aesthetic – as it becomes more explicit in his notebooks and belles lettres in the last decade of his life

> – is the image of Christ. . . . 'The moral ideal is Christ.' Yet again, 'not Christ's morality, not his teaching will save the world, but precisely faith that the Word became flesh. This faith is not alone intellectual recognition of his teaching, but direct attraction. One must believe precisely that this is the final ideal of man, the whole embodied Word, God embodied.' . . . Christ came so that mankind might know that the human spirit can be in heavenly glory 'in fact and in flesh, and not only in the dream and in the ideal.' 'Beauty will save the world,' Dostoevsky observed in his notebooks to *The Idiot*. 'The world will become the beauty of Christ,' we read in the notebooks to *The Devils* (Jackson 1978, 56).

In *The Brothers Karamazov*, beauty becomes salvific when it shines from the visage and resonates in the words of those who themselves *iconically* reflect the beauty of Christ.

The icon represents the full recovery of human beauty – a person's participation in divine beauty by the recovery of her or his divine likeness. The icon can thus help us to understand what Zosima means when he says that "On earth, indeed, we are as it were, astray and if it were not for the precious image of Christ before us, we should be altogether lost, as was the human race before the flood" (276). Dostoevsky's earliest memory was of reciting his prayer before the icon of the Mother of God (Kjetsaa 1987, 1). From Sunday worship he would have known the entrance prayer of *The Divine Liturgy According to St. John Chrysostom*, in which the priest and deacon "go before the icon of Christ, and kissing it, say: 'We venerate Thy most pure image, O Good One, and ask forgiveness of our transgressions, O Christ, our God'" (John of Chrysostom 1977, 5).

The icon calls the Christian viewer to repent and re-turn to God. It reminds us that in our pilgrimage in this life, we are called to holiness, to become saints and thus icons of Christ for each other, much as Zosima and Alyosha are in the novel. Exemplary here is the famous sixth-century icon of Christ Pantocrator from St. Catherine's monastery in Mount Sinai – painted not long after the Council of Chalcedon forged the definitive statement on the Incarnation, that Christ is both man and God, finite and infinite, "without separation or confusion." In this icon we get a sense of what this calling might mean, and the way it takes shape in the lives of Zosima and Alyosha.

Observe the asymmetry of Jesus' face in the icon. Jesus' right eye is open, receptive. It gazes into ours with tenderness and merciful acceptance. We are found, loved, and redeemed as we are, in our fallenness. Here is the Christ of whom Alyosha reminds Ivan, when Ivan has insisted that no one dare forgive the torturer of an innocent child: here is the "Being [who] can forgive everything, all *and for all*, because he gave his innocent blood for all and

everything" (213, italics in text). In contrast, Jesus' left eye challenges: *we* are responsible for the violence that blights our world. Zosima articulates this challenge of responsibility in his last discourse, moments before he speaks of the "precious image of Christ": "There is only one means of salvation, then take yourself and make yourself responsible *for all* men's sins. . . ." (276, italics added). From the *Divine Liturgy's* Eucharistic Prayer, Dostoevsky draws the phrase that is crucial in understanding *how* the image of Christ is represented as salvific in the novel. That phrase is "of all and for all."[3] "For all" is the linguistic key. The phrase links two claims: first, that Christ's redemptive work was accomplished *for all* and second, that, in cooperative response, we must therefore work in active love *for all.*

Christ forgives *for all* and yet we are responsible *for all.* How can the promise of salvation be simultaneously taken up and imposed by Christ? The paradox grows clear a few lines later in Zosima's discourse: the only way in which we can accept and enact this imposition of responsibility is in conforming to the image of Christ, which stands before us as both model ("Go and do likewise") and gracious ground, the Word that creates, sustains, and enters the world, and thus provides the warrant for an analogical conception of being. In grace, "in touch with other worlds," we must by our responsible example challenge each other to be responsible. Responsibility entails active love, which Zosima starkly contrasts to the unrealistic "love in dreams" which is exemplified by fantasy, a denial of duration, and a greedy desire for immediate applause (55). Active love is a "harsh and dreadful thing" and always entails work, endurance, and sometimes suffering. In such suffering we participate in the redemptive suffering of Christ (Col. 1.24). When we fail to love actively, we are called to articulate responsibility for our failure in confession – a complex but crucial practice in *The Brothers Karamazov*.[4]

This icon in particular suggests that the person who would conform to its image must sustain a belief in divine mercy and grace, and, concomitantly, the need for personal responsibility and work. To borrow from Mikhail Bakhtin, the icon calls us to respect the *unfinalizability* and freedom of the other person, to retain a hope in the other's capacity to change, to surprise (Bakhtin 1993, 63). But it also reminds us of the need to embody our intentions in concrete deeds (Bakhtin 1984, 51–52).

Incarnational Realism

Dostoevsky described himself as "a realist in the higher sense" who aimed in his writing to reveal "the man in the man"[5] – the deepest self called to conform to the model of the Word made flesh. Indeed, the saving image of Christ is so much at the center of *The Brothers Karamazov* that Dostoevsky's "higher realism" might more precisely be called "incarnational realism," grounded as his art is in what Dostoevsky believes is the Word made flesh.[6] Thematically and formally, this realism is embodied in numerous, interrelated ways throughout the novel, five of which I will discuss here. First, Alyosha, Zosima's disciple and the novel's hero, is described as "more of a realist than anyone" (28). Alyosha's realism, like Zosima's, entails an ethics of prudential decision-making marked by a careful assessment of particular circumstances and cases. Second, the novel represents time as transformed by Christ's incarnation, embodied in the novel by recapitulations of the image presented in the novel's epigraph from John 12:24: the corn of wheat that falls into the ground and dies, and that thereby brings life. Third, the novel reprises a descent-ascent pattern, imaged most vividly in Zosima's kissing the earth before he dies, and Alyosha kissing the earth after his dream of Cana. Fourth, the novel recalls the patristic tradition of the *sermo humilis*, the low and humble style of narration, a style authorized by the humility of the incarnation, and embodied by the narrator's (and author's) humble acceptance of his character's freedom and complexity. Fifth, the novel presents an image of embodied active love, one that unites both *agape* and *eros* in the incarnational synthesis of *caritas*. I'll briefly discuss each of these embodiments of Dostoevsky's incarnational realism, with more extensive attention given to the fifth, in the final part of the essay where I'll turn to Alyosha's meeting with Grushenka.

First: Alyosha's "realism" – which develops in the course of the novel, especially in his first three days as a "monk in the world" – is a *spiritual* realism. Early on, the narrator insists that Alyosha is a "realist" and not a mystical fanatic. He's got his feet on the ground ("he knew every inch of [it]"; when the limits of time and prudence dictate it, he knows how to take a shortcut (93). In his explanation, the narrator suggests that Alyosha's realism and faith are inseparable:

> Alyosha was more of a realist than any one. Oh, no doubt, in the monastery he fully believed in miracles, but, to my thinking, miracles are never a stumbling-block to the realist. . . . Faith does not, in the realist, spring from the miracle, but the miracle from faith. If the realist once believes, then he is bound by his very realism to admit the miraculous also. The Apostle Thomas said that he would not believe until he saw, but when he did see he said, 'My Lord and my God!' Was it the miracle forced him to believe? Most likely not, but he believed because he desired to believe and possibly he fully believed in his secret heart even when he said, 'I shall not believe except I see.' (28)

For Thomas (as for Alyosha) beholding Christ's image fosters an already-present faith in the Word made flesh.[7] Faith itself grounds realism: Thomas can see the physical and spiritual reality of the risen Christ *because* he believes. So too Alyosha who thus stands in stark contrast to Rakitin, whose egotism blinds him to the spiritual transformations of others. Rakitin is an "unbelieving realist"[8] whose materialism reduces human freedom to the chemical reactions of nerve cells (497). Rakitin sneeringly refers to Alyosha's encounter with Grushenka as a "miracle" (308); in fact, in the way in which the two image Christ for the other, their encounter *is* a miracle. Fundamentally, realism recognizes the reality of the world as created and redeemed by God. In the words of Andrew Moore, Christian realism "confesses the reality of the triune God revealed in Jesus Christ" (9). Such faith lends a believer like Alyosha the "ability to see what God chooses to show and which cannot be seen without faith" (von Balthasar, 175).

Second: The incarnation of Christ transforms time. In *Dante: The Poetics of Conversion*, John Freccero helpfully elucidates a passage from St. Paul's Letter to the Ephesians, in which "Christ is described as 'the fullness of time'" (Freccero 1986, 267). All that precedes Christ's Incarnation can be understood as figural anticipation of that decisive joining of divine and human. All that proceeds from that event can be understood as its recapitulation, specifically the human drama of conversion and confession, which recapitulates the descent and ascent, death and resurrection of Christ, but also in the drama of the saint, especially those, like Zosima and Alyosha, who serve as confessors for others: each descends, empties him or herself in kenotic attentiveness to the other. A number of the novel's best readers have observed a similar figural pattern in *The Brothers Karamazov.* Nina Perlina observes that

> The authority of the Bible subordinates and structures the entire sum of individual 'moralities' in The Brothers Karamazov. . . . Within the framework of Erich Auerbach's theory [articulated in his essay "Figura"], Biblical narrative, the most authoritative and universal text that has ever existed, engulfs all the individual discoveries made by Dostoevsky's heroes. A figural interpretation of the novel tends to saturate occurrences of everyday life with the spirit of eternity" (Perlina 1985, 12–13).

Diane Oenning Thompson also sees the image of Christ as central to the novel,[9] and the foundation of figural and recapitulative readings. She emphasizes the role of memory as crucial to the process of conversion, and contrasts Dostoevsky's realism with that of his contemporaries (Thompson 1991, 223). Similarly, Harriet Murav (1992) claims that "the basic proposition of Dostoevsky's novel [is] that human history can be touched by God, that we are not limited to the horizontal time frame. Our world and other worlds converge, to use the language of the novel" (134). This feature is seen vividly in the final scene of the novel, "The Speech at the Stone," which in a Eucharistic sense both remembers little Ilyusha, whose suffering and death participates in Christ's, and makes present God's redemptive grace in the apostolic community, the little church forged by Alyosha and the boys.[10]

The third feature of incarnational realism is the novel's repeated descent / ascent pattern. Drawing on Freccero's analysis of the pattern of conversion in Dante, Murav observes a similar pattern in *The Brothers Karamazov*, specifically in its repeated pattern of descent and ascent, which she links to the structure of certain icons. She calls the novel a "narrative icon in which the stories of the brothers and the structure of the novel mirror each other. The icon consists of three parts: *katabasis*, or descent into hell; trial; and resurrection, or ascent" (Murav 1992, 135). In *Christ and Apollo*, William F. Lynch (1975) sees in this passage of descent and ascent "the great fact of Christology, that Christ moved down into all the realities of man to get to his Father" (13). Lynch traces this passage in the experience of Alyosha in the wake of Zosima's death, and readers can discern it in the lives of Zosima, Dmitri, Grushenka, Ivan, and Kolya.

These repetitions – recapitulations of Christ's descent and ascent – create in part what Robin Feuer Miller calls "a novel of rhymes": "[T]he very rhyming or interconnectedness of the parts of *The Brothers Karamazov* becomes the reader's own thread through [its] labyrinth of events and ideas. . . . Characters, fragments of plot, fragments of time – all echo and reverberate in unexpected ways and places" (Miller 1992, 13). In the chapter entitled "An Onion," in which Alyosha begins his ascent, the novel itself provides an aptly humble symbol of layering for these rhymes and recapitulations. In the chapter, the kind attentiveness offered by Grushenka to the grieving Alyosha surprises and consoles him. "[I've only given] away one onion" (303), Grushenka claims, drawing on an old Russian folk tale in which a stingy old woman's guardian angel discovers the one redeeming deed in her life: the giving of an onion to a poor peasant. Grushenka's gift of active love is small, ordinary, humble – and redemptive.

Indeed, the humility of the earthy onion metonoymically suggests the fourth dimension of Dostoevsky's formal incarnational realism in *The Brothers Karamazov*: the humble style with which the novel is so often narrated. The narrator is an ordinary townsperson of Skotoprigonevsk, the novel's setting, and remembers events that occurred there thirteen years earlier. Early in the first chapter, he describes Fyodor Pavlovich as "in fact an evil buffoon, and nothing more" (12). His tone is insistent, judgmental. But in the final paragraph of that first chapter, his tone grows less certain as he describes Fyodor's reaction to his first wife's departure and eventual death:

> Fyodor Pavlovich was drunk when he first heard of his wife's death, and the story is that he ran out into the street and began shouting with joy, raising his hands to Heaven: "Lord, now lettest Thou Thy servant depart in peace," but others say he wept without restraint like a little child, so much so that people were sorry for him, in spite of the repul-

> sion he inspired. It is quite possible that both versions are true, that he rejoiced at his release, and at the same time wept for her who released him. As a general rule, people, even the wicked, are much more naive and simple-hearted than we suppose. And we ourselves are, too (13).

The narrator relaxes his earlier judgment upon Fyodor, and suggests, humbly, that he just doesn't know. As Victor Terras (2002) points out, "The narrator's manner is that of a 'conversation with the reader,' and his vocabulary and syntax tend to be those of an oral narrative: sentences and paragraphs are not well-constructed and well-balanced. . ." (87). Robin Feuer Miller (1992) describes the narrator-chronicler as "chatty, often digressive" (16).[11]

The humility of this narrative style – which alternates with a more conventionally omniscient one – harkens back to another manifestation of patristic Christian realism: the *sermo humilis* or low style of preaching and writing. As Erich Auerbach (1965) explains, such a low style, in which "humble everyday things" (37) and language were employed in rhetoric concerning the most sublime subjects such as God, grace, redemption, was authorized by the event of the Incarnation. Auerbach observes that "*Humilis* is related to *humus*, the soil, and literally means low, low lying, of small stature" (39). The word "*humilis* became the most important adjective characterizing [Christ's] Incarnation" (40). For the patristic literary imagination, "The humility of the Incarnation derives its full force from the contrast with Christ's divine nature: man and God, lowly and sublime, *humilis et sublimis*; both the height and the depth are immeasurable and inconceivable . . . " (43). "The *sermo humilis* is: accessible to all, descending to all men in loving-kindness, secretly sublime, at one with the whole Christian congregation" (65).

If we return to the narrator's voice in Chapter One, we can observe such a "descent to all men in loving-kindness." By pointing to the possibility of the two conflicting responses – histrionic, buffoonish exultation; authentic, childlike grief – the narrator acknowledges Fyodor's possibilities, and descends from a position of limiting omniscience above Fyodor, to a position alongside him. He slows down, pauses, and gives Fyodor a more attentive look. The narrator's negative capability allows him to resist an all-too-neat explanation of Fyodor's apparently contradictory behavior, and reveals a respect for the complex unfinalizability of this other person, Fyodor Karamazov. "But who knows[?]" the narrator muses earlier in the paragraph, commenting on conflicting explanations of Fyodor's antics: the narrator – and Dostoevsky behind him – accept a less-than-omniscient stance in relation to the characters in his story. And in his final sentence he reminds us that we ought to follow suit.

The narrator's "loving descent" from a finalizing position above Fyodor, to an open position beside him is analogous to the *kenosis* or self-emptying of

Christ, as Saint Paul describes that emptying in his Letter to the Philippians. "Make your own the mind of Christ Jesus," he exhorts,

> Who, being in the form of God,
> did not count equality with God
> something to be grasped.
> But he emptied himself,
> taking the form of a slave,
> becoming as human beings are;
> and being in every way
> like a human being,
> he was humbler yet,
> even to accepting death,
> death on a cross.
> And for this God raised him high,
> and gave him the name which is above all other names;
> so that *all beings*
> in the heavens, on earth
> and in the underworld,
> *should bend the knee* at the name of Jesus
> and that *every tongue should acknowledge*
> Jesus Christ as Lord,
> to the glory of God the Father. (Phil. 2:5–11, *New Jerusalem Bible*)

In their pioneering biography of Mikhail Bakhtin, Katerina Clark and Michael Holquist first suggested this analogy. If Flaubert situates himself in a controlling distance above his characters, Dostoevsky, "in the best kenotic tradition, . . . gives up the privilege of a distinct and higher being to descend into his text, to be among his creatures. Dostoevsky's distinctive image of Christ results in the central role of polyphony in his fiction" (Clark and Holquist 1984, 249). In its attunement to the complex reality of personhood, polyphony can thus be seen as a crucial aspect of the form of incarnational realism.

Form deeply reflects content here, for one of the key thematic affirmations of *The Brothers Karamazov* is the sacred dignity of human freedom. Dostoevsky's respect for his character's freedom is analogous to divine respect for human freedom. Freedom is intrinsic to human identity, given the human person's created reality as *imago Dei*. The novel's central critique of Christ is uttered by the Grand Inquisitor, whose complaint is that freedom overwhelms human beings in their weakness: "Respecting him less, Thou wouldst have asked less of him. That would have been more like love, for his burden would have been lighter" (223). But Christ's silent love respects even the perverse freedom of the demonic Inquisitor; the active love exemplified by Zosima and Alyosha likewise respects the freedom of those who seek their help.

Alyosha and Grushenka: Sharing Onions

Active love is the foundational theme of the novel, and the fifth and final aspect of incarnational realism that I will discuss here, and it is related to the theme of beauty, as well as to the novel's own polyphonic, beautiful form. Theme and form are both suggested in "The Onion" chapter, in which Alyosha receives a gift of active love from the beautiful Grushenka, is restored to his vocation as a "monk in the world," and reciprocates with a gift of his own.

The concept of active love is first articulated by Father Zosima, Alyosha's mentor – the monastic elder who commissions him to serve as "a monk in the world" – when he tells Madame Khokhlakov that her faith in eternal life will be nourished

> . . . [b]y the experience of active love. . . . If you attain to perfect self-forgetfulness in the love of your neighbor, then you will believe without doubt, and no doubt can possibly enter your soul . . . . [Active love] is a harsh and dreadful thing compared with love in dreams. Love in dreams is greedy for immediate action, rapidly performed and in the sight of all. Men will even give their lives if only the ordeal does not last long but is soon over, with all looking on and applauding as though on the stage. But active love is labor and fortitude, and for some people too, perhaps, a complete science (54-55).

With its emphasis upon the sheer hard work of love, and the renunciation of any selfish inclination, active love recalls Kant's insistence in *Grounding for the Metaphysics of Morals* that an act of love for or duty to the neighbor must be bleached clean of any stain of "dear self" if that act is to have any moral worth.[12] This insistence upon "perfect self-forgetfulness" seems consonant with the image of the kenotic, self-emptying Christ so vital to Dostoevsky's Orthodox tradition, and to his own artistic imagination. The novel's epigraph from John's gospel itself suggests that harsh and dreadful self-renunciation is indeed the novel's prescription: "Except a corn of wheat fall into the ground and die, it abideth alone; but if it die, it bringeth forth much fruit." Such self-giving, embodied by Christ, is designated *agape*, and as Anders Nygren insists, *agape*, exemplified most purely by God's self-giving, can have nothing to do with *eros*, the human desire by which – in *The Symposium*, for example – the Platonic pilgrim scales the ladder of love in a quest for immortal beauty.

However, the organic image from John's gospel, with its promising image of final fruition, suggests that desire, *eros*, and its satisfaction may itself have a place in active love. An organic image provides the title of "An Onion," arguably the turning point of the novel in its depiction of Alyosha's transformative response to Grushenka's active love. This chapter makes especially clear that active love partakes of both *agape* and *eros*. As such, it produces the synthesis of *caritas* which Anders Nygren rejects and Martin D'Arcy and Benedict XVI affirm, and which Dostoevsky suggests is the most deeply human need and deed.[13] Dostoevsky works from an incarnational anthropology which understands the human person as created in the image and likeness of God. Sin distorts this image but Christ's redemption restores both spirit *and* body (that which Plato saw as "perishable rubbish"). Faith in the incarnation, and the sacramental sense of immanent grace that follows from that faith, fosters trust. As David Tracy writes, "As grounded in that gift of trust, *eros* will be transformed but not negated by divine *agape*. That transformation is *caritas*" (432). In Dostoevsky's artistic vision, the person is drawn to and by beauty to restore the beauty of his own divinely-endowed image. In this chapter, Grushenka and Alyosha become iconic images for each other.

As "An Onion" begins, Alyosha's image is distorted: his face is irritable and the cynical Rakitin observes how uncharacteristic this is: "Do you know your face is quite changed? There's none of your famous mildness to be seen in it" (294). Alyosha's trust in the goodness of the created world has been shaken: the body of his beloved elder has decayed prematurely. As did his brother Ivan on the previous day, Alyosha questions divine justice, and in a fit of *nadryv* – that de-formative, infernal self-laceration in which one hurts oneself to hurt another, or vice-versa – allows Rakitin to lead him to the temptress Grushenka, willfully casting his spiritual discipline to the wind, as if into God's face. Alyosha, fearful of sexuality, fears Grushenka. Two days earlier, she had used her sexual allure to humiliate Katerina, right before Alyosha's eyes. When he arrives at Grushenka's, Alyosha expects to find Sodom – to use Dmitri's image when he agonizes to his younger brother about the ambivalence of beauty: "I can't endure the thought that a man of lofty mind and heart begins with the ideal of the Madonna and ends with the ideal of Sodom" (98). To his surprise, however, Grushenka, twice described as "beautiful" (296), presents an image of the Madonna, the face that most resembles Christ's, to borrow words from Dante's *Paradiso*. Thus, Grushenka points up the falsity of Dmitri's Sodom/Madonna dichotomy: The Madonna, who bore Christ in her womb, cannot be reduced to an abstract, completely spiritual antithesis to fleshly disorder. Mary is herself body and soul, like her son, Jesus Christ.

Dante's *Commedia* tells the story of a man whose soul is risen from the depths by the mediation of a beautiful woman, Beatrice, whom Dante loves, body and soul. So too is Alyosha's. At first, when Grushenka sits "beside Alyosha on the sofa," Alyosha notices a change in *her* face: "Her lips glowed, her lips laughed, but it was a good-natured, merry laugh. Alyosha had not expected to see such a kind expression on her face. . . " (299). His expectations are further overturned when Grushenka "suddenly skipped forward and jumped, laughing, on his knee, like a nestling kitten, with her right arm about his neck. 'I'll cheer you up, my pious boy'" (300). When we look at this scene,

I ask my students, is there any sexual attraction on Alyosha's part in this scene? "Oh no," an earnest student usually replies, and points to the text for support: Even with flirtatious Grushenka on his lap, Alyosha "felt numb. . . . [T]here was nothing in his heart such as Rakitin, for instance, watching him malignantly from his corner, might have expected or fancied. The great grief in his heart swallowed up every sensation that might have been aroused, and, if only he could have thought clearly at that moment, he would have realized that he had now the strongest armor to protect him from every lust and temptation" (300). But another student might point out that the next word is "yet." In that "yet" we see that active love in *The Brothers Karamazov* ought be understood as *caritas*, an incarnational image of love which partakes of both *agape* and *eros*. Here is the passage:

> *Yet* in spite of the vague irresponsiveness of his spiritual condition and the sorrow that overwhelmed him, he could not help wondering at a new and strange sensation in his heart. . . . [T]his woman, dreaded above all women, sitting now on his knee, holding him in her arms, aroused in him now a quite different, unexpected, peculiar feeling, a feeling of the intensest and purest interest without a trace of fear, of his former terror. That was what instinctively surprised him (300, my emphasis).

Alyosha's pure and intense interest is *eros*. He is powerfully *drawn to* Grushenka's beauty, but not only the beauty of her physical form, but that beauty of the form in which she responds to Alyosha, bound up as that response is with her truthfulness and kindness. Thus Alyosha's "eyes involuntarily [rest] on her with attention" (326).

Grushenka's beauty is manifested most fully in her *attentiveness* to Alyosha when she learns of Zosima's death:

> "Good God I did not know!" She crossed herself devoutly. "Goodness, what have I been doing, sitting on his knee like this at such a moment!" She started up as though in dismay, instantly slipped off his knee and sat down on the sofa. Alyosha fixed a long wondering look upon her and a light seemed to dawn in his face. (302)

In her essay on "School Studies," Simone Weil claims that attentiveness to the afflicted neighbor entails an emptying of self that asks of the neighbor, "What are you going through?" Grushenka feels and respects what she imagines Alyosha is going through, and empties herself of her merry flirtation – and the anxiety that it cloaks – to attend to Alyosha. The gesture of crossing herself is apt as her self-emptying reflects the *kenosis* of Christ, as sung by St. Paul (Phil. 2:6–8). Reflecting Christ's image, Grushenka is iconic: she reveals the transfigured glory of what seems forsaken, only "harsh and dreadful," to recall Zosima's description of active love. In this crucial scene, *kenosis*, the painful self- renunciation always entailed in active love, emerges as beautiful. The theological project of Hans Urs von Balthasar largely entails the restoration of beauty to its honored place not only as a transcendental category, but as the means by which "sight and hearing can be fused into one . . . assent to God's gifts of creation and revelation" (Oakes 1997, 142). Von Balthasar emphasizes the paradox of beauty in *kenosis*: "To the unity of his humiliation and exaltation, God brings his own form and proper beauty. Isaiah's phrase, 'he had neither form nor beauty' determines the precise locus from which God's unique beauty radiates. . . ." (von Balthasar 1982, 55–56). Further, von Balthasar stresses the beauty of holiness which draws us toward the other.

The radiant look on Alyosha's face – "a light seemed to dawn in his face" – suggests the transformative power of such beauty, the spiritual *metanoia* that the icon seeks to inspire in its beholder. The transformation is manifested in the impassioned declaration of Alyosha that follows. His voice, broken before by *nadryv*, is now "firm" as he first implores Rakitin to "look at" Grushenka as a means of transforming his hardened heart. Alyosha's *metanoia* is then given form by his own confession: "I came here to find a wicked soul – I felt drawn to evil because I was base and evil myself, and I've found a true sister, I have found a treasure – a loving heart." Finally, he acknowledges the manifestation of grace in Grushenka as he tells her: "You've raised my soul from the depths" (302).

Grushenka tells Alyosha that she has only given him an onion, referring to a folk tale in which a guardian angel appeals to God on behalf of a woman condemned to hell, reminding God that the wicked woman had once given an onion to a beggar woman.[14] Inspired by Alyosha's restored, iconic image, Grushenka also makes a confession, and confides in Alyosha the crisis of decision she faces. Alyosha assists her in making her decision by respecting her freedom and attending to that which she herself most deeply wishes. In response to her declaration of love, he says, "I only gave you an onion": the verbal echo sensitively recalls and affirms Grushenka's own imagining, through narrative, of her capacity for active love (307).

The onion is an apt image as it suggests, finally, what is so mysteriously beautiful about the form of *The Brothers Karamazov*: scenes like this, in which repetitions sound, but in slightly different keys, chime throughout the entire novel. As Robin Miller eloquently observes:

> An onion, like a seed, is a living organism . . . . A slice along its diameter shows its carefully structured and separate layers; to unravel it is to discover that each layer recapitulates all the others. *The Brothers Karamazov* embodies these attributes of the onion. . . . [C]orrespon-

> dences – of which there are literally thousands in the novel. . . – give the novel its surprising unity, its miraculously open metonymy (Miller 1992, 86).

I would add that they give the novel its beauty. Readers, our students, perceive and are drawn to this beauty. And, like Dostoevsky's contemporary readers who said to the author, "We've become better people since we read *The Karamazovs*," they are often transformed by it.

. . .

In moments like "The Onion" chapter and in its onion-like recapitulations throughout the novel (Miller 1992, 85), Dostoevsky provides an answer, "in oblique artistic form,"[15] not only to Ivan's despair regarding the human possibility of Christ-like love, but to Mitya's agonized confession that the beautiful form of literary art has never re-formed him. By the end of the novel Mitya *is* re-formed, a "new man." And the novel's beauty invites us to change with him. The novel's transformational power lies in the way it assists its reader to perceive the reality of things – the way the Incarnation has linked the earthly with the infinite, the "mystery of the earth" and "the mystery of the stars" (312). It doesn't present us with Rilke's impossibly ideal "archaic torso of Apollo." In the novel, the burden of false ideals and self-divinization takes the distorted form of *nadryv* ("laceration" or "strain").[16] Instead, the novel's "prosaics of conversion" present the humble, sublime image of Christ, in whom Dostoevsky saw "nothing more beautiful," who descends into the limited and particular contours of human life and – in the words of Gerard Manley Hopkins – "plays in ten thousand places," including the "limbs" and "eyes" and "face" of Grushenka. In the incarnational realism of *The Brothers Karamazov*, the salvific image of Christ calls the reader to behold and contemplate this presence – and, possibly, to be re-formed in the process. In the three Christian universities in which I have taught this novel – Notre Dame, Valparaiso, and Pepperdine – I have been blessed to teach many students who have witnessed to this possibility.[17]

Paul J. Contino

References

Auerbach, Erich 1965. "Sermo Humilis" in *Literary Language and Its Public in Late Antiquity and in the Middle Ages*. Trans. Ralph Manheim. Princeton University Press.

Bakhtin, Mikhail 1984. *Problems of Dostoevsky's Poetics*. Ed. and trans. Caryl Emerson. Minneapolis: University of Minnesota Press.

——— 1993. *Toward a Philosophy of the Act*. Trans. and Notes Vadim

Liapunov. Ed. Vadim Liapunov and Michael Holquist. Austin: University of Texas Press.

——— 1961. "Toward a Reworking of the Dostoevsky Book" in *Problems of Dostoevsky's Poetics*. Minneapolis: University of Minnesota Press. 283–302.

Balthasar, Hans Urs von 1982. *The Glory of the Lord: A Theological Aesthetics*. Volume I: Seeing the Form. Trans. Erasmo Leiva-Merikakis. Ed. Joseph Fessio, S.J., and John Riches. San Francisco: Ignatius Press.

——— 1988. *Dare We Hope "That All Are Saved"?* Trans. David Kipp and Lothar Krauth. San Francisco: Ignatius Press.

Belknap, Robert L. 1989. *The Structure ofThe Brothers Karamazov*. Evanston: Northwestern University Press.

Benedict XVI 2005. *Deus Caritas Est [God is Love]*. http://www.vatican.va/holy_father/benedict_xvi/encyclicals/documents/hf_ben-xvi_enc_20051225_deus-caritas-est_en.html

Clark, Katerina and Michael Holquist 1984. *Mikhail Bakhtin*. Cambridge: Harvard University Press.

Connelly, Julian W. 2010. "Confession in *The Brothers Karamazov*." *The Brothers Karamazov: Art, Creativity, and Spirituality,* edited by Pedrag Cicovacki and Maria Granik. (Universitätsverlag C. Winter Heidelberg.

Contino, Paul J. 2010. "Incarnational Realism and the Case for Casuistry: Dmitri Karamazov's Escape." *The Brothers Karamazov: Art, Creativity, and Spirituality,* edited by Pedrag Cicovacki and Maria Granik. (Universitätsverlag C. Winter Heidelberg.

————— 2009. "William Lynch's *Christ and Apollo* and the Field of Religion and Literature," *Religion and Literature* 41, 2: 237–44.

——— 1995. "Zosima, Mikhail, and Prosaic Confessional Dialogue in *The Brothers Karamazov*," *Studies in the Novel* 27, 1: 63–86.

Cunningham, David S. 2001. "The Brothers Karamazov and Trinitarian Theology" in *Dostoevsky and the Christian Tradition*. Ed. George Pattison and Diane Oenning Thompson. Cambridge University Press.

D'Arcy, M.C. 1956. *The Mind and Heart of Love*. New York: Meridian Books.

Dostoevsky, Fyodor 2011. *The Brothers Karamazov*. Ed. Susan McReynolds Oddo. Trans. Constance Garnett, revised by Ralph E. Matlaw and Susan McReynolds Oddo New York: Norton Critical Edition, Second Edition.

——— 2011. "Selections from Dostoevsky's Letters" in *The Brothers Karamazov*. Norton Critical Edition. 653-66.

——— 1971. *The Notebooks for* The Brothers Karamazov. Ed. and Trans. Edward Wasiolek. University of Chicago Press.

——— 1987. *Selected Letters of Fyodor Dostoyevsky*. Eds. Joseph Frank and David I. Goldstein. New Brunswick, New Jersey: Rutgers University Press.

——— 1993. *A Writer's Diary*. Volume One 1873–1876. Trans. Kenneth Lantz. Evanston: Northwestern University Press.

——— 1994. *A Writer's Diary*. Volume Two 1877–1881. Trans. Kenneth Lantz. Evanston: Northwestern University Press.

Emerson, Caryl 1989. "The Tolstoy Connection in Bakhtin" in *Rethinking Bakhtin.* Evanston: Northwestern University Press. 149–72.

Fanger, Donald 1965. *Dostoevsky and Romantic Realism*. Cambridge: Harvard University Press.

Flath, Carol A. 1999. "The Passion of Dmitri Karamazov," *Slavic Review*, 58, 3: 584–99.

Frank, Joseph 2002. *Dostoevsky: The Mantle of the Prophet, 1871–1881*. Princeton University Press.

Freccero, John 1986. *Dante: The Poetics of Conversion*. Ed. Rachel Jacoff. Cambridge: Harvard University Press.

Jackson, Robert Louis 1978. *Dostoevsky's Quest for Form: A Study of His Philosophy of Art*. Second edition. Bloomington: Physsardt.

John of Chrysostom 1977. *The Divine Liturgy According to St. John Chrysostom*. South Canaan, Pennsylvania: St. Tikhon's Seminary Press.

Kjetsaa, Geir 1987. *Fyodor Dostoevsky: A Writer's Life*. Trans. Siri Hustvedt and David McDuff. New York: Fawcett Columbine.

Linner, Sven 1967. *Dostoevskij on Realism*. Stockholm: Almqvist and Wiksell.

Lossky, Vladimir 1997. *The Mystical Theology of the Eastern Church*. Crestwood, New York: St. Vladimir's Seminary Press.

Lynch, S.J. William F. 1975. *Christ and Apollo. The Dimensions of Literary Imagination*. University of Notre Dame Press.

Miller, Robin Feuer 1992. The Brothers Karamazov: *Worlds of the Novel*. New York: Twayne.

——— 2007. "The Gospel According to Dostoevsky: Paradox, Plot, and Parable" in *Dostoevsky's Unfinished Journey*. New Haven, CT: Yale University Press. 68–85.

Milosz, Czeslaw 2001. *Milosz's ABC's*. Trans. Madeline Levine. New York: Farrar, Straus and Giroux.

Moore, Andrew 2003. *Realism and Christian Faith: God, Grammar, and Meaning*. Cambridge University Press.

Morson, Gary Saul 1993. "Introduction" in *Dostoevsky, A Writer's Diary*. Volume One. Evanston, IL: Northwestern UP. 1–121.

Murav, Harriet 1992. *Holy Foolishness: Dostoevsky's Novels and the Poetics of Cultural Critique*. Stanford University Press.

The New Jerusalem Bible. 1985. Garden City: Doubleday.

Nygren, Anders 1982. *Agape and Eros*. Chicago: University of Chicago Press.

Oakes, Edward T. 1997. *Pattern of Redemption: The Theology of Hans Urs von Balthasar*. New York: Continuum.

Perlina, Nina 1985. *Varieties of Poetic Utterance: Quotation in* The Brothers Karamazov. Lanham: University Press of America.

Scanlan, James P. 2000. "Dostoevsky's Arguments for Immortality," *The Russian Review* 59: 1–20.

Scarry, Elaine 1999. *On Beauty and Being Just*. Princeton University Press.

Schmemann, Alexander 1997. *For the Life of the World*. Crestwood, NY: St. Vladimir's Press.

Soloviev, V.S. 2000. "Seven Paschal Letters: XI. Christ is Risen!" in *Politics, Law, and Morality: Essays by V. S. Soloviev*. Ed. and Trans. Vladimir Wozniuk. Yale University Press. 91–7.

Terras, Victor 2002. *A Karamazov Companion*. Madison: University of Wisconsin Press.

Thompson, Dianne Oenning 1991. The Brothers Karamazov *and the Poetics of Memory*. Cambridge University Press.

Tracy, David 1980. *The Analogical Imagination: Christian Theology and the Culture of Pluralism*. New York: Crossroad.

Ward, Bruce 2010. *Redeeming the Enlightenment: Christianity and Liberal Virtues*. Grand Rapids: Eerdmans.

Ware. Timothy 1993. *The Orthodox Church*. New York: Penguin.

Weil, Simone 2000. "On the Right Relation to School Studies with a View toward the Love of God" in *Waiting for God*. Trans. Emma Craufurd. New York: Harper.

Williams, Rowan 2008. *Dostoevsky: Language, Faith and Fiction*. Waco, TX: Baylor University Press.

"*Christ Pantocrator*, sixth-century icon (reproduced by permission of the Holy Monastery of Saint Catherine, Sinai, Egypt.)"

Nietzsche
On the Genealogy of Morals

We shall not cease from exploration
And the end of all our exploring
Will be to arrive where we started
And know the place for the first time.
T. S. Eliot

Active Forgetfulness

What role does reading the works of Friedrich Nietzsche play in a great texts curriculum, particularly within a Christian university? If a great texts program is anything, it is an educational exercise in collective memory or recollection. It considers those texts and themes that have been particularly formative of the culture within which students find themselves. If it is to be anything more than an exercise in antiquarian interests looking back nostalgically at texts that happen to be of particular interest to the faculty, the curriculum must have an order and purpose beyond the idiosyncratic interests of individual faculty members, a curriculum that looks forward to the life of its students within the culture they have come to understand through this process of recollection. The exercise of examining the great texts of one's culture must help students understand how their present culture and the thoughts and beliefs they have formed in that culture have shaped them as they ask themselves where and how their lives will proceed, and how they will shape their culture in turn. To achieve this goal, a great texts program must *recollect with an eye forward*. Within a Christian education, it must also ask what relationship that recollection has to the truths that God has revealed about Himself, the creator and redeemer of all that is other than God. Christianity is not external to the culture in which our students have grown up, but in many ways formative of it. So finally, the curriculum must aid recollection of what God has revealed about human beings made "in the beginning" "in the image and likeness of God."

Nietzsche is particularly useful in such a curriculum for the questions he raises about the very tradition that is recalled. He announces at the beginning of *On the Genealogy of Morals* that

> We are unknown to ourselves, we men of knowledge – and with good

> reason. We have never sought ourselves – how could it happen that we should ever *find* ourselves? . . . So we are necessarily strangers to ourselves, we do not comprehend ourselves, we have to misunderstand ourselves . . . . (Nietzsche 1967, Preface 15)

As a work of self-understanding, the *Genealogy* is particularly concerned with accounting for the origin of morality among human beings, by providing a genealogy of moral notions, a kind of natural history of the descent of moral species to the present time. To do this it provides a sweeping account of Western culture in its past and present, as well as the influence of significant historical figures, philosophers among them, who have given shape to the moral features of our culture. The opening passage makes it clear that the work is an exercise in coming to self-understanding, both individually and culturally, through a process of recollection so that we may no longer be "strangers to ourselves." But, as we will see, this genetic search for the birth of morality has an ironic flavor, since Nietzsche will argue that a certain kind of forgetfulness of the past, not recollection, is necessary for human flourishing or happiness. The recollection is propaedeutic for its being cast off in our process of truly coming to ourselves. Here I will not examine the details of Nietzsche's genealogy, but rather examine the play of memory and forgetfulness in Nietzsche, as a way of showing the work's irony and its relationship to the tradition that it attempts to overcome, particularly the tradition stemming from Augustine.

In *On the Genealogy of Morals*, Nietzsche comments on the importance of forgetfulness:

> To close the doors and windows of consciousness for a time; to remain undisturbed by the noise and struggle of our underworld of utility organs working with and against one another; a little quietness, a little *tabula rasa* of the consciousness, to make room for new things, above all for the nobler functions and functionaries, for regulation, foresight, premeditation (for our organism is an oligarchy) – that is the purpose of active forgetfulness, which is like a doorkeeper, a preserver of psychic order, repose, and etiquette: so that it will be immediately obvious how there could be no happiness, no cheerfulness, no hope, no pride, no *present*, without forgetfulness. The man in whom this apparatus of repression is damaged and ceases to function properly may be compared (and more than merely compared) with a dyspeptic – he cannot "have done" with anything. (Nietzsche 1967, II.57–58)

This passage occurs near the beginning of the second essay of the *Genealogy* entitled "'Guilt,' 'Bad Conscience,' and the Like," and offers a window into the entire text and to a "common thread" that binds Nietzsche to other great texts.

Nietzsche is concerned in the essay to give an account of how, through purely naturalistic means, nature gives rise to such phenomena in human beings as the experience of guilt and the formation of a bad conscience. But he begins by meditating on the process by which nature "breed[s] an animal with the right to make promises" (Nietzsche 1967, II.57). He thinks promise-making requires memory. And yet Nietzsche wants to examine how the struggle between memory and what he describes as "active forgetfulness" generates those who can make promises. Indeed, forgetfulness is not something that happens to us, or that we undergo. It is something we must do.

The passage I cited interests me not so much for the role it will play in Nietzsche's account of the development of guilt and a bad conscience, but for what it says about this active power of forgetfulness and its relationship to the purpose of great texts in a Christian education. The passage contains the familiar power of Nietzschean images. The background image of consciousness closing up the doors to the outer world of turmoil reminds us of Descartes. Indeed, the concern to talk about a creature capable of making promises is the worthy inheritor of Cartesian methodology. When, in the *Discourse on Method*, Descartes describes the procedure one has to go through in order to be rational, he gives four *Maxims* or rules of thumb necessary to live one's life in the absence of, but in anticipation of acquiring methodological reason. The first is to obey the laws and customs of one's country, and to avoid all extremes. "In particular, I counted as excessive all promises by which we might give up some of our freedom" (Descartes 1988, III.32). Descartes suggests that, short of having achieved the rationality promised by the method, one is not really capable of making promises, which is why they ought to be avoided. So, presumably, one result of acquiring methodological reason will be that one need no longer avoid making promises, having become a creature capable of and with "the right to make promises" in Nietzsche's language. In that respect, Nietzsche is the worthy inheritor of the Cartesian project. Descartes will play a significant role in the recollections that follow.

The passage also contains the background image of the Lockean view of the mind as a kind of "dark room" with windows that allow in some light (Locke 1959, II.11.17, 212) coupled with the equally Lockean account of the mind as a *tabula rasa* (II.11.17, 121). There is also the underworld of bustling organic functions, as if a boiler room or grimy factory of the 19th century industrial revolution. Our calm and quiet mind stands above nature with the hustle and bustle of its underlying mechanisms. So we see the dichotomy of mind and nature that is played out in different ways in Western thought from Plato, Augustine, Anselm, Descartes, Locke, and Kant, among others. All of this stands in the background of Nietzsche's image. So the text itself, to be understood, ironically requires active memory, not the active forgetfulness that Nietzsche recommends, for if we do not remember these earlier texts we cannot understand Nietzsche, either in this passage particularly, or throughout Nietzsche's work generally. If we are to understand him, even as we may have to close off the doors to the outside world and engage in active forgetfulness, we must actively remember whom he is inviting into the dark room of consciousness as his interlocutors.

But what is necessary for there to be peace in that inner chamber of the mind that Nietzsche describes? How can it avoid the turmoil outside, achieving a spirit that can rule and instill order; how can it shed light upon itself; how can it become the autonomous moral agent of Kant's Enlightenment with the courage to think for itself, and release itself from the yoke of "self-incurred tutelage?"[1] (Kant 1963, 3). It must forget, not passively, but by actively shutting out the past to make room for the future, "for the nobler functions and functionaries, for regulation, foresight, premeditation . . . . ." Without this active forgetfulness, the influences and teachings of others are no more than part of the mechanical cacophony of unruly nature that impinges upon the mind – unruly, because the mind does not rule over its mechanisms. Again we recall Descartes' various descriptions in the *Discourse on Method* of the influence of conflicting traditions of classical texts in his education, the result of which was his general skepticism except in the quiet and peace of mathematical method.

Thus Nietzsche's forgetfulness looks actively forward. This active forgetfulness is a necessary condition for happiness, progress and achievement. "There could be no happiness, no cheerfulness, no hope, no pride, no *present*, without forgetfulness. The man in whom this apparatus of repression is damaged and ceases to function properly . . . cannot 'have done' with anything." Here we hear an echo of a theme essential to Nietzsche that runs throughout his work – active self-creation as an answer to the looming nihilism of the habits of custom and the mechanisms of nature as conceived by modern science. The man who cannot forget is bound to the past, a Prometheus incapable of looking ahead creatively to a future of new challenges and new ways of meeting them. Active forgetfulness, then, is a form of "strong health," the strong health of Milton's Apostate in *Paradise Lost* who forgets the fact of his creatureliness:

> That we were formed, then, saist thou? & the work
> Of secondarie hands, by task transferd
> From Father to his Son? strange point and new!
> Doctrin which we would know whence learnt: who saw
> When this creation was? Rememberst thou
> Thy making, while the Maker gave thee being?
> We know no time when we were not as now;
> Know none before us, self-begot, self-rais'd . . .
> (Milton 2007, V.856–860, 159)

The point here is the explicit rejection of memory in the Apostate's response to the rhetorical question "Rememberst thou Thy making?" To remember is to recognize that one is a creature, dependent upon that which one does not control and that which precedes one.

Nietzsche contrasts this faculty of active forgetting with the breeding of an equally active memory that generates human beings entitled to make promises. It is not a mere inability to be rid of some fact of the past, but is "an active *desire* not to rid oneself, a desire for the continuance of something desired once, a real *memory of the will*" (Nietzsche 1967, II.58). A promise is an act that looks toward the future, when one will fulfill the promise. Of course it looks equally toward the past, since it binds one's future to the past act of promising and sustains the act of will that constituted it. So this is not an active memory of all that precedes one, and upon which one is dependent. It is a memory of oneself as expressing one's will.

Nietzsche goes on to point out that the condition of making a promise requires that one be able to recognize the predictability of the future in the face of unruly events that impinge upon the consciousness of the one who promises; and so the promiser must make himself predictable, at least to himself. This predictability among humans generates a "morality of custom," the "laws and customs of one's country" as Descartes describes it in the first maxim.

However, Nietzsche agrees with Descartes that this morality of custom is not sufficient to undergird genuine promise-making. With Descartes' first maxim, this morality of custom is only a necessary "means" to a further end – a stage in the development of the *methodical man* (Descartes) or the *autonomous man* (Nietzsche). The autonomous man will go beyond this "morality of custom," free himself from it, and stand surety for his promises by force of will itself. The man who is bound by the "morality of custom" presumably has had bred within him a *desire* to be capable of fulfilling his promises. But insofar as he is bound by an external force, he is not yet capable of doing so – he does not have the genuine *will* to do so. For this he must actively forget the "morality of custom," in order to actively remember only the act of will that promises. His fulfillment of his promise must not be a binding of his will by something outside his consciousness, but the self-conscious expression of his own will. If Nietzsche disagrees with Descartes about the autonomy of promise-making, it is over the role of reason in guiding the will. I will return to this point.

Thus the present memory of the promise will be an act of the autonomous will, as will be its fulfillment. The autonomous man's promise-keeping will not be a product of social custom, a yoke of tutelage, governing him from the outside, but an act of self-creation and thus of nobility and human greatness. His is not the autonomous will of Kant that throws off the yoke of tutelage only to recognize through reason a moral law it did not create in order freely to bind itself to that law. How can one be freely bound? No. His is the autonomous will that creates its own law, that cannot be bound because through its active forgetfulness it has left behind the binding ties of the moral law that is nothing other than custom. It is not bound to the law, but expresses, indeed creates, it. Nietzsche writes:

> If we place ourselves at the end of this tremendous process, where the tree at last brings forth fruit, where society and the morality of custom at last reveal what they have simply been the means to: then we discover that the ripest fruit is the *sovereign individual*, like only to himself, liberated again from the morality of custom, autonomous and supramoral (for "autonomous" and "moral" are mutually exclusive), in short, the man who has his own independent, protracted will and the *right to make promises* – and in him a proud consciousness, quivering in every muscle, of *what* has at length been achieved and become flesh in him, a consciousness of his own power and freedom, a sensation of mankind come to completion. (Nietzsche 1967, II.59)

The German says "*das nur sich selbst gleiche*." "Something that is like only itself." To the extent that this translation of Nietzsche is accurate, the translator recognizes in Nietzsche a deliberate word play when he says that this noble man is "like" only himself, that is, he copies only himself, which is not to be a copy at all. To have copied another would be to fail to forget the other in one's own actions, and to live according to the morality of custom – the man of custom is a copy of another. But the sovereign autonomous individual is not a copy at all; he is not an image; he is the exemplar.

Autonomy and sovereignty thus require active forgetfulness. And here it is important to emphasize again that forgetfulness is not a failure but an achievement. One cannot fail *by* forgetting; one can only fail *to* forget. Now, however, we want to ask what it is specifically that Nietzsche actively forgets in positing the noble human being as a likeness only of himself.

Memory of the Tradition

These themes of recollection and forgetfulness have a long history in Western culture. Beginning with Plato, we see philosophy, the love of wisdom, portrayed as a process of recollection. In the *Meno* Socrates interrogates a slave boy to show that he understands a form of Pythagoras' theorem. The fact that he is a slave boy serves at least two purposes. First and most obvious, it provides an individual who cannot be expected to have learned that geometric truth before the encounter with Socrates. Thus, as we observe the slave's display of the knowledge of that truth through the Socratic inquiry, we are to conclude that he has always been in possession of the knowledge, and has merely forgotten it. The general conclusion is that there is no learning in this life, only recollecting. Knowledge of truth is gained by recollecting what one already knows but has forgotten from a previous existence of the soul in the presence of the truth. The forms are a "given" in the sense of preceding the philosopher, and only in need of recognition, that is re-cognition. This forgetting was presumably passive, while the recollection is active under the questioning tutelage of a sage.

The second important purpose of the boy's being a slave is metaphorical and concerns the nature of philosophy. We do not have to accept the argument of the *Meno* that there is no genuine learning, since it is as likely that through leading questions Socrates is in fact conveying the information to the slave boy, who learns it through the language of the questions. Nevertheless a seed of a theme of recollection or memory remains essential to philosophy. After all, even if Socrates is conveying the knowledge to the slave boy through the language of the questions, it is a knowledge that exists and is preserved in the social memory of the community that the slave boy must come to grasp; in that respect it remains a "given" prior to the individual soul. And of course, while that social memory may be preserved in oral traditions, it may also be preserved in texts, as we ourselves encounter it in the *Meno*.

Now philosophy is the love of wisdom, and Plato has Socrates tell us in the *Republic* that Wisdom is the governing science, the knowledge of the highest causes of things, that allows one to rule oneself and rule the world around one. In that respect, Nietzsche is as interested in this development of wisdom in our passage from the *Genealogy of Morals* as Plato's characters are in the *Republic*. He is interested in developing a ruling knowledge, wisdom. A slave is neither sovereign nor autonomous. The reader has to ask himself what the fate of the slave will be if he becomes the companion of Socrates, and does not simply recollect geometric truths, but engages in active recollection of the highest of all truths, and becomes a lover of wisdom. His character as a slave is a metaphor for his ignorance and the ignorance of all who do not engage in philosophy. His coming to know through the Socratic inquiry is a metaphor for all who would love wisdom. The Platonic love of wisdom is a coming to have an active memory of the truth by those who are otherwise enslaved by ignorance which is forgetfulness. But we have already seen that Nietzsche's account of wisdom involves an active memory not of truth, but of an originary act of will. In stark contrast to the Platonic ideal, Nietzschean wisdom requires forgetfulness, not passive but active forgetfulness, active forgetfulness of any truths that may be the result of the morality of custom.

In addition, in thinking about Nietzsche and the role of active forgetfulness in the process of self-creation, it is important to keep in mind Aristotle's discussion of the great-souled ("proud") man in the *Nichomachean Ethics*. The great-souled man is supposed to be a kind of superlative and exemplary instance of the virtuous man.

> Now the proud man, since he deserves most, must be good in the highest degree; for the better man always deserves more, and the best man most. Therefore the truly proud man must be good. And greatness in every excellence would seem to be characteristic of a proud man. (Aristotle 1984, 1123b28–33, 1773)

The great-souled man possesses all the virtues, but is concerned with the greatest of things and deeds in a way that the ordinary virtuous man is not. So he is the best man. However, there is a problem with this great-souled man that Nietzsche's account of active forgetfulness can solve. The great-souled man has a strong sense of his own superiority and the inferiority of others. And yet, as a human being he is a social animal and will have in his life benefited from the aid of others. But to benefit from others rather than benefit them is to stand in a relation of inferiority to them. So Aristotle writes:

> And he is the sort of man to confer benefits, but he is ashamed of receiving them; for the one is the mark of a superior, the other of an inferior. And he is apt to confer greater benefits in return; for thus the original benefactor besides being paid will incur a debt to him, and will be the gainer by the transaction. [Great-souled people] seem also to remember any service they have done, but not those they have received (for he who receives a service is inferior to him who has done it, but the proud man wishes to be superior), and to hear of the former with pleasure, of the latter with displeasure. (Aristotle 1984, 1124b7–15, 1774)

Notice the role of memory here in the life of Aristotle's great-souled man. He tends not to remember the ways in which he has benefited from the aid of others. Indeed, being made to remember by hearing of such aid in the past is a source of displeasure. As receiving he is passive and inferior, and the memory of such passivity and inferiority is painful.

This displeasure, however, is a problem for Aristotle's account. Virtue at its most basic is supposed to be a kind of strength, the strength to deal well with the contingencies of life that face one in different areas. And the great-souled man is supposed to be superlatively virtuous, capable of dealing with the greatest of events. Yet the great-souled man appears weak in the face of the memory of his dependence upon others. In addition, the virtuous are supposed to find pleasure in the exercise of their virtue. And yet here the one possessing magnanimity [great-souledness] experiences displeasure at the passive memory of his inferiority with respect to what he has received from another. So Aristotle's account of the great-souled man appears inconsistent with his general account of virtue.

However, Nietzsche's transformation of the great-souled man in possession of active forgetfulness can overcome this problem. Aristotle's great-souled man *suffers* the memory of his dependence upon others, a memory of a given in human life. It is a passive recollection, for it is upon hearing of his dependence that he is made to recollect such dependence, and that passive recollection causes him displeasure. But Nietzsche's great-souled man will have the power to put such passive recollection and displeasure out of mind by actively forgetting it, and he will not listen to those who would make him recall – they will be actively forgotten as well. So we see Nietzsche in his own way dealing with lasting difficulties inherited from Plato and Aristotle, in the first instance rejecting Plato, and in the second overcoming Aristotle.

Centuries after Plato and Aristotle, Augustine picked up the theme of memory and active recollection in his works, including the *Confessions*, particularly Book 10, *The Trinity*,and *Concerning the Teacher*. Of course he rejected the idea of the pre-existence of the soul that comes out of the *Meno*, for reasons stemming from both his Christian faith and his reading of Cicero's *Tusculan Disputations*. But the theme of memory transformed remains in Augustine in the process of recollecting one's inner self as the mind made in the image of God. This recollection is not of a temporal past but of an ontological priority. The mind of the human being, created in the image and likeness of God, consists of three activities in one being, the activities of memory, intellect, and will. It is from memory that understanding within the intellect proceeds or even "pours over" into an act of love that proceeds from the will, as the Son as *Logos* proceeds from the Father, and the Spirit as love proceeds or "pours out" from both. Memory is the foundation, or better, font of understanding, and understanding is the seed of love; what the mind comes to know and understand and love in itself is the active memory of its being an image of God. Again, as with Plato's Forms, the image is "given." But it is the givenness of being a creature, a creature that is the image of God, the givenness and image that Milton's Apostate actively forgets.

For Augustine, in this life we find that this image of God, which Augustine, echoing St. Paul, calls a mirror, is smudged and obscured by sin. So the mind, in a false love of self that identifies itself with the life of the outer man consumed by bodily engagement with the world, forgets itself as the image of God when it finds itself occupied with the obscurity of sense and bodily desire. But this is no active forgetting – it is the result of original sin, a condition into which one has been born (another given). But this given is the condition of the creature himself in his nature. As a given it is passive forgetfulness.

In summary, the mind, the image of God, the soul of the human being, must turn away from the "outer man" through a process of turning in toward the "inner man," the mind. Here we can see an element of active forgetfulness, the active forgetting of the "outer man" ordered toward an active memory of the inner man. Only then can it recall that it is an *imago dei*, an exercise of memory making manifest what has always been present to it – the Triune God, the Trinity of Persons. This memory is not present to it in a former existence (as in Plato), but in the core of its being from the moment of its creation as the image of God. The Trinity has always been there, "more inward than my most inward part" (Augustine 1991, III.vi, 43), only obscured and forgotten. Thus Augustine can write, "late have I loved you, beauty so old and so new" (Augustine 1991, X.xxvii, 201).

> See how widely I have ranged, Lord, searching for you in my memory. I have not found you outside it. For I have found nothing coming from you which I have not stored in my memory since the time I first learnt of you. Since the day I learnt of you, I have never forgotten you. Where I discovered the truth there I found my God, truth itself, which from the time I learnt it, I have not forgotten. And so, since the time I learnt of you, you remain in my consciousness, and there I find you when I recall you and delight in you. These my holy delights you have given me, in your mercy looking upon my poverty. (Augustine 1991, X.xxiv, 200)

Through this active memory of the ever present Triune God, the soul through the intellect can truly understand itself and through the will truly love itself. This self-love is nothing other than the love of itself, not apart from God, but as the mirror image of God carried to God. And with this Trinitarian memory, it can then return as ruler and sovereign over the "outer man" engaged with the world. Plato's vision of Wisdom as the governing science putting order into the soul and the world is recovered not by a recollection of the forms but by a recognition of the given image of the Trinitarian God. Thus the love of wisdom, philosophy, is nothing other than the love of God, and the love of oneself and other human beings in God given as creaturely images of God.

Like Nietzsche, Augustine proposes a process of closing off the windows of the mind to the hustle and bustle of what is outside, in order to find wisdom and happiness. But unlike Nietzsche, what is discovered in this wisdom is that the mind is a copy, an image, and *like something other than itself*. This image is not like the forms, and not even Nietzsche's image of the morality of custom, but the image of God himself. We are God-like. So through our active memory of Augustine we begin to perceive the depth and boldness of Nietzsche's counter assertion that as wisdom enters the inner chamber of the mind, it discovers that it is a copy of nothing other than itself; indeed it is a memory of nothing other than its own will. It actively forgets that it is God-*like*. So, much more has been actively forgotten by Nietzsche in this apparently simple reflection on promise-making than merely the morality of custom.

Returning then to Augustine, a key feature of this internal memory of God was that it took place within the context of recalling the teaching of the church expressing its faith in holy scripture, in particular the trinitarian teachings that had come out of Nicaea. Augustine never forgets that his internal act of remembrance of the image of God within is guided by what as a Christian he has come to believe from without, from the faith of the church in the word of God, namely, that the trinitarian God is one being in three persons. While *Concerning the Teacher* echoes the *Meno* in arguing that any learning is prompted by the action of the teacher, Christ, within the mind of the student, it does not exclude that the understanding of the external teaching of the church through scripture is what is made possible by that internal teaching.

The method of recollection and remembrance is not forgotten at the dawn of modern philosophy in Descartes. It is well known that Descartes is heavily indebted to Augustine for some of his most important arguments.[2] The *Cogito* recalls Augustine's *Dubito* as found in *Against the Academics*, while the argument for the distinction of mind from body looks nearly plagiarized from a parallel text in *The Trinity*. Indeed, the character of the *Meditations* calls to mind the method of the *The Trinity* in its reflections. Descartes, like Augustine, advises the inquiring mind to turn away from the world and the concerns of the body to get a more accurate understanding of human nature within the mind. And according to Descartes, in the process an image of God is found in the mind in the "idea of God."

But we begin also to see here seeds of the process of active forgetfulness. As Descartes reflects in the *Discourse on Method* on the opinions of scholars that he found so often in conflict, he informs the reader that the opinions of men are so confused on any particular topic that they are a prime source of confusion and doubt, and for that reason he must set out on his own, as if from scratch. So he must forget what he has been taught by other men, for it cannot survive the first rule of the method which is to accept as true only those beliefs that are in no way subject to doubt. But experience shows that few things are more subject to doubt than the discourses of the scholars, and in general what others have related to us. Thus, as Descartes sets out on his meditations, even as he attempts to show what can be indubitably understood of the Catholic faith he holds, he will not be guided by the teaching of the church and its "scholars" that guided Augustine's memories.

As a result, we see a second difference from and forgetfulness of Augustine. While Augustine began with a belief in the trinitarian God that allowed him to recall the nature of his own mind as an *imago dei*, the mind with its acts of memory, intellect, and will as the image of Father, Son, and Holy Spirit, Descartes finds an idea of God in his mind, but it is not an idea of a trinitarian God. Descartes' idea of God is the idea of "a substance that is infinite, [eternal, immutable], independent, supremely intelligent, supremely powerful, and which created both myself and everything else (if anything else there be) that exists" (Descartes 1988b, III, 93). Of course Augustine would not disagree with this description. But what has been forgotten in the idea of God available to Descartes in his method is the understanding of God as trinitarian, the understanding of God that Augustine had learned by faith in God's revelation as taught by the church.

Still, Descartes does not forget the Augustinian search for the *imago dei* in the mind. His idea of God is effectively the product of the *imago dei* within the human mind. Having argued that only a being that could be described by the idea he has of God could in fact produce that idea, and thus having argued for the existence of God, Descartes asks himself how God has implanted this idea of himself within Descartes' mind. Here Descartes explicitly raises the theme of the *imago dei*, arguing that the idea of God is implicitly contained within the idea he has of himself. He argues that since God is his creator, it is "probable" that God has created him in his "image and likeness, and that I perceive that likeness, which includes the idea of God, by the same faculty which enables me to perceive myself. That is, when I turn my mind's eye upon myself" (Descartes 1988b, III, 98).

Descartes' idea of himself is of "a thing which is incomplete and dependent on another and which aspires without limit to ever greater and better things" (Descartes 1988b, III, 98). The idea of God is tacitly implicated in this idea, because "I also understand at the same time that he on whom I depend has within him all those greater things, not just indefinitely and potentially but actually and infinitely, and hence that he is God" (Descartes 1988b, III, 98). In short, Descartes does not discover or even come to a recollection of himself as the *imago dei* by a prior understanding of God. On the contrary, he comes to the idea of God from a prior understanding of himself, having begun with the "probable" thought that he is an *imago dei*. So his idea of God is in effect a product of his idea of himself projected through the lens of the *imago*. And thus while he has remembered the topic of Augustine's *The Trinity*, he has forgotten Augustine's method of being guided by his faith and the belief of the church – indeed he has *actively* forgotten it with the substitution of his own method which is to be guided only by oneself and beliefs that are in no way subject to doubt.

And yet there is a clear inconsistency here, since his appeal to the notion of *imago dei* was merely to a "probable" idea. It is understandable that Descartes would call this line of argument "probable" insofar as the theme of "*imago dei*" comes to him from the teaching of *Genesis*. But it is also a little odd that he would speak of this as "probable" reason, since by the rules of the method its being merely probable undermines the reasoning. Presumably a "probable" idea is an idea that can be doubted, and ought not to remain in the mind at this point in the *Meditations*.

Descartes' forgetfulness of Augustine continues in a way crucial for understanding Nietzsche as the heir to Descartes, indeed the image of Descartes. When Descartes picks up again the theme of the *imago dei* to tell us just what it consists in, he tells us that nothing is to be found in the idea of the *imago dei* other than the image of an unrestrained will.

> If I examine the faculty of memory or imagination, or any other faculty I possess, I discover that in my case each one of these faculties is weak and limited, while in the case of God it is immeasurable. It is only the will, or freedom of choice, which I experience within me to be so great that the idea of any greater faculty is beyond my grasp; so much so that it is above all in virtue of the will that I understand myself to bear in some way the image and likeness of God. For although God's will is incomparably greater than mine, both in virtue of the knowledge and power that accompany it and make it more firm and efficacious, and also in virtue of its object, in that it ranges over a greater number of items, nevertheless it does not seem any greater than mine when considered as will in the essential and strict sense. This is because the will simply consists in our ability to do or not do something. (Descartes 1988, IV, 101)

So Descartes remains like something other than himself. But the image of God is not to be found in the unity of memory, intellect, and will as it was in Augustine. No, it is found in the indifferent will itself. Memory will not guide it, as memory is a prime source of doubt. And Descartes allows that intellect may guide will, indeed intellect must guide will if Descartes is to act as God wills him to act – if only will will confine itself to going no further than methodologically purified intellect makes clear, Descartes will always act as God wills that he act.[3] And yet, in so acting in accord with the deliverances of intellect, Descartes is not properly concerned with the image of God, for the image of God is to be found primarily in the sovereign will indifferent to any of the contrary possibilities presented to it by intellect.

At the beginning of *Beyond Good and Evil* Nietzsche implicitly raises the specter of Descartes as the figure to be overcome. "It has not even occurred to the most cautious among them to raise doubts right here at the threshold where it is surely most necessary: even if they vowed to themselves, '*de omnibus dubitandum*'" (Nietzsche 1966, I, 10).[4] As we have seen, Descartes can be said still to "want" truth, insofar as he thinks the image of God within him, his indifferent will, ought to be guided by the truth that his methodically oriented intellect grasps. But if to be God-like is to be an indifferent will, Nietzsche poses the obvious question:

> *What* in us really wants "truth"? – Indeed we came to a long halt at the question about the cause of this will – until we finally came to a com-

> plete stop before a still more basic question. We asked about the *value* of this will. Suppose we want truth: *why not rather* untruth? . . . The problem of the value of truth came before us . . . it finally also seems to us as if the problem had never even been put so far – as if we were the first to see it . . . (Nietzsche 1966, I, 9).

If Descartes is simultaneously actively recalling and actively forgetting Augustine's search for the *imago dei*, the search that had been so deeply impressed to that point upon the character of Western culture, then Nietzsche wants to press this Cartesian active forgetfulness even further. Why this clinging to the value of truth, and not doubting it? "*Omne dubitandum est.*" Clinging to the value of truth in Descartes is what makes the indifferent will *merely* the vague residue or dregs of the image of the trinitarian God that Augustine had remembered. But such a will is not autonomous if it is bound by something extrinsic to itself, namely the truth that the intellect discovers. It must forget this residue, if it is to cease to be a copy of something other than itself, cease to be God-*like*, and become an image, a likeness of only itself.

This fact about the will is no less true in Kant than in Descartes, when Kant proclaims that enlightenment requires throwing off the self-imposed yoke of tutelage to establish an autonomous will that will nonetheless bind itself to a moral law that it discovers, the moral law that functions as a "given" for the genuinely rational mind. It is no surprise that even Kant leaves us with a vestige of the *imago dei* when he presents God as the regulative ideal of a rational being. But recalling Nietzsche, we can ask, what is this act of will that precedes or constitutes enlightenment by throwing off the yoke, if not an act of pure will prior to the acknowledgement of the moral law by the subsequently enlightened rational agent? Enlightenment begins with an act of the will alone that is the condition for the possibility of enlightened reason. However, for Nietzsche autonomy can only be achieved when the will refuses to be so guided – but "why not untruth?"

And so Nietzsche tells us in the famous "will to power passage" from *Beyond Good and Evil*:

> *Genuine philosophers, however, are commanders and legislators*: they say "thus it *shall* be!" They first determine the Whither and For What of man, and in so doing have at their disposal the preliminary labor of all philosophical laborers, all who have overcome the past. With a creative hand they reach for the future, and all that is and has been becomes a means for them, an instrument, a hammer. Their "knowing" is *creating*, their creating is a legislation, their will to truth is – *will to power*. (Nietzsche 1966, VI, 136)

Just before this passage, Nietzsche had appealed to Kant as the exemplar of a "philosophical laborer," one who takes some former dominant value, which is really nothing other than the prior "creation" of some value by someone – we might say the failure to forget the achievement of someone else – and reduces it to a "formula" and calls it "truth." Here again we see the underlying theme of the discussion of the "morality of custom" that we saw in our discussion of promise-making and bad conscience. And Nietzsche acknowledges that the genuine philosopher may need these "philosophical laborers" for his education; memory *is* necessary. But like the morality of custom, these laborers are a means toward the end of the genuine philosopher, which is to create values and thus to create what will come to be called "truths" by subsequent "philosophical laborers." And so the genuine philosopher must also actively forget the work of these laborers who have made possible his love of wisdom. The genuine lover of wisdom, the philosopher that Plato, Augustine, Descartes, and Kant have been looking for, is not an image of God – he is not God-like – he is rather a god, having thrown off the yoke of creatureliness in which he is merely an image of the creator, to take on the mantle of creator himself and of himself.

So recalling now our original passage about those who are capable of making promises, Nietzsche goes on to assert that "'autonomous' and 'moral' are mutually exclusive terms." Consider that assertion carefully. Nietzsche is himself engaged in an act of active forgetfulness. He recalls that the driving force of the modern lover of wisdom has been the longing for autonomy. And yet he believes that that longing has been frustrated by the lingering memory of the image of God in the philosophers, whether that God goes by the name of the Trinity, Truth, Value, The Moral, Grammar,[5] or The Given. What the modern philosopher of autonomy must do then is actively forget every trace of the image of God, so that he can be, in terms of our original passage, an image of none other than himself – not an image at all in fact, but the divine exemplar. Nietzsche, in pursuing the moderns' project of enlightenment and autonomy, is willing to forget more than the modern philosophers he recalls dared to imagine. To be a god one must actively forget the image of God. The death of God is the death of the image of God. That is the only prospect of happiness. But as we have seen, this active forgetfulness must play ironically with a certain memory or recollection as the condition for self-knowledge, a recollection that will nonetheless be actively and so ironically forgotten.

The Memory of a Promise

What then in our own quest for self-understanding should we make of Nietzsche? Some will object at this point that this destruction of the image of God within us is precisely the reason we ought not to have students in a Christian university read Nietzsche, so that they may be protected from this active forgetfulness of the image of God advocated by Nietzsche. However, this would be like saying that they ought not to be taught the doctrine of original sin, to protect them from it. That is impossible. Just as one cannot be protected from original sin, but only redeemed from it, one cannot be protected from the forgetfulness that Nietzsche describes and even advocates. This is why it is so important for great texts education to recall the figures Nietzsche is himself recalling in his work. It was the genius of Nietzsche to demonstrate for modern thought that it had long ago forgotten (without realizing it) Augustine's recollection of the creaturely image of God, so that all it was left with was the morality of custom.

> Have you not heard of that madman who lit a lantern in the bright morning hours, ran to the market place, and cried incessantly: "I seek God! I seek God!" – As many of those who did not believe in God were standing around just then, he provoked much laughter. Has he got lost? asked one. Did he lose his way like a child? asked another. Or is he hiding? Is he afraid of us? Has he gone on a voyage? emigrated? – Thus they yelled and laughed.
>
> The madman jumped into their midst and pierced them with his eyes. "Whither is God?" he cried; "I will tell you. *We have killed him* – you and I. All of us are his murderers." (Nietzsche 1974, III.125, 181)

Nietzsche is not the seed; he is the fruit. What he preaches, as our opening quotation suggests, is the need to become self-conscious of one's passive forgetfulness, and thus make it active. Nietzsche, like Augustine, wants to remind us that we have already forgotten the image of God – that is the given for a human being living in our age. Nietzsche will not make the students forget. He will only remind them that they have already forgotten, long before they ever read him.

To attempt to ignore Nietzsche and what he diagnoses is like attempting to ignore the fact of original sin. Indeed, after Nietzsche, to ignore Nietzsche is in a way to become an image of him, because the act of ignoring him embodies the very "active forgetfulness" that he suggested is the necessary condition of happiness. So, like original sin, there is no avoiding Nietzsche; he makes clear to us the condition we are in. One can only actively remember. But contrary to Nietzsche, and like Augustine, one can be redeemed from forgetfulness by recalling that one is in fact made in the image and likeness of God.

This essay began with Nietzsche's reflection on promise-making. He asserted that genuine promise-making is nothing other than an act of the will binding itself to its prior act, an act that requires a certain amount of active forgetfulness. Looking back at that discussion, one feature of promising that Nietzsche forgets is the other to whom the promise is made. It is as if in Nietzsche's account of promise-making, the promise is made to oneself – one wills to remain faithful to one's own act. The problem with acknowledging the other in a promise is that the other is a given – the promise is given to "a given" in the sense of another who is simply present to oneself as not created by oneself or by one's act of will.

But acknowledging that given raises another element in the analysis of promise-giving that Nietzsche forgets, no doubt actively. Implicated in the notion of promising is faithfulness. I noted above that in Nietzsche it is as if promise-giving involved being "faithful to one's own act," having forgotten the other. In remembering and reasserting the originary act of the will, one is a being capable of "making promises." So one might also say that in Nietzsche there is no promise-giving, only promise-"making." But if one does not forget the other as Nietzsche does, it becomes apparent that promise-making is always a promise-giving. And that raises the specter of faithfulness toward another. Keeping faith with another. Binding one's will, not to itself, but to another.

Nietzsche has given us an image of a god that is incapable of giving, for giving is an acknowledgement of the other, the given in life. His is an impotent god. The God in whose image Augustine is made is powerful enough to give being to something other than his own will; Nietzsche's god is not. Augustine's God gives being to those others that he acknowledges – indeed his acknowledgement of them is their being. As a result, Augustine's God both creates creatures capable of making and thus giving promises by acknowledging and being faithful to the others, and can make and thus give them a promise, having acknowledged them. It is Augustine's God who can breed a creature capable of making promises. Nietzsche's god is no god at all, for he is powerless to create anything other than himself, and he is powerless to make a promise that is a gift given to the given.

By reading Nietzsche we have the opportunity to remember our own faithlessness to the image of God, that is, our faithlessness to ourselves, to become self-conscious, and to know ourselves. And recalling that faithlessness, we have the opportunity with Augustine to recall ourselves to that image, and thus with him to recall ourselves to a faithfulness to the God whose image we understand ourselves to be. Like Augustine in the *Confessions*, who surveyed all those elements of his culture and education that had led him to his forgetfulness, so also Nietzsche enables us actively to recall our own culture in a way that places us with Augustine ready to make our confessions. "Consequently modern, noisy, time-consuming, proud and stupidly proud industriousness educates and prepares precisely for 'unbelief' more than anything else does?" (Nietzsche 1966, III, 69). Augustine did not write that, but Nietzsche. And what the peaceful quiet remembrance of ourselves as images of God, chastened by Nietzsche's recollections, may achieve is that we become capable of making a promise to God and to one another as images of God. Perhaps it is only as an image of God, a God who is Memory, Logos, and Will as One, that we can make a promise to another that is genuinely autonomous, and thus, God-like – not a genealogy, but rather a genesis, of morals.

John P. O'Callaghan

References

Aristotle 1984. *The Complete Works of Aristotle.* Ed. Jonathan Barnes. Princeton: Princeton University Press.

Augustine 1951. *Against the Academics* in *Ancient Christian Writers*. Vol. 12. Trans. John J. O'Meara. Westminster: The Newman Press.

——— 1991. *Confessions*. Trans. Henry Chadwick. Oxford: Oxford University Press.

——— 1938. *Concerning the Teacher*. Trans. George G. Leckie. New York: Appleton-Century-Crofts.

——— 1991. *The Trinity*. Trans. Edmund Hill, O.P. Brooklyn: New City Press.

Descartes, Rene 1988a. *Discourse on the Method* in *Selected Philosophical Writings*. Trans. John Cottingham, Robert Stoothoff, Dugald Murdoch. Cambridge: Cambridge University Press.

——— 1988b. *Meditations on First Philosophy* in *Selected Philosophical Writings*. Trans. John Cottingham, Robert Stoothoff, Dugald Murdoch. Cambridge: Cambridge University Press.

Kant, Immanuel 1963. "What is Enlightenment" in *On History*. Trans. Lewis White Beck. Indianapolis: The Bobbs-Merrill Company.

Locke, John 1959. *An Essay Concerning Human Understanding*. Vol. 1. New York: Dover Publications.

Matthews, Gareth B. 1992. *Thought's Ego in Augustine and Descartes*. Ithaca: Cornell University Press.

Menn, Stephen 1998. *Descartes and Augustine*. Cambridge: Cambridge University Press.

Milton, John 2007. *Paradise Lost: A Poem Written in Ten Books*. Pittsburgh: Duquesne University Press.

Nietzsche, Friedrich 1966. *Beyond Good and Evil*. Trans. Walter Kaufmann. New York: Random House.

——— 1974. *The Gay Science*. Trans. Walter Kaufmann. New York: Random House.

——— 1967. *On the Genealogy of Morals*. Trans. Walter Kaufmann and R. J. Hollingdale. New York: Random House.

——— 2004. *Twilight of the Idols*. Trans. Thomas Common. Mineola: Dover Publications.

Plato 1961. *Collected Dialogues*. Eds. Edith Hamilton and Huntington Cairns. Princeton: Princeton University Press.

James Joyce
A Portrait of the Artist as a Young Man

The Restless Mind

The journey has been a pervasive motif in Western literature since at least the time of Homer. Adapting the odyssey of wandering and return to biblical typology, medieval writers depicted individuals as pilgrim figures en route from this world to their heavenly home. With the rise of the novel, however, the practice of figural realism receded into the background as the narrative focus shifted from homesickness (*nostos*) to "transcendental homelessness" (Lukács 1971, 61) as the normative human condition. The new sojourner roamed the earth without "the memory of a lost home or the hope of a promised land," as Camus observed (Camus 1975, 6), and experienced an incurable sense of alienation. Cast adrift in a cosmos without a divine center, the modern figure of the stranger, according to Lukács, chose to withdraw into the inner world of the self: "the novel tells of the adventure of interiority . . . of the soul that goes to find itself" (Lukács 1971, 89). Twentieth-century novelists employed the fictional mode of psychological realism with the aim of altering the trajectory and primary goal of the old journey from salvation to individuation.

James Joyce penned one of the most striking depictions of the search for unique selfhood in *A Portrait of the Artist as a Young Man*. What makes this landmark modern novel distinctive is the unprecedented manner in which the author modulates style to reflect the developing consciousness of the hero, Stephen Dedalus, from infancy to adolescence. In the memorable opening, for example, the narrative is couched in the idiom characteristic of a child listening to a fairy-tale: "Once upon a time and a very good time it was there was a moocow coming down along the road …and this moocow met a nicens little boy named baby tuckoo…He was baby tuckoo" (Joyce 1968, 7). As the small and sensitive boy grows in his understanding of the world around him, the language continues to mirror the later stages of his development. Stephen's first romantic yearnings are accordingly described in sentimental prose, his short-lived practice of faith in the vocabulary of religious piety, the discovery of his artistic calling in a euphoric lyricism, and his aesthetic theory in the intellectual lexicon of a revamped Thomism. In all of these instances, an indirect stylistic affinity exists between the third-person narrator and the protagonist in the presentation of his fluctuating perceptions of external reality. The narrative switches to direct internal monologue only in the final pages when Stephen logs his diary entries. The almost exclusive focus on the inward-turning consciousness keeps the subjective point of view in the foreground to such an extent that it becomes virtually solipsistic. The strategy of combining "an impersonal manner and . . . profound self-approval," which Joyce adopted in the earlier version of the novel titled *Stephen Hero* (Joyce 1969, 45–6), is modified somewhat in the final *Portrait* through the use of irony at key moments in the story. The most important of these occurs when Stephen unlocks the mystery of his mythical name, Dedalus, and goes into "an ecstasy of flight" that makes "radiant his eyes and wild his breath and tremulous and wild and radiant his windswept limbs" (Joyce 1968, 169). The exalted mood of the soaring artist is immediately undercut, however, by the seemingly innocuous cries of some boys playing nearby on the beach: " – One! Two! . . . Look out! – O, cripes. I'm drownded" (Joyce 1968, 169). The subtle allusion to the abortive flight of Icarus which ended in death by water sends Stephen's lofty aspirations tumbling down to earth. The juxtaposition of contrapuntal voices helps to create some distance between the narrator and protagonist, but the irony at work in this scene remains partial, not pervasive. Joyce's deft handling of point of view always affords the reader a double perspective on the predicament of his fictitious younger self. While most literary critics agree that Stephen fails to fulfill his artistic ambitions, they nevertheless maintain that his struggle to throw off the burden of religion, which culminates in his decision against entering the Catholic priesthood in favor of becoming a "priest of eternal imagination" (Joyce 1968, 221), elicits sympathy from readers.[1]

Hart Crane registered an early sympathetic response to Stephen's plight by hailing *A Portrait of the Artist* as "spiritually the most inspiring book" he had ever read "aside from Dante" (Crane 1970, 124), even surpassing Bunyan in artistic excellence. Although the young American poet did not elaborate on his remarks, his positive spiritual response to the novel's vision of achieving self-transcendence through art is notable because it resonated decades later with what might be called "the school of critical wishful thinking."[2] Like-minded critics who read the novel along similar religious lines seemed to imagine Joyce as the character in Flann O'Brien's *The Dalkey Archive* whose sideline was writing pamphlets for the Catholic Truth Society. Crane and his successors failed, however, to note that Joyce inverts the paradigm of life-pilgrimage established by early Christian writers in order to accentuate the "individuating rhythm" (Joyce 1968, 258) that marks his hero's loss of faith. Joyce painted, in effect, a portrait of the artist as a young rascal. The story of Stephen Dedalus accordingly takes the shape of an un-divine comedy charting the pilgrim's regress towards apostasy. The aspiring artist registers the temper of his upside-down pilgrimage in a telltale diary entry:

> Began . . . a discussion with my mother . . . . [S]he said I would come back to the faith because I had a restless mind. This means to leave church by backdoor of sin and reenter through the skylight of repentance. Cannot repent. (Joyce 1968, 248)

Mrs. Dedalus believes her son will follow in the footsteps of a famous convert, who, in spite of his spiritual deviations, eventually fulfilled the restless yearning of his heart to be at rest in the source of his being. By refusing to play the role of Augustine to his mother's Monica, however, Stephen authorizes a poetics of counter-conversion. He banishes the thought of becoming another prodigal son who will return to the fold like his putative prototype. Augustine revealed that during most of his adolescence he found himself in "an immense forest...full of snares and dangers," but succeeded in gradually paring away countless sins from his soul through the mercy of God's grace (Augustine 1984, X.35, 242). In stark contrast, Stephen believes that the innocent soul, once enticed by the irresistible power of sin, lapses irreversibly since "not to fall was too hard, too hard" (Joyce 1968, 162). In this unhopeful scenario, the fallen individual does not sin his way to God, as the saying goes, descending in humility before ascending to truth (Augustine 1984, IV.12, 83). Stephen deliberately averts the downward path to salvation so that he can wander aimlessly and continually in the dark wood of error: "He was destined to learn his own wisdom apart from others or to learn the wisdom of others himself wandering amid the snares of the world. The snares of the world were its ways of sin" (Joyce 1968, 222).

Sin becomes the pulse of Stephen's art, for the act of writing provides him, as it provided Rousseau, with a forum for confession without repentance. By making evil his good, however, Stephen adopts the contradictory logic of Milton's Satan. Sin breeds "inconsistency," as Kierkegaard observed (Kierkegaard 1966, 64), constraining the sinner to evade the truth about his actual mode of being. The subjectivity of erratic thought directs the eyes of the soul inward to a deceptive self, rather than outward to a true Other. The self-justified sinner gazes away from the One who is Truth in person in order to contemplate "his own soul going forth to experience, unfolding itself sin by sin" (Joyce 1968, 103), and curving back upon itself in the endless circularity of its own solipsism. Joyce transposes the traditional quest for identity, based on casting the self in the pattern of *imitatio Christi*, into the distinctively modern key of self-fashioning. Taking his cue from Rousseau, who ventured to say he broke the mold of the *imago Dei* and was therefore "like no one in the whole world" (Rousseau 1953, 17), Stephen harbors the strong conviction that he, too, is "different from others," for the fierce "pride of his spirit . . . always made him conceive himself as a being apart in every order" (Joyce 1968, 65, 161). To affirm his uniqueness and the isolation of the soul in its own selfhood, Stephen replaces the biblical idea of *kenosis*, or self-emptying, with a private *gnosis* which empowers the singular individual to achieve, in Irving Howe's lapidary phrase, "a salvation of, by, and for the self" (Howe 1967,14).

As opposed to the truth-seeking pilgrim, the erring nomad seeks the wisdom of forbidden knowledge. Stephen notes the grave concern his transgressive impulse caused his mother: "[She] [s]aid I have a queer mind and have read too much. Not true. I have read little and understood less"(Joyce 1968, 248). Despite his disclaimer, Mrs. Dedalus attributes her son's backsliding to an excess of learning, the vice that caused Marlowe's Faustus to become so "swollen with cunning" that his "self-conceit" propelled his waxen wings "to mount above his reach" (Marlowe 1969, I, 20–21) and, after melting under the sun, left the over-reacher, like Icarus, floundering in a sea of his intellectual hubris. Joyce captures the Faustian movement of rise and fall by having his Irish Dedalus double as an Icarus who attempts through the stratagem of "cunning" (Joyce 1968, 247) to fly by the net of his Catholic upbringing. Augustine described his passionate pursuit of "the wisdom of eternal truth" metaphorically as a flight from the abyss upward to his Father's house: "I began to climb out of the depths to which I had sunk . . . . My God, how I burned with longing to have wings to carry me back to you" (Augustine 1984, III.4, 58–9). Stephen counterpoints Augustine's mental itinerary by declaring with Faustian audacity that the pursuit of error will make him free: "I am not afraid to make a mistake, even a great mistake, a lifelong mistake and perhaps as long as eternity too" (Joyce 1968, 247).

While Dante discovered, when he scaled the mountain of Purgatory and the heights of Paradise, that true freedom consists, paradoxically, in one's voluntary submission to God's will (Dante 1955, 16.80; 27.140; Dante 1962, 3.85; 33.143–5), Stephen gets caught in the snare of illusory freedom when he makes Lucifer's declaration of independence, "I will not serve" (Joyce 1968, 117, 246–7), his own. His flight towards existential alienation from church, family, and community sends him, ironically, plummeting back into the infernal labyrinth he set out to escape. The idea of damnation no longer terrifies the presumptuous individualist who empowers the mind, like Milton's Satan, to make a heaven out of hell. When contraries meet, there is no straight line of progression, no orderly Daedalian ascent or Icarian downward spiral, for, according to Blake, "In Equivocal Worlds Up & Down are Equivocal" (Blake 1969, 785–6). Stephen therefore moves in a relativistic universe in which he can apply his mind, in the words of the epigraph to the novel taken from Ovid, to unknown arts. The "restless mind" of the "fabulous artificer" (Joyce 1968, 169) serves as a trope for the artist's refusal to settle within established modes of thought. The possibility of obtaining "secret knowledge and secret power" (Joyce 1968, 159) appeals to his mind's characteristic activity of "[winding] itself in and out of the curious questions" (Joyce 1968,106) it formulates. Fuelled by curiosity, Stephen embarks on an intellectual quest beyond the confines of the known world: "There was a lust of wandering in his feet that burned to set out for the ends of the earth" (Joyce 1968, 170). Joyce links his protagonist here with Dante's impious Ulysses, whose "mad flight" (Dante 1949, 26.125) past the utmost bounds of human knowledge led to the shipwreck of his soul.

Whatever he gained by ruthless curiosity, he lost through overweening arrogance. Stephen also identifies his project with that of Giordano Bruno, "the terrible heretic" who was "terribly burned" (Joyce 1968, 249) for pursuing to the end "his path of triumphant defiance on behalf of *curiositas*" (Blumenberg 1983, 382–3) against the limits placed on the cognitive drive by the wisdom of truth. The perpetual mental restlessness (*evagatio mentis*) of curiosity-seekers, as Mrs. Dedalus correctly intuited, directly affects their disposition towards the texts they read. Augustine figured the act of reading as an odyssey wrought with peril for the seafarer who takes circuitous routes instead of following Christ, who is both the "way" home and the native country (the "truth") itself (Augustine 1958, I.4.4; I.11.11), the One "in whom are hidden all the treasures of wisdom and knowledge" (Col 2:3). The errant frame of mind, on the other hand, turns readers into "nomads poaching their way across fields they did not write," to use Michel de Certeau's analogy, "despoiling the wealth of Egypt to enjoy it themselves" (de Certeau 1984, 174). Stephen overturns the well-known principle involving "Egyptian gold" enunciated by Augustine (Augustine 1958, II.40.60) by appropriating Christian ideas for his own pagan ends.

Although Stephen imagines himself as one of the nomadic clouds "voyaging across the deserts of the sky...high over Ireland" (Joyce 1968, 167) towards the Continent, he sets out to undermine the common heritage of western culture that T.S. Eliot called the "mind of Europe" (Eliot 1972, 16). Joyce associated modernity with "the breaking-up of tradition" (Joyce 1959, 100), and he has his artist-hero follow suit. Unlike Dante, who joined the ranks of the great poets of antiquity, and was pleased to be counted "one of their company" (Dante 1949, 4.79–108) so as to gain access to the accumulated wisdom of the ages, Stephen keeps "company [with] subversive writers" whose textual violence filters into his own "crude writings" (Joyce 1968, 78). Although cultural ancestors form nothing more than a chorus of "hollowsounding voices" (Joyce 1968, 84) vying for the unswerving allegiance of the disaffected intellectual, his disinherited mind remains so haunted by the "the anxiety of influence" that it feels compelled to ruin the sacred truths contained in foundational Christian texts. Among the most significant of these, I suggest, are the classic works of Augustine[3] and Dante. Stephen therefore attempts to transcend the Augustinian dichotomy between the city of man and the city of God dramatized in *The Divine Comedy* by imagining a masterful, godlike entry into a Blakean "City of Art."[4]

The Restless Heart

Before reaching the artifice of eternity, however, the anomic pilgrim explores all the labyrinthine ways of error in the terrestrial city. Joyce draws on the venerable medieval tradition that linked the idea of a pilgrimage with the labyrinth, the image that was etched as a mosaic on the floor of Gothic cathedrals on which pilgrims knelt to start their journey. This striking figure, often referred to as a "house of Daedalus," functioned as a symbol, on the one hand, of "the perplexities and intricacies which beset the Christian faith," and, on the other, of "the entangling nature of sin" (Matthews 1971, 66–7). Although Stephen strolls through the physical space of Dublin, Joyce initially sets his protagonist's spiritual movement in the narrative mode of an Augustinian tale of two cities, one founded on charity (*caritas*), the other on cupidity (*cupiditas*). Love moves the pedestrian's feet in the direction either of the heavenly Jerusalem, pictured as a bride, or of the earthly Babylon, pictured as a whore. As he walks through the multicursal "maze of narrow and dirty streets" (Joyce 1968, 100) of his native city, Stephen is forced to "take wrong turns and feel [his] way by trial and error" (Howard 1980, 8).

The main type of moral error the modern Daedalus confronts there is the minotaur of lust. The outer maze of the cityscape reflects the inner maze of the stroller that is generated by his own sexual desire: "A figure that had seemed to him by day demure and innocent came towards him by night through the winding darkness of sleep, her face transfigured by a lecherous cunning, her eyes bright with brutish joy" (Joyce 1968, 99). His pace quickens as he comes closer to meeting the shadowy image his soul constantly beheld: "His blood was in revolt. He wandered up and down the dark slimy streets peering into the gloom of lanes and doorways, listening eagerly for any sound. He moaned to himself like some baffled, prowling beast" (Joyce 1968, 99). Ironically, a brothel becomes the center of the maze: "He would follow a devious course up and down the streets, circling nearer and nearer in a tremor of fear and joy, until his feet led him suddenly around a dark corner" (Joyce 1968, 102).

As his "sinloving soul" (Joyce 1968, 102) descends further into the vicious circles of his cupidity, Stephen realizes the foul nature of his moral offense upon hearing a fiery sermon while on retreat in which the preacher describes a hell inhabited by "goatish creatures" moving "in slow circles, circling closer and closer to enclose, to enclose" (Joyce 1968, 137–8). Here Stephen envisions sin in the traditional manner as self-enclosure, as a prison-house. Although he confesses his sins at this juncture, the increasingly keen sense of his "mild proud sovereignty" (Joyce 1968, 168) prompts Stephen to alter the course that, under the tutelage of the Virgin Mary, would have brought him "*across the bleak wilderness . . . home*" to Jesus (Joyce 1968, 139). The ambages of sin will later provide the fledgling artist with the supposed escape route out of the labyrinth of his religion.

This transgressive impulse allows the minotaur of lust to roam freely in the dark wood of Stephen's imagination. Rather than seeking the spiritual release of the believing pilgrim, Stephen remains a willing captive of the mythical creature. Joyce employs circling and winding images repeatedly to link the topography of Dante's hell to the Cretan labyrinth (Fortuna 1998, 204). At the climax of his soul's descent into evil, the Irish Dedalus beholds a "bovine god" (Joyce 1968, 111), the product of Pasiphae's brutish passion for a white bull. This demonic vision, a reflection of Stephen's own "monstrous reveries" and dispositions (Joyce 1968, 90), recalls Dante's portrayal of the half-man, half-beast as an "infernal parody" of the Incarnation (Doob 1992, 295).[5] The lustful who rupture the incarnational harmony between *eros* and *agape* (cf. Williams 1970, 161) "make reason slave to appetite" (Dante 1949, 5.39). By surrendering the "intellect to the disordered sensualism of the moment," in the words of Charles Williams, they "dehumanize" their sexual cravings in hell instead of "transhumanizing" them to heaven (Williams 1994, 134, 124). Joyce overturns the traditional moral significance attached to these otherworldly destinations by having Hume's psychological imperative, "reason is, and ought only to be the slave of the passions" (Hume 1962, II.iii, 156) inform Stephen's rite of passage towards aesthetic beatitude.

The inability to distinguish between aesthetic and sexual pleasure disqualifies Stephen from being a Dantesque threader of the labyrinth, as Marshall McLuhan once suggested (McLuhan 1971, 20). Dante's pilgrimage counterpoints Ulysses's vain attempt to transform the oars of his vessel into "wings" (Dante 1949, 26.125), a mad flight that re-enacted the fall of Icarus (Dante 1949, 17.109). The double catastrophe prompted Dante to ask an overwhelming question: "O human race, born to take flight and soar / Why fall ye, for one breath of wind, to earth?" (Dante 1955, 12.95–6). The slightest sin thwarts the soul's ascent. The lowliness of human nature can be elevated only through grace, just as the earthbound worm, naturally destined to become an "angelic butterfly" (Dante 1955, 10.124–5), cannot pretend to fly without wings. Like the human soul that yearns for immortal beauty in Plato's *Phaedrus* (Plato 1952, 92) and begins to grow wings to fly upward towards its transcendent object, Dante is lifted up on the "wings of desire" (Dante 1955, 4.28–30), fortified in the hope of attaining "the end of all desires" (Dante 1962, 33.47).

To keep on this divine path, the pilgrim repents of his past sins, and decides not to spread his wings too widely (Dante 1955, 22.44). The exercise of moderation requires a right ordering of one's desires since love is "the seed of every virtue and of all acts deserving punishment" (Dante 1955, 17.104–5). When Beatrice takes over from Virgil as Dante's guide, the pilgrim confesses to her that he was led astray by falling in love with "transitory things" and by failing to follow "the ideal lady of his mind" towards heaven (Dante 1955, 31.34–6). Beatrice, for her part, rebukes her prodigal lover for having harbored false affections that "weighed down [his] wings" (Dante 1955, 31.58–60). He succumbed for a time not only to physical lust but also figuratively to the siren charms of philosophy, abandoning the riches of divine Revelation that Beatrice represented. Virgil helped Dante recover the natural light of reason, but deferred to Beatrice, "the light between [the] mind and truth" (Dante 1955, 6.45), when the pilgrim aspired to knowledge of higher things. Beatrice accordingly clothed her pupil with the plumes of grace for the lofty flight (Dante 1962, 15.53–4, 72) towards "that heaven which is pure light alone" (Dante 1962, 30.39). She turns out to be a better craftsman than Daedalus for her artistic Icarus. The beauty of a wise woman, then, awakened the spirit of an ennobling love in Dante's heart (Dante 1992, 20.39). Beatrice's *caritas*, like Ariadne's the antithesis of Pasiphae's perverse lust (Doob 1992, 302), provided the thread that eventually led her beloved out of hell and towards contemplation of the first author of beauty.

Joyce recasts Dante's epiphanic meeting with Beatrice in a climactic scene from his novel. In *A Portrait* the "epiphany" functions as a secular equivalent to the instantaneous and mysterious action of grace. Stephen apprehends the splendor of one such moment when he spots a girl wading on the beach. In this well-known tableau, Joyce reproduces the Beatrician moment Williams defined as "a moment of revelation and communicated conversion by means of a girl" (Williams 1994, 123) only to subvert its theological implications. Dante's new life began, as Eliot pointed out (Eliot 1972, 427), once he rejected sinful desire and celebrated human love as a step to the divine. Stephen, on the other hand, resists *metanoia*, the sinner's radical change of heart, preferring instead to transmute the self through "palingenesis," or death and rebirth leading to *gnosis*:

> What were they now but cerements shaken from the body of death . . . cerements, the linens of the grave?
>
> His soul had arisen from the grave of boyhood, spurning her graveclothes. (Joyce 1968, 169–170)

Joyce demythologizes the gospel narrative of the resurrection of the body and reinterprets it as a trope of sexual awakening. Stephen's counter-conversion holds out the promise of *jouissance*, of erotic rather than beatific bliss. Small wonder his soul exclaims, "Heavenly God! . . . in an outburst of profane joy" (Joyce 1968, 171). The bodily presence of the beloved, no longer a vehicle of grace as in the *Vita Nuova* (Dante 1992, 26, 56–8), transports Stephen into "a wild new life" (Joyce 1968, 170) that beckons him to make sin itself the cadence and keynote of his art. He emerges out of his endless erring in the dark labyrinth of his soul to experience – in the punning phrase of Mark C. Taylor – the phenomenon of "mazing grace" (Taylor 1984, 73).

This defining moment inspires the young artist to try his hand at writing poetry. Although Aquinas serves as a major source for his aesthetic theory, Stephen's poetic practice contradicts the ethical principles of the medieval philosopher as well as those of Dante (cf. Fortuna 1998, 207). A tremendous visionary power transforms an ordinary girl on the strand into the temptress-muse of the villanelle sequence Stephen composes: "While his soul had passed from ecstasy to languor where had she been? Might it be, in the mysterious ways of spiritual life, that her soul at those same moments had been conscious of his homage?" (Joyce 1968, 223). Stephen's homage is in fact autoerotic; like Pygmalion, he is aroused by the work of his own hands:

> Conscious of his desire she was waking from odorous sleep, the temptress of his villanelle. Her eyes dark and with a look of languor, were opening to his eyes. Her nakedness yielded to him, radiant, warm, odorous and lavish-limbed, enfolded him like a shining cloud. (Joyce 1968, 223)

Locked within the confines of his being, the muse becomes an interior paramour who facilitates the sexual transfiguration of her male creator. The poet exhibits a natural affinity with Rousseau, for whom writing was an analogue of masturbation (Rousseau 1953, 109). Stephen falls in love with the image of his own creation, his own desire answering his own desire, not with a true other. The "false image of Beatrice" nourished by his interior desire (Williams 1994, 7, 165) excites Stephen's "kinetic emotions," not the "esthetic stasis" or contemplative spirit he deems a necessary product of a "proper art" (Joyce 1968, 205–6). The artist associates *eros* primarily with the sexual urge as in Freud rather than with the aspiration to what is true, good, and beautiful as in Plato. Unlike Dante, who renounced the disordered loves that made the "crooked road seem like the straight" (Dante 1955, 10.3), Stephen finds himself in a twisted moral labyrinth where, as Nietzsche puts it, "all that is straight lies . . . all truth is crooked" (Nietzsche 1968, 270). The "wild angel . . . of mortal youth and beauty" who appears to the artist in the seascape throws open before him "all the ways of error and glory" (Joyce 1968, 172). Consequently, the erotic focus of the aesthetic moment leaves Stephen stranded in a beauty maze of his own making.

The "End Beyond the End" of Art

In the process of depicting Stephen as an apostle of beauty, Joyce subverts Dante's sacramental poetics. To explain why the medieval master presents Beatrice as a figure of the eucharist when she appears in a solemn procession at the end of the *Purgatorio*, Charles Williams cited Coventry Patmore's gloss on the scene: "the Holy Eucharist, in the beginning, is desired because it resembles the lower but still 'great' sacrament of human affection; afterwards the lower sacrament is explained by its resemblance to the higher" (Williams 1994, 188n.). For Dante, "a transubstantially-minded man" (Sinclair 1971, 416), the contemplation of the beloved reflected the communion of the soul with the Author of grace and established "a state of *caritas*, of pure love, the mode of expansion of one moment into eternity" (Williams 1938, 90). In sharp contrast to Aquinas's *Adoro te devote*, composed in honour of the sacred host exposed during benediction, Stephen's irreverent "eucharistic hymn" commemorates his fleeting sensual communion with an imaginary seductress. A priest of eternal imagination, he refuses to communicate at the sacrament of the altar, and yet, through the alchemy of the word, transmutes the daily bread of experience into the radiant body of ever-living life (Joyce 1968, 243, 221). Like Rimbaud, the modern symbolist worships the man-made sign, his art, "as if the chalice were the reality, and the Real Presence the symbol" (Symons 1958, 36). Ovidian metamorphosis functions as the aesthetic equivalent of transubstantiation.

In this way Stephen elevates art to the "supreme end he was born to serve" (Joyce 1968, 169). Whereas Bunyan's faithful pilgrim in the course of his journey finds a peaceful room in the House Beautiful to rest, to peruse rare old books and to reflect on the texts of Sacred Scripture under the guidance of an authentic Interpreter, Joyce's protagonist waits in his study chamber for a profane annunciation. He follows Pater and the Victorian aesthetes in turning Christian's allegorical mansion of divine wisdom into a sanctuary of aestheticism where the artist-critic takes solace in acknowledging no anterior Logos. Stephen rejects Augustine's statement that "we were made by the Word after the likeness of the Word" (Augustine 1996, 483), and becomes, in fact, his own *verbum* since the word is made flesh in the virgin womb of the artist's imagination (Joyce 1968, 217). As a "counter-creator" competing with the primal fiat, in George Steiner's telling phrase (Steiner 2001, 109), the godlike artist begets a new, self-referential word before which he bows down on the altar of his imagination. The modernist who perceives no "end beyond the end" of art, Jacques Maritain remarked (Maritain 1953, 170), falls into the "deadly error" of expecting his own word "to provide the supersubstantial nourishment of man" (Maritain 1943, 37). The failure to distinguish between means and end, between perishable food and the bread of life, makes art the object rather than a channel of worship. The "idolatry of the beautiful," as Levinas put it, leads one to adore "a work of art [that] substitutes itself for God" (Levinas 1981, 199n.21).

Dante, the consummate artist of pilgrimage, chose a writer like himself to be his mentor, but realized he must leave his Latin precursor behind in order for his journey to be fruitful in its fullest sense. "It is ultimately the function of art," Eliot later commented on this pivotal scene, "to bring us to a condition of serenity, stillness, and reconciliation; and then leave us, as Virgil left Dante, to proceed toward a region where that guide can avail us no further" (Eliot 1967, 87). Art points to a truth beyond itself, a grace that exceeds its grasp, but there is a definite frontier the artist or critic should not cross unless he is guided, as Eliot insisted, by "sound theology" (Eliot 1975, 150). The human logos can only go so far, and should defer to the transcendent poet who is "Alpha and Omega" (Dante 1962, 26.17) the boundaries of the letters of the alphabet which can be combined in and produce all possible words in an infinite text. It is therefore necessary in this context to preserve Kierkegaard's austere distinction between the "apostle" who finds peace in being a faithful servant of the eternal Word he announces, and the "genius" who frets constantly that the words he invents will soon be eclipsed by those of other writers. The Danish philosopher was concerned principally with the anti-Christian bias of a (Nietzschean) "purely aesthetic metaphysics." "If the sphere of [Christianity] is abolished, or explained away in aesthetics," he wrote in *The Present Age*, "an Apostle becomes neither more nor less than a genius, and then – good night, Christianity! *Esprit* and the Spirit, revelation and originality, a call from God and genius, all end up meaning more or less the same thing" (Kierkegaard 1962, 89).

Modern culture, Chesterton indicated long ago, has been "using and using up . . . the truths that remain to it out of the old treasury of Christendom" (Chesterton, 1939, 16). Perhaps one of Joyce's greatest unintended ironies in *A Portrait* concerns the extent to which Stephen lives on borrowed spiritual capital. Unabashedly, he continually employs the conceptual riches and classic texts of Christianity to sustain his movement from pilgrimage to voluntary exile. The usually unreliable Cranly is nevertheless perceptive enough to point out the inconsistency of the budding poet's position: "your mind is supersaturated with the religion in which you say you disbelieve" (Joyce 1968, 240). Ironically, even the iconoclast necessarily depends on the sacred tradition he seeks to demolish in order to make sense of his own act of rebellion.[6]

The inescapable irony affected one unusual reader of *A Portrait* in a surprising manner. This was none other than Thomas Merton, who became known as the "man who was converted to the [Christian] faith by reading James Joyce" (Merton 1951, 386). The pivotal turning point recorded in his autobiographical *The Seven Storey Mountain* demonstrates that artists can sometimes play an unwitting role in the transformative process of salvation. Although Stephen Dedalus intended to "hit the conscience" (Joyce 1968, 238) of future readers and influence them with the account of his defection, Merton's response serves as a useful reminder that the reception-history of a work of art often lies outside the control of its author. The Trappist monk recalled how the description of the young Dubliner's spiritual crisis had left him "discouraged, bored and depressed," while the dramatic sermon on hell Stephen heard during his retreat had made an immediate and indelible impression on his soul:

> Now, instead of being repelled by the thought of such preaching – which was perhaps the author's intention – I was stimulated and edified by it. The style in which the priest in the book talked, pleased me by its efficiency and solidity and drive." (Merton 1951, 211)

Joyce meant to expose the terror of the religion Stephen eventually rejects, but the vivid realism of the scene prompted Merton to put down his book and attend Mass at a nearby church in order to experience first-hand what he had just read about. The sermon delivered on that occasion was equally powerful: "For behind those words you felt the full force not only of Scripture but of centuries of a unified and continuous and consistent tradition. And above all, it was a vital tradition" (Merton 1951, 209). Merton draws our attention in this epiphanic episode to the function of literature as a mediation of desire. In *De Doctrina Christiana*, Augustine famously articulated the fundamental distinction between "enjoying" a text "for its own sake" and "using" its literal sense in order to understand spiritual truth (Augustine 1958, I.3.3–I.4.4). The first approach results in carnal enjoyment, the kind illustrated by Augustine himself in the *Confessions* (Augustine 1984, I.xiii.33–5) when he recounts his seductive reading of the story of Dido in the *Aeneid*. In similar fashion, Stephen's literal identification with Mercedes, the romantic heroine of *The Count of Monte Cristo*, precedes his so-called "holy encounter" with a prostitute (Joyce 1968, 64–5, 99). Stephen undertakes his erratic quest for the wisdom of the sensual man in obedience to the "wayward instinct" (Joyce 1968, 165) that leads him to turn his words into an anti-Gospel, whereas Augustine's restlessness helps him attain the wisdom of the spiritual man who acknowledges the eternal Word as the end of all desire. The restless mind of the truth-seeker opens the door of his heart to Love. Merton's charitable reading of Joyce's text also reflects the tranquility of ordered desire the pilgrim achieves when he sees himself as a character in search of his divine Author.

Dominic Manganiello

References

Augustine 1984. *Confessions*. Trans. R.S. Pine-Coffin. Harmondsworth: Penguin Books.

——— 1958. *On Christian Doctrine*. Trans. D.W. Robertson, Jr. New York: Liberal Arts Press.

——— 1996. *Sermons on Selected Lessons of the New Testament* in *The Nicene and post-Nicene Fathers*, Ed. Philip Schaff. Grand Rapids: Eerdmans.

Blake, William 1969. "Notes on the Illustrations to Dante" in *Blake: The Complete Writings*, 785–6. Ed. Geoffrey Keynes. London: Oxford University Press. Vol. VI, 241–545.

Blumenberg, Hans 1983. *The Legitimacy of the Modern Age*. Trans. Robert M. Wallace. Cambridge: M.I.T. Press.

Boyle, Robert, S.J. 1978. *James Joyce's Pauline Vision: A Catholic Exposition*. Carbondale: Illinois University Press.

Camus, Albert 1975. *The Myth of Sisyphus and Other Essays*. Trans. Justin O'Brien. New York: Alfred A. Knopf.

Chesterton, G.K. 1939. *The Thing*. London: Sheed and Ward.

Crane, Hart 1970. "Joyce and Ethics" in *James Joyce: The Critical Heritage*, Ed. Robert H. Deming. London: Routledge and Kegan Paul. Vol. I, 124.

De Certeau, Michel 1984. *The Practice of Everyday Life*, trans. Steven Rendall. Berkeley: University of California Press.

Dante Alighieri 1949. *The Divine Comedy I: Hell*. Trans. Dorothy L. Sayers. Harmondsworth: Penguin Books.

——— 1962. *The Divine Comedy III: Paradise*. Trans. Dorothy L. Sayers and Barbara Reynolds Harmondsworth: Penguin Books.

——— 1955. *The Divine Comedy II: Purgatory*. Trans. Dorothy L. Sayers. Harmondsworth: Penguin Books.

——— *Vita Nuova*. 1992. Trans. Mark Musa. Oxford: Oxford University Press.

Doob, Penelope Reed. 1992. *The Idea of the Labyrinth from Classical Antiquity to the Middle Ages*. Ithaca and London: Cornell University Press.

Eliot. T.S. 1967. "Poetry and Drama" in *On Poetry and Poets*. London: Faber.

——— 1972. *Selected Essays*. London: Faber and Faber.

——— 1975. *The Use of Poetry and the Use of Criticism*. London: Faber and Faber.

Fortuna, Diane 1998. "The Art of the Labyrinth" in *Critical Essays on James Joyce's 'A Portrait of the Artist as a Young Man'*. Ed. Philip Brady and James F. Carens. New York: G.K. Hall. 187–212.

Howard, Donald R. 1980. *Writers and Pilgrims. Medieval Pilgrimage Narratives and their Posterity*. Berkeley: University of California Press.

Howe, Irving 1967. "The Idea of the Modern" in *Literary Modernism*. Ed. Irving Howe. New York: Fawcett. 11–40.

Hume, David 1962. *A Treatise of Human Nature*, Vol. 2. Ed. Pall S. Ardal. London: Fontana.

Joyce, James 1959. *The Critical Writings of James Joyce*. Ed. Richard Ellmann and Ellsworth Mason. New York: Viking Press.

——— 1968. A *Portrait of the Artist as a Young Man: Text, Criticism, and Notes*. Ed. Chester G. Anderson. Harmondsworth: Penguin Books.

——— 1969. *Stephen Hero*. London: Jonathan Cape.

Kierkegaard, Soren 1966. *The Concept of Irony*. Trans. Lee Capel. New York: Harper and Row.

——— 1962. *The Present Age*. Trans. Alexander Dru. New York: Harper and Row.

Levinas, Emmanuel 1981. *Otherwise Than Being, or Beyond Essence*. Trans. Alphonso Lingis. The Hague: Martinus Nijhoff.

Litz, A. Walton 1966. *James Joyce*. New York: Twayne.

Lukács, Georg 1971. *The Theory of the Novel*. Trans. Anna Bostock. Cambridge: M.I.T. Press.

Manganiello, Dominic 1993. "Reading the Book of Himself: The Confessional Imagination of St. Augustine and Joyce" in *Biography and Autobiography:*

Essays on Irish and Canadian History and Literature, ed. James Noonan. Ottawa: Carleton University Press. 149–162.

Maritain, Jacques 1943. *Art and Scholasticism*. Trans. J. F. Scanlan. London: Sheed and Ward.

——— 1953. *Creative Intuition in Art and Poetry*. Princeton: Princeton University Press.

Marlowe, Christopher 1969. *Doctor Faustus*. Ed. Sylvan Barnet. New York: New American Library.

Matthews, W.H. 1971. *Mazes and Labyrinths: Their Development and History*. New York: Dover.

McLuhan, Marshall 1971. *The Interior Landscape: The Literary Criticism of Marshall McLuhan*. Ed. Eugene McNamara. New York: McGraw-Hill.

Merton, Thomas 1951. *The Seven Storey Mountain*. Garden City: Garden City Books.

Nietzsche, Friedrich 1968. *Thus Spake Zarathustra*. Trans. R. J. Hollingdale. New York: Viking Press.

Percy, Walker 1991. *Signposts in a Strange Land*. Ed. Patrick Samway. New York: Picador.

Plato. 1952. *Phaedrus*. Trans. R. Hackforth. Indianapolis: Bobbs-Merrill.

Raleigh, John Henry 1987. "*Ulysses*: Trinitarian and Catholic" in *Joyce's Ulysses: The Larger Perspective*. Ed. Robert D. Newman and Weldon Thornton. Newark: University of Delaware Press. 98–122.

Rousseau, Jean-Jacques 1953. *Confessions*. Trans. J. M. Cohen. Harmondsworth: Penguin Books.

Sinclair, John D. 1971. Trans. *The Divine Comedy 2: Purgatorio*. London: Oxford University Press.

Steiner, George 2001. *Grammars of Creation*. New Haven: Yale University Press.

Symons, Arthur 1958. *The Symbolist Movement in Literature*. New York: E. P. Dutton.

Taylor, Mark C. 1984. *Erring: A Postmodern A/Theology*. Chicago: Chicago University Press.

Williams, Charles 1994. *The Figure of Beatrice: A Study in Dante*. Cambridge: D. S. Brewer.

——— 1938. *He Came Down from Heaven*. London: Heinemann.

——— 1970. *The Image of the City and other Essays*. Oxford: Oxford University Press.

Flannery O'Connor
The Violent Bear It Away

Introduction

The title of Flannery O'Connor's *The Violent Bear It Away* contains both a conundrum and the key for unlocking it. The novel's name is taken from the Douay-Rheims translation of Matt. 11:12. "And from the days of John the Baptist until now, the kingdom of heaven suffereth violence, and the violent bear it away." Many recent biblical scholars interpret this passage as a reference to those who would impatiently seize the divine kingdom by force, brutally laying hold of it as if it were a means of destruction rather than redemption. The phrase may in fact refer to Jewish Zealots who wanted to rout the Romans, or else to Jewish religious authorities who bullied their way into control of the synagogues or, even more particularly, to arrogant leaders of the Jewish temple with its wealth, prestige, and political power. In every case, it seems that the biblical claim about seizing the kingdom is negative in its import, referring to evil (perhaps even satanic) attacks on the radically alternative community established by Jesus.

Yet this is only a single way of reading Matthew's strange saying about the violence that besets the reign of God. Another is offered in the gloss on Matt. 11:12 found in the 1899 Challoner version of the Douay-Rheims Bible that O'Connor herself used: "*[The Kingdom] is not to be obtained but by main force, by using violence upon ourselves, by mortification and penance, and resisting our perverse inclinations*" (http://www.drbo.org/chapter/47011.htm; italics in the original). The violence that makes raids on the rule of God is here regarded not as satanic and inimical but as salutary, indeed as necessary. It is not a call for Christians to attack others so much as to practice spiritual and moral violence against their own sinfulness.

The burden of this essay is to demonstrate that both interpretations of the violence done to the kingdom of God – both the satanic and the holy – are at work in *The Violent Bear It Away*, and that their difference is obscured by demonic guile, especially concerning the nature of evil. The task of undeceiving the Deceiver thus becomes a crucial act of moral and religious no less than literary discernment. Hence the division of the essay into three parts: (1) a concise summary of the Christian understanding of evil; (2) an analysis of the demonic raids on the divine domain that occur in the novel; and finally (3) an account of the blessed assaults that justify the book's title, as the kingdom of God is borne away with "the terrible speed of Mercy."

A Christian Conception of Evil

St. Augustine famously understood evil as *privatio boni*, the privation or absence of true being, the perversion or deformation of the good. The paradoxical Christian claim is that, while evil has horrific power and devastating effect, it is ultimately to be regarded as emptiness and nothingness. It is something alien rather than essential to God's good creation. It has no power to create, only to damage and destroy; indeed, it exists only parasitically, leeching off the good, as the very name of C. S. Lewis's demonic Screwtape makes evident: he is akin to a pernicious tapeworm feeding off his host. Evil, it follows, literally cannot *be*. Evil cannot assume true form because it is literally nothing.

Yet what even Christian theologians often fail to discern is perhaps the most important matter of all: Exactly because Satan has no substance or essence, he can feign numerous *appearances*, the less obvious the more deadly. Indeed, he *must* assume these many masks, since he always acts in the semblance of some alleged good, having no positive identity of his own. Not by happenstance is he regarded as the supreme Illusionist, the "subtlest beast of the field," "the Father of Lies." Therein lies both the perverse power of the evil as well as the key to interpreting the guises he is given in scripture. He appears as a snake in Genesis, as Lucifer in Isaiah, as Beelzebub in Luke, as Belial in 2 Corinthians, and as Satan himself in many other places – not only as he tempts Jesus in the wilderness, but also as he is finally defeated in the apocalypse: "the great dragon . . . that ancient serpent, who is called Devil and Satan, the deceiver of the whole world – he was thrown down to the earth, and the angels with him" (Rev. 12:9).

For Flannery O'Connor, it is an error – for Christian self-understanding as well as Christian witness to the world – not to identify the Evil One by means of his particular names and voices, the concrete images and persons that he inhabits. Such failure to undeceive Satan's deceptions could enhance his victories. Indeed, the domestication of the Devil into a mere symbol or principle may constitute his most significant modern triumph:

> To insure our sense of mystery, we need a sense of evil which sees the devil as a real spirit who must be made to name himself, and not simply to name himself as vague evil, but to name himself with his specific personality for every occasion. Literature, like virtue, does not thrive in an atmosphere where the devil is not recognized as existing both in himself and as a dramatic necessity for the writer. (O'Connor 1970, 117)[1]

It thus becomes evident that for Flannery O'Connor as for ancient Christian tradition, Satan is something far more sinister than the sum total of human ill will; he is a ravaging presence who stalks his prey like an exceedingly clever deceiver – except as he is driven out, whether sooner or later, by undeception.[2]

Demonic Violence Practiced against the Coming of the Kingdom[3]

The fiction of Flannery O'Connor, especially her novel *The Violent Bear It Away*, resists the relegation of Satan to an abstract principle and thus to his ultimate irrelevance. She envisions Luciferian evil in traditional terms as a personal power determined to achieve his own supremacy. When Satan appears in her fiction, she candidly observed, he is not to be understood as "this or that psychological tendency" (O'Connor 1979, 360). She cites Baudelaire's celebrated dictum that the Devil's greatest wile is to convince us he does not exist, and she acknowledges his considerable success in our own time. Yet for all that is traditional in her conception of Satan, she is concerned not to make him obvious, lest he be easily dismissed as a bogeyman. In fact, her demons disguise themselves in thoroughly Freudian and Jungian terms. Freud regarded Satan as nothing other than a symbol, albeit a powerful one, of repressed erotic desires or else of neuroses lying deep within the unconscious, often negatively projected "onto individuals or groups that we identify as enemies or potential enemies" (Russell 1986, 229). In the work of Jung, Freud's student, Lucifer represents the massive destructive energy resident in the universe as it stands over against the equally enormous constructive powers that Jung links to the divine. Yet for Jung, Lucifer's name still applies: He is the light-bearer whose demonic negativity dwells in a mandala-like complementarity with divine positivity. Only as good incorporates evil into itself, Jung teaches, can higher wisdom and wholeness be attained (Russell 1986, 229, 233–34). It is noteworthy that, when I ask students to identify the voice that speaks inwardly to young Francis Marion Tarwater from the very beginning of the novel, they respond in Jungian and Freudian ways. They almost always answer that this "stranger" who gradually becomes Tarwater's "friend" is the boy's sub-conscious mind, his inward self, his alter ego.

Young Tarwater is the grandnephew of Mason Tarwater, an eighty-four-year-old backwoods prophet who has commissioned the fourteen-year-old youth to become his successor in the life of prophecy. The boy's first task of filial loyalty is to provide a reverent burial for old Mason when he dies. The elderly Elijah instructs his would-be Elisha to bury him deep enough to prevent the dogs from digging him up, and also to plant the cross of his Savior at the head of his grave. Francis's second summons is to baptize his cousin Bishop, the imbecile child of his uncle George Rayber. Rayber is an atheist school psychologist who believes that, like all other religious practices, baptism is a vain and useless rite, especially when conferred upon a cretinous child. Yet according to old Mason, young Francis's obedience to these commands will set the boy on his way to becoming a baptizing prophet of the kingdom that always hurries near.

It is noteworthy that the elder Tarwater had not promised his nephew a life of prophetic glory or delight, but rather of pain and ignominy. Far from putting him on the road to American ministerial fame and success, the old prophet had called the stripling to a life of fearful suffering and awful wrestling with God – indeed, to a holy violence:

> He had schooled him in the evils that befall prophets; in those that come from the world, which are trifling, and those that come from the Lord and burn the prophet clean; for he himself had been burned clean and burned clean again. He had learned by fire. (O'Connor 1988, 332)

The boy dreads a calling that would make him serve as a rod for earthing the holy lightning. He dreams, instead, of far more awesome feats of power: Moses striking water from a rock, Joshua making the sun stand still, Daniel staring down lions in a pit. Eager to perform such thrilling, even glamorous acts, the young Tarwater is disappointed that old Mason orders him to undertake these seemingly mundane tasks of burial and baptism.

Young Tarwater looks forward to neither of his callings. When the old man dies, the boy labors for a day and a half at scooping out his great-uncle's grave. Yet gradually the gorge of rebellion rises within him. It has risen before, whenever the old man had spoken not of the prophet's power and glory, but "of the sweat and stink of the cross, of being born again to die, and of spending eternity eating the bread of life" (O'Connor 1988, 334). The defiant youth finally abandons his spadework and heads off to the whiskey still, where his bootlegging great-uncle had manufactured not divine but earthly lightning, there to partake of alcoholic waters that will numb his conscience, while quenching neither his spiritual nor physical thirst.

Tarwater does not undertake his spiritual rebellion alone; he is also prompted by an inward interlocutor. My students are partially justified in reading this inner voice as the product of Tarwater's unconscious longings and frustrations, and thus as the boy's alter ego. As a thoroughgoing Thomist, O'Connor discerns the profound intersection of nature and grace, so that the human world is either elevated or degraded by the human reception or refusal of the divine summons. Yet she leaves open another and more penetrating perception – namely, that this alien and intrusive speaker is the impersonator of Satan himself, the Tempter who operates not only by human permission but also by demonic invasion. Here lies O'Connor's signal theological breakthrough: She depicts this subjective voice as arising from within the boy's own mutinous will, but also as assaulting him from without as a satanic force.

Because young Francis's Christian conscience has been so deeply formed by the religious teachings of his great-uncle, this Luciferian speaker at first seems strident and strange. Initially, the boy resents its insults against his dead uncle's life of prophecy. Old Mason had taught his great-nephew to have a deep reverence for the dead, the huge silent majority who constitute the authentic human *patria*. Not only did they literally father us; their rotted bodies also constitute the very humus beneath our feet, thus prompting, as the word suggests, a life of humility.

> "The world was made for the dead. Think of all the dead there are," [Mason] said, and then as if he had conceived the answer for all the insolence in the world, he said, "There's a million times more dead than living and the dead are dead a million times longer than the living are alive." (O'Connor 1988, 339)

Gradually, however, young Tarwater welcomes the inward mouthpiece who enunciates the insolence the old prophet had condemned. It is the voice of theological rebellion, and it speaks with Dostoevskyan clarity about the relationship between parricide and deicide: If the boy can slay his immediate obligations to his dead great-uncle, he can be rid of all other constraints as well. All things will be permitted, including wanton havoc: "'Now I can do anything I want to,' he said, softening the stranger's voice so that he could stand it. Could kill off all those chickens if I had a mind to, he thought, watching the worthless black game bantams that his uncle had been fond of keeping" (O'Connor 1988, 345). These are the accents of nihilistic autarky, even if they are given to a backwoods youth who has never heard of Friedrich Nietzsche or Ivan Karamazov. Once the demonic is permitted entrance, O'Connor shows, it assumes complete control. From having been an alien intruder, the devilish voice gradually becomes Tarwater's affectionate familiar:

> He didn't search out the stranger's face but he knew by now that it was sharp and friendly and wise, shadowed under a stiff broad-brimmed panama hat that obscured the color of his eyes. He had lost his dislike for the thought of the voice. Only every now and then it sounded like a stranger's voice to him. He began to feel that he was only just now meeting himself, as if as long as his uncle had lived, he had been deprived of his own acquaintance. (O'Connor 1988, 352)

O'Connor's Devil is all the more canny for being a comic figure rather like the fiend who appears in Dostoevsky's *The Brothers Karamazov*. He is a brittle rationalist and literalist, for example, denying the bodily resurrection of the faithful dead on the grounds that many of them have been so thoroughly mangled that God could not possibly reconstitute their risen flesh into human form. "And lemme ast you this: what's God going to do with sailors drowned at sea that the fish have et and the fish that et them et by other fish and they et by yet others?" (O'Connor 1988, 352). This countrified Satan also argues – in accord with a good deal of modern politics and psychology – that young Tarwater's authentic selfhood depends on his complete independence and self-sufficiency. He must deny all divinely ordered authority in order to be free. And in complete fulfillment of Baudelaire's dictum about demonic deception, Francis must learn to deny the Devil himself, as in the hilarious counsel that this satanic voice provides:

> The way I see it, [the inner voice] said, you can do one of two things. One of them, not both. Nobody can do both of two things without straining themselves. You can do one thing or you can do the opposite.
>
> Jesus or the Devil, the boy said.
>
> No no no, the stranger said, there ain't no such thing as a Devil. I can tell you that from my own self-experience. I know that for a fact. It ain't Jesus or the Devil. It's Jesus or you. (O'Connor 1988, 354)

In appealing to experience as the ultimate criterion for authenticity, this demonic impersonator is a thoroughly modern subjectivist, one who locates truth only in the private and inward realm. Far more delusory is this cornpone demon's insistence that human flourishing stands in rivalistic competition with obedience to God: "It's Jesus or you." The central Christian claim is exactly to the contrary: only by participating in the triune life of God through Jesus and the church, losing one's life for the sake of the kingdom, does one truly find one's life (Mark 8:34–37).

The all-too-eagerly yielding Tarwater soon follows the command of his inner voice to abandon his grave digging and to imbibe his great-uncle's illicit whiskey. At first, the satanic speaker recommends that the boy drink moderately, as if he were learning a well-mannered social practice; indeed, the wise-sounding demon recommends the golden mean in all things: "I wouldn't pay too much attention to my Redemption if I was you. Some people take everything too hard" (45). With every success in subduing the boy's will, the demonic voice ceases to sound like an invasive stranger and becomes Tarwater's alleged friend. The mutinous youth soon becomes so thoroughly wasted with his great uncle's home-brew that he is able to "finish up" only by attempting the one thing that his dead uncle had strictly forbidden: the desecration of the old man's body by reducing it to ashes.

It is altogether fitting that, when the fourteen-year old Francis Tarwater abandons Powderhead in revolt against the fierce and sweated Christianity that the elderly prophet had taught him, he should flee his rural home to live in the city with his uncle George Rayber once again. Rayber, in turn, is eager to give Tarwater a crash course in civic life – its amenities as well as its responsibilities – so as to counteract the prophet's violently religious rearing of young Francis:

> In four days they had been to the art gallery and the movies, they had toured department stores, ridden escalators, visited the supermarkets, inspected the water works, the post office, the railroad yards and the city hall. Rayber had explained how the city was run and detailed the duties of a good citizen. (O'Connor 1988, 397–98)

The "natural" means of such civic salvation, as Rayber tells Tarwater, is "through your own efforts" (O'Connor 1988, 451). "If there's any way to be born again," he adds, "it's a way that you accomplish yourself, an understanding about yourself that you reach after a long time, perhaps a long effort. It's nothing you get from above by spilling a little water and a few words" (O'Connor 1988, 450–51). Indeed, the psychologist counsels the rebel anti-prophet with advice almost identical to that given by the satanic voice: "You want to avoid extremes," he tells the youth. "They are for violent people" (O'Connor 1988, 420).

Despite his cool counsel, George Rayber is consumed by an anti-Christian zealotry of his own, as he makes his own bitter assault on the kingdom of God and what he regards as its sorry products. Like Ivan Karamazov, he is not an atheist so much as an anti-theist. Rayber believes that, if God exists at all, he is surely a monster. Together with his Dostoevskyan predecessor, Rayber is determined to deny and refute this evil deity, this gnostic demiurge. Rayber resembles Ivan in another way: he is not deliberately demonic; he does not declare with Milton's Satan, "Evil, be thou my good." On the contrary, he regards himself as a compassionate altruist. Believing his own life to have been blighted by the religious fanaticism of the old prophet, George Rayber has become a school psychologist who wants to rescue other childhood victims of Christian fanaticism. O'Connor's novel poses an acute question: To what extent is Rayber so obsessed with a desire to serve as a secular savior that he actually loses his humanity and becomes demonic? Already in the fourth century, St. Athanasius warned against the destruction of the divine image in which we are made, as if we could actually extinguish our humanity, returning to the nothingness from which we came. Hence Athanasius' dire reference to "this dehumanizing of mankind, this universal hiding of the knowledge of [God] by the wiles of evil spirits" (Athanasius 2002, 40). Is Rayber such a subhuman no-thing, a creature who becomes not a humanoid animal but a devil in disguise?

The answer lies, I believe, in Rayber's conflicted regard for his own child, the imbecile Bishop. On the one hand, he can behold his son with utter coldness of heart, as if he were the mangled mistake of nature, a biological botch. "His normal way of looking upon Bishop was as an *x* signifying the general hideousness of fate. He did not believe that he himself was formed in the image and likeness of God but that Bishop was he had no doubt" (O'Connor 1988, 401). On at least one occasion Rayber has tried but failed to drown the "useless" Bishop. He also prophesies, quite accurately, that in future ages the birth of such "defective" children will be prevented. Rayber's genuine-seeming humanism is thus characterized by something quite frightening – namely, by a demonic nihilism.

Insofar as God is dead for Rayber, he is the harbinger of what Pope John Paul II called "the culture of death." "The twentieth century will have been an era of massive attacks on life," he wrote in his hallmark encyclical, *Evangelium Vitae*, "an endless series of wars and a continual taking of innocent human life" (*Ev. Vit.* 17). For Flannery O'Connor as for the late pope, there is an undeniable link between the huge collective horrors of our age and such individual evil acts as Rayber commends. The church is also complicit in these abominable evils, she suggests, whenever it fails to teach and preach and enact "the Gospel of Life," as John Paul II named it. The demonic triumphs, she suggests, through such deceptive terms as "compassion" and "caring" – whether in preventing "unwanted" births or ending "useless" lives:

> One of the tendencies of our age is to use the suffering of children to discredit the goodness of God, and once you have discredited his goodness, you are done with him. . . . In this popular pity, we mark our gain in sensibility and our loss in vision. If other ages felt less, they saw more, even though they saw with the blind, prophetical, unsentimental eye of acceptance, which is to say, of faith. In the absence of this faith now, we govern by tenderness. It is a tenderness which, long since cut off from the person of Christ, is wrapped in theory. When tenderness is detached from the source of tenderness, its logical outcome is terror. It ends in forced labor camps and in the fumes of the gas chambers. (O'Connor 1988, 830–31)

Fearing that old Mason has bequeathed to him an irresistible instinct for inward violence, Rayber has determined to spend his life walking a tightrope of self-control, so that when he is finally forced to choose between the only two options – belief and unbelief – he will elect a noble kind of nothingness:

> He was not deceived that this was a whole or full life, he only knew that it was the way his life had to be lived if it were going to have any dignity at all. He knew that he was the stuff of which fanatics and madmen are made and that he had turned his destiny by his bare will. He kept himself upright on a very narrow line between madness and emptiness, and when the time came for him to lose his balance, he intended to lurch toward emptiness and fall on the side of his choice. (O'Connor 1988, 402)

Even if Rayber cannot believe, he remains a troubled unbeliever, unable to bask in his nihilist faith. It is hard to imagine his becoming an Adolf

Eichmann.[4] Though he knows that his virtually mindless child will never be able to "make a contribution to society," Rayber loves Bishop in his very uselessness. In fact, almost every created thing – precisely because of its otherness, its unnecessity, its sheer gift-character – can overwhelm Rayber with boundless charity: "It could be a stick or a stone, the line of a shadow, the absurd old man's walk of a starling crossing the sidewalk. If, without thinking, he lent himself to it, he would feel suddenly a morbid surge of love that terrified him – powerful enough to throw him to the ground in an act of idiot praise." Rayber is least able to control his "insane" love when he beholds Bishop in his stark gratuity: "It was love without reason, love for something futureless, love that appeared to exist only to be itself, imperious and all demanding . . . " (O'Connor 1988, 401).

Rayber also fails to maintain his serene self-control when he hears the dying scream of Bishop as Tarwater drowns him. Having vowed to lurch toward nothingness when he is pushed to a final bitter choice, Rayber faints. His breakdown may seem to indicate that he has at last succeeded in electing nihilism as his final fate. Yet this scene is open to another and much more positive reading. A truly nihilistic triumph of the Devil would surely have entailed Rayber's celebration, if only in exhausted relief that Bishop is at last dead and that he himself can now live in peace. Rayber's collapse into unconsciousness may indicate, instead, the truth of O'Connor's own surmise "that he is not going to be able to sustain his choice" (O'Connor 1979, 484). The reason for Rayber's potential failure at the end is that the "madness" of divine charity does not have its counterpart in demonic emptiness, as if they were equals. The holy "violence" that old Mason had practiced on young Rayber – by baptizing and schooling him in the ways of prophecy during an intense four-day tutelage – is rooted in Reality as Rayber's election of the void is not. He can take no nihilistic pleasure in Bishop's death.

The Holy Violence that Bears Away the Kingdom

The novel's two main bearers of holy violence are Mason Tarwater and his unwilling protégé, Francis Marion Tarwater. Yet both of them also practice a savagery that cannot be called sacred. Mason's brutality is negligible as compared to the cruelty of the younger Tarwater. Whereas the old prophet acts as Peter to Rayber's Malchus by virtually deafening him with a gunshot wound to the ear, his rebel successor has actually committed murder. The satanic character of Tarwater's murder of Bishop cannot be mistaken, as his inward "friend" gives him Nietzschean encouragement throughout the death-scene, urging him to "be a man" and to drown the dimwit. Yet in the very act of sending Bishop to his watery grave, young Tarwater also finds himself uttering the baptismal formula – thus fulfilling, against his own defiant and demonic will, the vocation he has determined to deny.

This episode has left many readers perplexed, even outraged. The most indignant of O'Connor's interpreters is surely the French critic André Bleikasten. He accuses O'Connor of being a misanthrope whose God is hardly distinguishable from the Devil:

> O'Connor's heroes are indeed sleepers: they traverse life in a dream-like state, and with the sense of impotence and anxiety experienced in nightmares. They go through the motions of revolt, but their violent gestures toward independence are all doomed to dissolve into unreality. They are nothing more than the starts and bounds of a hooked fish. Tarwater and Motes both act out scenarios written beforehand by someone else. (Bleikasten 1978, 53)

Not only for hostile critics such as Bleikasten, but also for many O'Connor sympathizers as well, the will of Francis Marion Tarwater seems to have been scripted by a procrustean author in the service of a domineering deity. Holy violence, alas, seems indistinguishable from its unholy counterpart, as O'Connor appears to have answered demonic nihilism with a divine determinism of her own.[5]

Such charges would have merit if Francis Marion were able, after submerging Bishop in a liquid death, to assume a career of his own "Christian" violence in the fashion, for instance, of a Jim Jones or a David Koresh, spiritually mesmerizing his followers until they became slaves of his own demonic will. Tarwater undertakes no such program. Instead, he gradually comes to penetrate the satanic guises that have gulled him. And since it has taken a virtual miracle to rescue him from the clutches of the inward Satan as he baptizes little Bishop, so is something akin to an anti-miracle required to deliver Tarwater from the spiritual grip of the Devil – namely, a sodomitic rape by "a pale, lean, old-looking young man" who has given the boy a ride. That O'Connor does not intend the nameless rapist to represent homosexuals as a group is made evident in his willfully caricatured features. He drives a lavender-tinted car, wears a lavender shirt, carries a lavender handkerchief, and possesses lavender eyes – the adjectival color being a standard symbol for decadence of all kinds, especially the sensual.[6] After drugging the boy into unconsciousness, the sodomite emerges from his (unnarrated) sexual violation of Tarwater as if he were a veritable vampire: "His delicate skin had acquired a faint pink tint as if he had refreshed himself on blood" (O'Connor 1988, 472).

Such a horribly anti-sacramental act, such sanguinary feasting on a boy's bodily fluids, is a sign that the image of God can indeed be effaced, as Athanasius declares, "by the wiles of evil spirits." No longer an inward voice, the Devil has assumed outward human likeness in a horribly intimate and violent manner. When the awakening Tarwater discovers the evil that has been perpetrated on him, he responds with appropriate apocalyptic fury:

> The boy's mouth twisted open and to the side as if it were going to displace itself permanently. In a second it appeared to be only a gap that would never be a mouth again. His eyes looked small and seedlike as if while he was asleep, they had been lifted out, scorched, and dropped back into his head. His expression seemed to contract until it reached some point beyond rage or pain. Then a loud cry tore out of him and his mouth fell back into place. (O'Connor 1988, 472)

This is a remarkable scene because it involves the actual appearance of the Devil in American literature at a time when he has largely disappeared from serious cultural discourse. There is no other way to account for Tarwater's multiple assaults on the Gospel of Life except by identifying the Prince of Death, as O'Connor says, "with his specific personality for every occasion" – in this case, for the occasion of Tarwater's at last being able to name the stranger who has been the catalyst for evil from the moment he first refused old Mason's prophetic summons.

In the boy's final driving out of the Devil, the legacy of the elder Tarwater has at last triumphed, and he remains O'Connor's chief exemplar of the holy violence that bears away the kingdom. Old Mason is, in fact, her most convincing fictional portrait of the Christian life as a summons to make startling witness for Christ in the world. As we have seen, the old man is obsessed with his calling as a prophet. Like a latter-day Jonah, he urges God to rain his fury on a world that has forsaken its Savior. He warns this "generation of vipers," as Jesus called it, "to flee from the wrath to come" (Matt. 3:7). To Tarwater's immense dismay, the world does not listen. Far worse, even the Lord himself seems oblivious to Mason's reproaches. The flames do not fall, nor do the wicked writhe. Instead, the sun "rose and set, rose and set, on a world that turned from green to white and green to white and green to white again" (O'Connor 1988, 332). It is not Matthew but Ecclesiastes who seems to comprehend the divine inaction: "The sun also riseth, and the sun goeth down . . . and there is no new thing under the sun" (Eccl. 1:5, 9).

In his own primitive way, Tarwater is forced to confront the problem of historicism – the terrible successiveness of human events. History seems altogether as heartless as nature, a repetitive round of one-thing-after-another, a tale told by an idiot except for the patterns we arbitrarily impose on it. Far from being a perplexity intrinsic to modernity, the bootlessness of history was an assumption that the early Christians took for granted. Paul, for example, believed that all events were mysteriously linked, yet not forming any chain of unbroken progress but rather constituting a steady deterioration and imminent collapse. Christian vocation has always been set against all assumptions about order and progress; it is, instead, a summons to a drastically different reading of history, as William Beardslee makes clear:

> Paul does not think of Christ as calling men to find meaning in or to renew the vitality of that pattern of human tradition and life which we call 'culture'. The social, intellectual, moral and aesthetic forms which constitute culture were for him primarily manifestations of the 'wisdom of this world', and stood in opposition to the new life given by Christ. . . . For him, men cannot find life through culture, or through its enrichment or renewal. Not only individual loyalties, but all the interlocking structures of power and of standards and values stand under the condemnation of God. (Beardslee 1961, 12)

Mason Tarwater's condemnations would seem, in their unremitting ire, to be thoroughly Pauline. Yet they are not. Paul does not regard the divine Word as relentlessly negative and admonitory. Pauline censures are directed only at the sinful and collapsing world; he also insists that God is positively at work within history. First in the Hebrew and Jewish people, then in the life and death and resurrection of Christ, and finally in his set-apart people called the church, God acts within space and time. Since the very origin of things, the Father and Son and Spirit have been creating the one universal community. The scope of divine action has an ever-narrowing focus, until it arrives at Golgotha; for this tenanted tree of divine mercy and judgment, as O'Connor said, has roots deep enough to encircle all the dead, and arms wide enough to embrace all the living. The old prophet's "rage of vision" was not given, he learns, to damn the unfaithful and to justify himself. As his name indicates, Mason is meant to build up and not to tear down – to edify, to construct something good with the stones of redeemed human recalcitrance. He is called, as the narrator makes evident, to a life devoted to "saving and not destruction . . . . He had learned enough to hate the destruction that had to come and not [to hate] all that was going to be destroyed" (O'Connor 1988, 332–33).

As a lone prophet who belongs to no visible church, this holy assailant on God's radically communal kingdom appears to be a contradiction in terms. How can a backwoods solitaire be a prophet of shared life in Christ? The answer lies in his obsession with baptism. Even when baptism is a freely chosen deed rather than the decision of parents and godparents, it signifies much more than one's own solitary decision to follow Jesus. Baptism is to Christians as circumcision is to Jews: a public sign that the universal God of Israel and Jesus and the church has claimed believers for the body of Christ through a life of outward and visible practices. Baptism is a sacramental and regenerative rite precisely because it is not a merely human choice; it is the church's own adoption and incorporation of believers into Christ's community. Baptism is thus a political act through and through: It is a radical transfer of allegiance and citizenship from one regime to another, from a polity that is corrupt and perishing to the only one that is being redeemed and shall stand forever.

Even so, how can Mason Tarwater be anything other than a hermit-baptizer, a solitary John the Baptist who heralds no coming of the communal kingdom? Exceedingly eccentric though he surely is, this wilderness prophet is not an *isolé*. In fact, he seeks serious Christian commonality, if only with his elder and younger nephews. He recognizes that, unlike any benefit the world might bestow, their baptism will make them members of the universal Christian family – his kinsmen in faith far more than blood. Mason understands, albeit in a quite inarticulate way, that the triune Lord wills not to confine himself within the Godhead but to gather a people to himself in order that they might participate in his own communal life.

In his holy seizure of the kingdom, this uncouth *vates* is a wildly exemplary teacher of the fundamentals of the faith. For instance, he rejects the attempt of modern educators to produce future autonomous adults who will make up their own private minds, deciding and defining things for themselves. Such training is not meant to form moral character but to produce good consumers, choosers of one's own "lifestyle" from a smorgasbord of options wherein religious faith becomes merely another "preference." Tarwater seeks, instead, to help his grandnephew to live according to the commitments that are intrinsic to baptismal life in Christ. He believes that time has order and meaning because God is orchestrating the true course of history – from creation and fall, on to incarnation and redemption, finally to consummation. Yet this positive temporal line has its negative counterpart, the horrendous legacy of evil. As we have seen, the demonic also embodies itself in particular individuals and events. The prophetic task of discernment, Mason teaches, is to identify the divergent lineages: the bright red line of redemption which is the boy's true legacy, and the dark arc of evil which would lead to his utter damnation. Accordingly, Tarwater has taught the boy "two complete histories, the history of the world, beginning with Adam, and the history of the schoolteacher . . . " (O'Connor 1988, 366).

Mason Tarwater is too orthodox a Christian to grant evil any sort of dualistic equality with good, making Rayber's unbelief equal to the faith of the saints. He has not schooled the younger Tarwater in the full ancestry of the world's evildoers, therefore, but rather in the roll call of biblical figures who have been radically summoned by God: "Abel and Enoch and Noah and Job, Abraham and Moses, King David and Solomon, and all the prophets, from Elijah who escaped death, to John whose severed head struck terror from a dish" (O'Connor 1988, 340). This list does not consist of those who were morally pure, but of a drunk and a doubter and a deceiver, a whiner and an adulterer and a schemer. As the maker and seller and consumer of illegal whiskey, Mason himself belongs in their line. Yet he has a profoundly biblical understanding of faithfulness. To be a Christian is not to become an ethically untainted person, much less a well-adjusted anthropoid such as Rayber imagines to be a true human being. To live faithfully is to become a person who dwells *coram Deo* – constantly before God – in repeated repentance and lifelong conversion.

Like Jesus and the prophets, moreover, old Tarwater had retreated to the backcountry for direct engagement with the Lord. O'Connor's narrator reports that he would emerge from the woods looking "as if he had been wrestling with a wildcat." Like a latter-day Ezekiel, he was "full of the visions he had seen in [the wildcat's] eyes, wheels of light and strange beasts with giant wings of fire and four heads turned to the four points of the universe" (O'Connor 1988, 334). Whether in prophets ancient or modern, such dreadful confrontations cannot be discounted as the surfacing of mere sub-conscious fears. Young Tarwater recognizes this terrible truth when the old prophet returns from one of his wilderness wrestlings with the Lord: "There was no fire in his uncle's eye and he spoke only of the sweat and stink of the cross, of being born again to die, and of spending eternity eating the bread of life . . . " (O'Connor 1988, 334). Mason Tarwater is like Ezekiel in another regard. Whether the captive Israelites heed or spurn his message matters much less than that God's presence be decisively marked: "And they, whether they will hear, or whether they will forbear, (for they are a rebellious house) yet shall know that there hath been a prophet among them" (Ezek. 2:5).

Ironically, it is through George Rayber's anger at his prophet-uncle for laying the "curse" of Christianity on him that we discover the authenticity of Mason Tarwater's witness. As a school psychologist determined to expose his uncle as a religious fraud, Rayber approaches his scientific studies with alleged objectivity, dispassionately refusing to allow any ties of gratitude or familial regard to limit his research. In the name of "charity," therefore, he invited the aging prophet to live in his home. Yet for the three-month duration of the old prophet's stay, Rayber had covertly analyzed him, observing all his actions and asking sly questions "that meant more than one thing, planting traps around the house and watching him fall into them . . . " (O'Connor 1988, 331). Rayber's cold conclusion, duly published in a scholarly journal, was that the elderly prophet is a throwback to a primitive age, "a type that [is] almost extinct." In perhaps his most heartless act, Rayber asks the unsuspecting Mason to read the conclusion of his academic report: "This fixation of being called by the Lord had its origin in insecurity. He needed the assurance of a call and so he called himself" (O'Connor 1988, 378).

Mason Tarwater is enraged by this reductive reading of his holy calling – by Rayber's psychoanalytic contention that, subconsciously unable to accept his own insignificance, he manufactured his vocation in order to achieve a certain worldly grandeur. The elderly prophet is convinced, on the contrary, that his gospel witness springs from his painful encounters with the unknown and humanly unknowable God, the Deity who has miraculously identified himself in Israel and Christ. Mason complains, for instance, that Rayber the rationalist is cursed for not knowing that there are things he does not know. Yet Mason remains undaunted by Rayber's attempt to reduce his violent vocation to a pathetic psychological need.

> "Called myself!" the old man would hiss, "called myself!" This so enraged him that half the time he could do nothing but repeat it. "Called myself. I called myself. I, Mason Tarwater, called myself! Called myself to be beaten and tied up. Called myself to be spit on and snickered at. Called myself to be struck down in my pride. Called myself to be torn by the Lord's eye. Listen boy," he would say and grab the child by the straps of his overalls and shake him slowly, "even the mercy of the Lord burns." (O'Connor 1988, 341–42)

For all his ranting, the old prophet goes to the heart of the universal Christian calling as Dietrich Bonhoeffer described it in his most celebrated single statement: "Whenever Christ calls us, his call leads us to death" (Bonhoeffer 2001, 87).[7] Rarely does the Christian life in the West constitute a summons to physical death by way of the physical persecution; yet it always remains a subpoena to die to one's own arrogant presumption and to suffer the world's obloquy. Old Mason confessed that he has faced both kinds of violence – his conscience seared by divine judgment and his calling ridiculed by secular contempt. Like the early Christians accused of being atheists because they believed in only one God, Mason refuses to tolerate those who ignore the profoundest of mysteries – the tabernacling of God in our midst. Though no historian of modern culture, he boils with contempt for the Enlightenment idea of benign tolerance, based as it is on a fundamental division of body and soul – the omnicompetent nation-state governing all outward and public affairs from a supposedly neutral stance, while the churches attend to the inward and spiritual matters of the soul that pertain chiefly to the afterlife.[8]

Just as a reverence for mystery opens life to infinite possibility, so does a repudiation of mystery produce a closed cosmos and a clamshell existence. It also reduces others to mere ciphers, to calculable units, to statistical numbers. Rayber's attempt to shrink the prophet's rich and complex and troubled life leaves old Tarwater feeling paralyzed, trapped, even mummified – much as young Tarwater would later feel after being sodomized by the Devil:

> For the length of a minute, he could not move. He felt he was tied hand and foot inside the schoolteacher's head, a space as bare and neat as the cell in the asylum, and was shrinking, drying up to fit it. His eyeballs swerved from side to side as if he were pinned in a straight jacket again. Jonah, Ezekiel, Daniel, he was at that moment all of them – the swallowed, the lowered, the enclosed. (O'Connor 1988, 378)

The elder Tarwater had learned the hard consequences of his unapologetic and intolerant faith when he was sent to a prison for the insane, there to serve a four-year sentence for abducting the youthful Rayber in order to baptize and catechize him. He could have been released much earlier had he been keen enough to recognize that his prophesying on the psychiatric ward served to prolong his incarceration. Yet the prophet's problem was not a mere lack of perception, as young Tarwater thinks. Like John Bunyan, Mason Tarwater had too much integrity to seek his release at the cost of his witness. His faith is as tough as an oak knot, and he is determined to fulfill his divine calling with Pauline disregard for outward conditions. As a preacher of the Word, he is "instant in season, out of season" (2 Tim. 4:2). He is a quite unwitting adherent to the claim of Adrienne von Speyer, a Swiss Catholic mystic and collaborator in Hans Urs von Balthasar's theological work, that Christ's disciples have no holidays from proclaiming the Word, no permission to take time out (von Speyer 1986, 60).

Neither is there any time out for Francis Marion Tarwater since, as Mason had taught him, God's kingdom "hurries terribly near." Having begun his religious life in rebellion against Mason Tarwater's summons to holy violence, so must young Tarwater end his revolt in relation to the elderly prophet who had so drastically embodied it. Nor will it suffice to purge the evil visited upon him by the lavender-colored sodomite, though the youth seeks to drive out the satanic presence by setting the woods afire. He must also confront the scene of his original betrayal. And so he heads home for Powderhead, expecting to meet the awful judgment that he deserves for having incinerated – so he believes – the body of his dead uncle. The farmhouse indeed lies in ashes, but the corn crop has been freshly laid by.

To his immense astonishment and even greater gratitude, Tarwater finds a newly mounded grave with a crude cross planted at its head. Buford, a black farm worker, had dragged the huge prophet from the burning house and given him the reverent burial that the old man had demanded. This utterly unbidden and unmerited gift of grace, this act of sheer transcendent mercy that spares the boy a lifetime of overwhelming guilt, at last frees Tarwater to become the prophet that he is meant to be. The flaming woods that he has set on fire no longer betoken the heat of the boy's anger but the ardor of God's summons:

> He knew that this was the fire that had encircled Daniel, that had raised Elijah from the earth, that had spoken to Moses and would in the instant speak to him. He threw himself to the ground and with his face against the dirt of the grave, he heard the command. GO WARN THE CHILDREN OF GOD OF THE TERRIBLE SPEED OF MERCY. (O'Connor 1988, 478)

That prophets repent in sackcloth and ashes, abasing themselves in abject humility, does not make them immune to being slain by the very people they are sent to save. In a letter commenting on Francis Marion Tarwater's postfictional fate, O'Connor observed that "the children of God . . . will dispatch him pretty quick" (O'Connor 1979, 342). Even if the young prophet dies in order to realize his mission, his death will not invalidate his calling. He has seen what ultimately counts – that the cross is not a knife driven into the heart of the world to rend its life; it is the only tree, as we have heard O'Connor confess, whose roots encircle all the dead and whose branches embrace all the living. In the end, young Tarwater's vision reaches even to paradise, for he is given a glimpse of Old Mason feeding eagerly among the great heavenly throng of the redeemed, as the multiplied loaf is passed among them. The boy knows that this hunger for the bread of life is also his own craving, that it belongs not to him alone but to every living soul, and that, as St. Augustine said, no one can rest until this longing is satisfied:

> He felt his hunger no longer as a pain but as a tide. He felt it rising in himself through time and darkness, rising through the centuries, and he knew that it rose in a line of men whose lives were chosen to sustain it, who would wander the world, strangers from that violent country where the silence is never broken except to shout the truth. (O'Connor 1988, 478)

That O'Connor can envision the beatific realm as "violent country" inhabited by violent men who are strangers on the earth reveals her abiding conviction that there are two kinds of violence, one earthly and the other heavenly. As we have seen, there are those who make a violent assault on Christ's kingdom by seeking to vacate it. They would replace our fumbling, struggling but finally redemptive existence before God with a simulacrum. In the name of freedom and autonomy, the Raybers of this world would create an allegedly benign system wherein the scientific mastery of the physical order is violently applied to the moral order, if only with a subtle inward violence whose outward consequences become only slowly evident. To treat human beings as impersonal objects having no transcendent *telos*, controlling and manipulating them for the alleged immanent good of anthropoid contentment, is to produce the greatest of calamities.[9]

That such a sub-human vision often passes as a truly human accomplishment is proof, for O'Connor, that it is both demonically deceptive and satanically successful – indeed, that it is the largely unacknowledged cause of misery in the modern world.[10] Hence her attempt, in *The Violent Bear It Away*, not only to name the demonry but also to provide an alternative to it. For we have also witnessed a second and salutary kind of assault on the kingdom as fictionally embodied by both Mason and Francis Tarwater. They are indeed scandalous figures. Yet their offense lies not chiefly in the violence that they visit on others but in the holy ferocity that they subject themselves to. Only because they have been "torn by the Lord's eye" of divine judgment can they become prophets of divine mercy, bearing away the kingdom of Heaven, not selfishly for themselves, but for whosoever else will come – baptismally shaming the Devil by participating in the Christian pilgrimage, first in its this-worldly intensity, and finally in the fierce blessedness of life in the world to come.

Ralph C. Wood

References

Athanasius, Saint 2002. *On the Incarnation*. Crestwood, New York: St. Vladimir's Seminary Press.

Balthasar, Hans Urs von 1988. *Dare We Hope "That All Men Be Saved"?* Trans. David Kipp and Lothar Krauth. San Francisco: Ignatius.

Beardslee, William A. 1961. *Human Achievement and Divine Vocation in the Message of Paul*. Naperville, Illinois: Alec R. Allenson.

Bonhoeffer, Dietrich 2001. *Discipleship*. Trans. Barbara Green and Reinhard Krauss. Minneapolis: Fortress.

Daniélou, Jean 1956. *The Bible and the Liturgy*. Notre Dame: University of Notre Dame.

Lewis, C. S. 1996a. *The Abolition of Man*. New York: Simon & Schuster.

——— 1996b. *Screwtape Letters*. New York: Simon & Schuster.

O'Connor, Flannery 1988. *Collected Works*. New York: Library of America.

——— 1979. *The Habit of Being*: Letters ed. Sally Fitzgerald. New York: Farrar Straus Giroux.

——— 1970. *Mystery and Manners*. Selected and edited by Robert and Sally Fitzgerald. New York: Farrar, Straus & Giroux.

——— 1964. *Three*. New York: New American Library.

Russell, Jeffrey Burton 1986. *Mephistopheles in the Modern World*. Ithaca: Cornell University Press.

von Speyer, Adrienne 1986. *They Followed His Call: Vocation and Asceticism*, tr. Erasmo Leiva-Merikakis. San Francisco: Ignatius.

von Speyer, Adrienne 1986. *They Followed His Call: Vocation and Asceticism*. Trans. Erasmo Leiva-Merikakis. San Francisco: Ignatius.

Wood, Ralph C. 2004. *Flannery O'Connor and the Christ-Haunted South*. Grand Rapids: Eerdmans.

——— 2009. "Hospitality as the Gift Greater than Tolerance: G. K. Chesterton's *The Ball and the Cross*." Logos 12:4: 258–85.

Wright, N. T. 2006. *Simply Christian: Why Christianity Makes Sense*. San Francisco: HarperSanFrancisco.

Endnotes

1 Introduction

1 It seems, nevertheless, that what scientists and historians actually seek from their work is largely understanding, and not knowledge in a narrow sense, though, like the ancient Greeks, whose words for knowledge (*epistêmê, gnôsis*) included and even stressed understanding, we often quite properly use the word "knowledge" to *include* understanding. See Roberts and Wood 2007, especially chapters 1 and 2. According to the *Oxford English Dictionary*, the word "epistemology" was first coined around the middle of the 19th century. But philosophers had been discussing the nature and value of knowledge since almost the beginning of philosophy, and the ancients thought its value vested primarily in what we call understanding and wisdom. See, for example, Plato's *Republic*, Books 6 and 7, Aristotle's *Metaphysics*, Book 1, and Aristotle's *Nicomachean Ethics*, Book 6.

2 We associate "therapy" and "the therapeutic" especially with the past century and the present one, and we may be inclined to think psychotherapy – strategies for improving the functioning of our thoughts and affections through talking, learning, and a special kind of relationship with a therapist – a distinctly modern phenomenon. But in this we suffer from historical myopia. The ancient world was populated by many approaches closely analogous to the modern therapies. They differed slightly from modern therapies in the kind of outcomes they aimed for and to some extent in the strategies employed. In both the modern and the ancient contexts many therapies compete for clients – in the modern context, Rogerian, psychodynamic, Jungian, Adlerian, cognitive-behavioral, family therapies, etc., and in the ancient Stoic, Epicurean, skeptic, cynic, and peripatetic, to name the most famous schools. Christians had their own brand(s) to offer. (Note the medical language that surfaces from time to time in Kruschwitz's paper on the tradition of the seven "deadly" sins.) For a survey of the modern therapies, see Corsini and Wedding 2003; on the Hellenistic therapies, see Nussbaum 1992; on ancient Christian therapy, see the "soul-therapy" of Prudentius, *Psychomachia* (4th century) and Boethius (6th century), *The Consolation of Philosophy*. All of the above therapies, including the Christian, can be seen as purveyors of one kind of "wisdom" or another, where that wisdom is seen as a kind of cognitive-affective *health* or wellbeing. If we think that reading great texts in the Christian university can and ought to contribute to a therapy of desire, then we suppose the outcome we aim at is a kind of health and wellbeing, and that the foolishness it overcomes is (at least a potential) pathology and sickness.

Homer

1 In 1998, The Modern Library Board named Joyce's *Ulysses* first on the list of "100 Best Novels" of the Twentieth Century. The Radcliffe Publishing Course placed Joyce's work sixth.

2 Homer, *The Odyssey* trans., Robert Fagles (New York: Penguin Books, 1996), I, 112. Text references are to book and line numbers of this edition unless otherwise indicated.

3 Douglas V. Henry, David Lyle Jeffrey, and Robert C. Roberts made numerous helpful suggestions to this essay for which I am grateful.

Plato

1 Lucy Beckett makes the point with beautiful reference to Scripture. With Psalm 67:4 of the Latin Vulgate in mind, she writes, "If we transpose Plato's answers into words we know well, we find that they tell us we should live in the love of God, so as to live at last in the sight of God, *in conspectu Dei*, with the full force of the double meaning of the words: 'in God's sight of us; in our sight of God'" (Beckett 2006, 49). The Psalm text Beckett cites reads *Et iusti epulentur exultent in conspectu Dei*. In words laden with prayerful longing, the text might be rendered in English as: "And let the just feast and rejoice in God's sight." Most English translations of Protestant provenance have the same text at Psalm 68:3.

2 Scripture quotations marked (ESV) are from *The Holy Bible*, English Standard Version® (ESV®), copyright 2001 by Crossway Bibles, a publishing ministry of Good News Publishers. Used by permission. All rights reserved.

3 My translations. References to Plato's texts follow the numbering convention of Henricus Stephanus. Where other classical and patristic sources are cited I include book, chapter, and line references as appropriate. When not of my own translation, particular editions cited are included in the reference list.

4 Cf. Clement of Alexandria 1994, 5.14, where Clement offers the certainly unsound argument that Plato, *inter alia*, plagiarized from the Hebrews. He goes so far as to intuit an inchoate doctrine of the Trinity in the *Timaeus*. The point to be taken is not that "Plato read Moses," as Clement's position is sometimes described, but rather that Plato's philosophical theology was deemed compatible with Christian doctrine.

5 Pieper makes a similar point. ". . . Plato is not only giving expression to something that has been passed down to him from long ago . . . but is at the same time imparting to that tradition, now firmly entrenched, a powerful impetus, so much so that his great disciple, the more 'critically' and 'pragmatically' minded Aristotle, will explicitly take up this thought and elaborate on it: Not only is the wisdom sought in philosophy actually the property of God alone, but what the philosophizing person is actually inquiring after is God himself" (Pieper 2006, 159).

6 See Hunter 2004, 99 where he notes that "detailed parallels between the two speeches [of Diotima and Alcibiades] have been noted by many," including Bury 1932, lx–lxii; C. Riedweg 1987, 14–16; and Sheffield 2001, 196–7.

7 Cf. Steiner 1996, 89–111.

Aristotle

1 I am grateful to Scott Moore for comments on an earlier draft of this paper that led to its improvement. Quotations are from the translations of H. Rackham, W. D. Ross, and Roger Crisp.

2 I owe this last point to Talbot Brewer (2009, especially chapter 4).

3 It seems that we must take "fearless" to mean, not *completely without fear*, but *without excessive fear*.

4 Socrates seems to allow for courage (*andreia*) in facing dangers at sea, illness, poverty, and affairs of state, as well as in fighting desire and pleasure (Plato 1997, 191d–e).

5 Another possible remark relates courage to pleasure or pain. In 2.3 he tells us that "the person who enjoys facing up to danger, or at least does not feel it painful to do so, is courageous, while he who does find it painful is a coward" (1104b7–9, Crisp transla-

tion, 26). But at 3.9 he says, "people are called courageous for enduring what is painful; so courage involves pain, and is justly praised, since it is more difficult to endure what is painful than to abstain from what is pleasant" (1117a32–34). "So it is not true, then, except in so far as one achieves the end [that is, whatever one is aiming at in the virtuous action], that the exercise of every virtue is pleasant" (1117b15–16, Crisp translation, 54). Perhaps these sayings are ultimately consistent, but in the absence of further explanation it looks as though Aristotle vacillates on this question.

6 All Bible quotations are from the Revised Standard Version.

7 For example, Rackham translates *ou gar timôrêtikos ho praos, alla mallo sungnômonikos* "the gentle-tempered man is not prompt to seek redress for injuries, but rather inclined to forgive them" (231). Martha Nussbaum (1996, 315) translates "for the mild person is not given to revenge, but is inclined to be forgiving." Crisp translates "because the even-tempered person is inclined not to revenge so much as to forgiveness" (73).

8 See Griswold 2007, 4–8.

Virgil

1 Ziolkowski 1997, vii. On the reception of Virgil, see especially Comparetti 1997 (originally published 1885); Thomas 2001; Kallendorf 2007; Putnam and Ziolkowski 2008.

2 Written about forty years before the birth of Christ, this Eclogue prophesies the birth of a miraculous child who will usher in a new Golden Age in human history; see Benko 1980. Virgil died two decades later, in 19 BC, before performing his final revisions on the *Aeneid.*

3 For a comprehensive treatment of Virgil's importance to Augustine, see MacCormack 1998.

4 On this sort of reductionist "Christian" reading of the Dido episode in late antiquity and the Middle Ages, see, e.g., Watkins 1995, 39–40.

5 Unless otherwise noted, all translations are my own; I have aimed for literalness rather than poetic merit. Of the many good translations available for reading and teaching, I generally recommend either Fitzgerald 1990 or Fagles 2006.

6 See Mackie 1990; Hejduk 2009b.

7 Lewis 1942, 19.

8 On the ongoing debate between "optimistic" and "pessimistic" readings of the *Aeneid* (crude and now unfashionable terms, occasionally useful but always to be put in scare quotes), see Harrison 1990, 1–20; Perkell 1999, 14–22; Schmidt 2001.

9 See especially Reckford 1961; Harrison 1989; Panoussi 2009.

10 Jenkyns 1985, 65.

11 In my opinion, the importance of this aspect of the *Aeneid*'s "intertextuality" is underappreciated even by many Classicists, and so I beg my reader's forgiveness for the rather extensive citation of my own work in this section.

12 See Dyson 2001, 29–49.

13 See Dyson 2001, 50–54.

14 The best introduction to Servius is Goold 1970, which has one of the most winsome openings of any scholarly article: "The principal issue discussed in this article permits of a simple formulation, 'Is the Helen Episode authentic?' and of a simple answer, 'No'. But the road which leads from the enunciation of the thesis to the final QED of the proof is long and winding, typical less of the unswerving advance of a Euclidean theorem than of the anfractuousness of a drunkard's homeward path" (60).

15 Reckford 1974 is another article that should not be missed, especially by lovers of Tolkien.

16 See Dyson 2001, 184–94.
17 See Dyson 2001, 210–27.
18 The best introduction to Virgil's "epic successors" is that of Hardie 1993.
19 On Ovid's comic treatment of Jupiter here, see Segal 2001.
20 See Hejduk 2009a, 51.
21 On Juturna as a voice of protest in the *Aeneid*, see Perkell 1997.
22 Shippey 2000, vii, for instance, lists Le Guin along with Tolkien, Orwell, Golding, Vonnegut, and Pynchon as one of the authors of the twentieth century's "most representative and distinctive works."
23 See Lyne 1987, 114–22; Dyson 1999.
24 See Thomas 1988, 126–46; Dyson 1996, 209–10.
25 See Hawkins 1991, 117–21.
26 See Ball 1991.
27 On the counterpoint of "voices" in the *Aeneid*, see Parry 1963; Lyne 1987.
28 See Hejduk 2009b.
29 See Mazzotta 1979, 220–21, and Ps. 119: 105, "Thy word is a lamp unto my feet and a light unto my path."
30 As Allan 1989 argues, there may be hope yet for Virgil's soul – but only as a result of the incessant prayer inspired by this pain.

Augustine

1 I am thinking of Augustine's wry observation, after he has riveted the reader with his own livid story of sin and redemption, that "Men are a race curious to know of other men's lives, but slothful to correct their own" (*Confessions* 10.3.3). All translations of the *Confessions* are taken from Augustine 2006.
2 Other scenes include, but are not limited to, Augustine's journey to Carthage (*Conf.* 3.1.1 vs. *Aen.* 4), Augustine's rejection of marriage as incompatible with his mission (*Conf.* 6.12.21 vs. *Aen.* 4.440, 449), and Monica as Euryalus's mother (*Conf.* 6.1.1 vs. *Aen.* 9.491–96). Cf. Bennett 1988, 61–65; O'Meara 1963, 259, 260.
3 Marrou later retracted this statement (Marrou 1949, 665–72).
4 Augustine summarizes this in terms of the three parts of the soul at the end of book one: "But in this lay my sin: that I sought pleasure, nobility, and truth not in God but in the beings He had created, myself and others. Thus I fell into sorrow and confusion and error. Thanks be to Thee, my Joy and my Glory and my Hope and my God: thanks be to Thee for Thy gifts" (1.20.31). The appetite for physical pleasure is ultimately a groaning for happiness in God, and thus the attempt to satisfy it with created goods instead of the creator ends in sorrow rather than joy (used here as an epithet for God Himself). The same is true both with the desire for nobility – which when pursued outside of God results in confusion and humiliation rather than glory – and with the desire for truth, which when misdirected leads to error rather than hope or confidence (*fiducia*), the fruit of faith.
5 Augustine even goes out of his way to say that he took St. Paul's epistle off of a *lusoria* or gaming table (8.6.14).
6 The word is *balaneion* – a bath (9.12.32). Augustine mentions it in order to explain its etymological meaning as something that drives out [*ball?*] sorrow from the mind [*anua*]. In 3.4.8 Augustine also discusses the meaning of another Greek concept, "philosophy," but most manuscripts have this word in its Latinized form.
7 For more on Augustine's use of Virgil in the *Confessions*, q.v. note 2 above.
8 The following section has been excerpted in large part from Foley 2003.
9 *et quid mihi proderat quod annos natus ferme viginti, cum in manus meas venissent aristotelica quaedam, quas appellant decem categories... legi eas solus et intellexi?*

10 *quid hoc mihi proderat, quando et oberat, cum etiam te, deus meus, mirabiliter simplicem atque incommutabilem, illis decem praedicamentis putans quidquid esset omnino comprehensum, sic intellegere conarer* (4.16.29).

11 O'Donnell posits that the *Categories* are mentioned here to account for the bad thinking that will culminate in Augustine's book *de pulchro et apto* (*ibid.*).

12 The *Categories*, it should be remembered, are concerned with the various ways to predicate the presence of concrete things, especially with respect to human beings and animals. Harold P. Cooke notes as much in introducing his English translation of the work: "Hence we may infer that when Aristotle lays down the Ten Categories… the Subject which he has wholly, or at least principally, in his mind is an individual Man" (Aristotle 1938, 3, 4).

13 Interestingly enough, the same point emerges years later in Augustine's arguments against Julian of Eclanum. Julian, a young, proud, and talented defender of the Pelagian heresy, cites the *Categories* several times to justify his positions (cf. *Against Julian* 1.4.12, 2.10.37, 3.2.7). Augustine replies that while the teaching of the *Categories* is correct, Julian is misusing it (5.14.51, 6.20.64, resp.).

14 Q.v. Cleary 2002, 29.

15 *aeternitate, sicut deus omnia; tempore, sicut flos fructum; electione, sicut fructus florem; origine, sicut sonus cantum* (*ibid.*).

16 Augustine does not mention the fifth priority most likely because its subject matter is not germane to his present concerns.

17 Augustine's development of this priority in terms of matter and form (*sonus eius materies eius est… formatur… ut cantus sit* [12.29.40]) most likely accounts for his changing the name.

18 "La priorité selon l'éternité comporte en effet que l'on saisisse le paradoxe d'un Dieu créant immuablement des êtres muables; c'est une priorité *de transcendance*…" (trans. mine).

19 For two possible objections to this thesis and my response to them, see Foley 2003, 619–21.

20 O'Donnell counts approximately two hundred references in the *Confessions* to a Ciceronian oratorical work or philosophical dialogue (O'Donnell 1992, 3: 454, 455).

21 As "Cicero," 3.4.7, 8.7.17; as "Tully" (*Tullius*) 3.5.9, 5.6.11.

22 *Sed liber ille ipsius exhortationem continet ad philosophiam, et vocatur Hortensius. Ille vero liber mutavit affectum meum, et ad teipsum, Domine, mutavit preces meas, et vota ac desideria mea fecit alia. Viluit mihi repente omnis vana spes, et immortalitatem sapientiae concupiscebam aestu cordis incredibili; et surgere coeperam ut ad te redirem* (3.4.7).

23 *At ego adulescens miser, valde miser, in exordio ipsius adulescentiae etiam petieram a te castitatem, et dixeram: Da mihi castitatem et continentiam, sed noli modo* (8.7.17). Augustine's testimony here about the *Hortensius'* advice on continence, incidentally, is corroborated by fragment 81 (Mueller).

24 *non te cogitabam, deus, in figura corporis humani: ex quo audire aliquid de sapientia coepi, semper hoc fugi.*

25 Cf. 8.2.3. Elsewhere Augustine interprets St. Paul's warning against philosophy "according to the elements of the world" (Col. 2:8b) as a warning against any philosophy incapable of understanding "another world utterly remote from the senses," i.e., a philosophy that understands all reality as material (*On Order* 1.11.32; cf. *Against the Academics* 3.19.42,).

26 Cf. Epistle 118.4.23–25, where Augustine, offering a careful analysis of *De natura deorum* 1.10,11.26, concludes that Cicero was a "true" Platonist who knew how and why

the various materialist philosophies of the pre-Socratics – to say nothing of the Stoics and Epicureans – were false.

27 Cf. *On the Trinity* 14.19.26 and *Against Julian* 4.14.72, 4.15.78, all of which presuppose that the *Hortensius* distinguishes spiritual goods from corporeal.

28 *ita enim et mihi liquido sensisse videbantur, ut vulgo habentur, etiam illorum intentionem nondum intellegenti* (italics added). Cf. his similar qualification at 5.14.24.

29 *eos putarem longe in alia, quam vulgo creditum est, fuisse sententia.*

30 Ep. 1.1; Ep. 118.3.16,17; cf. *Against the Academics* 3.17.38.

31 Cf. *Against the Academics* 3.17.38.

32 *carni deditos homines* (Ep. 118.3.20).

33 *Quid enim convenientius pecori est, quam putari animam corpus esse?* (Ep. 1.1).

34 Like his fellow Academics, Cicero also wrote esoterically – at least in Augustine's opinion (cf. Ep. 118.4.23–25; *Against the Academics* 2.18.60, 3.16.36, 3.18.41). In fact, it is uncertain whether Augustine read any other Academic besides Cicero. In any event, Augustine took seriously the likelihood of esotericism among non-Christians. He lingered with the Manicheans for as long as he did because he incorrectly suspected that they were being esoteric. "I did not agree with them," Augustine writes, "but thought they were concealing in these veils some important secret they would later divulge" (*On the Happy Life* 1.4).

35 Cf. Strauss 1952, especially the introduction and second chapter; Strauss 1989; Strauss 1959; and Bagley 1992.

36 With a rise of interest in the occult, the "Bible code," and other such bizarre fare, "esotericism" is becoming an increasingly muddled term. Although Strauss's usage, which I am following, risks becoming lost in this muddle, it does have the advantage of restoring the term to its original meaning. According to Varro the distinction between esoteric and exoteric may be traced to Pythagoras, who distinguished his advanced students, to whom he told his most profound teachings, from his less advanced, from whom he kept certain things. The former he called *esoterikoi,* the latter *exoterikoi*. See *Oxford English Dictionary*, 2nd ed., s.v. "Esoteric, a. and n.," and Crosson 2005, 76–79.

37 Cf. *Against the Academics* 2.10.24; Ep. 1.2. The issue of esotericism raises the question whether Augustine himself wrote esoterically; the answer depends on how one defines esotericism. If esotericism is the art of concealment by means of noble lies (which seems to be Strauss's operative definition), then Augustine was not an esoteric writer. He was one of the few Church Fathers who categorically condemned lying, and there is no evidence that his writings point in one direction exoterically and in a contradictory direction esoterically. While Augustine is sympathetic to the ancient philosophers who felt it necessary to write esoterically to avoid persecution, he cannot join them for one simple reason: the incarnation. God's humbling Himself and taking the form of man allows not just the few but the many for the first time to "return to their very selves and even gaze upon their fatherland without the bickering of disputations" (*Against the Academics* 3.19.42). This places a certain onus on the believer to bear witness to the truth, and hence to avoid incurring any suspicion that the doctrine which he is preaching is in any way concocted. For a Christian to use a medium which relies heavily on noble lies would do exactly that. Esotericism after the Incarnation is thus not only superfluous for the Christian, but counterproductive. Augustine views the literally duplicitous character of classical esotericism, with its use of noble lies and its assumptions regarding an unbridgeable gap between the few and the many, as essentially different from sacred scripture's literary and typological polysemy, from the church's discipline of the secret (*disciplina arcani*), and from Christian literature in general.

However, Augustine does not deny that there is a difference between the few and the many, nor does he think that the Incarnation eliminates the fallen world's hatred of the light. Thus, great discretion and caution in expressing the truth are still necessary. I give one example of how Augustine exercises such caution in the conclusion to this essay when I speak of the *Confessions*' "revisal" quality and its silence about the positive value of the authors whom he earlier on excoriates. Note, however, that this example does not involve lying, for failing to mention a truth and uttering a lie are, Augustine points out, two different things, and only the latter is inherently sinful (*On Lying* 10.17; *Against Lying* 10.23).

38 *immo quaeramus diligentius et non desperemus. ecce iam non sunt absurda in libris ecclesiasticis, quae absurda videbantur, et possunt aliter atque honeste intellegi (ibid).*

39 *iam quidem servientibus tibi, sed adhuc superbiae scholam tamquam in pausatione anhelantibus* (9.4.7).

40 *Against the Academics* 1.1.4, 3.4.7, 3.14.31; *On the Happy Life* 1.4, 2.10.

41 On Augustine's conscious imitation of the Academics, see Epistle 1.1. On the relationship between the Ciceronian and Cassiciacum dialogues, see Foley 1999.

42 See Robert Roberts's introduction to this volume.

43 Like the rest of Augustine's writings, however, the *Confessions* is able to do this without the use of lies and is thus decisively different from the writings of the Academics and of other esoteric authors. See note 37.

Marie France

1 The annotated bibliography edited by Glyn Burgess (1977–2007) is a very useful reference tool for teachers of Marie de France.

2 Early Old French works include the epic *Song of Roland* and hagiographic *Life of Saint Alexis*, for example. It is worth noting that the development of the vernacular canon took a unique turn in Anglo-Norman England. After the conquest of England by William the Conqueror and the ensuing installment of French-born officials to important offices at court and in the Church, French quickly eclipsed English as the official spoken language. Along with Latin, it also became one of the official written languages of the clergy, government, and universities.

3 For an overview of studies on the General Prologue, see Logan Whalen 2008, esp. 35–54.

4 "Quant uns granz biens est mult oïz,/ dunc a primes est il fluriz,/ e quant loëz est de plusurs,/ dunc a espandues ses flurs" (vv. 5–8).

5 "Ki de vice se vuelt defendre,/ estudïer deit e entendre/ e grevos uevre comencier;/ par ceo s'en puet plus esloignier/ e de grant dolur delivrer" (vv. 21–27).

6 Ovid was widely read and commented upon in twelfth-century schools, where tales from the *Metamorphoses* formed the basis of grammatical exercises (see Glendinning 1986). The discussion of *Guigemar* that follows draws heavily on Murray and Yancey 2010.

7 "Le livre Ovide, u il enseigne/ coment chascuns s'amur estreigne" (vv. 239–40).

8 All biblical quotations are from the Douay-Rheims translation of the Vulgate. Marie and her audience would have read the Bible in Jerome's Latin version.

9 "N'i trueve clef ne serreüre" (v. 675).

10 "Il la saisist par le mantel/ od lui l'en meinë el chastel. Mult fu liez de la troveüre,/ kar bele esteit a desmesure" (vv. 705–08).

11 "Ieo la trovai, si la tendrai!/ Encuntre vus la defendrai!" (vv. 851–52).

12 See Murray and Yancey 2010.

13 The following pages take up, and summarize, my arguments in "Marie de France, Ethicist?" forthcoming in *Modern Philology*.

14 "…un bachelers,/ bien conëuz entre ses pers/ de pruësce, de grant valur,/ e volentiers faiseit honur./ Mult turneoit e despendeit/ e bien donot ceo qu'il aveit./ La feme sun veisin ama." (vv. 17–23).
15 "Tant pur le bien que ele oï/ tant pur ceo qu'il ert pres de li" (vv. 27–28).
16 "Tant i estut, tant i leva/ que sis sire s'en curuça/ e meinte feiz li demanda/ pur quei levot e u ala" (vv. 79–82).
17 " 'Lasse,' fete le, 'mal m'estait!/ Ne purrai mes la nuit lever/ n'aler a la fenestre ester/ u ieo soil mun ami veer" (vv. 126–29).
18 Teachers of British Literature may be interested in assigning, in addition to Marie's *lai*, the Middle English translation; see Archibald 2000 and McCreesh 1999.
19 "En Bretaigne jadis maneient/ dui chevalier; veisin esteient./ Riche hume furent e manant,/ e chevalier pruz e vaillant" (vv. 3–6).
20 Envy is also a major theme in the Prologue to *Guigemar*.
21 "Kar ele ert feinte e orguilluse/ e mesdisanz e enviüse" (vv. 27–28).
22 "Ki sur altrui mesdit e ment,/ ne set mie qu'a l'oil li pent" (vv. 87–88).
23 "Un des enfanz m'estuet murdrir" (v. 92).
24 "Mielz le voil vers deu amender/ que mei hunir e vergunder" (vv. 93–94).
25 "S'entur li fussiez enceintiee/ durement en iert curuciee" (vv. 293–94).
26 "En un cofre les enferma/ le cofre fist od sei porter,/ nel volt lessier ne bliër" (vv. 314–16).
27 "Jadis par ma grant vileinie/ de ma veisine dis folie./ De ses dous enfanz mesparlai:/ vers mei meïsmes mesdit ai./ Veritez est, ieo enceintai,/ dous filles oi, l'une en celai./ A un mustier la fis geter/ e vostre paile od li porter/ e l'anel que vus me donastes/ quant vus primes od mei parlastes./ Ne vus puet mie estre celé:/ le drap e l'anel ai trové./ Nostre fille ai ci conette/, que par ma folie oi perdue./ E ja est ceo la dameisele/ qui tan test pruz e sage e bele,/ que li chevaliers a amee,/ ki sa serur a espusee" (vv. 477–94).
28 Named after the ash tree, which, in contrast to the hazel (La Codre), does not bear material fruit, Fresne has, through her great act of charity, exhibited spiritual fruit.
29 Even La Codre "later made a rich marriage" (Marie 1999, 67).
30 It is not surprising, then, that *Eliduc* incorporates far more secondary characters than the other *lais* (Brumlik 1997).
31 "Amurs i lance sun message/ qui la sumunt de lui amer,/ palir la fist e suspirer" (vv. 304–06).
32 "De sa femme li remembra,/ e cum il li asseüra/ que bone fei li portereit/ e leialment se cuntendreit" (vv. 323–26).
33 It is interesting to note that Eliduc thinks only of the recent promise he made to his wife, whereas his marital vows do not seem to preoccupy him in the least.
34 "A las, fet il, mal ai erré!" (v. 585). Note how Marie's choice of verb (*errer*), translated by Burgess and Busby "I have behaved badly," might also be rendered as "how badly I have erred" or "strayed from the true path," echoing the popular *topos* of the paths of the righteous and the wicked in Psalm 1.
35 "Trop ai en cest païs esté!/ Mar vi unkes ceste cuntree!/ Une meschine i ai amee,/ Guilliadun, la fille al rei,/ mult durement e ele mei./ Quant si de li m'estuet partir,/ un de nus estuvra murir/ u ambedous, ester ceo puet./ E nepurquant aler m'estuet;/ mis sire m'a par brief mandé/ e par sairement conjuré,/ e si ma femme d'altre part./ Or me covient que ieo me guart!/ Ieo ne puis mie remaneir,/ ainz m'en irai par estuveir" (vv. 586–600).
36 "S'a m'amie esteie espusez,/ nel suffereit crestiëntez" (vv. 601–02).
37 I agree with Maurizio Virdis (1993), who views the storm as the moment in *Eliduc* when the text undergoes a significant thematic shift.

38 Femme leial espuse avez/ e sur cele altrë en menez/ cuntre deu e cuntre la lei,/ cuntre dreiture e cuntre fei" (vv. 835–38).

39 "Lessiez la nus geter en mer/ si poüm sempres ariver" (vv. 839–40).

40 "Desur sun vis cheï pasmee,/ tute pale, desculuree./ En la pasmeisun demura,/ qu'el ne revint ne suspira" (vv. 853–56).

41 And, by killing the sailor prior to throwing him overboard, there is no room for a miraculous intervention by the Christian God, who saves Jonah in the Old Testament by sending him the great fish. Seen in this light, Eliduc's ability to take control of the ship and steer it to land does not imply that God sanctions his actions. Instead, I believe we must read the boat's sailing back and forth along the coast prior to the sailor's murder (Marie 1999, 121) as a sign that Eliduc can still, at that point, reveal the truth to Guilliadun. Instead, by throwing the sailor overboard, he effectively charts another, radically different, course.

42 On the role of tombs and memory in Marie's *Lais* (including *Eliduc* and *Laüstic*), see Callahan (1999–2000).

43 Françoise Denis (2002) views the renunciation and self-sacrifice of Guildelüec as a form of feminine heroism.

44 "Del tut le voil quite clamer,/ e si ferai mun chief veler" (vv. 1101–02).

45 The full passage (*Patrologia Latina* 1844–45 and 1862–65), vol. 182, cols. 998B-C). "Verumtamen quia carneles sumus, et de carnis concupiscentia nascimur, necesse est ut cupiditas vel amor noster a carne incipiat; quae si recto ordine dirigitur, quibusdam suis gradibus duce gratia proficiens, spiritu tandem consummabitur: quia non prius quod spirituale, sed quod animale, deinde quod spirituale (I Cor. XV, 46). Et prius necesse est portemus imaginem terrestris, deinde coelestis" (since we are carnal and are born of the flesh, it must be that our desire and our love shall have its beginning in the flesh. But rightly guided by the grace of God through these degrees, it will have its consummation in the spirit: for that was not first which is spiritual but that which is natural; and afterward that which is spiritual. And we must bear the image of the earthly first, before we can bear the image of the heavenly.)

Aquinas

1 Brian Davies explains the difference between the frequent private disputations that were designed by the master, and the less common, more formal public disputations that included guests and might be ordered by their questions, in his "Introduction" to Aquinas 2003, 10–11.

2 For an excellent introduction to this movement, see Harmless 2004.

3 Only recently has a complete English translation of the important texts become available in Evagrius 2003.

4 Evagrius employs the Stoic distinction between "that which depends on us" and "that which does not depend on us" to describe the roles of thoughts and demons. See Stewart 2005, 5.

5 Soon after his death in 399, Evagrius and others were accused of heresy in the first Origenist controversy. Following a second controversy that arose in Palestine a century later, his speculative writings were condemned at the Second Council of Constantinople in 553. Nevertheless, he had an immense influence on the theology of Maximus the Confessor (c.580–662), though Maximus labeled him a heretic. Four of Evagrius's ascetical works were mistakenly (or perhaps cautiously) attributed to Nilus of Ancyra (d. c.430) and anthologized in the *Philokalia* (1782), the major collection of spiritual guidance in Eastern Orthodoxy. For an account of how Evagrius's name was virtually occluded in the history of Christian theology until the rediscovery of his ascetical writings in the twentieth century, see Harmless 2008.

6 Since Evagrius calls the vices "passions" (*path?*), using the negative connotation of this term pioneered by the Stoics, he sometimes identifies the goal of ascetic self-examination as the "passionlessness" (*apatheia*) that makes selfless love (*agap?*) and knowledge (*gnosis*) of God possible. Jerome scurrilously lampoons Evagrius for publishing "a book of maxims on apathy" that instructs monks to become "either a stone or a God" (*Letter to Ctesiphon, 133.3*). Cassian avoids this line of objection to *apatheia* by substituting "purity of heart" (*puritas cordis*) – a term related to Jesus' beatitude "Blessed are the pure of heart, for they will see God" (Matt. 5:8). Other scripture passages support Cassian's usage (e.g., 1 Tim.1:5 and 2 Tim. 2:22). See Driscoll 1999.

7 While Aquinas refers directly to Cassian's works only four times in *On Evil*, he cites Gregory's *Morals on the Book of Job* ninety-six times. In the parallel passages on virtues and vices in *Summa Theologiae* II.I and II.II, he cites Cassian nine times and Gregory almost five hundred times.

8 Gregory streamlines Cassian's list of vices in three ways: (1) he removes pride (*superbia*) from the list and describes it as the spiritual source of the other seven, for Scripture teaches "pride is the beginning of all sin" (Sirach 10:13); (2) he drops spiritual apathy (*acedia*) from the list, presumably because it is close in meaning to sadness (*tristitia*); and (3) he inserts envy. Gregory lists the vices in (almost) inverse order from the earlier tradition: "But seven principal vices, as [pride's] first progeny, spring doubtless from this poisonous root (*de hoc virulenta radice proferuntur*), namely, vain glory (*inanis gloria*), envy (*invidia*), anger (*ira*), sadness (*tristitia*), avarice (*avaritia*), gluttony (*ventris ingluvies*), lust (*luxuria*)" (Gregory 1844–1850, XXXI, 45, n. 87). In *On Evil*, Aquinas generally follows Gregory's list, but replaces sadness (*tristitia*) with spiritual apathy (*acedia*) and puts this vice after envy. He works the concept of sadness (*tristitia*) back into the discussion by defining envy and spiritual apathy as forms of sadness in response to the good in other people and to "a divine and interior good" (i.e., at God's presence in one's life) respectively.

9 Job 39:25. Scripture quotations are the *New Revised Standard Version Bible*, copyright © 1989 National Council of the Churches of Christ in the United States of America. Used by permission. All rights reserved.

10 For a remarkable glimpse of this form of teaching in the early seventh century, see Dorotheos of Gaza 1977.

11 Textual criticism carried out by the Leonine Commission, which was appointed by Pope Leo XIII in 1880 to produce critical editions of Aquinas's writings, traces the entire manuscript tradition of *On Evil* to a single Parisian copy with Questions 1–15. Probably this original manuscript was written in 1270, and Question 16 on demonology was appended with Aquinas's permission before his departure from Paris in 1272. For arguments concerning the date of the original manuscript, see Torrell 1966, 202–203. The Leonine critical edition of *De malo* (1982) is available online at *www.corpusthomisticum.org.*

12 For advanced students who are familiar with Aquinas's methods, there is value in reading the text "forwards." As they read the many objections, they can anticipate which ones will influence his answer and which he will dismiss easily. Nevertheless, in the private disputations this approach can become tedious for even the most knowledgeable and committed Aquinas scholars!

13 Both available English translations of *De Malo* use "evil" for *malum*, even though the Latin word simply refers to the privation of good (*bonum*) and does not connote wickedness. In this essay I will follow Richard Regan's translation in Aquinas 2003. This text, which includes a philosophical introduction by Brian Davies, is the one I recommend to undergraduates. It is more readable, though less literal, than the translation

by John and Jean Oesterle in Aquinas 1995, and in electronic form in the *Past Masters* database (Charlottesville, VA: Intelex Corporation). For a helpful comparison of the two translations, see Robert Pasnau 2004.

14 Aquinas borrows these examples of evil and sin (which he also mentions in *On Truth,* Q 24, a 12, arg 4) from Augustine, *On the Perfection of Man in Righteousness*, Chapter 2.

15 I have paired envy with spiritual apathy to highlight Aquinas's evaluation of sadness, envy with vainglory to discuss the role of self-image in the capital vices, gluttony with lust to feature the distortion of bodily desires, and gluttony with avarice to emphasize the social construction of these disorders.

16 To the works of Evagrius, Cassian, and Gregory mentioned above, one might add Gregory the Great, *Pastoral Rule*; Maximus Confessor, *Four Centuries on Love*; John Climacus, *Ladder of Divine Ascent*; Dante Alighieri, *Purgatorio*; Petrarch, *My Secret Book*; Geoffrey Chaucer, *The Parson's Tale*, the paintings of Hieronymus Bosch, and so on.

17 Bondi 1987; DeYoung 2009; and Fairlie 1978, 1995.

18 Funk 1999; Kreeft 1986, 1992, and Willimon 2005.

19 Several titles in the New York Public Library, *The Seven Deadly Sins* series (New York: Oxford University Press, 2003–2006); Schimmel 1997; Solomon 1999; and Taylor 2006.

20 In addition to the great literature and art mentioned in note 18, see the short stories in Born, Levine, and Whitfield 2007 and Born, Benningfield, McCue, Mitchell, Tigue, and Whitfield 2009.

21 Bonnie Kent considers this an important lacuna in the capital vices tradition and suggests it is a major reason why academic theologians largely abandoned the tradition in the late thirteenth century (Kent 2003, 244–245). It is also a reason, I suspect, for the eclipse of *De Malo* as a major sourcebook for Aquinas's moral theory. Not until the recent revival of virtue-based moral theory was it translated into modern languages. Currently it is available in French (1992), Spanish (1997), Italian (1999), and the two English editions by John and Jean Oesterle (1995) and Richard Regan (2003).

22 Though DeYoung 2009 tracks Aquinas's discussions of the capital vices in *Summa Theologiae* II.II, it is also the best general guide to his analyses in *De Malo*.

23 An act is "a mortal sin by reason of its kind" when it is essentially contrary to the love of God or neighbor. Aquinas says acts motivated by spiritual apathy typically are mortal sins because they are opposed to love of God, and acts motivated by envy or anger typically are mortal sins in opposition to love of neighbor. On the other hand, acts motivated by gluttony or lust typically are venial sins. Avarice and vainglory are more complicated: they come in several species and some are typically mortal while others are venial. Circumstances can make a difference too: actions that are typically venial will become mortal if, in doing them, one intends to harm others or deny God; and actions that are typically mortal can be only venial if the actions are "incomplete" (done without consent) or "trivial" in their object.

24 These lines come from John Greenleaf Whittier's long narrative poem, "The Brewing of Soma," *The Atlantic Monthly* (April 1872), that critiques the use of a drug (the "soma" of the title) to manufacture religious experiences.

25 Bondi 1987.

Dante

1 I am deeply grateful to David Lyle Jeffrey for supplying the opening frame and notes for this paper.

2 Jacques Maritain and, in turn, Henri de Lubac, S.J., have used this term to distinguish the thought of nihilists such as Feuerbach and Nietzsche as well as hard materialists such as Marx from mere "secularism." See de Lubac 1995.

3 See Auerbach 1974, especially "Farinata and Cavalcante," 174–202.

Catherine of Siena

1 Subsequently Thérèse of Lisieux became the third woman and youngest doctor of the church.

2 Raymond of Capua, *The Life of Catherine of Siena* II.1.121, cited by O'Driscoll 1993, 9.

3 See Cavallini 1998, 108–30, Tylus 2009, 23–33.

4 Concerning the emergence of women's literacy, see Tylus 2009, 33–45.

5 As we shall see, Catherine employs this image of a bridge in *The Dialogue*, but in its context has a very different sense to it.

6 As this pericope suggests, the language of interiority has a long history in the Christian tradition, but its sense has changed substantially over the centuries. With Augustine, the boundary between inner and outer does not fall between the mind and the body, but between that part of the mind which is dependent on the body for the exercise of its powers, including imagination, and that part which is not so dependent, viz., reason. See Turner 1995, 90–92.

7 During the canonical process that led to her being named a doctor of the church it was often asserted that her theological wisdom was divinely infused rather than humanly acquired. For example, Pope Paul VI, in his Apostolic Letter of October 4, 1970, declared that her learning came "without benefit of human teacher." In her editorial notes to *The Dialogue*, Noffke cites a long list of influences on her work: Augustine, Cassian, Gregory the Great, Bernard, Francis, Aquinas, Ubertino, Passavanti, Cavalca, and Colombini (Catherine 1980, 10).

8 There is a debate over the extent to which Catherine's writings were edited and perhaps augmented, and even whether she should be considered an author, as opposed to an orator, at all. See Tylus 2009 for an exhaustive discussion.

9 For the most part, Catherine did not use the metaphors of interiority, darkness and light, and ascent, which are the dominant tropes to describe the journey to God in the Western Christian tradition.

10 Catherine affirms the sacramental presence, stating at one point that "you leave yourself with us as food to strengthen our weakness, so that we forgetful fools should be forever reminded of your goodness. Every day you give us this food, showing us yourself in the sacrament of the altar within the mystic body of holy Church" (Catherine 1980, 72).

11 In a fascinating allegorical turn of phrase Catherine then construes Jesus' saying as pointing to the co-inherence of the two commandments to love God and neighbor with the three powers of the soul: memory, understanding and will. This is but one example of Catherine's use of medieval biblical exegesis.

12 Indeed, says Catherine, every evil is grounded in this selfish love of oneself, blotting out the light of reason in which the light of faith is held (Catherine 1980, 103).

13 Catherine here exhibits an awareness of the principle of *dominium utile*, in which property may be procured and disposed of in good faith, but only and always with an eye to its use toward the common good. See Aquinas, *Summa Theologiae* IIa.IIae.66.1, 2.

14 Once again we see how the path of knowing, which is also the path of love, culminates with the knower/lover becoming identical with its object/beloved.

15 Gregory the Great, "Gregory to Ethelbert, King of the Angels," XI.37, cited by McGinn 1998, 64.

16 As Hans Urs von Balthasar observes, the fathers (both individually and in councils) made effective use of all the rational methods of distinguishing and defining for the clarification of concepts in their many controversies with heretics. These methods, however, were not the determining factor in their theology: "Even polemical works such as Irenaeus' *Adversus Haereses*, Athanasius' *Contra Arianos*, Hilary's *De Trinitate*, Gregory of Nyssa's *Contra Eunomium* were embedded in a spiritual, sapiential setting which became more and more pronounced as the decisive element." von Balthasar 1989, 214.

17 Statements about the need for true, heartfelt, and perfect contrition and sorrow for sin are of course not absent from earlier theologians and spiritual masters, but shorn of the connection to eschatology and the works of mercy they take on a decidedly different connotation.

18 See also McIntosh 1998, 64–5 and McGinn 1987, 7–24.

19 Denys the Carthusian, *Difficultatum Praecipuarum Absolutiones*, a5, in *Doctor Ecstatici D. Dionysii Cartusiani Opera Omnia* XVI (Tournai: Typis Cartusiae S. M. de Pratis, 1902), 494D, cited by Turner 2004, 77.

20 See also Turner 1995, 186–273, and Coakley 2002, 78–82.

21 In the words of McGinn, "No mystic (at least before the [twentieth] century) believed in or practiced 'mysticism'. They believed in and practiced Christianity (or Judaism, or Islam, or Hinduism)." McGinn 1992, xvi.

Chaucer

1 Guido delle Colonne (de Columnis) was a twelfth-century Sicilian jurist who wrote this once-celebrated prose history of the Trojan War. He was also a vernacular poet, whose work is praised by Dante (*De vulgari eloquentia* 2.5). See here McCall, "The Trojan Scene in Chaucer's *Troilus*".

2 Wyclif, *De Ecclesia*, 37 ff., offers a view of these matters by one of Chaucer's close contemporaries who was, like him, under the patronage of John of Gaunt.

3 See Peck, "Number Symbolism in the Prologue to the Parson's Tale," for the best, most detailed general analysis of the prologue.

4 For example, if Boethius's *Consolation of Philosophy* is an anchor text the approach to cognition and wisdom makes much sense; if St. Bernard or Dante's *Vita Nuova* have been read then an approach through the theological virtues should work well.

5 *On Christian Doctrine* is a text that teachers of Chaucer should consider using early in the curriculum; *On the Sermon on the Mount* provides a particularly useful vocabulary for considering progressions of intention.

6 The General Prologue describes the knight as both "worthy" and "wise," one who "lovede chivalrie,/ trouthe, honour, freedom and curteisie" (Chaucer, 1992, General Prologue, 45–6).

7 Severs, in *Literary Relationships*, was one of the first to show how indicative of purpose are some of the changes Chaucer makes from his originals. Among the notable changes in this tale are significant additions from the Epistle of St. James.

8 Harry Bailey is the fictive "literary critic" of the Canterbury pilgrimage.

9 In the Great Texts curriculum a text such as the Everyman Library edition conveniently rectifies this problem.

10 Medieval legends of the Blessed Virgin had sometimes an anti-Semitic character, and while the Jews had been exiled from England since 1290, there is no reason to suppose that this element would not have been attributed by Chaucer to the Prioress, whose unflattering General Prologue description associates her with excessive sentimentality and affected mannerisms drawn directly from the characterization of the old whore in

Jean de Meun's continuation of the *Roman de la Rose* (which Chaucer also translated). Some of these elements are discussed in Beichner 1961, 302–7, and Gaylord 1962, 613–36.

Teresa of Avila

1 See Dominic Manganiello's chapter in this volume where he cites this passage from Lukács in his analysis of *A Portrait of the Artist as Young Man*.

2 Here I am using the word "gnostic" to refer to the conviction that one's real self is spiritual rather than material. Gnosticism, while variously expressed, is the belief that salvation lies beyond the material world of time and space. It thus seeks an inner, "pure," and immaterial knowing (gnosis) that will save the soul from a corrupt creation.

3 Brown 2000. In the novel, papal authorities banish the Bernini statue to an "obscure chapel" because it is apparently too risqué for the magisterium. Langdon, the hero of the novel, describes Bernini's Teresa as "on her back in the throes of a toe-curling orgasm. Hardly Vatican fare" (337).

4 Heidi Shlumpf 2007. For a similar understanding of Teresa, see Mirabai Starr in a recent translation of *Interior Castle* as well as Caroline Myss in *Entering the Castle: An Inner Path to God and Your Soul*.

5 Cited in Shlumpf 2007, my emphasis. Mujica is the author of the novel *Sister Teresa* and of *Teresa de Avila, Lettered Woman*.

6 This is not to deny that the Inquisition directly affected Teresa. Three of her books were examined by the ecclesiastical tribunal, under direct control of the Spanish monarchy at the time. In 1485, the Inquisition accused Teresa's paternal grandfather, Juan Sanchez, of being a *judaizante*, a Christian convert who secretly practiced Jewish customs. He was found guilty and sentenced to walk with his children in penitential processions to Toledo's churches on seven consecutive Fridays. Soon after this humiliation, he moved his family to Ávila, and by 1493 he was successfully running a rich shop of woolens and silks. For an account of this, see especially, Jodi Bilinkoff, 1989.

7 This familiar phrase is from Kant's classic definition of "enlightenment": "Enlightenment is man's release from his self-incurred tutelage," in Kant 1959, 85. By tutelage, Kant meant our inability to use our minds without guidance from another.

8 My thanks to Jacob Goodson for assistance in making this point. This is another way of saying that "spirituality" and "religious experiences" are not generic, but formed by larger stories and practices. One can no more have a purely private spiritual experience than one can have a private language. For a philosophical argument against the possibility of a private language, see Ludwig Wittgenstein's *Philosophical Investigations*.

9 "You pierced my heart with your word, and I fell in love with you," writes Augustine 1997, 10.6.8. It is against the backdrop of God's word "piercing" Teresa that we ought to interpret her description of the Holy Spirit "wounding" her (in contrast to a Freudian reading). For a wonderfully rich analysis of Augustine's *Confessions*, see the essay by Michael P. Foley in this volume.

10 Teresa is citing Proverbs 8:31. The context that Teresa is focusing on at this point is particularly the Sacrament of the Mass: "How You desire, Lord, thus to be with us and to be present in the Sacrament," Teresa 1995, 14:10, 86. This is significant because it displays how *both* the Word and the Sacrament form and transform Teresa.

11 The Augustinian nuns of Our Lady of Grace was the convent where Teresa had stayed as a layperson.

12 "Late have I loved you, Beauty so ancient and so new, late have I loved you! Lo, you were within, but I outside, seeking there for you, and upon the shapely things you have made I rushed headlong, I, misshapen" (Augustine 1997, 10.27.38).

13 Teresa does, though, write *Meditations on the Song of Songs* in Kavanaugh and Rodriguez, trans. 1980, 207–60.

14 "Doctrine" means teaching and "doctor," in this context, means teacher. I return at the conclusion of this essay to discuss the significance of Teresa's ecclesial title *doctor ecclesiae*.

15 In describing the practice of scriptural reasoning, Jacob Goodson writes, "The goal is not to use Scripture but to be healed by Scripture" (Goodson, unpublished 13). Scriptural reasoning is the practice whereby Christians, Jews and Muslims read Scripture together not in spite of, but out of, their unique commitments.

16 W. A. Bienert as quoted in Peter W. Martens 2008, 290. As J. J. O'Keefe notes, this way of reading scripture was referred to by the fathers as "spiritual." Two figures are brought into association for the purpose of illuminating the "perceived fit" of the whole. See Martens 2008, note 42, 294.

17 Augustine famously related remembering, knowing and loving to our being created in the image of the triune God; the image is realized as God is remembered, known and loved. See especially his *On the Trinity*.

18 My emphasis. Hart describes this restoration of human beauty again when he states, "In Christ God brings about a return of the gift he has given in creation by himself giving it again, anew, according to that Trinitarian dynamism in which donation and restoration are one; Christ effects a recapitulation . . . that refashions the human after its ancient beauty and thus restores it to the Father" (Hart 2003, 325).

19 Du Boulay (2004, 72) uses this phrase in telling about Teresa's dreadful vision of hell.

20 Cited by Steinmetz 1988, 136. Similarly, William Cavanaugh writes, "The individual consumer of the Eucharist does not simply take Christ into herself, but is taken up into Christ" (Cavanaugh 2008, 54).

21 Hauerwas and Baxter 1995, 211. The authors are describing the rationale given in *Quas primas* by Pope Pius XI for the establishment of Christ the King Sunday, a rationale resting ultimately on the Nicean doctrine of the Son's consubstantiality with the Father.

22 See footnote 6.

23 Teresa needs the money of her backers to support her foundations, yet she will decide (under the influence of the Franciscan reformer Peter of Alcantara) to accept no fixed income. This frees Teresa and her convents from having to please benefactors to secure donations. Not having to "strive to please those who are in the world," Teresa states, gives the reformed Carmelites a holy freedom (*santa libertad*).

24 Teresa in a sense retrieves the politics and practices of the early church as described in Acts 2:42, "They devoted themselves to the apostles' teaching and fellowship, to the breaking of bread and the prayers."

25 For a fuller account of the Teresa's reception as *doctor ecclesiae*, see Egan 1981.

Shakespeare

1 Northrop Frye cautions against judging these two sisters too harshly: "It's true that Goneril and Regan are being hypocrites when they patter glibly through the declarations of love they are required to make, but we should not forget that it is a genuine humiliation, even for them, to have to make such speeches. At no time in the play does Lear ever express any real affection or tenderness for Goneril or Regan" (Frye 1986, 103).

Milton

1 E.g., Forsyth (2003). Compare Donnelly (2009b, 86–88, 117–141).

2 Citations and quotations from the *Republic* are from the Grube-Reeve translation and will be cited parenthetically throughout.

3 The introductory claims in the first part of this essay are very limited in scope. For fuller introductions to Milton's writing, see Corns (2001), Danielson (1999), Dobranski (2009), and McDowell and Smith (2009).
4 Parker (1996, 593–97, 567–77). Compare von Maltzahn (1996, 479–81).
5 E.g., Perkins (1607, 2–3). Milton would eventually reject the Calvinism that Perkins represents, but the conception of "prophecy" as biblical interpretation was not limited to Calvinists.
6 All quotations and citations from *Paradise Lost* are from Campbell (1992). Campbell's edition follows the now-standard twelve-book edition of 1674. The ten-book first edition was published in 1667, but see Shawcross and Lieb (2007). Although I later refer to the poem's ten-book version, all citations follow the customary twelve-book numbering.
7 For a detailed treatment of how *Paradise Lost* deploys typology and adapts these and other biblical narratives, see chapters 4–6 in Donnelly (2009b).
8 Compare Rumrich (1996, 2–10) and Fish (1967, 1–91).
9 The specific formulation of Epicurus's argument was preserved in Lactantius and cited by Milton in his *Commonplace Book* (1953–82, 1:363). The extent to which *Paradise Lost* is properly a "theodicy" is considered more fully in Donnelly (2009b, 77–86).
10 Regarding "assert," see *Oxford English Dictionary* Definition III. 7: "To declare formally and distinctly, to state positively, aver, affirm . . . a thing *to be*, or *that* it is."
11 Regarding "justify," see *OED,* Definition 3: "To show (a person or action) to be just or in the right."
12 "God not only foresaw the fall of the first man, and in him the ruin of his posterity; but also at his own pleasure arranged it" (Calvin 1989, bk. 3, chap. 23, par. 7).
13 My characterization of divine making is indebted to David B. Hart (2003, 249–318).
14 Regarding this series of distinctions, compare Donnelly (2007, 177).
15 Regarding Milton's relation to Platonic texts generally, see Baldwin (1994); Donnelly (2007, 161–65); Fallon (1991, 81–84); and Samuel (1947). Compare Jayne (1995).
16 This outline adapts the diagram presented in Brann (2004, 117).
17 The next three paragraphs draw upon arguments first advanced in Donnelly (2007).
18 Regarding explanations for the ten-book arrangement, see Donnelly (2007, 159–60; 258–59).
19 Compare Donnelly (2009b, 100).

Kant

1 I am also the only contributor with no experience of teaching at a Christian institution, which no doubt places me at some disadvantage with respect to the subject matter.
2 John E. Hare supplies a notable exception to the prevailing negative attitude among Christian scholars. See Hare 1996, 2001, and 2007.
3 See, e.g., *The Genealogy of Morals,* Second Essay, Section 2. It should be said that, even while he places "the autonomous individual beyond morality" and asserts that "'autonomous' and 'moral' are mutually exclusive terms," Nietzsche here ties autonomy to responsibility and the making (and presumably keeping) of promises. John O'Callaghan takes up the Nietzschean notion of autonomy in his essay in this volume, under the auspices of "active self-creation."
4 See his account of his method in the Preface of the *Groundwork.*
5 In particular Kant writes against his own Pietist Lutheran background. One could very productively trace a lineage from the apostle Paul, through Augustine and Luther, to Kant.
6 See Lundin, p. 11: "This is nature seen as an amoral realm where desiring, acquiring selves meet and compete free of social restraint and cultural precedent…" and Lundin's reference to Frye on p. 16.

7 He also takes it to be identical to a third question, "Is reason practical in us?" Reason is practical, in Kant's sense, if we can be motivated by the thought of what we have most reason to do. If we can be motivated that way, then it is possible for us to act against our desires. If not, then we are limited to acting as these desires dictate, are thus merely part of the causal order, and the moral law is an illusion.

8 In fact, Kant's entire project, not just the moral philosophy, can be understood as an attempt to locate a place for morality, and ultimately for meaning, in a world that science conceives as mechanistic. But, like any claim about the overall aims of Kant's work, this one is controversial.

9 I cite Kant's works according to the volume and page numbers in *Kants gesammelte Schriften* (published by the *Preussische Akademie der Wissenschaften,* Berlin). The *Akademie* pages are noted in the margins of most contemporary editions of Kant's works. Quotations are from the Cambridge Texts in the History of Philosophy listed in the references section.

10 Or, as he says. "a good will seems to constitute the indispensable condition even of worthiness to be happy" (Kant 1997a, 4:393).

11 Thus Kant affirms both parts of the thesis that Robert Roberts attributes to Aristotle in this volume's introduction: Satisfaction of desires is not itself the goal of life. It is important also to desire the right things (Roberts, 5).

12 This reading makes the best sense of Kant's description of the person as one who "take[s] delight in the satisfaction of others." However, the interpretation of the sympathetic man as vainglorious explains why his delight in others' sympathy would meet the qualification: "…insofar as it is [his] own work." And it would explain why he takes satisfaction in *spreading* joy, not just in observing it. There is surely something suspicious about the emphasis on his own agency here.

13 For more on this example see Christine M. Korsgaard's Introduction to the *Groundwork,* p. xii–xv and Herman, 1993a.

14 Aristotle thinks that the person who is subject to desire to act wrongly is deficient in virtue, even if he manages to overcome temptation and act rightly in every case. The truly virtuous person, in this view, not only engages in right action, but also has right desire. Kant may be less confident than Aristotle that this model of virtue is achievable for human beings, and thus he uses the idea of "virtue" to designate the state of moral strength that allows us to overcome countervailing temptation (Kant 1996a, 6:380, 6:405). But he is not unfriendly towards Aristotle's model conceived as an ideal. Kant treats these matters in much more detail in *The Doctrine of Virtue,* the second part of *The Metaphysics of Morals.*

15 "A good will is not good because of what it effects or accomplishes . . . . Even if, by a special disfavor of fortune or by the niggardly provision of a stepmotherly nature, this will should wholly lack the capacity to carry out its purpose . . . then like a jewel, it would still shine by itself, as something that has full worth in itself" (Kant 1997a, 4:394).

16 Some would not count Autonomy as a separate formula, since Kant's articulation of it is so close to that of the Universal Law: "The principle of autonomy is, therefore: to choose only in such a way that the maxims of your choice are also included as universal law in the same volition" (Kant 1997a, 4:440). In addition, some regard the Natural Law Formulation, "act as if the maxim of your action were to become by your will a universal law of nature" (Kant 1997a, 4:421) as a separate formula.

17 See Korsgaard 1996a. And compare O'Neill 1989, Herman 1993b, 1993c, 1993d, and Wood 1999, especially chapter 3.

18 There are some items in the world that seem not to fit neatly in this division, including

animals, ecosystems, and objects of natural beauty like the Grand Canyon. This calls for an amendment to Kant's two categories, but doesn't undermine his central contention about the special, non-fungible value of persons.

19 See Aristotle's treatment of slavery in the *Politics* (1254a18ff).

20 This mode of thinking marks much of contemporary economics and is also embodied in utilitarian and other consequentialist approaches to ethics. For some discussion of this idea see Taylor 1992.

21 "... every rational being must act as if he were by his maxims at all times a lawgiving member of the universal kingdom of ends" (Kant 1997a 4:438).

22 The discussion that I have in mind here ranges from *Groundwork* 4:432, where Kant first introduces the concept of autonomy, to 4:448, where he completes his first argument attempting to vindicate the moral law.

23 We act, as Kant says, under the idea of freedom (Kant 1997a, 4:448).

24 It is because of this ability to direct ourselves that we are responsible for what we do. Since you are able to reflect on the justifications for your actions, it is reasonable and fair to call you to account for these actions, to ask for the justification that you took to be compelling.

25 A more sophisticated take on the idea that I may do whatever I want would read it as claiming that I may do whatever I *judge best*. In this version, I think that Kant does endorse the claim. This might look problematic to someone who thinks that the proper practical stance is one of submission of one's own will to the will of God, but the foregoing argument about descriptive autonomy could be taken to show that ultimately acting on our own judgment is inescapable. I return to related issues below.

26 This is clearer and spelled out in more detail in Kant's work *Religion within the Boundaries of Mere Reason* than it is in the *Groundwork*. See especially Kant 2000, 6:29–39.

27 Kant claims not just that indefensible practical principles can't be *justifiably* willed as laws, but that such principles cannot, in some sense, be willed at all. He believes that the unjustifiability of a principle of action in conflict with the moral law shows up as a kind of contradiction in the practical commitments of the person who is attempting to will it. Much as someone could not, at least in a straightforward way, believe both conjuncts of a contradiction, so one cannot will impermissible principles as laws. For more details on this puzzling but intriguing idea see Korsgaard 1996a, 1996b.

28 The whole of Kant's practical thought makes this clear, but he discusses the particular categories of vice that he recognizes at *Religion,* 6:29–32.

29 Perhaps the most famous interpretation and defense of the tight connection is found in Allison 1996. Korsgaard 1996b provides another helpful treatment. Compare James 1:25 and 2:12.

30 The element of humility that I find here is different from the one that Jeanine Grenberg identifies as a central aspect of Kantian virtue. See Grenberg 2005. For some concerns that Grenberg's reading results in an overly secularized Kant, and that this causes internal problems with her view, see Frierson 2007.

31 Kant also thinks that all such principles are heteronomous. Their authority depends on the goodness of their end, but there is no guarantee that the person who is purportedly bound by them can perceive this goodness or take an interest in the end in question. In that case the motivation to follow the principle would have to derive from some incentive external to the principle itself, such as social pressure or threats of punishment.

32 It is thus correct to understand Kant as a deontologist where this is contrasted with views that make good outcomes fundamental, and understand right action as just that which brings about good outcomes. The utilitarianism of Bentham and Mill and con-

temporary consequentialism more generally form the contrast class here. It is less clear that Kant's way of thinking should be contrasted with virtue-based theories. Not only does Kant have a rich understanding of virtue that is in many ways similar to Aristotle's, but as we have seen he begins the development of his moral system in the *Groundwork* by reflecting on the good or virtuous person. Thus it may be right to treat him as a virtue theorist in the sense that he takes virtue to be first in the order of moral explanation. His view does, however, differ from those who think that there is no moral principle more informative than "act as the virtuous person would act," a view sometimes attributed to Aristotle.

33 Kant affirms this most notoriously in his essay "On a Supposed Right to Lie from Philanthropy." Here he argues that the obligation not to lie applies even when you are faced with a murderer who demands to know whether you are hiding his intended victim. Though I am not affirming the substance of Kant's moral judgment here, I find the relation between his moral rigorism and his religious hope interesting and helpful.

34 This is an argument that Kant revisits several times. Compare Kant, 1998b, A797–A830; 1997b, 5:107–148; and 2000, 5:416–485.

35 E.g., Kant 1998a, 6:99: "Therefore only [God] can be thought of as the supreme lawgiver of an ethical community, with respect to whom all *true duties*, hence also the ethical, must be represented as *at the same time* his commands."

36 This power might be thought to be the central characteristic of authority of any kind.

37 For my own attempt to work out this connection see Ebels-Duggan 2009.

38 The epistemological restriction is also less limiting than it may appear on its face. Chignell 2007 argues that Kant allows for a broader range of propositional attitudes towards claims about God than most commentators have realized. In particular he defends the claim that "Kant is not opposed to the idea of rational, speculative, assertoric assents regarding things-in-themselves [including God]; he's just claiming that they don't count as Knowledge" (349–50). Nevertheless, even on this more liberal view, Kant will not countenance the attitudes needed for the extension that we are here considering.

39 But this line of thought, even if more fully developed, would not yet silence the worry that Kant cannot account for the distinctive import of God's special authority. In the inter-human case, a Kantian view yields only that others' choices give me reasons to act, not that these reasons are sufficient to determine what I should do. This is just what we want in that case, since it would be impossible to act for all other people's ends. But in the God-human case the traditional Christian makes a more radical claim: God's command doesn't just give us one reason to be tallied up among others, but determines what we ought to do.

To close the gap we might try drawing on the status and value of our relationship with God. In the inter-human case more intimate and developed relationships generate more demanding reasons. It is one thing to forgo helping some stranger across town, another to forgo helping my neighbor, and yet another to forgo helping my husband. I argue that a Kantian framework supports these aspects of our ordinary thought (Ebels-Duggan 2009). If so, then the special status and value of our relationship with God might account for God's special authority. This is, of course, far from a full answer to our question, but I think that the answer may lie in this direction.

40 I appeal here to "the Kantian" rather than Kant himself, since it is quite clear, again on epistemic grounds, that Kant himself would reject the idea that I could ever have knowledge of such a command.

41 And we might also appeal, again, to the thought that my relationship with God is of special value.

42 Robert Adams endorses Kant's interpretation in Chapter 12 of *Finite and Infinite*

Goods. He also suggests that we should not even entertain the question of what we should do were God to issue such a command, saying that to do so "does not honor God." He goes on, "So long as it is possible for us at all to dismiss them, I think that it is the better part of religious as well as moral wisdom to dismiss all thoughts of our actually being commanded by God to practice something as horrible as human sacrifice. The question of whether God commands such a thing should stay off our epistemological agenda as long as it possibly can, which I expect will be forever" (291). Contrast Hare, 2007, 269–270.

43 The text of Genesis does not so much as raise the question of how Abraham knew that the command was from God, much less tell us how Abraham resolved it.

44 It is instructive to compare Kant's response to Kierkegaard's in *Fear and Trembling.* Kierkegaard acknowledges the utter unintelligibility of what God asks Abraham to do. In fact, he emphasizes this unintelligibility, because he fears that familiarity has dulled his readers' sense of it. Yet he countenances the possibility that Abraham did as he ought to do in his willingness to sacrifice Isaac, that faith in God may demand even this most radical trust.

45 See, for example, his remarks in the Preface at *Groundwork* 4:389. And see the references to the *Critique of Practical Reason* in n 49, below.

46 See Kant 1998a, 6:29–39, in which Kant defends something akin to the doctrine of original sin.

47 Compare the psalmist: "Your word is a lamp to my feet and a light to my path" (Ps. 119:10). The whole of the Psalm celebrates God's law, and voices the psalmist's need and gratitude for its guidance.

48 No doubt some will find great irony in Kant, of all people, issuing a warning against complexity.

49 This view comes out most clearly in the *Critique of Practical Reason.* For example, Kant writes that "The most common understanding can distinguish without instruction what form in a maxim makes it fit for the giving of universal law" (5:27). And later, "What is to be done in accordance with the principle of autonomy of choice is seen quite easily and without hesitation by the most common understanding . . . what *duty* is plain to everyone" (5:36, and compare the whole of this "Remark."). Compare Paul in Rom. 2:14. Occasionally, Kant seems somewhat less confident of our ability to determine what we ought to do. Our need for others' help in working out our obligations is one reason that Kant thinks that we have a moral need for friends. See Kant 2001, 27:427, 27:683.

Dostoevsky

1 Here and elsewhere I use the Norton Critical Second Edition of the novel, translated by Constance Garnett, revised by Ralph E. Matlaw and Susan McReynolds Oddo (2011). All subsequent references are to this edition and will be cited parenthetically in the text. The first part of this essay appears, in slightly different form, in my "Incarnational Realism and the Case for Casuistry: Dmitri Karamazov's Escape" (2010)

2 In that letter, Dostoevsky also wrote: ". . . if someone succeeded in proving to me that Christ was outside the truth, and if, *indeed*, the truth was outside Christ, then I would sooner remain with Christ than with the truth" (Dostoevsky 1987, 68). Czeslaw Milosz criticizes this claim: "Those who would choose the truth are probably more honorable, even if the truth appears on the surface to deny Christ (as Simone Weil argued). At least they are not relying on their fantasy and not constructing idols in their own image" (Milosz 2001, 102). James P. Scanlan, however, insists that Dostoevsky's claim in this

letter is "far from an unqualified rejection of rational demands. The full statement consists of three clauses, the second of which is typically overlooked: '[1] If someone were to prove to me that Christ were outside the truth, and [2] it *really* were the case that the truth is outside Christ, [3] I would prefer to remain with Christ than with the truth.' . . . By the second clause Dostoevsky requires in effect that it genuinely be *true* that the truth lies outside Christ before he will choose the latter – a confused and no doubt unintentional bow to the authority of truth even when, in a transport of religious enthusiasm, he sought to dramatize his devotion to faith by sacrificing truth to it. And of course he did *not* think that the truth lay outside Christ" (17). I agree with Scanlan and would add that in *The Brothers Karamazov*, Christ and the truth are seen as synonymous. (The problem of Dostoevsky's conception of a particularly *Russian* Christ is another issue, and one that Soloviev tried to address with the less ecumenically minded Dostoevsky.)

3 Alexander Schmemann explains, "As we stand before God, there is nothing else we can remember and bring with us and offer to God but this self-offering of Christ, because in it all thanksgiving [the root meaning of Eucharist], all remembrance, all offering – that is, the whole life of man and of the world are fulfilled." Schmemann cites the Orthodox Eucharistic prayer:

> Remembering this commandment of salvation
> And all those things which for our sakes were brought to pass,
> The Cross, the Grave, the Resurrection on the third day,
> The Ascension into Heaven, the Sitting on the right hand,
> The Second and glorious Advent –
> Thine own of thine own we offer unto Thee,
> *In behalf of all and for all. . . .* (Schmemann 1997, 41, italics added).

4 See Contino 1999 and Connelly 2010. Dianne Oenning Thompson (1991) writes: "In Dostoevsky's fiction salvation begins with confession" (110).

5 Fanger (1965) cites Dostoevsky's self-description as a "realist in a higher sense"; in his literary art Dostoevsky sought "to find the man [or the human] in a man" and to "depict all the depths of the human soul" (215).

6 "Christian realism" is the term V. N. Zakharov uses. See "Preface 2002" in Terras 2002.

7 For a reading of the "doubting Thomas" story from the Gospel of John, chapter 20 that is quite close in spirit to his friend Dostoevsky's, see Vladimir Soloviev's "Seven Paschal Letters" in which he writes: "If the unbelief of Thomas had resulted from a crude materialism which reduced all truth to sensory evidence, then having been convinced palpably in the fact of the resurrection, he would have invented for himself some kind of materialistic explanation and would not have exclaimed, 'My Lord and My God!'" (Soloviev 2000, 96). Soloviev contrasts Thomas' "conscientious unbelief," "thirsting only for a complete and final attestation in perfected truth" with the "cunning unbelief" which is "consciously indulged to excess with various half-truths out of a hostile fear before the full truth" (97). In my reading of the novel, Rakitin, who stands in stark contrast to Alyosha, represents this latter, willful "cunning unbelief."

8 As Victor Terras writes: "A 'realist,' according to Dostoevsky, is a person who lives and thinks in terms of an immediately, or intuitively, given reality. The opposite, then, is the 'theoretician' (*teoretik*), who seeks to create and to realize a subjective world of his own." (Terras 2002, 137). Dostoevsky's distinction between "realist" and "theoretician" is analogous to Gary Saul Morson's contrasting of "prosaics" with "theoretism" (Morson 1993) and to William Lynch's distinction between the analogical and univocal imaginations (Lynch 1975). See Contino 2009 for further discussion of these ideas.

9 In the opening of her chapter on "The Christological poetic memory system," Thompson (1991) writes: "The ideal of Christ was the first cause and aim of

Dostoevsky's poetic work and aesthetic thought. . . . Every aspect of poetic memory ultimately leads to the memory of Christ" (273).

10 More recently, Rowan Williams (2008) has pointed to the Christological dimension of the novel's dialogic form, and David S. Cunningham (2001) and Bruce Ward have also noted its Trinitarian form. Ward writes: "*The Brothers Karamazov*, in particular, can be regarded as a sort of 'hymn' to the Trinity: it is indeed one of the most significant expressions of Trinitarian thought to be found in any modern text" (Ward 2010, 202). Any discussion of Christology is, inevitably, linked to discussions of the Trinity.

11 Joseph Frank, drawing on the work of V. E. Vetlovskaya, observes: "The fumbling, tentative quality of [the narrator's] assertions, his uncertainty about details, his moralistic judgments and evaluations, his emotional involvement in the lives of his characters (especially Alyosha), his relative lack of literary sophistication, and the heavy-handedness of his expository technique – all can be seen as an up-to-date of the pious, reverent, hesitant, hagiographic style of the Russian religious tradition. Such a narrator would be apt to produce a sense of trust in the reader by his very awkwardness and simplicity; and his constant appeal to the opinion of the community also imparts a chorus-like quality to the testimony that he offers" (Frank 2002, 573).

12 For a nuanced reading of Kant's understanding of desire, and its relation to the moral life, see Kyla Ebels-Duggan's essay in this volume.

13 For these opposing views of the place of *eros* in the Christian life see Anders Nygren 1982 and D'Arcy 1956. D'Arcy's understanding of the relation between agape and eros is clearly closer to Dostoevsky's: "The proper way to state the problem [of the interrelation between God's agape and human eros] is surely this: that God must act with sovereign power and freedom, and we know from the New Testament and all Christian teaching that God has freely offered to man a way of life which is His own, the way of what Nygren calls Agape. God, therefore, has the initiative and by His grace does lift man up into an order of love which is above that which Nygren delineates in terms of Eros. But God does this without constraint or defiance of what is best in human nature; He makes man a co-heir with His own Divine son without destruction of his freedom or his human personality. Grace perfects nature and does not undo it. How this can be so is precisely the mystery" (D'Arcy 1956, 83). In the same vein, Pope Benedict XVI writes, in his 2005 encyclical, "Deus Caritas Est": "*Eros* and *agape* – ascending love and descending love – can never be completely separated. The more the two, in their different aspects, find a proper unity in the one reality of love, the more the true nature of love in general is realized" (Benedict XVI 2005, 7).

14 See von Balthasar's discussion of "The Onion," in von Balthasar 1988, 57.

15 See August 24, 1879 letter to K.P. Pobedonostsev, describing Book 6, in Dostoevsky 2011, 662.

16 See the quotation from Dostoevsky in Morson 1993: "'The man-god encountered the God-man, Apollo Belvedere encountered Christ' (8/80, 3.30)" (Dostoevsky 1994, 34). Robert Belknap (1989) provides a helpful discussion of the theme of *nadryv* in the novel. I would add that the willful assertion of the man-god, exemplified by characters like Ivan, his Grand Inquisitor, Smerdyakov, and the "proud and fierce" souls in hell (Dostoevsky 2011, 279), provide the novel's ultimate images of *nadryv*. But, as Zosima observes, God continues to call them (279), a reality that even Ivan recognizes, as seen in the way in which his "poem" culminates: the soft kiss that Christ gives to the Grand Inquisitor, which "glows in [the Inquisitor's] heart," even as he "adheres to his idea" (228).

17 I develop my discussion of prudence in "The Prudential Alyosha Karamazov: The Russian Realist from a Catholic Perspective." Forthcoming in "Dostoevsky and Christianity: Art, Faith, and Dialogue," a special volume of *Dostoevsky Monographs*,

Eds. Susan McReynolds and Jordi Morillas. (St. Petersburg, Russia: Dmitry Bulanin). 2012.

Nietzsche

1 "Enlightenment is man's release from his self-incurred tutelage. Tutelage is man's inability to make use of his understanding without the direction of another" (Kant 1963, 3).
2 See Matthews 1992 and Menn 1998.
3 Showing that a failure to act in this way is the source of error is a large part of the burden of Meditation IV.
4 It was of course Descartes who has said, "everything ought to be doubted" as the starting point for developing methodologically purified reason.
5 "I fear we do not get rid of God, because we still believe in grammar . . . ," (Nietzsche 2004, 17).

Joyce

1 A. Walton Litz's observation is typical in this respect: "We see Stephen as a sterile egoist, cut off from humanity by his lonely pride; yet we also appreciate his imaginative powers, and sympathize with his plight" (Litz 1966, 72).
2 Among many examples of literary criticism that attempted to rehabilitate Joyce as a Catholic writer, see the entries by Boyle and Raleigh.
3 For an extended treatment of Joyce's *Portrait* and Augustine's *Confessions* see Manganiello 1993.
4 In William Blake's mythology, Golgonooza is Los's city of "Art & Manufacture." See "Milton, A Poem," 24:50 (Blake 1969). The City is foursquare, like the New Jerusalem.
5 In *Purgatory* 29.43–150, Dante witnesses a splendid procession during which a chariot, representing the Church, is drawn by a griffin, a mythical beast, part eagle and part lion, whose dual nature symbolizes the human and divine natures of Christ (Dante 1955).
6 Walker Percy maintained that the Christian view of man as a wayfarer provided "a recipe for the best novel-writing from Dante to Dostoevsky." "Even an excellent atheist novelist like Sartre," he added, borrowed "from this traditional anthropology for the upside-down pilgrimage of his characters into absurdity" (Percy 1991, 369). The same can be said of Joyce's depiction of Stephen's this-worldly journey.

O'Connor

1 O'Connor reveals that it is ever so easy to slip into the language of existence when referring to the devil, even though, strictly speaking, he has no substantive being at all.
2 It is likely that O'Connor developed her particular regard for the satanic from the church's baptismal liturgy, with its exorcism of the Devil and all his pomps. This exorcism is no general renunciation of evil as a way of life, but a quite specific acknowledgment of the struggle between Christ and Satan for the souls of the faithful. Baptism has been closely linked to demonic temptation because it entails a transfer of allegiance from Satan to Christ, an appropriation of Jesus' own wilderness foreswearing of fealty to the Evil One. The baptismal liturgy of the early church came to its climax as the catechumens were literally re-oriented, as Jean Daniélou explains: "The profession of faith made while facing the East completed the abjuration made while facing the West" (Daniélou 1956, 30).
3 The remainder of this essay constitutes a wholesale reworking of my treatment of *The Violent Bear It Away* in Wood 2004.

4 Yet it is quite possible to imagine Francis Marion, if he were not reborn into his baptismal life at the novel's end, becoming something far more sinister. With his Nietzschean strength of will, he could take Rayber's teachings to their ultimate conclusion, becoming not so much an Eichmann as perhaps a Himmler or even a Mengele.
5 I have sought to justify Tarwater's unintended baptism of Bishop theologically as being not a breach so much as an enabling of his freedom (Wood 2004, 190–92).
6 It is noteworthy that the word "purple" is never used to describe the pervert, not only because it is not the same as "lavender," but also because it is the liturgical color of penitence.
7 This is a more faithful rendering of "Jeder Ruf Christi fährt in den Tod" than Reginald Fuller's more famous and dramatic version: "When Christ calls a man, he bids him come and die."
8 I have sought to address this quandary in Wood 2009.
9 Flannery O'Connor agreed with C. S. Lewis that such assaults on the kingdom of God will end with the abolition of our very humanity: "Man's conquest of Nature turns out, in the moment of its consummation, to be Nature's conquest of man" (Lewis 1996a, 76).

About the Authors

Introduction – Robert C. Roberts (robert_roberts@baylor.edu)

Bob Roberts is Distinguished Professor of Ethics at Baylor University. He is an author (with Jay Wood) of *Intellectual Virtues: An Essay in Regulative Epistemology* (Oxford U. P., 2007) and *Emotions: An Essay in Aid of Moral Psychology* (Cambridge U. P., 2003), among other books. He has published articles in the *Philosophical Review*, *Philosophical Studies*, the *American Philosophical Quarterly*, *Philosophy and Phenomenological Research*, the *Emotion Review*, *Inquiry*, *Philosophy*, the *Journal of Religious Ethics*, *Faith and Philosophy*, and other journals.

Homer (9th century B.C.) – *The Odyssey*
[Scott H. Moore (Scott_Moore@baylor.edu)]

Scott Moore is Associate Professor of Philosophy and Great Texts and Director of the Great Texts Program in the Honors College at Baylor University. His recently published book is *The Limits of Liberal Democracy: Politics and Religion at the End of Modernity* (IVP Academic, 2009).

Plato (427-327 B.C.) – *The Symposium*
[Douglas Henry (Douglas_Henry@baylo.edu)]

Doug Henry is Associate Professor of Philosophy in the Honors College, Master of Brooks Residential College at Baylor University, and former director of Baylor's Institute for Faith and Learning. He is the editor (with Bob Agee) of *Faithful Learning and the Christian Scholarly Vocation* (Eerdmans, 2003) and editor (with Michael Beaty) of *Christianity and the Soul of the University: Faith as a Foundation for Intellectual Community* (Baker Academic, 2006) and *The Schooled Heart: Moral Formation in American Higher Education* (Baylor U.P., 2007). He has published articles in *Faith and Philosophy*, *Logos*, *Philosophia Christi*, and the *Christian Scholar's Review*.

Aristotle (384-322 B.C.) – *Nicomachean Ethics* [Robert Roberts]

See above.

Virgil (70–19 B.C.) – *The Aeneid*
[Julia (Dyson) Hejduk (Julia_Hejduk@baylor.edu)]

Julia Hejduk is Associate Professor of Classics at Baylor University. She is the author of *King of the Wood: The Sacrificial Victor in Virgil's Aeneid* (University of Oklahoma Press, 2001) and *Clodia: A Sourcebook* (University of Oklahoma Press, 2008). She has published articles in *Classical Philology*, the *Classical Journal*, the *Classical Quarterly*, the *American Journal of Philology*, *Classical World*, and *Vergilius*.

Augustine (354-430) – *Confessions*
[Michael Foley (michael_foley@baylor.edu)]

Michael Foley is Associate Professor of Patristics in the Great Texts Program of the Honors College at Baylor University. Forthcoming from University of Notre Dame Press are his translations and commentaries on Augustine's *Against the Academics*, *On the Happy Life*, *On Order*, and *Soliloquies*. Foley is the editor of F. J. Sheed's translation of Augustine's *Confessions* (Hackett, 2006) and has published articles in such journals as *Thomas More Studies*, *Logos*, *Antiphon*, *History of Political Thought*, *The Thomist*, *AVGVSTINVS*, the *Journal of Theological Studies*, and *Studia Liturgica*.

Marie de France (late 12th century) – *Lais*
[Sarah-Jane Murray (SJ_Murray@baylor.edu)]

Sarah-Jane Murray is Associate Professor of Medieval Literature and French, Baylor University. She is the author of *From Plato to Lancelot: A Preface to Chrétien de Troyes* (Syracuse, NY: Syracuse University Press, 2008), and has published articles in *MIFLC Review, Oeuvres et Critique, Cahiers de civilisation médiévale, Romance Quarterly, Philological Quarterly, Babel, Modern Philology*, and other journals and scholarly collections. In September, 2011, Murray became the recipient of a $210,000 fellowship from the National Endowment for the Humanities to translated the *Ovide Moralisé*, a 14th century Christian edition of Ovid's *Metamorphoses*, from Old French into English.

Thomas Aquinas (1225–1275) – *On Evil*
[Robert Kruschwitz (Robert_Kruschwitz@Baylor.edu)]

Bob Kruschwitz is Professor of Philosophy and director of the Center for Christian Ethics at Baylor University. Since coming to Baylor, he has developed ethics courses centering on the virtues and vices, with special attention to teaching texts of Aquinas. He is the editor of a quarterly journal *Christian Reflection* and co-editor (with Bob Roberts) of *The Virtues: Contemporary Essays on Moral Character* (Wadsworth, 1987).

Dante Alighieri (1265–1321) — *The Divine Comedy*
[Anthony Esolen (aesolen@yahoo.com)]

Anthony Esolen is Professor in the Department of English at Providence College. He is the author of many scholarly articles, books, and translations, including *Ten Ways to Destroy the Imagination of Your Child* (ISI Press, forthcoming), *The Politically Incorrect Guide to Western Civilization* (Regnery), and a translation of Dante's *Divine Comedy* (Modern Library).

Catherine of Siena (1347–1380) – *The Dialogue*
[Barry Harvey (Barry_Harvey@baylor.edu]

Barry Harvey is Professor of Theology in the Honors College at Baylor University. He has published four books, including *Can These Bones Live? A Catholic Baptist Engagement with Ecclesiology, Hermeneutics, and Social Theory*. Grand Rapids, MI: Brazos Press, 2008 and *StormFront: The Good News of God*, with James V. Brownson, Inagrace T. Dietterich and Charles C. West. Grand Rapids, MI: Wm. B. Eerdmans, 2003 and about 30 articles in collections and such journals as *Modern Theology*, the *Scottish Journal of Theology*, the *Journal of Scriptural Reasoning*, *Perspectives in Religious Studies*, *Review and Expositor*, and *First Things*.

Geoffrey Chaucer (1343–1400) – *The Canterbury Tales*
[David Lyle Jeffrey (David_Jeffrey@baylor.edu)]

David Lyle Jeffrey (Ph.D. Princeton; Fellow of the Royal Society of Canada) is Distinguished Professor of Literature and Humanities at Baylor University. He is also Professor Emeritus of English Literature at the University of Ottawa, and has been Guest Professor at Peking University (Beijing) since 1996 and Honorary Professor at the University of International Business and Economics (Beijing) since 2005. Jeffrey is best known as a medievalist and as a scholar of biblical tradition in western literature and art. His books include *A Dictionary of Biblical Tradition in English Literature* (1992), *The Early English Lyric and Franciscan Spirituality* (1975); *Chaucer and Scriptural Tradition* (1984); *English Spirituality in the Age of Wesley* (1987; 1994; 2000); *The Law of Love: English Spirituality in the Age of Wyclif* (1988; 2001); *People of the Book: Christian Identity and Literary Culture* (1996), a co-authored book on *The Bible and the University* (2007) and, with Greg Maillet, *Christianity and Literature: a Philosophical Approach to Literary Criticism* (forthcoming, 2010). His articles have appeared in Chinese as well as western academic journals, including *Foreign Literature* (BeiDa), the *Journal for Biblical Literature Studies* (Henan) and the *Journal of Christian Culture Studies* (RenDa).

Teresa of Avila (1515–1582) – *The Interior Castle*
[Elizabeth Newman, Baptist Theological Seminary of Richmond (bnewman@btsr.edu)]

Elizabeth Newman is Professor of Theology and Ethics at Baptist Theological Seminary at Richmond. She is the author of *Untamed Hospitality: Welcoming God and Other Strangers* (Brazos, 2007) and the editor of the Paternoster Series *Studies in Baptist History and Thought*. She has written on the spirituality and ethics of hospitality.

William Shakespeare (1564–1616) – *King Lear*
[Roger Lundin, Wheaton College (Roger.Lundin@wheaton.edu)]

Roger Lundin is the Blanchard Professor of English at Wheaton College (IL). He has written extensively on 19th century American literature, the relationship of Christianity to literature, and modern intellectual history. He recently directed a multi-year project on American literature and religion sponsored by the Pew Charitable Trusts and the Erasmus Institute of the University of Notre Dame. His most recent books include *Believing Again: Doubt and Faith in a Secular Age* (Eerdmans, 2009), *Invisible Conversations: Religion in the Literature of America*, editor (Baylor University Press, 2009), *There Before Us: Religion, Literature and Culture from Emerson to Wendell Berry*, editor (2007), *From Nature to Experience: The American Search for Cultural Authority* (Rowman & Littlefield, 2005) and *Emily Dickinson and the Art of Belief* (2nd edition, revised and expanded, Eerdmans, 2004).

John Milton (1608–1674) – *Paradise Lost*
[Philip Donnelly (Phillip_Donnelly@baylor.edu)]

Phillip Donnelly is Associate Professor of Literature in the Honors College at Baylor University, where he teaches in the Great Texts Program and the English Department. He is the author of *Milton's Scriptural Reasoning: Narrative and Protestant Toleration* (Cambridge U. P., 2009) and *Rhetorical Faith: The Literary Hermeneutics of Stanley Fish* (English Literary Studies Monograph Series, Vol. 84, Victoria, BC: University of Victoria, 2000). He has published articles in distinguished collections and such journals as *Milton Studies*, the *George Herbert Journal*, and *Christianity and Literature*.

Immanuel Kant (1724–1804) – *Groundwork for the Metaphysic of Morals*
[Kyla Ebels Duggan, Northwestern University (kebelsduggan@gmail.com)]

Kyla Ebels-Duggan is Assistant Professor of Philosophy at Northwestern University. She works on moral and political philosophy and their history, especially the work of Immanuel Kant. She has published articles in

Philosophers' Imprint, *Ethics*, and the *Philosophical Quarterly* and has held the Laurance S. Rockefeller Visiting Fellowship at the Princeton University Center for Human Values.

Dostoevsky (1821–1881) – *The Brothers Karamazov*
[Paul Contino, Pepperdine (paul.contino@pepperdine.edu)]

Paul J. Contino is Professor of Great Books at Pepperdine University. With his wife, Maire Mullins, he serves as Co-editor of the journal *Christianity and Literature*. With Susan Felch, he edited and introduced *Bakhtin and Religion: A Feeling for Faith* (Northwestern UP, 2001). His work on Dostoevsky has appeared in *Studies in the Novel*, *Renascence*, and *Augustine and Literature* (Lexington, 2006). Other work has appeared in *Religion and the Arts*, *Comparative Literature Studies*, *The Cresset*, *Commonweal*, *America*, *The Christian Century*, *Image*, and *Religion and Literature*.

Nietzsche (1844–1900) – *On the Genealogy of Morals*
[John O'Callaghan, Notre Dame (o'callaghan.1@nd.edu)]

John O'Callaghan is Associate Professor of Philosophy, University of Notre Dame. His books include *Recovering Nature: Essays in Honor of Ralph McInerny*, edited with Thomas Hibbs (1999) and *Thomistic Realism and the Linguistic Turn: Toward a More Perfect Form of Existence* (University of Notre Dame Press, 2003). He has published articles in the *Thomist*, the *American Catholic Philosophical Quarterly*, and the *Review of Metaphysics*.

James Joyce (1882–1941) – *Portrait of the Artist as a Young Man*
[Dominic Manganiello (domeng@uottawa.ca)]

Dominic Manganiello is Professor of English at the University of Ottawa. He is the author of *Joyce's Politics* (Routledge, 1980) and *T.S. Eliot and Dante* (St. Martin's, 1989), and co-author (with David Lyle Jeffrey) of *Rethinking the Future of the University* (University of Ottawa Press, 1998). He is at work on *Making Dante New* on the twentieth century reception of *The Divine Comedy*. In addition, he is the author of many articles on Joyce, Dante and modern literature, Yeats, Wilde, Walter Miller, Jr., Tolkien, biblical tradition in English literature, Chesterton, T. S. Eliot, I. A. Richards, C.S. Lewis, university education, life writing, C.H. Sisson, Dorothy L. Sayers, Seamus Heaney. Marshall McLuhan, Evelyn Waugh, and Wendell Berry.

Flannery O'Connor (1925–1965) – *The Violent Bear It Away*
[Ralph Wood (ralph_wood@baylor.edu)]

Ralph Wood is University Professor of Theology and Literature at Baylor

University. He is the author of *The Comedy of Redemption: Christian Faith and Comic Vision in Four American Novelists* (Notre Dame, 1988), (Baylor U.P., 2003), *The Gospel According to Tolkien*: *Visions of the Kingdom in Middle-earth* (Westminster John Knox, 2003), and *Flannery O'Connor and the Christ-Haunted South* (Eerdmans, 2004), as well as countless essays and reviews in book collections and such journals as the *Anglican Theological Review*, the *Christian Century*, the *Flannery O'Connor Bulletin*, *Perspectives in Religious Studies*, the *Journal of Literature and Theology*, the *Poetry Nation Review*, *Books and Religion*, and *Theology Today*.